THE COLLECTED LETTERS OF
KATHERINE MANSFIELD

VOLUME ONE

1903–1917

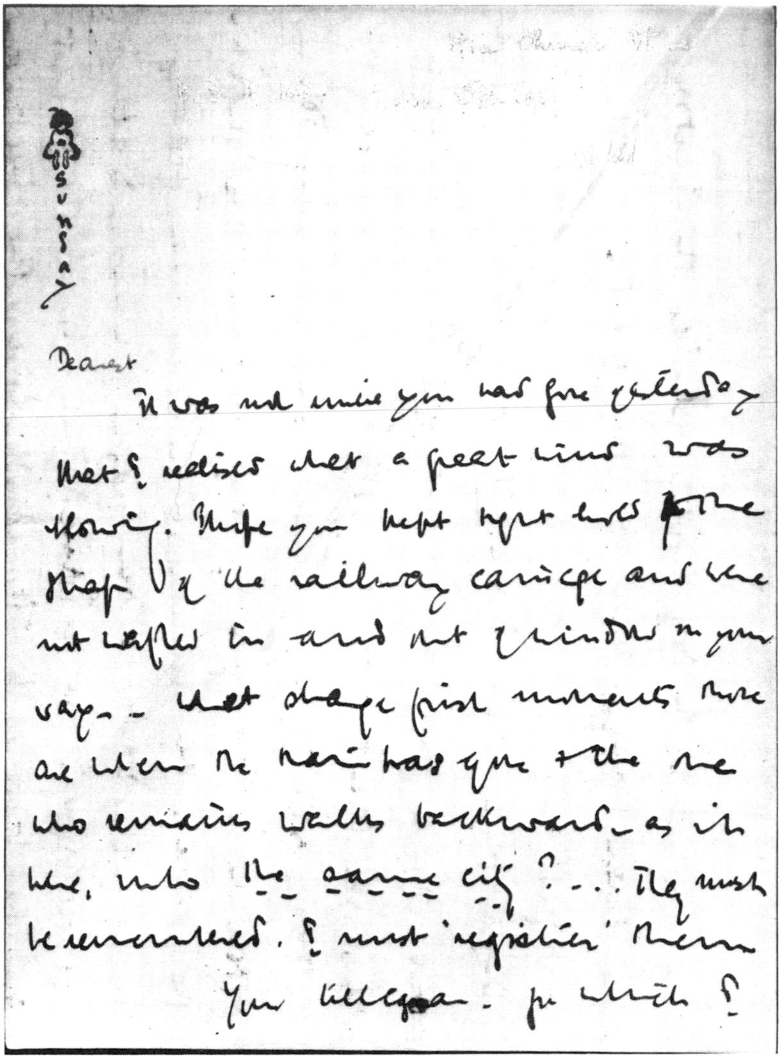

Sunday

Dearest

It was not until you had gone yesterday that I realised what a great tide was flowing. Perhaps you kept right back to the strap of the railway carriage and then [illegible] on your way—what strange first moments those are when the train has gone & the one who remains walks backward—as it were, into the same city?... They must be remembered. I must 'register' them.

Your telegram—for which I

From a letter of 25 November 1917 to John Middleton Murry
(Alexander Turnbull Library, Wellington)

THE COLLECTED
LETTERS OF

KATHERINE
MANSFIELD

EDITED BY
VINCENT O'SULLIVAN
AND
MARGARET SCOTT

VOLUME ONE

1903–1917

C. 1

CLARENDON PRESS · OXFORD
1984

Oxford University Press, Walton Street, Oxford OX2 6DP

London Glasgow New York Toronto
Delhi Bombay Calcutta Madras Karachi
Kuala Lumpur Singapore Hong Kong Tokyo
Nairobi Dar es Salaam Cape Town
Melbourne Auckland
and associated companies in
Beirut Berlin Ibadan Mexico City Nicosia

Oxford is a trade mark of Oxford University Press

Published in the United States
by Oxford University Press, New York

British Library Cataloguing in Publication Data
Mansfield, Katherine
The collected letters of Katherine Mansfield.
Vol. 1: 1903–1917
1. Mansfield, Katherine — Biography
2. Novelists, New Zealand — Correspondence
I. Title   II. O'Sullivan, Vincent, 1937–
III. Scott, Margaret
823   PR6025.A572/
ISBN 0-19-812613-1

Library of Congress Cataloging in Publication Data
Mansfield, Katherine, 1888–1923.
The collected letters of Katherine Mansfield.
Contents: v. 1. 1903–1917.
Includes indexes.
1. Mansfield, Katherine, 1888–1923 — Correspondence.
2. Authors, New Zealand — 20th century — Correspondence.
I. O'Sullivan, Vincent.   II. Scott, Margaret, 1928–
III. Title.
PR9639.3.M258Z48 1984   823'.912 [B]   83-12189
ISBN 0-19-812613-1 (v. 1)

Typeset by Hope Services, Abingdon
and printed in Great Britain
at the University Press, Oxford

CONTENTS

INTRODUCTION

The parents of Katherine Mansfield, born Kathleen Mansfield Beauchamp in Wellington on 14 October 1888, preserved in the names of their children their links with a mobile assortment of ancestors. The middle name given to their third daughter was the maiden name of her maternal grandmother, who would come to mean more to the young child than did her mother. By 1888 both sets of grandparents had lived in New Zealand for almost twenty years, although Kathleen's own parents, Annie Burnell Dyer and Harold Beauchamp, were born in Australia. Both grandfathers and one grandmother were English. Kathleen's special 'Grandma' was Australian. The grandfathers were of the stuff from which colonial stock was often drawn — honest, the begetters of large families, enterprising, but not blessed with much luck when they ventured into business. Her father's father was said to have been charming, good-humoured, and garrulous, and served as a member of Parliament. Young Harold Beauchamp felt, at least a little, that he was conferring an honour on Joseph Dyer, manager of an insurance company, when he married Dyer's handsome twenty-year-old daughter in 1878. His own forebears he traced back to an eighteenth-century silversmith; one grandfather claimed an acquaintance with Constable, and his wife had sat for her brother-in-law C. R. Leslie RA. Annie Dyer's family may have boasted eminent Baptist missionaries early in the century, but Harold's mother-in-law was the daughter of a successful Sydney publican. Her children believed there was Irish somewhere in the background. Yet for both families there were relatives in England who amply bore witness to sound connections.

From the start the Beauchamp offspring — two girls older than Kathleen, a younger sister, and the only brother — were encouraged to see themselves as quite properly part of two worlds. One was the Wellington of daily life, a city of 30,000 people, the capital of Britain's furthest domain, where the recent Land Wars between Maoris and the British Army had touched the lives of both Beauchamps and Dyers. 'The Empire City', as it called itself, was set on a magnificent harbour, but its high surrounding hills were raw, recently cleared of bush and scarred with road-works. 'The houses are built of light painted wood. They have iron roofs coloured red. And there are big dark plumy trees massed together, breaking up those light shapes, giving a depth — warmth — making a composition of it well worth looking at.'[1] Father, who was energetic, clever, and

[1] From 'Daphne', an incomplete story by Katherine Mansfield, written in 1921.

without funds to set him off, had bought a simple two-storeyed house in the suburb closest to the city. Harold Beauchamp rose quickly. There was a partnership in an importing firm by the time he was thirty, an invitation from his friend the Premier to accept a directorship of the Bank of New Zealand before he was forty. He was also kind, and always more important to his daughter than Kathleen cared to admit. She wrote to John Middleton Murry in early May 1913: 'Thank you for Pa's letter. He was cheerful and poetic, a trifle puffed up but very loving. I feel towards my Pa man like a little girl. I want to jump and stamp on his chest and cry "you've *got* to love me." When he says he does, I feel quite confident that God is on my side.' She once wrote a poem about him in which she imagined she was sitting on God's knee.

Mother was remote, delicate, witty, and rather conscious that she had married well. She was also grateful that Harold Beauchamp had given a home to her widowed mother and two unmarried sisters, and that he took one of her brothers into the firm. But Annie and Harold were happy, it seems, and devoted to each other. Their marriage was a paradigm their daughter returned to more in envy than emulation. A good deal of her fiction examines them over and over, seeking to find flaws, mercilessly revelling when she does. Until the end of her life, she was held by that small world in which their affections are constantly the reward, and their closeness to each other the barrier, for the child who fears that her siblings exert more charm and so have greater power.

The Beauchamps' other world was 'home'. The family quite re-garded themselves as heirs to a London where one of their mother's cousins was a distinguished surgeon and scholar, and to which their father's uncle had returned to enjoy the fruits of his Australian wealth, presiding over a household of cultured tastes and gifted children. Most important for the young Kathleen, her cousin Mary had married a German aristocrat, and written a famous book, *Elizabeth and Her German Garden* (1898). After their years at Karori Primary School, Wellington Girls' High School, and the socially superior Miss Swainson's private school, Harold Beauchamp decided it was time for the girls to come into their other inheritance. England was now to be theirs as certainly as Wellington, and Queen's College, Harley Street, was to polish the antipodean nuggets.

The first letter in this volume is from a fourteen-year-old who, after a month in London, having been drilled to think of England as the natural repository of traditions and values, found it as much hers for the taking as Karori or Thorndon. There is only a hint in the schoolgirl Kathleen's letters of that sense of displacement that would frequently mark the writing of the mature woman. For the time being, she happily enough believed she could hold two worlds in balance, that quite literally the best of both were her due. But other traits are already there in the letters to Sylvia Payne, cousin on her mother's side and fellow Queen's Collegian. There is at once that desire to enchant, to call the terms of a friendship, although Sylvia is not as tractable as Kathleen would like her to be. And there is the first stirring of what in time would bewilder her closest friends, and fuel the charges that were brought of insincerity, of 'performance': 'I am enjoying this Hotel life. There is a kind of feeling of irresponsibility about it that is fascinating. Would you not like to try *all* sorts of lives — one is so very small — but that is the satisfaction of writing — one can impersonate so many people.' (To Sylvia Payne, 24 April 1906.)

It would be easy enough, yet far too simple, to draw a line from there to the variety of names the writer of that letter takes on during the years covered by this first volume: to her publishing or living at times as Julian Mark, K. Bowden, K. Bendall, Matilda Berry, as well as Katherine Mansfield; to her signing letters variously as Katerina, Kissienka, Wig, Tig, and so on. That she was an accomplished actress, a known 'performer', was something her family early had to accept. Her youngest sister recently recalled Kathleen coldly setting out to make an elderly friend of the family weep with her recitation of 'Evelyn Hope'; her certainty, at least in her later Wellington years, that men were there to double as audience and victims. Commentators who place the actress at the centre of her character have evidence enough to make their case. But there is another line that must be allowed. She also told her cousin on 23 December 1903: 'they call me false, and mad, and changeable. I would not show them what I was really like for worlds.' She advised Murry fifteen years later against taking the same risk: 'Its a terrible thing to be alone — yes it is — it is — but dont lower your mask until you have another mask prepared beneath — As terrible as you like — but a *mask*.' (Late July 1917.)

From her adolescence, self-defence was almost inseparable from the way she behaved. This went with the sense that she was not to be bound quite as others were bound, that her gifts backstage, so to speak, permitted her the freedom of choosing from a range of voices in public. For the rest of her life, she would feel herself to be an 'outsider' in almost every context, so that the local rules did not necessarily apply. Already, as a schoolgirl in England, she made something of not being *simply* English. Shortly, back in New Zealand, she would make much of not being at ease in the town that was her family's milieu.

The small city that the eighteen-year-old Kathleen came back to in 1906 was indeed provincial, although it was not uncultivated. For the daughters of a prosperous merchant there were music lessons, soirées, visiting celebrities, concerts and theatre, the social round of teas and dances — and no obligation to earn a living. Harold Beauchamp worked hard to provide such things. Annie Burnell Beauchamp dressed her children well, and passed on the little snobberies, those glancing condescensions, that Kathleen would never lose. Mainly because of her father, one supposes, the large, fashionable house in Fitzherbert Terrace was open to Catholic priests, to Jewish business friends, to visiting artistes. Harold even made a point of speaking Maori. For its day, and its place, the family was spared the grosser prejudices of its community. For all Kathleen's complaining, her parents were tolerant, the girls supervised rather than ruled.

In the twenty months between her return to New Zealand and her final departure, Wellington gave Kathleen Beauchamp a store of experiences that would surface in some of her finest stories. That time also hardened her decision to become an artist — at the moment either musician or writer would do — and to establish herself in London. There could not be one without the other. As a few years earlier the young James Joyce, in another provincial capital, had written verses like Ernest Dowson's, and worked 'towards life through corruption',[2] Kathleen took Oscar Wilde as her mentor, and his epigrams as a code of wisdom. Life itself was there to be shaped, to be crafted, much as works waited to be written. 'I thank Heaven that at present, though I am damnable, I am in love with nobody, except *myself*' (23 October 1907; *Journal of Katherine Mansfield*, ed. Murry [1954], 22).

A teenage daughter basing herself on a convicted Irish homosexual was rather more than a Wellington family could easily stomach in 1907. Father already was cast as the dragon who guarded the treasure. He had also to double as sexual guardian. On the ship back from England he had occasion to warn her that 'he wouldn't have me fooling around in dark corners with fellows'. Now she wondered just how closely she was bound with 'the Oscar-like thread'. (November 1906, June 1907; *Journal*, 6, 16.) Her one intellectual peer in her own country was the sophisticated and handsome Maori schoolfriend, Maata Mahupuku. While the Beauchamp girls were being 'finished' at Queen's College, Maata's wealthy father had sent her to Paris. The two girls had begun to keep journals. Only a fragment of Maata's survives, but at times it is indistinguishable from what Kathleen was writing. For tutor they had read Marie Bashkirtseff, dead of consumption at twenty-four. The Russian aristocrat and painter left behind her the journals in which she reflected with endless fascination

[2] James Joyce, *Stephen Hero*, ed. Theodore Spencer (1975), 41.

over her own development, as did her pupils over theirs at the other end of the earth a generation later. Maata and Kathleen, at least briefly, were lovers. Then, in one busy year, Kathleen flirted with several men, published her first stories, convinced her father that she must leave New Zealand, and settled on 'Katherine Mansfield' as the name she would live by professionally.

In London at twenty, independent, ambitious, the world before her as she thought, Mansfield found her life assuming narrow horizons when, only six months away from home, she became pregnant by the twin brother of the man she had been in love with the year before, and made the briefest possible marriage — of one afternoon — to another man she barely knew. Her later letters will be wittier, shrewder, far more self-aware than those she wrote to young Garnet Trowell. None will be so open, or place her so vulnerably. The last of those letters marks in a sense the conclusion to her girlhood.

After a miscarriage in Germany, Mansfield returned to London with enough 'material' to write over the next year her first book of stories, *In a German Pension* (1911). In those months at Wörishofen she seems to have learned from Chekhov, as well as developed the cold eye of a satirist. Shortly she would blaze to her family, through the title of her book, that she was quite in the same street as cousin Elizabeth. She returned to England more confident, more ambitious, and again entangled with men. Soon she had met Orage, editor of the intellectual weekly the *New Age*, and began to write for him her sketches of Bavarian life. She allowed Beatrice Hastings, Orage's witty and malicious mistress, to instruct her in swank and bitchiness. In all the Mansfield correspondence, the letters she wrote to the *New Age* are the ones that most pretentiously take on the role of *enfant terrible*.

Something of a pattern was emerging, in that almost every close friendship Mansfield made with a woman over the next ten years was to be with one who was not, in any usual sense, English. Hastings was a South African, unrestrained by the metropolis. Ida Baker, already in harness as lifetime confidante and unpaid servant, had spent her early life in Burma, and her family later settled in Rhodesia. Anne Estelle Rice came from Philadelphia, Beatrice Campbell from Dublin. Lady Ottoline Morrell was almost beyond categorizing, the Hon. Dorothy Brett from a similar background that had not much to do with ordinary English life. Mansfield did not much like most English people, although she became an impressive hand at taking what they offered her. There may be sparkle and even warmth in her dealings with Virginia Woolf, but on both sides there were alert suspicions. The 'Blooms Berries' and the Garsington 'Deaders' were sets she wanted to possess. But she knew that any act of possession would come, as it were, by a kind of ventriloquism, almost by an emotional stealth. Behind her charm and wit, perhaps inseparable from them, were the 'dark hatreds' that so repelled Bertrand Russell when they were on the brink of an affair.

In many of her letters we see Mansfield 'casting' her correspondents – creating for each of them a role that assists the one she has assumed herself: 'dearest woman friend' for Lady Ottoline, pressing at times a little too hard; fellow artist for Brett; intimate fellow outsider for Beatrice Campbell. Ida Baker is kept in line with calls across the years of friendship, and sharp reproofs when she makes a bid for independence. And so with men as well. Frederick Goodyear, in the one letter that survives, is held at arm's length, yet drawn closer by the *risqué* voice that is scarcely heard elsewhere. Koteliansky, dependable and severe, is given avuncular status, with the occasional hint that he may expect a little more. Russell is flattered as intellectual adventurer, until boredom rang that particular curtain down. Fergusson is there briefly as bohemian and chum. Yet one of Mansfield's gifts as a letter-writer is that she seldom sounds false, even as she writes in the parts for her friends. With tact, and usually with great warmth, she sets the boundaries within which the moves of friendship are to be conducted. In her own terms a mask is lowered, another is ready there behind.

Those balanced feelings of revelation, and yet control, are what bring her letters so frequently into the domain of literary craft, without their losing a beat to spontaneity, the effect of good talk. Only Murry, and he only at certain times, is permitted to see the woman who is uncertain, easily moved and easily hurt, trying (as will be seen in the later volumes) to move towards a purity whose sense Murry himself subsequently distorted. She would aspire to an openness, without demands or expectations, that *received* rather than judged the tragic crossings of time and loneliness, of desire and loss, that she saw about her. And saw with a cool, unsentimental eye. What she offered to the friends she wrote to was the sense not just of life being grabbed at so eagerly, but its particulars picked out for that friend, on that day. 'I like always to have a great grip of Life,' she told Garnet Trowell, 'so that I intensify the so-called small things – so that truly everything is significant' (8 November 1908).

Before Mansfield wrote that in 1908, she had finished the first of her stories that stakes out one kind of narrative as very much her own. By the time she was twenty her letters, notebooks, and pieces of fiction move to that constellation of themes – perhaps obsessions – that thread her writing until the end. There is her belief, still bearing whiffs of the *fin de siècle*, that art, like sensitivity, has its price in suffering. There is the sense of isolation that intensifies what surrounds it, the joy one might say of the solitary, observing mind. There appear, as there will continue, the ambiguous sexual perceptions, and the feeling that friendships, places of residence, fidelities of one sort or another, are more in the nature of campsites than enduring edifices. Her temperament and reading seem early to place her squarely in the tide of late Impressionism: the drift of experience that asks for vividness, the accuracy of momentary things, 'that strange, perpetual weaving and unweaving of ourselves', as her favourite Walter Pater had put it at the beginning of that tide.[3] Her best writing over the next half-dozen years takes her towards a kind of fiction which is there as Modernism gathers pace. Her work will always move closely against the grain of her own experience, but she will shake it free from conventional plot, from the usual expectations of character. She is after a style that will hold the glancing of intimations, a form that catches rather than sets. By the time she completed *Prelude* in 1917, she had brought her prose to the point at which some of her contemporaries were then directing poetry — to the order in what appears random, the unity possible in the apparently disparate.

But *Prelude* was a long way off when Mansfield returned to England after Bavaria. The years between 1909 and 1912 are the ones from which least remains. Apart from the German pension stories, there is little else of interest. The diaries and notebooks were destroyed, only a couple of dozen letters survive from the hundreds she must have written. She herself tended to regard these as her lost years, and she seldom referred to them. In the little that does remain, one sees her trying out, or sustaining for a time, her various parts as cynic, entertainer, satirist, aesthete, sentimentalist. Russia and Japan, Nietzsche and Christianity, at different times played in the spotlight. But Mansfield was utterly serious in her belief that she was a writer or nothing, as she continued searching for the style that best suited her. There is an interesting example of how deftly she could change tack in her earliest dealings with the man she would love for ten years. Before they met, she had sent Murry a fairy story for his magazine *Rhythm*. He judged the piece fey, not at all what he had in mind when he made his editorial claim that his paper was the true organ of modernism. Along with marching under the colours of Mahler, post-Impressionism, and Bergson, Murry was out for 'guts and bloodiness'.[4] Mansfield obliged by writing for him over the next year stories which went back to her own country, settings that

---

[3] *Studies in the Renaissance* (1873), 'Conclusion'.
[4] F.A. Lea, *The Life of John Middleton Murry* (1959), 24.

variously took up murder, hysteria, and insanity in a tough frontier world. This was no more Thorndon than it was Maida Vale, but it fitted the editorial call. Within a few months, Murry was her lover, and she was co-editor. Jointly they wrote essays that asked for 'seriousness' in art, and uncharacteristically she shared, at least briefly, and for the only time, her young critic's pomposity.

Mansfield's love for John Middleton Murry dominated her life, and so the shape of her *Collected Letters*. He was slightly younger than she, and when they met it must have been very clear that while formal brilliance certainly was on his side, 'life' was on hers. Mansfield would soon come under Orage's fire in the *New Age*, in a splenetic series of caricatures[5] in which she was depicted as worldly, not as clever as she thought, and knocking men about for the sport of it. By contrast, even his friends thought Murry naïve and trusting. Mansfield struck him as both brilliant and beautiful. She made Oxford and a scholarly career seem limiting and dull, and he was drawn by her apparent freedom from convention. She encouraged him to chance his arm as a free-lance writer, rather than settle for university life.

Because Murry himself so assiduously stage-managed Mansfield after her death, there is perhaps a sense of the almost too well-thumbed about the romance between the clever scholarship boy from Wandsworth and the break-away merchant's daughter from the antipodes. Criticism of Murry especially so often reads as though the commentator were obliged to live with him, and so finds him wanting on scores whose relevance is not always obvious. As literary history stands at the moment, Murry has had what may be the worst press of any writer among his contemporaries, apart from Aleister Crowley. Yet there is one central fact that makes most other remarks pretty much beside the point. There is no doubt whatever that Mansfield loved him for the ten years they were together. That is the fact which dictates the reading of these letters, compelling us to take the Mansfield-Murry correspondence for what it was — a dialogue of troubled, intense, and continuing affection. Her letters to him are extraordinary in how much they cover of what a relationship over so many years may involve. Woven always through her feelings for Murry are those other two constants — her delight in the natural world; and her commitment to her writing, a passion for clarity in the midst of that strong sense she carried of the flickering transience of life. The range of wit and invective, of intimacy and longing and support, are there from early 1913 to the last letters of 1922. There is the packing of detail, often from week to week, at times day by

---

[5] 'A Fourth Tale for Men Only', published under the pseudonym of 'R.H. Congreve' in six instalments. The *New Age*, 2 May-6 June 1912.

day. There is also a shape that emerges only with the years.

There is an unpublished entry in Murry's diary[6] in February 1915: 'Lawrence said I was so uneasy when meeting persons because I made the social, instead of the personal approach to people. Katherine because she felt herself an outlaw, and felt that wealth and ease were her birthright.' If we take that back to the evidence of how Mansfield felt something of an outsider in whatever social context, an outsider open to its advantages yet excused its limitations, then D.H. Lawrence's remark is shrewdly just. Mansfield needed to manipulate to feel at ease. That is true even with Murry. Distress in her letters usually is bound to her feeling that their relationship is somehow sliding from what she expects. A late postman can become a flaw across existence, the delight from an unexpected letter absolve her from the bitterness she has levelled at him perhaps earlier that day. The troubled tone in so much of their love for each other has much to do with their wanting the certainties of childhood in a world which quite simply will not admit them. They encouraged each other's belief that what set them apart was in fact what made them special. They began early on a game they believed in, the game of Mansfield and Murry versus the Rest. Its pattern became more set after the death of Mansfield's brother in October 1915, when his spectre joined the exclusive club. 'We are in a world apart', she told Murry,' & we shall always be in a world apart — in our own Kingdom which *is* finer and rarer. Shut the gates of it for a minute — & let us stand there. Let us kiss each other, we three.' (19-20 December 1915.) For his part, Murry had just written to her, 'For that is our business in life, my dearest, to . . . walk hidden from the world, beneath the big leaves' (17 December 1915, ATL).

After 1916, they seldom really trusted anyone else. There is no friend who did not come in for his or her share of accusation. They wrote frequent warnings to each other about the uninitiated world, the threat from others who had to be kept at arm's length. They began to plan together for 'the Heron', a small house in the country that Mansfield especially yearned for but would never have, partly because Murry seemed not to want it as much as he said. His war work, and then his journalism, demanded that London remain his centre. But he encouraged Mansfield to hope for it — 'my life is absolutely built on it, because it is to me the solid symbol of our love, the symbol, the fortress, the hiding place' (6 March 1918, ATL).

Yet there was a darker motive she and Murry fed in each other. Early in 1916, Murry wrote to Lady Ottoline Morrell, 'I've passed beyond the world nowadays. I hate it and it hates me, or rather us.

[6] In the possession of Colin Middleton Murry.

But we are a great deal too happy to be upset — and one of these days we shall get our own back handsomely. It's awfully childish to dream of revenge, I know, but I do continually.' Murry had begun his vocation of being persecuted. In a rare flash of light-heartedness, he admitted to Lady Ottoline the next year, 'I feel that. . .I should have worn a card, like the policemen who give notice of air-raids, "LIABLE TO COMIC DEPRESSIONS AND METAPHYSICAL ENNUIS" ' (26 March 1916, 6 September 1917, Texas). Part of Mansfield's task was to keep the cloud from settling: 'I will stretch a lovely rainbow wing over you & not let them make you hate life' (30-31 December 1915).

Inevitably, there were times when the game of precious separateness broke down, times when Mansfield would flare out against its confinement.

Whose fault is it that we are so isolated — that we have no real life — that everything apart from writing and reading is "felt" to be a waste of time. . . .Why haven't I got a real "home", a real life. . . .Im not a girl — Im a woman. I *want* things. Shall I ever have them? To write all the morning and then to get lunch over quickly and to write again in the afternoon & have supper and *one* cigarette together and then to be alone again until bed-time — and all this love and joy that fights for outlet — and all this life drying up, like milk, in an old breast. Oh, I want life — I want friends and people and a house. I want to give and to spend (the P.O. savings bank apart, darling.)

(? 7 May 1915)

This gift for inflicting a reproach, then pulling it up short with a final turn to wryness or affection, shapes many of the letters. So does that sequence of mood when Mansfield temporarily leaves London and settles in a new place. At first there is elation in the excitement of travel and novelty, then loneliness, and then anger alternating with protestations of love.

Yet merely to note the recurrent pattern of separation and grief is at once to distort it. The broader tendencies are leavened with the immediacy and vitality that each Mansfield letter brings. The weight of her recriminations is deflected by the certainty, page after page, that however much Murry may be striking her as 'a guarded and careful little Bogey' (15 May 1915), enjoying himself as she believes while she is away, healthy while she is ill, circumspect when she wants him to fly out, he is still always the one person she longs to be with — 'You are so grown into my heart that we are like the two wings of one bird' (23-24 December 1917). While in writing to any of her friends, as much as to Murry, there is the *élan* that lifts from the page, the 'infinite delight and value in *detail*' she remarked on to Koteliansky, 'not for the sake of detail but for the life *in* the life of it' (17 May 1915).

When Mansfield wrote the first letter in this volume she was a schoolgirl freshly arrived in London. When she wrote the last, fourteen years later, she was a woman of twenty-nine, about to leave England because the disease that slowly would kill her was established in her left lung. In any normal sense the most active years of her life were over. In those that remained she more and more would be preoccupied with how best to snatch at intervals of health. Her life with Murry, her stories, and how she is to outmanœuvre and then to accept decay, will become the matters that finally obsess her. This first of four volumes contains only a quarter of her surviving letters. Yet already there are enough to place her with those whom her friend for a time, Lytton Strachey, saw as the finest correspondents:

. . . to be a really great letter-writer it is not enough to write an occasional excellent letter; it is necessary to write constantly, indefatigably, with ever-recurring zest; it is almost necessary to live to a good old age. What makes a correspondence fascinating is the accumulative effect of slow, gradual, day-to-day development — the long, leisurely unfolding of a character and a life.[7]

Vincent O'Sullivan

[7] 'Walpole's Letters', The *Athenaeum*, 15 August 1919.

CHRONOLOGY: KATHERINE MANSFIELD 1888–1923

1888	14 Oct: Kathleen Mansfield Beauchamp (KM), third daughter of Harold and Annie Burnell Beauchamp, born at 11 Tinakori Road, Wellington.
1895–8	Attends Karori village school.
1898–9	At Wellington Girls' High School.
1899–1902	At Miss Swainson's School, Wellington.
1903–6	29 Jan 03: Beauchamp family sail for London on S.S. *Niwaru*. Spring 1903–June 1906: KM at Queen's College, Harley Street; meets Ida Baker (LM). 18 Oct 06: Family sail for New Zealand on S.S. *Corinthic*. KM begins spasmodic journal.
1907	Oct–Dec: First published stories in the *Native Companion* (Melbourne). Nov–Dec: With camping party in the North Island.
1908	6 July: Sails for London alone, on the S.S. *Papanui.* 24 Aug: At Beauchamp Lodge, a hostel in Paddington. Sept: Begins love affair with Garnet Trowell.
1909	2 Mar: Marries George Bowden at Paddington Register Office, leaving him the same day. *c.* 10–28 Mar: Joins Garnet Trowell on tour in Glasgow and Liverpool, becoming pregnant at this time. June–Dec: At the Bavarian spa of Bad Wörishofen, where she miscarries in ?late June.
1910	Jan: Returns to London, living briefly with George Bowden at 62 Gloucester Place, Marylebone. 24 Feb: First 'Bavarian Sketches' in the *New Age*. Mar–?July: At Rottingdean, Sussex, with LM, after operation, 29 July: Staying with A.R. Orage and Beatrice Hastings at 39 Abingdon Villas, Kensington. Autumn: At 131 Cheyne Walk, Chelsea.
1911	Jan: Moves to 69 Clovelly Mansions, Gray's Inn Road. Dec: Meets John Middleton Murry (JMM), editor of *Rhythm*. *In a German Pension* published by Stephen Swift & Co.
1912	Apr: JMM her lodger, and shortly thereafter her lover; she is assistant editor of *Rhythm*. Sept: They move to Runcton Cottage, near Chichester. Oct–Nov: *Rhythm*'s publisher absconds, leaving JMM responsible for its debts. KM and JMM in office-cum-flat at 57 Chancery Lane.
1913	Mar: Move to The Gables, Cholesbury, Bucks. May–July: Last three issues of *Rhythm*, renamed the *Blue Review*. Meeting (June) with D.H. Lawrence. Move (1 July) to Chaucer Mansions, Barons Court. Dec: To Paris, where they take a flat at 31 rue de Tournon. Meeting with Francis Carco.
1914	Feb–Sept: JMM declared bankrupt, they return (26 Feb) to London; at various addresses in Chelsea until autumn. Oct: Move to Rose Tree Cottage, The Lee, Great Missenden. Meeting with S.S. Koteliansky.
1915	15–25 Feb: KM to France, to join Carco at Gray (Saône et Loire) for four days; in Paris *en route*. 18–31 Mar and 5–19 May: In Paris, staying alone at Carco's flat on the Quai aux Fleurs; has begun to write *The Aloe*. June: With JMM, moves to 5 Acacia Road, St. John's Wood. 7 Oct: Leslie Beauchamp killed in France. Nov: KM and JMM leave for the South of France, staying first at Cassis, then at Bandol. 7 Dec: JMM returns to England; KM alone at Hôtel Beau Rivage, Bandol.
1916	Jan–Mar: With JMM at the Villa Pauline, Bandol. 7 Apr: They return, to join the Lawrences at Higher Tregerthen, near Zennor, Cornwall. June: Move to Sunnyside Cottage, Mylor, near Penrhyn. July: KM's first visit to Garsington. Sept: JMM begins work (4 Sept) in the War Office as a translator. Move to

3 Gower Street, Bloomsbury (29 Sept), sharing the house with the Hon. Dorothy Brett and Dora Carrington. Autumn: KM meets Virginia Woolf; is meeting and corresponding with Bertrand Russell.

1917   Feb: KM moves to a studio at 141A Old Church Street, Chelsea; JMM near by at 47 Redcliffe Road. Nov-Dec: JMM ill from overwork; KM falls ill with 'pleurisy'. KM's TB diagnosed (12 Dec); advised to go abroad.

1918   7 Jan: KM leaves alone for Bandol, where LM joins her. 19 Feb: First lung haemorrhage. 21 Mar: KM and LM leave for England; detained three weeks in Paris under bombardment. 11 Apr: KM joins JMM at 47 Redcliffe Road. 3 May: Her divorce from Bowden final, KM and JMM are married at South Kensington Register Office. May-June: KM at Headland Hotel, Looe. July-Aug: *Prelude* (formerly *The Aloe*) published by the Hogarth Press (10 July). KM's mother dies (8 Aug) in Wellington. KM and JMM move to 2 Portland Villas, East Heath Road, Hampstead. Sept: KM first consults Dr Sorapure.

1919   Feb: JMM appointed editor of the *Athenaeum*; KM begins reviewing fiction for it. Sept-Dec: With JMM and LM to San Remo, Italy (11 Sept). With LM at Casetta Deerholme, Ospedaletti, where they are joined by JMM on 16 Dec.

1920   Jan-Apr: After JMM's return to England (2 Jan), KM goes with LM to Menton (21 Jan) to stay with a cousin, Connie Beauchamp. May-Aug: At 2 Portland Villas. 11 Sept: Returns to Menton; with LM at Villa Isola Bella. Dec: *Bliss and Other Stories* published by Constable. (10 Dec) Last review for the *Athenaeum*.

1921   Jan-Apr: At Menton; joined by JMM *c.* 20 Feb. May-Dec: At Montreux and Sierre; after ? 23 June with JMM at the Chalet des Sapins, Montana-sur-Sierre; LM living near by.

1922   30 Jan: To Paris with LM, to begin treatment with Dr Manoukhin; joined by JMM on 9 Feb. Feb-May: With JMM in Paris. *The Garden Party and Other Stories* published (23 Feb) by Constable. June-July: At Sierre with JMM; LM in attendance. 14 Aug: Makes her will at Sierre. 16 Aug: Returns to London with JMM and LM, to stay with Brett at 6 Pond Street, Hampstead. Oct: To Paris (2 Oct) with LM; on 16 Oct to Le Prieure, Avon, Fontainebleau, for treatment by Gurdjieff. LM leaves her (20 Oct) to work at Lisieux.

1923   9 Jan: JMM arrives at Fontainebleau to visit KM; that evening she has a massive haemorrhage and dies.

EDITORIAL NOTE

It is to our good fortune, if not Katherine Mansfield's own intentions, that her husband accepted as he did the brief which she enjoined on him five months before her death: 'Please destroy all letters you do not wish to keep and all papers. You know my love of tidiness. Have a clean sweep, Bogey, and leave all fair — will you?' In her formal will she made the same request, asking that 'as few traces of my camping ground as possible' be left.[1] The kind of instinctive reserve — or self-protection — which made acquaintances so often believe that Mansfield faced them with a mask, which compelled her several times to warn Murry against showing too much of what really mattered to him, seems to have been in her mind when she considered what she wished to be left behind.

Almost at once, Murry began to think of an edition of her letters. Five years after her death, he published two volumes that drew both on the letters she had written to him, and on those he could borrow from her family and friends. As title to this enterprise, 'Selections from' would have been more appropriate than 'Letters of. . .'. Murry in fact had garnered for an anthology of *aperçus*, moments of insight and suffering, generally untarnished glintings of friendship and warmth. The editing was skilful, but as evidence of the woman Mansfield was, at the least it was misleading. Yet for a generation that edition served as the basis for estimating her. Murry appreciated its limitations, and in 1948 he noted,

For many years I have cherished the intention of publishing a fuller edition of Katherine Mansfield's letters. When they were originally published . . . it was necessary to edit them severely; and I suppressed many passages and many entire letters — particularly among those addressed to myself. The passage of time has removed that necessity. Letters which seemed twenty-two years ago too painful for publication now appear to be part of the texture of experience.[2]

When Murry found that substantial numbers of Mansfield's letters were already dispersed, he settled for what in 1951 his publishers called 'a virtually new book'. *Katherine Mansfield's Letters to John Middleton Murry* offered almost in full the letters she had written to him over a span of ten years, the frequent cross-grain of their love now quite as much there as the earlier surface sheen. Again, Murry

---

[1] Letter of 7 August 1922, quoted by F.A. Lea, *The Life of John Middleton Murry* (1959), 95; will dated 14 August 1922, quoted by Antony Alpers, *The Life of Katherine Mansfield* (1980), 366.

[2] Note in the possession of Mrs Mary Murry.

'corrected' spelling, punctuation, and passages in foreign languages; he deleted names, and frequently references to people who were still alive; occasionally he omitted what he regarded as lapses of taste. That 1951 volume, and his own 1928 first selection, are the two editions of her letters of any significance. The few selections by other and later hands have been fairly effortless quarryings from Murry's work.

The present edition, which includes all the extant letters which are now available, will run to four volumes. The first prints letters from the beginning of her writing life (the earliest in 1903) to the end of 1917. Volume II will cover the years 1918-19; Volume III, 1920-1; Volume IV, 1922-3. As Mansfield's illness more and more made its claims, and as she spent longer periods away from England, she became increasingly dependent on correspondence to give her life what sociability it had — 'God! What it is to count on letters, so' (5 February 1918; *Letters to J.M. Murry* [1951], 152).

Although sentiment, friendship, an eye for quality, then later, the efforts of collectors, have done their share in preserving the letters this edition draws on, it is probable that a good deal less than half of her correspondence has been retrieved. Most surprising, perhaps, is how few of the numerous letters she wrote to her immediate family have come to light, although on the evidence of her nephew, the late Andrew Bell, it seems that those to her parents, at least, may be in the hands of an untraced collector.

There are other groups of letters which this edition is the poorer for not having, and it now seems almost certain that few of these will surface. As a schoolgirl and young woman, Mansfield wrote to her friends with irrepressible eagerness. Letters to Maata Mahupuku — her one intellectual peer among New Zealand friends — were probably destroyed because their intensity embarrassed, once their occasion had cooled. Those to other Wellington and English acquaintances have simply disappeared in the way of most communications, as did Mansfield's handwritten school newspapers held on to by a few, but finally discarded 'as she never was heard of again'.[3] Only Sylvia Payne, cousin as well as fellow pupil, preserved letters that put Mansfield the schoolgirl before us, and Garnet Trowell's keeping over twenty letters from their early love affair provides the one bridge between her youth and maturity.

Other batches of letters were quite deliberately destroyed. When Floryan Sobieniowski, Mansfield's friend in Bavaria in 1909 and her suitor in 1910, ten years later produced what she had written to him and demanded payment, she instructed Murry to hand over £40 for

---

[3] Ruth E. Mantz and J. Middleton Murry, *The Life of Katherine Mansfield* (1933), 152.

those letters 'I would give any money to recover' (16 September 1920; *Letters to J.M. Murry*, 536). A severer loss were the many hundreds of letters kept by Ida Baker, detailed bulletins sent weekly for a year and a half from New Zealand, then for two years again when Ida went to Rhodesia in 1914. She made the mistake of offering back the parcel of letters — 'quite a foot square' — sometime in 1918, believing they might serve as material for Mansfield's work. 'I gave them back to Katherine. She opened the parcel, glanced at one or two letters, and cried: "What dreadful rubbish — burn them *all!*"'[4]

Of her other friends, A.R. Orage did not believe in preserving private correspondence; D.H. Lawrence presumably thought her letters not worth keeping. Francis Carco held on to his at least long enough for extracts to appear usefully in his books, although one must be wary of accepting what he quotes as completely authentic. Beatrice Hastings, who for a time exercised some kind of dominion over Mansfield, perhaps needed only her own obsessive jealousy to make her destroy what letters she had received — or they may have been part of that collection of private papers offered to the British Museum in 1943, and not accepted. One letter to Frederick Goodyear survives; others, one supposes, were dispersed with the effects of a man who died in the Great War.

From what does survive, it seems that apart from letters meeting family, business, and social obligations, Mansfield's correspondence after her twenty-first year was with a small number of people. Of the more than 300 letters collected in this volume, a little less than one third are to Murry — a proportion which increases greatly in subsequent volumes. More than 50 come from the files of careful archivists like Bertrand Russell and Lady Ottoline Morrell; nearly 30 are to the closest of her few devoted friends, Dorothy Brett and S.S. Koteliansky. The handful written to such people as William Orton and Edna Smith are distinctive enough to make it very clear that when letters to a particular correspondent have been lost, a particular style of letter has been lost as well. No two recipients of letters are permitted to see quite the same face.

A problem in editing Mansfield, and one which editors at least of twentieth-century writers are usually spared, is the difficulty of much of her script. When she made the effort, she could of course produce a fair copy, for she was quite aware that often what she wrote could not be read with ease. But usually when she took up her pen it was in haste, or in enthusiasm, or to someone she believed was familiar with her hand. A recollection her first biographer constantly

[4] Ida Baker, *Katherine Mansfield: The Memories of LM* (1971), 126-7.

encountered among her teachers was of 'compositions . . . poorly written'.[5] That was a handicap she did not outgrow. Within two months in 1915, she explained to Koteliansky, 'I would write you a long letter but I am afraid you cannot read my handwriting,' and Murry wrote to her, 'Oh Tig, what wonderful letters you do write — they're worth every bit of the trouble of making them out.' (22 March 1915, *Letters of Katherine Mansfield,* ed. J.M. Murry [1928], I. 12-13; 10 May 1915, ATL.)

A glance at transcripts of her letters made by various of her friends bears out that not only was the trouble considerable, it was often taken with something less than total success. Even her husband ran into confusions which years of acquaintance with her papers did not dispel. Although one may attain a working familiarity with her hand, one can never assume final consistency in the shaping of her letters, the manner of contractions, or the outcome of recurrent puzzles. Her style is at all points too individual to permit anticipation.

One aspect a reader may remark on initially in this edition is the difference between the present text and those that have been pub-lished heretofore. The present editors have worked towards re-producing as closely as possible what Mansfield wrote, preserving her occasional oddities in spelling, her idiosyncratic paragraphing, and her very personal disposal of punctuation. She quite saw that this last was problematic. 'No, my dash isn't quite a feminine dash. (Certainly when I was young it was) . . . . The truth is — punctuation is infernally difficult . . . . Its boundaries need to be enlarged.' (To Murry, end of November 1920; *Letters to J.M. Murry,* 603-4.) Many times in the manuscripts the precise boundary between a dash, a comma, and a full stop simply cannot be asserted, nor can the exact location of a paragraph break. When such problems arise, editorial decisions have been made in the light of overall tendencies in the letters.

The bristling of ampersands throughout a printed page can be an irritation, but as Mansfield was not consistent in choosing either to write out 'and' or to use the conventional symbol, it was decided to reproduce exactly what she wrote. Similarly, when apostrophes are omitted in the manuscript they have not been supplied in the printed text. Mansfield did not always omit them, but when she did it seems a small personal mark on a letter that deserves to be kept.

The occasions on which there has been editorial intervention are in providing full stops, when their omission was clearly inadvertent; in regularizing single and double inverted commas when these are omitted or mismatched; and in silently emending occasional and very obvious slips of the pen. When a word or a phrase has finally

[5] Mantz and Murry, op. cit., 152.

resisted attempts to read it, the word 'illegible' appears in italics, within square brackets. Doubtful readings also appear in square brackets, preceded by a question mark. On the few occasions when a phrase has been crossed out, the deleted words are enclosed in angle brackets (< >). Any words supplied are in square brackets.

Mansfield's emphases have been rendered in the conventional manner, with words underlined once printed in italics, those underlined twice in small capitals, and with further underlinings printed as in the manuscript. The little sketches with which she occasionally adorned her letters have been reproduced as they occur in the manuscripts.

In the dating of letters also this edition departs considerably from previous publications. It was unusual for Mansfield to date a letter, or to head it with an address, and those who kept her letters did not as a rule keep as well the envelopes in which they were posted. Even when postmarked envelopes do survive, they have frequently become separated from the original letters, and so another kind of confusion is introduced. Murry's datings were often inaccurate, but since his side of their correspondence survives, and he was more consistent in indicating at least the day of the week, it has usually been possible to arrive at precise dates for the letters Mansfield wrote to him. For the dating of most other letters, the editors have had to depend on internal evidence, references to public events, a sequence established by earlier letters, or ancillary correspondence by other people.

Where Mansfield did not herself date a letter, the date supplied by the editors is enclosed in square brackets; where that date is uncertain or approximate it is preceded by a query or by the conventional 'c.' for *circa*. Where an address has been supplied, it too is given in square brackets. Printed or blind-stamped addresses are rendered in small capitals, and the layout of address, date, and complimentary close has been standardized, with vertical rules indicating the original line breaks. Postscripts, marginal notes, and addenda are invariably printed at the end of a letter, with a bracketed indication of their original position in the manuscript.

The greater part of the letters in this edition have been transcribed directly from the manuscripts or, when those were not accessible, from photocopies provided by the various institutions and individuals who own the originals. In only a few cases, where no manuscript survives, has it been necessary to reproduce a secondary or printed version. Where the text of a letter has been reproduced from Mansfield's notebooks or loose papers in the Alexander Turnbull Library, it has been identified as a draft, and the recipient's name given in square brackets; usually it is impossible to establish whether or not a fair copy of the letter was sent.

The provenance line at the foot of each letter describes the copy-text and gives the owner or location of the manuscript. Where a letter has been previously published, in whole or in substantial part (even though here transcribed afresh from the manuscript), a reference is given to the publication in which it first appeared; when only a sentence or a brief extract has been published, the word 'cited' precedes the reference. On occasion, three or four published works may be listed, when different portions of the same letter found their way into print at different times. When no published source is given, the letter is previously unpublished.

The annotation at the foot of each letter has been kept to what seems necessary to identify individuals, places, or publications, and to elucidate references and events. Middleton Murry's own correspondence has often been drawn on to clarify allusions, and the sum of such quotations proposes something of the relationship between himself and Mansfield.

Mansfield's correspondents are briefly identified at the first letter to each, with an initial cross-reference to that note if the individual figures in the text before being written to. When personages as well known as Debussy or Whitman or Yeats are mentioned in passing, it has seemed impertinent or absurd to append an identifying note. Similarly, when the young Mansfield visits Versailles, and writes of it in rather guide-book fashion, it would be unnecessarily pedantic to expand her own references. But even familiar personalities from the worlds of Bloomsbury, Garsington, and literary London are given a cursory identification, for in those instances the scale of fame is perhaps smaller, and the references more directly relevant to the details of Mansfield's life. On a few occasions it has not proved possible to track down an individual referred to, or to offer the context for a quotation or an event. Like any editors, we must regret those times when a particular reader feels either under- or overinformed.

At several points in the volume, the sequence of letters is interrupted by a longer explanatory note. These headnotes usually occur at times of emotional or physical transition in Mansfield's life. They offer information that may not emerge from the letters themselves, but is pertinent to their writing or their context. The Chronology at p. xix gives the main events of Mansfield's life in a condensed form which the reader may find useful.

V. O'S.

Wellington
March 1983

ACKNOWLEDGEMENTS

As with any edition of letters, the editors are obliged, first of all, to those individuals and institutions who have allowed the inclusion of letters or transcriptions in their possession: the Alexander Turnbull Library, Wellington; Mrs George Bemis; the Henry W. and Albert A. Berg Collection of the New York Public Library; Mr G.C. Bowden, the Trustees of the British Library; Mr Owen Leeming; Mrs Lulu McIntosh; the Bertrand Russell Archives, McMaster University, Hamilton, Ontario; the Mitchell Library, Sydney; the Newberry Library, Chicago; Mr R.E.D. Rawlins; Mrs Dorothy Richards; the Smith College Library Rare Book Room, Northampton, Massachusetts; the Stanford University Library, Stanford, California; the Strachey Trust, London; the Library of Sussex University; the Humanities Research Center, the University of Texas at Austin; Mrs Shirley Weber; Windsor University Library, Windsor, Ontario; Viking Press for a letter quoted from Antony Alpers, *The Life of Katherine Mansfield* (1980); Yale University Press, for part of a letter quoted from Sylvia Berkman, *Katherine Mansfield: A Critical Study* (1951).

All unpublished material by Katherine Mansfield and John Middleton Murry is copyright by the respective Estates of Katherine Mansfield and of John Middleton Murry, and is quoted here by permission of the copyright owners. We are especially grateful to the late Mrs Mary Murry, and to Mr Colin Middleton Murry, for continued kindness over several years. Some of Middleton Murry's letters to Katherine Mansfield, quoted here from the manuscripts in the Alexander Turnbull Library, will have appeared in print before this volume is published, in C.A. Hankin's selection, *The Letters of John Middleton Murry to Katherine Mansfield* (London: Constable, 1983).

For extracts from material by other authors published here for the first time, and quoted by permission of the copyright owners, we are indebted to Mr Luke Gertler, executor of Mark Gertler; the Bertrand Russell Archives, McMaster University, Hamilton, Ontario; the Strachey Trust, London.

This edition was first undertaken several years ago, at the suggestion of Mr D.M. Davin, then Academic Publisher to the Oxford University Press, and Dr Eric McCormick. Both have been constant in their encouragement. Since then, many people have assisted in many ways, and the editors gladly acknowledge them: the late Miss Ida Baker; the late Mrs Vera Mackintosh Bell; Mrs Anne Bennett; Mrs Gill Body; Ms Ellen Dunlap, of the Humanities Research Center, the

University of Texas at Austin; Ms Alexia Galt; Professor I.A. Gordon; the late Miss Ruth Herrick; Ms Ann Hollander; Dr Frank McKay; the late Mrs Maude Morris; Mr Norman Morris; the New Zealand High Commission, London; Mlle Christiane Mortellier; Professor Frederick Page; Mrs Jeanne Renshaw; Miss Mary Ronnie; Mr Dermot Sullivan; Mr Michael Taylor; Mr John Mansfield Thompson; Dr W.R. Trumble, Science Editor of the *Oxford English Dictionary*; Mr Dunstan Ward; Mrs Diane Wards; Ms Lydia Wevers; Professor F. Wood; Mrs Irene Zohrab.

There are some persons the editors must thank very particularly: Mr A.G. Bagnall, formerly Librarian, Alexander Turnbull Library, Wellington; Miss Aileen Claridge, of the New Zealand National Library; Mrs Elizabeth Caffin, formerly resident in Paris; Dr Michael Freyne, of the University of New South Wales; Dr Peter Russell, of the German Department, Victoria University of Wellington; Mr J. Traue and his staff at the Alexander Turnbull Library, Wellington. Ms Caroline Macdonald prepared the Index to the volume. And there are two people without whom the editors cannot imagine the completion of this volume: one is Miss Catharine Carver, expert and tactful editor; the other is Professor Antony Alpers, the benign and endlessly generous *doyen* of Mansfield scholars.

Vincent O'Sullivan was able to visit libraries and collections in the United States through a grant from the New Zealand National Library, and to work for a time on the material in New Zealand with assistance from the Trustees of the Alexander Turnbull Library. Margaret Scott was aided by the Katherine Mansfield Memorial Fellowship, an ICI Bursary, and a grant from the Department of Internal Affairs, Wellington.

V.O'S.
M.S.

Wellington
March 1983

LIST OF ABBREVIATIONS AND MANUSCRIPT SOURCES

KM = Katherine Mansfield

The following abbreviations and short forms are used in the description and provenance given at the foot of each letter:

MS	autograph original
TS	typescript original
draft	autograph draft
MSC	handwritten copy of original
PC	photocopy
TC	typed copy

MANUSCRIPT SOURCES

Institutions

ATL	Alexander Turnbull Library, Wellington
Berg	The Henry W. and Albert A. Berg Collection, New York Public Library, Astor, Lenox and Tilden Foundations
BL	British Library
McMaster	McMaster University, Hamilton, Ontario
Mitchell	The Mitchell Library, Sydney
Newberry	The Newberry Library, Chicago
Smith	Smith College, Northampton, Massachusetts
Stanford	Stanford University, Stanford, California
Sussex	University of Sussex, Brighton
Texas	The Humanities Research Center, University of Texas at Austin.
Windsor	University of Windsor, Windsor, Ontario
WDPT	Wellington District Public Trustee

Private owners

Alpers	Professor Antony Alpers
Bemis	Mrs George Bemis
Bowden	Mr George M. Bowden
Leeming	Mr Owen Leeming
McIntosh	Mrs Lulu McIntosh
Murry	Mr Colin Middleton Murry
Rawlins	Mr R.E.D. Rawlins
Richards	Mrs Dorothy Richards
Strachey	The Strachey Trust, London
Weber	Mrs Shirley Weber

SOURCES OF PREVIOUS PUBLICATION
and short forms used in the annotation

Adam 300	*Adam International Review*, No. 300 (1963–5)
Adam 370–375	*Adam International Review*, Nos. 370–375 (1972–3)
Alpers 1953	Antony Alpers, *Katherine Mansfield, a Biography* (New York, 1953)
Alpers 1980	Antony Alpers, *The Life of Katherine Mansfield* (1980)
Beauchamp	Sir Harold Beauchamp, *Reminiscences and Recollections* (Wellington, 1936)
Berkman	Sylvia Berkman, *Katherine Mansfield, a Critical Study* (New Haven, Conn., 1951)
BTW	John Middleton Murry, *Between Two Worlds, an Autobiography* (1935)

Carco 1916   Francis Carco, *Les Innocents* (Paris, 1916)
Carco 1938   Francis Carco, *Montmartre à vingt ans* (Paris, 1938)
Carrington   *Carrington, Letters and Extracts from her Diaries,* ed. David Garnett (1970)
CLDHL   *The Collected Letters of D.H. Lawrence,* ed. Harry T. Moore (New York, 1962)
Delany   Paul Delany, *D.H. Lawrence's Nightmare: The Writer and His Circle in the Years of the Great War* (New York, 1979)
Dickinson   John W. Dickinson, 'Katherine Mansfield and S.S. Koteliansky: Some Unpublished Letters', *Revue de littérature comparée,* no. 45 (1971), 79-99.
DVW   *The Diary of Virginia Woolf,* ed. Anne Olivier Bell, vols. I and II (1977-8)
Exhibition   *Katherine Mansfield: An Exhibition,* Humanities Research Center, University of Texas (Austin, Texas, 1973)
Glenavy   Beatrice [Campbell], Lady Glenavy, *Today We Will Only Gossip* (1964)
Journal 1927   *The Journal of Katherine Mansfield,* ed. John Middleton Murry (1927)
Journal 1954   *Journal of Katherine Mansfield,* Definitive Edition, ed. John Middleton Murry (1954)
LDHL   *The Letters of D.H. Lawrence,* ed. James T. Boulton, vol. I, ed. George J. Zytaruk and James T. Boulton, vol. II (1979-82)
Lea   F.A. Lea, *The Life of John Middleton Murry* (1959)
LJMM   *Katherine Mansfield's Letters to John Middleton Murry, 1913-1922,* ed. John Middleton Murry (1951)
LKM   *The Letters of Katherine Mansfield,* 2 vols., ed. John Middleton Murry (1928)
LVW   *The Letters of Virginia Woolf,* ed. Nigel Nicolson and Joanne Trautmann, vols. I and II (1975-6)
Mantz   Ruth Elvish Mantz and John Middleton Murry, *The Life of Katherine Mansfield* (1933)
Meyers   Jeffrey Meyers, *Katherine Mansfield, a Biography* (1978)
MLM   Ida Baker, *Katherine Mansfield: The Memories of LM* (1971)
Morrell   *Ottoline at Garsington 1915-1918,* ed. Robert Gathorne-Hardy (1974)
Orton   William Orton, *The Last Romantic* (1937)
O'Sullivan   Vincent O'Sullivan, *Katherine Mansfield's New Zealand* (Wellington, 1974)
UN   *The Urewera Notebook,* ed. Ian A. Gordon (Wellington, 1978)

The place of publication is London unless otherwise noted.

I

ENGLAND AND NEW ZEALAND:

1903–1908

Kathleen Mansfield Beauchamp was born on 14 October 1888 at 11 Tinakori Road, Wellington. She was the third daughter born in four years of marriage to Harold Beauchamp, a vigorous and ambitious thirty-year-old merchant, and Annie Burnell Beauchamp, née Dyer, who was beautiful, delicate, and already, at twenty-four, a little detached from her children. When Kathleen was a year old, she was left in charge of her maternal grandmother while her parents visited England for several months.

Beauchamp prospered in business, and in 1892 moved his family to a large house with extensive grounds at Karori, a thinly populated valley six miles from Wellington. Kathleen began her education at the local primary school when she was six. Three years later she attended Wellington Girls' High School, where she wrote her first stories. In 1899, when her father — already sole partner in J.M. Bannatyne & Co., a large importing firm, and a director of the Gear Meat Co. — was appointed a director of the Bank of New Zealand, the family was taken back to the city, to 75 Tinakori Road. Two more girls had been born meanwhile, only one of whom, Jeanne, survived, and a boy, Leslie Heron ('Chummie'). In Wellington the three eldest children, Kathleen and her older sisters Vera and Charlotte ('Chaddie') were transferred to Miss Swainson's School in Fitzherbert Terrace, a private establishment which claimed social superiority to the state school. The houses lived in over these years, the beaches of the summer holidays, and the small circle of family and friends were to furnish the details of most of KM's New Zealand stories.

On 29 January 1903 the Beauchamp family sailed from Wellington for London, the only passengers on board the *Niwaru*. 'It was really a glorified yachting cruise,' as Harold Beauchamp recalled in 1936, 'beginning with calls at Gisborne and Auckland and then via Cape Horn and Las Palmas, the whole voyage occupying 47 days' (Beauchamp, 87).

To Lulu Dyer,[1] *[12 March 1903]*

[Las Palmas]

This is such a lovely place,[2] darling, & we are having a very good time. Be a good little "Tweets."

From
Kass

MS (picture postcard) McIntosh.

[1] Lulu Dyer (b.1897), KM's young cousin, the daughter of her maternal uncle Frank Dyer.

[2] The card, posted from Plymouth on 17 Mar 1903, has a picture of Tenerife.

To [? Marion Tweed],[1] *16 April 1903*

27 St. Stephen's Sq.[2] | Bayswater. W.
April 16th 1903

My dearest Marius.

What a long time since I have had a talk to you? It seems years & years. Do you feel the same about it? I wish that I could give you an idea of London. It is totally beyond description. It is most marvellous!!! The traffic is so astounding. There is none other way to have a really splendid view, than to sit on the top of a bus, with a piece of strong elastic on your hat; Then it is superb!! The bus drivers are such cures. They look most beautifully comfy wrapped up in gloves and rugs, and are most talkative. My dear, I wish that you could see Westminster Abbey. It is so lovely!! It is utterly impossible to rush the Abbey, because immediately you enter you are held enthralled by some marvellous work of sculpture, and so it is the whole time that you are there. I fell in love with Sophia, daughter of James I, (I mean, I fell in love with her tomb.) She died when she was three days old. The tomb is of white marble. It is a baby's basinette with a hood and deep curtains, and a little child asleep inside. I bent over and kissed the baby; it looked so sad! Are you laughing dear? It was not funny. We went to St. Paul's Cathedral last Good Friday. What charmed me most was the beautiful paintings the exquisite arches, & the magnificence of the mosaic work. The service was fearfully impressive. The church was dim, and there was a wonderful anthem. It seems to go right through you, and made you quite choky. The building of St. Pauls is very fine but I don't like all the pigeons that are constantly flying about. They remind me of the time that Christ came and turned the dove merchants out of the

Temple. How interested you would be in the British Museum. My dear you could see enough Julius Caesar's to last you a lifetime, with noses, and minus noses, according to B.C. & A.D. All the sculpture everywhere, was a huge revelation, to me. O the indescribable beauty of form and attitude, that can be hewn out of a block of marble. And, O Marius, the pictures. My dear they take away all my adjectives!!!!!! I have fallen in love with all Watts pictures in the Tate Gallery. The most marvellous originality of colour is so striking, the depth of his reds, the calm peace of his blues, and his figures!!!! I think that the two most beautiful I saw were "Love and Life", & "Hope".³ On Bank Holiday Father & I did the correct thing & went to 'Appy 'Ampstead 'Eath. When we arrived there it grew most fearfully cold, and we had a bad snowstorm. I loved it. The whole place looked like a picture postcard. A place I am very fond of going to is Hyde Park. The carriages, horses and babies are most lovely, especially the last named. In their perambulators they remind me of little bits of wedding cake tied up with white ribbons. The motor cars are very fascinating. You see hundreds dodging about everywhere.

I never saw such beautiful curtains as the English have. Silk & silk lace of the most exquisite quality!!! I would just love some of them for dresses!!!

We three girls go to school on the 29th of this month (April.) We are going to Queen's College Harley Street. W. It is a most delightful school. The school headmistress is a Miss Croudace, and the house mistress a Miss Wood.⁴ They are both exceedingly nice. The school is most superbly furnished. The room where we study is carpets with thick Turkey carpeted, great armchairs everywhere, neat little tables, rugs, and charming pictures. Even Latin would be interesting in this room. And now dear, I must stop. Diddy⁵ will give you my address if you have not got it. The best of luck to your matric.⁶ With love

I am | Yrs truly

Kassius.

P.S. Do write me soon about everything. Love to all my friends.

MS Newberry. The *New Zealand Guider*, June 1936, 2-3.

¹ Evidently to a school friend in Wellington, this letter may have been to Marion Tweed, a contemporary of KM's at Miss Swainson's School. Both girls were members of the A.R. (ante-room) Club, which was limited to pupils with literary aspirations — a school rhyme began, 'A for A.R. Club confined to the fair'.
² Presumably a residence hotel, at which the Beauchamp family were staying until the girls entered school.
³ The allegorical paintings of George Frederick Watts (1817-1904), English painter and sculptor, were extraordinarily popular at this time.
⁴ Queen's College, Harley Street, at which KM and her sisters Vera and Chaddie were enrolled from April 1903, had been founded in 1848 by the Christian Socialists F.D. Maurice and Charles Kingsley, as the first English institution for the higher education of women. The

College was probably chosen for the Beauchamp girls because their cousins were already attending it; but one of the teachers at Miss Swainson's School in Wellington was related to Kingsley.

Camilla Croudace was Lady Resident at Queen's College from 1881 to 1906. Clara Wood leased no. 41 and the upper part of no. 43 Harley Street, where she boarded the 20 or so College girls who lived in, and were known as compounders. The Beauchamp girls were in Miss Wood's charge, and their Aunt Belle (Isobel Marion Dyer, later Mrs Trinder) was taken on as her assistant.

[5] Hilda Nathan, a Wellington friend and pupil at Miss Swainson's School; her family figures in *Prelude* as the Samuel Josephs.

[6] Marion Tweed was the only girl KM was close to at Miss Swainson's who took the entrance examination for the University of New Zealand (although she did not sit her Matriculation until the following year) and who also studied Latin. The 'Mar-' 'Kass-' play also lends weight to the identification of her as the recipient of this letter.

To Sylvia Payne,[1] *[25 August 1903]*

Brompton House[2] | Horngold Road | Malvern

My dearest Sylvia.

Thanks ever so much for your postcard which I received this morning. I am so glad that you are enjoying Minehead so much. It looks very pretty. We have been doing a good deal of walking since we came. The peculiar feature of this place seems that one cannot get tired. I earnestly believe that you could walk to, well, London, without feeling the slightest fatigued — I expect to come home quite thin, I am sure I quite deserve it. So far I can see no signs of "Skeletonism," I grieve to say. By the way, what would Evelyn[3] say to that word, if she saw it in my notes? We went to an open air concert, held in the Promenade Gardens, on Thursday night. I should imagine that only local talent had been employed. One capacious gentleman, who looked as though he had lived all his life on pork, cabbage, and stodgy suet puddings, played, or strictly speaking, made a great noise on the cornet. The effect was most harrowing!!!!! Another small prodigy (which is a type of mankind, that I particularly dislike, as a general rule), played 'Auld Lang Syne' on the harp. I had visions of the Pfeiffer Hall,[4] in my brain — and so did not particularly enjoy it.

The last I heard of Marion[5] was from Heidelberg. My dear, don't you envy her? I am greedy enough to do so. I am quite anxious for College to open again, much though I like holidays. I have heard from Cornwall twice already. Long, long, letters.[6] Now my dear, I must stop. I can see you politely suppressing a yawn. With love to all, and in particular to yourself

I am | Ever your loving friend

Kathleen

Should I have signed myself as cousin?

P.S. I am sure your age and discretion could suggest a poem much better than I ever could. Please do so!!!

MS ATL.

[1] Sylvia Payne (1887–1949), KM's cousin, was the daughter of Joseph Frank Payne (1840–1910), a distinguished physician, one-time fellow of Magdalen, medical historian, and Emeritus Harveian Librarian at the Royal College of Physicians. His mother was Eliza Dyer, the sister of KM's maternal grandfather.

[2] A private hotel where the Beauchamps stayed briefly during the summer of 1903.

[3] Evelyn Payne, Sylvia's older sister.

[4] The hall at Queen's College, where dances ended with the girls singing 'Auld Lang Syne'.

[5] Marion Creelman, a Canadian girl at the College.

[6] Probably from Eileen Palliser, another New Zealander at Queen's College, with whom KM shared a room after the Beauchamp girls had quarrelled among themselves. Eileen's father, Charles Palliser, then a banker in London, had been a boyhood friend of Harold Beauchamp.

To Lulu Dyer, [28 October 1903]

[Queen's College, Harley Street]

How do you like this,[1] Tweets dear? Do write old Kasslena a letter soon. Much love to Mother & Father from

Kass.

MS (picture postcard) McIntosh.

[1] The card has a picture of girls on a staircase at Queen's College.

To Sylvia Payne, 23 December 1903

The Retreat[1] | Bexley — Kent.
23/xii/03

Dearest Sylvia —

I want to write to you this afternoon, so here I am — I am not at all surprised at myself, I knew that I would not wait till you had written. Why should we lose any time in knowing each other, when we have lost so much already.

I cannot tell you how sorry I am that I shall not see you again. I like you much more than any other girl I have met in England & I seem to see less of you. We just stand upon the threshold of each other's heart and never get right in. What I mean by 'heart' is just this. My heart is a place where everything I love (whether it be in imagination or in truth) has a free entrance. It is where I store my memories, all my happiness and my sorrow and there is a large compartment in it labelled *"Dreams."* There are many many people that I like very much, but they generally view my public rooms, and they call me false, and mad, and changeable. I would not show them what I was really like for worlds. They would think me madder I suppose —

I wish we could know each other, so that I might be able to say "Sylvia is one of my *best* friends." Don't think that I mean half I look and say to other people. I cannot think why I so seldom am myself. I think I rather hug myself to myself, too much. Don't you? Not that it is beautiful or precious. It is a very shapeless, bare, undecorated thing just yet. I have been fearfully cross this morning — It was about my music. Yesterday I got a concerto from Tom[2] for a Xmas present and I tryed it over with Vera this morning. She *counted aloud* and said *wrong wrong*, called me a pig, and then said she would go and tell Aunt Louie[3] I was swearing at her. I laugh as I read this now. At the time I felt *ill* with anger. So much for my excellent temper!!

It is quiet here now. I am alone in my bedroom. O don't you just thank God for quiet. I do. If only it could last though. Something always disturbs it. There is a bird somewhere outside crying ♪ , yet for all this, I am sorry, very sorry, to have left London. I like it so very much. Next term I really shall work hard. I MUST — I am so fearfully idle & conceited.

Why I have written this letter, I do not know. Forgive me dear. I do not dare to read it through. I should burn it if I did. Goodbye for the present. I beg of you write soon to

Your very loving Friend
Kathleen

[*On back of last page*]

Private.
If you feel absurd or jolly don't read this.
Private.

MS ATL. Alpers 1953, 60–1.

[1] The home of Henry Herron Beauchamp (1825–1907), KM's great-uncle, who after twenty years amassing considerable wealth as a merchant in Australia, returned to England with his family in 1871. His daughter Mary Annette (1866–1941), known always as 'Elizabeth', married Count Henning von Arnim in 1891. Author of the extremely popular *Elizabeth and her German Garden* (1898), as well as further memoirs and novels, she was later the Countess Russell.

[2] Thomas Trowell, a young musician friend, see p. 16, n.1.

[3] Henry Beauchamp's wife, known as Louise or 'Louey', had been Elizabeth Weiss Lassetter, the daughter of a Baptist minister and the sister of Frederick Lassetter, a prominent Sydney businessman.

To Sylvia Payne, 6 January 1904

Wortley | Sheffield
6/i/04.

My dearest Sylvia

I cannot apologise for not having written before. I have no excuse except, *I could not.* Chad & I came here last Saturday because Bertha, Aunt Louey's maid has been very ill, and there were so many in the house — We are staying with cousins.[1] Really, I am not enjoying it at all, but I have to pretend I am. O, I do want to see you so. Chad & I shall be in London on Tuesday at 1.30. Do come and see me that afternoon, *if you have nothing else to do.* I have written a good deal these holidays, and practised, *and* worked, but I have grown no thinner!!!! I cannot write today. Please don't think me a pig! I am tired of the sight of paper and of pens. I have *had* to write 15 N.Z. letters. At present I am sitting in a small room with a large fire and

3 dogs

1 cockatoo

1 canary.

My head is thumping like an engine. I am almost too tired to do anything. O do write to me!!!! I know I deserve no letters at all but I *want* some. I have had *one* glorious letter from G.W.[2] Sylvia dear, if I did not love you very much I would not dare to write to you like this. —

With much love | Always your affectionate
Kass.

O I DO WANT TO SEE YOU SO!!!!!!

[*Enclosure*]

The Old Year and the New Year

31/xii/03

> Tonight we pass a Milestone on the road
> One nearer to the great one and the last
> Slowly we tread, for heavier grows our load
> And veils of mist are creeping o'er the Past.
>
> One Milestone nearer! do we understand
> We pass so many; sometimes we forget,
> We have crept closer to the dear Lord's hand
> Are we quite ready to receive it yet?

The night is dark; our way is hard to find
We stumble and alas! we often fall
But we have God to pity and to bind
Our wounds, if only we but faintly call.

O God, our Father, be with us tonight
And listen while to thee we feebly pray
Let there be all around us a great Light
Turning our darkness into brightest Day.

Written on New Years Eve.

MS (with enclosure) ATL.

[1] The Broughtons, with whom KM was staying in Sheffield, were English relatives by marriage. Harold Beauchamp's uncle, Craddock Beauchamp, married Harriet Broughton, whose elder brother Reginald (1837-1912), a graduate of Balliol College, Oxford, accompanied his sister to New Zealand. He was Headmaster of Nelson College in 1862, and of Christ's College, Christchurch, 1863-4, before returning to England, where he became a Fellow of Hertford College, Oxford, in 1878.

[2] Gladys Williams, an Australian student at Queen's College who later published fiction and verse as 'John Presland'. She had gone up to Girton College, Cambridge, at the beginning of the academic year.

To Sylvia Payne, 24 January 1904

[Queen's College] 41 Harley Street | W.
24/i/04.

Dearest Sylvia —

It was ripping of you to write to me such a long letter! I was very pleased to receive it. I certainly do *hate* fogs. They are abominable. Yesterday I did nothing but practise and I wrote to Gladys and to Tom. I heard from G. yesterday morning. It was a perfectly lovely letter, but *so* queer. Just exactly like her. I do wish that people did not think her fast, or empty. She has more in her than almost anyone else I know. She has the most glorious ideas about things, and is wonderfully clever — Her letters are just full of keen originality, and *power*. Do you understand? Perhaps other people would think them foolish. I don't. O, how thankful I am to be back at College, but, Sylvia, I am *ashamed* at the way in which I long for German.[1] I simply can't help it. It is dreadful. And when I go into class, I feel I must just stare at him the whole time. I never liked anyone so much. Every day I like him more. Yet on Thursday he was like *ice*! By the way, is not this *heavenly*: — "To every man, there come

noble thoughts which flash across his heart like great white birds."
(Maeterlinck.)[2]

O, that is wonderful. Great white birds. Is not that perfect?! I wish
there was not a night before College. O, I wish you were a boarder!!!
What times we would have together. I do love you so, much more
each time I see you. So little goes on here. All the girls are so very dull.

Is not the condition of the Poor just now awful. Miss Wood told us
all about [it] the other afternoon, so I have arranged a Celebrity
Evening for next Thursday night. Admission sixpence. Gwen Rouse[3]
is going to help me, and the money is to be sent to a poor parish —
On Friday afternoon I went to Mudie's.[4] What a fascinating place it
is!! I had some peeps into most lovely books, & the *bindings* were
exquisite. I always think that it is so sinful to publish "Bloody
Hands", by Augusta St. John, in green leather, & Bleak House, in,
paper for 6d. 'Tout marche de travers.' That is very true!

My writing this afternoon is most erratic. I do not know why.
You know you always say that you are not *17*, well, pardon me, I
think you *are quite*. I mean to *work* specially hard, this term. I am
taking *19* hours. Dear, I must finish this 'ego'. You must be tired
of it

With my love from | Your loving Friend
Kathleen —

MS ATL. Cited Alpers 1953, 62; Alpers 1980, 31.

[1] 'German' was Walter Rippmann (1869-1947), professor of German during KM's years
at Queen's College; he was an important influence, introducing her to the work of Oscar
Wilde and the 1890s.
[2] Quoted, with slight inaccuracies, from Maurice Maeterlinck's essay, 'The Deeper
Life', in *The Treasure of the Humble*, trans. Alfred Sutro (1897), 183.
[3] A contemporary of KM's at Queen's College, whom Ida Baker described as 'a tall,
languid girl from the Isle of Man . . . She had a mouth that might have belonged to one of
Dante Gabriel Rossetti's damsels' (*MLM*, 26-7).
[4] A bookshop in New Oxford Street.

To Sylvia Payne, 25 March 1904

[Queen's College] 41 Harley Street | W.
25:iii:04.

I am about to presume on your good nature, my dearest Sylvia. I
had to write to Mac Neile[1] tonight, and I don't know her address.
Would you be so kind as to address the letter I sent inclosed, and
post it as soon as possible. I am afraid this sounds so rude and
'familiar' of me, but you are the only person I would dare to ask to

do such a thing, so please, dear, forgive me. The letter is going to Mac Neile on Monday. That is why it is so urgent.

Hoping to see you on Monday, and also hoping that this won't give you any trouble.

Believe me to be | Ever your very loving friend

Kass

MS ATL.

¹ Bridget McNeile, a year senior to KM at Queen's College.

To Sylvia Payne, 1 April 1904

[Queen's College] 41 Harley Street | W.

1:IV:04

I am rather thankful dearest Sylvia, that the Fates did not give me my cue and bid me enter on the First of April. Though we, of this generation pride ourselves upon non superstition, and many other most delightful qualities that did not belong to our great grand-mothers, still I should not like to walk in and make my bow hand in hand with the first of April, however dear and mirthful he may be.

> And here is my holiday motto:—
> "The world is so full of a number of things
> I am sure we should all be as happy as Kings."¹

Well known?, you say. Yes, very well known. It vies in popularity with the word "feeble" or "help!" Still I think it is very excellent. I have only discovered very very lately how absurdly blind I am — I mean, concerning happiness. I shall print a huge advertisement and send a man all round London with it. This is what it shall be:—

> "The way to Happiness.
> Marvellous invention.
> Patent Food.
> Free on Payment of 1d stamp."

Then when I receive countless myriads of letters inclosing 1d stamp I shall send each person a nice dainty little box tied up with red ribbon. Inside they will find a dear little chubby Cupid with a large sized bow and arrows, and the direction shall be: — "Apply this to the heart. Money sent back if the result is not accomplished".

Sylvia forgive this nonsense if you can dear. I feel so happy myself. Why not be happy? We have so little time in which to live at all! Write and tell me what you think of this.

Ever yours with love
Kass

MS ATL.

[1] 'Happy Thought', from Robert Louis Stevenson's *A Child's Garden of Verses* (1885).

To Sylvia Payne, [before 10 July 1904]

[Queen's College, Harley Street] In my bedroom. I am so sorry to hear that you are ill, Sylvia dear. Ida[1] has been in just now to tell me that she called at lunch time! I am sure that Miss Harper[2] will miss you in Latin.

I am afraid I was very dull and silly last night. To tell you the truth I felt so 'played out'. College has been as dull as possible today. I suppose it was because of the holidays. I wrote to Gladys last night. I do hope to hear from her soon.

Dear, do take care of yourself, and come back to College soon.

Much love from | Your 'friend' (?)
Kathleen.

MS ATL.

[1] KM's lifelong friend Ida Baker (see p. 90, n.1); she and her sister May, daughters of a retired Indian Army doctor who lived in Welbeck Street, were day students at Queen's College.
[2] Barbara Harper, second mistress when KM attended Queen's College, served as Warden 1906-8.

To Sylvia Payne, [10 July 1904]

[Queen's College] 41 Harley St. | W.
Thursday

I was so glad to receive your P.C. tonight, dearest Sylvia. Ridge Cap[1] will do you ever so much good — How I envy you seeing country and hills and flowers and all the many good things that just delight my heart in the country.

Hills, especially are such dear friends of mine — they are so strong, so noble, and such an example to our wretched selves — if only we would take it.

There is someone playing on the violin next door. I can hear them so plainly. The lamp in the Mews[2] below is flickering & moving about restlessly, and my flowers in my window are nodding and talking to me at a great rate.

Funny how everything grows to be a friend if you live near it long enough! That lamp in the Mews I feel is an old old comrade of mine. In the evening I just wait to see it lighted, and it [is] so sociable it simply beams all over for the rest of the night.

If I had been a Cave Dweller I should have worshipped Light, I think. Wouldn't you? The Portland Square Gardens are very beautiful just now though, to my great sorrow the irises are over. I mourned for them very much for a day or two, but now I have transferred my affection to the copper beeches. Gladys comes home on Monday. How I long to see her! I have no news and my letter is dull so I shall not bore you longer.

Get strong dear and take care of yourself —

Your friend
Kathleen.

MS ATL.

[1] Miss Croudace had a cottage at Ridge Cap, Shottermill, Haslemere, where the College students sometimes stayed.
[2] Mansfield Mews, at the side of Queen's College.

To Sylvia Payne, 26 December 1904

'The Retreat' [Bexley, Kent]
26.xii.04.

My dearest Sylvia.

I received your sweet little Kalendar by the post this morning. It was dear of you to give it to me, and all the year it will be reminding me of you, wherever I am. So far, I have enjoyed myself immensely. The days have flown past, without one dull moment. There has been so much to do. I have had some good practises too, and my cousin who is staying here has a glorious tenor voice.[1] I am so fond of a tenor voice, it is so poetical, I think.

It is a very quiet day here. Do you know the kind of day when you can almost *hear* the grass growing.[2] I love days like that. I have been for a long long walk, and the ground was fresh and wet, and the hills, all brown and bare, were covered with a thin veil of mist. Every sound that broke the stillness seemed to come from thousands of miles away. I was thinking of you, too, and of how strange it is that we two, who wish to be friends so much, don't seem to be able to.

I wonder why. It seems as though the Fates did it on purpose. Yet the more I know you the more I want to. College is so full of work, and the days are so short, we don't seem to find time for talking together. It is only by your letters, that I really feel I know you.

Wouldn't it be glorious if we went to Ridge Cap together, and had long long walks down in the copse, and then talks at night, or if in the summer we went away to the same place. Sylvia, we must try to.

Among my Xmas presents I got a photo of the blessed German baby. I am longing to show it to you. I was so devoted to her. I have written another little tale about her. It is better than the others, so I am going to send it to the Mag. Some people seem to like those 'baby' stories, and I love writing them.[3] Your poem in this Mag, was just lovely.[4] I like it more and more. I do hope you will write a lot now, and send one regularly. I am sure that you could.

Isn't there a strange fascination about College? I am always thinking of it. It seems to become quite part of one's life in time. I don't know what I shall do when I leave, and think of it going on in the dear old way, and new girls coming, and the old ones all gone away. There is really not much news to tell you today, for little has happened, and as yet I have read nothing.

There is another baby here. She is four and a half. Her name is Estherelle.[5] She is beautiful, with long gold hair far past her waist, and great blue wonderful eyes. When she kneels in front of the fire with the light on her hair, & the heat flushing her dear little face, she is like a fairy or a little picture child. She sings in a little shaky voice about a black-bird, and says the drollest things. She has been telling me about an " 'a'gusting mis'able mouse" all the morning, and is so affectionate. Are you very fond of small children? They always will captivate me —

Dear, do write to me soon, and tell me about what you are doing, and about yourself. I am wanting to hear so much. Auf wiedersehen! Write *soon*, and

Believe me to be | Your very loving
Kass.

MS ATL.

[1] Henry Beauchamp (1864-194?), known in the family as Harry or 'Grief', was the official guardian of the Beauchamp girls in England, and referred to as 'Guardy'. He taught voice at the London Academy of Music.

[2] Cf. Wordsworth, 'The Idiot Boy' (11.295-6): 'The grass you almost hear it growing, / You hear it now if e'er you can.'

[3] The baby was Felicitas Joyce von Armin, born July 1899, fourth daughter of 'Elizabeth'. Two of KM's uncollected 'baby stories' had been published in the *Queen's College Magazine*, 'The Pine Tree, the Sparrow, and You and I' in December 1903, and 'Your Birthday' in December 1904. A third, 'One Day', appeared in July 1905.

[4] 'A Rondeau on Autumn', in the December 1904 *Magazine*.

[5] Esterel Beauchamp, daughter of cousin Harry.

To [?Thomas Trowell],[1] [31 December 1904]

[The Retreat, Bexley, Kent]

New Years Eve. It is 12.30. All the bells in the village Churches are pealing — Another year has come. Now at the entrance of this New Year, my dearest, I propose to begin my book. It will not be at all grand or dramatic but just all that I have done. You, who are so far away, know so little of what happens to me, and it is selfish of me not to tell you more — I have just returned from a Midnight Service — It was very very beautiful & solemn. The air outside was cold and bracing, and the Night was a beautiful thing. Over all the woods & the meadows, Nature had tenderly flung a veil to protect from the frost, but the trees stood out, dark and beautiful, against the clear, starry sky. The church looked truly very fit for God's House, tonight — It looked so strong, so invincible, so hospitable — <There were many many people there> It was only during the Silent Prayer that I made up my mind to write this — I mean this year to try and be a different person, and I want at the end of this year, to see how I have kept all the vows that I have made tonight. So much happens in a year. One may mean so much good, and do so little — I am writing this by the light of a wee peep of gas, and I have only got on a dressing gown — so dearie, I am so tired, I think I must go to bed. Tomorrow will be the 1st of January. What a wonderful and what a lovely world this is. I thank God tonight, that I *am*.

MS (draft) ATL, notebook 37. *Journal* 1954, 1-2.

[1] Thomas (or Arnold) Trowell (1889-1966) was the 'Caesar' to whom KM addressed passionate declarations — presumably never sent — in the early portions of her journal. The private subscription fund which enabled him and his twin brother Garnet (see p. 58, n.1) to study music abroad included a contribution of £25 from Harold Beauchamp. The brothers gave two farewell concerts before leaving Wellington at the end of June 1903, six months after KM. They studied for a year at the Hoch Conservatorium in Frankfurt; Thomas then went on to the Conservatorium in Brussels, where he won the Concours Prize for the violoncello. Later, in London, he became Professor of Cello at the Guildhall School of Music, 1924, was on the staff of the Royal College of Music from 1937, and enjoyed a modest success as a composer.

To Sylvia Payne, 15 February 1905

9 John Street | W[1]
15.II.05.

My dearest Sylvia.

Many many thanks for my Valentine. It is the first I have ever seen or received, so it is quite an occurrence — It was dear & good of you to have sent it me —

Well, here am I in bed propped up with pillows, surrounded with flowers & books and feeling quite 'perky' — Still I *long* for College, and for 2 *whole* feet! My first operation is an event that I shall ever look back to with horror *and* amusement — It is amusing to think of such an old carthorse as I am being in such a condition as not even able to do my hair!

The Nurses are all dears — I am quite D.V.[2] on the matron — What a day it is! The sparrows are having a Vocal Class outside my window, & the sky is blue.

There is a cab stand below my window — I never knew such cheerful souls as cabbies are — they do nothing but *shriek* with laughter. Sometimes I wake up in the night, and a cab comes, alone — 'Allo, Bill, 'ow are yer? calls a cab man, and straight way the whole number scream & guffaw. What dears they must be. I have had numbers of visitors, and that blessed Ida writes to me every day, & tells me about College. My head is full of plots for stories — I have not written any down yet, because it is so difficult in bed —

Elsa[3] came to see me yesterday looking beautiful. She brought me heaps of books, & this house appears to be full of them.

I have read Amiel,[4] & I am going to be frank. I like him in bits, but I do not think he is always logical — I hope I have not offended you dear.

There is no news from me, but I thought I must write & thank you for your dearness —

Much love from your loving friend Kass —

MS ATL.

[1] KM was in a nursing home run by her father's cousin, Connie Beauchamp, for a minor operation, apparently on one of her feet.
[2] A College expression, from the initials of a niece of Miss Croudace's, meaning, to have a 'crush' on someone.
[3] Elsa Cutler, a boarder at the school a year ahead of KM.
[4] The *Journal* of Henri-Frédéric Amiel (1821–81), French diarist and critic, was first translated by Mrs Humphry Ward in 1885.

To Sylvia Payne, 24 April 1906

30 Manchester Street | W.[1]
24.iv.06

My dearest Cousin,

I was so delighted to get your letter yesterday — and to hear what a fine time you are having. Truth to tell — I am just longing for the country — and especially for pine woods — they have a mystical fascination for me — but all trees have. Woods and the sea — both are perfect.

We have been staying here since last Friday with Father and Mother, and have had a very good time. I don't think I have ever laughed more. They are both just the same *and* we leave for New Zealand in October. Strange thought — for some things I am very glad, now — but I feel as though all my English life was over, already. Do you know — I have a fancy that when I am there, we shall write far more often and know each other far better than we do now. I do hope it will be so — dear — because I have always wanted us to be friends — and we never seem to pass a certain point — once a Term, perhaps, I feel "Sylvia & I really know each other now", and next time we meet — the feeling is gone.

A great change has come into my life since I saw you last. Father is greatly opposed to my wish to be a professional 'cellist or to take up the 'cello to any great extent — so my hope for a musical career is absolutely gone. It was a fearful disappointment — I could not tell you what I have felt like — and do now when I think of it — but I suppose it is no earthly use warring with the Inevitable — so in the future I shall give *all* my time to writing.[2] There are great opportunities for a girl in New Zealand — she has so much time and quiet — and we have an ideal little "cottage by the sea"[3] where I mean to spend a good deal of my time. Do you *love* solitude as I do — especially if I am in a writing mood — and will you do so — too. Write, I mean, in the Future. I feel sure that you would be splendidly successful —

I am so keen upon all women having a *definite* future — are not you? The idea of sitting still and waiting for a husband is absolutely revolting — and it really is the attitude of a great many girls. Do you know I have read none of the books that you mentioned. Is not that shocking — but — Sylvia — you know that little "Harold Brown" shop in Wimpole Shop [*for* Street] — I picked up a small collection of poems entitled "The Silver Net" by Louis Vintras — and I liked some of them immensely. The atmosphere is so *intense*. He seems to me to belong to that school which flourished just a few years ago — but which now has not a single representative — a kind of impressionist literature school. Don't think that I even approve of them — but they interest me — Dowson — Sherard — School.[4] It rather made me smile to read of you wishing you could create your fate — O, how many times I have felt just the same. I just long for power over circumstances — & always feel as though I could do such a great deal more good than is done — & give such a lot of pleasure — aber — — — — — —

We have not seen a great deal of the Bakers, but they are flourishing. Mother asks me if you know a house suitable for a lady two wee children and two maids anywhere near? It is just by the way. I am enjoying this Hotel life. There is a kind of feeling of irresponsibility about it that is fascinating. Would you not like to try *all* sorts of lives — one is so very small — but that is the satisfaction of writing — one can impersonate so many people —

Au revoir — dear friend.

Will you give my love to Cousin Ellie & Marjory[5]

I send you a great deal.

Your friend

K.

MS ATL. Alpers 1953, 70-1.

[1] Fripps Hotel, where the Beauchamp family were staying.

[2] During her time at Queen's College, KM took cello lessons at the London Academy of Music, and on her return to Wellington was encouraged by Thomas Trowell sen. (see p. 25, n.1) to take her music seriously; but her father's intransigent opposition had much to do with her eventual determination to become a writer. In January 1907 she wrote, 'Definitely I have decided not to be a musician. It's not my forte, I can plainly see. The fact remains at that — I must be an authoress.' (*Journal* 1954, 8.)

[3] At Downes Point, Days Bay, across the harbour from Wellington city.

[4] Louis Vintras's *The Silver Net* was published in 1903. Ernest Dowson (1867-1900), poet and fiction writer, became identified in the popular mind with 'decadence'. Dowson died at the home of Robert Harborough Sherard (1861-1943), novelist and critic. The two did not, as KM suggests, form any kind of 'school'.

[5] 'Cousin Ellie' was Sylvia's mother. 'Marjory' may have been Marjorie Wilensky, a school friend in the College Debating Society with KM.

To Lulu Dyer, 31 August 1906

[Queen's College] 43 Harley St., W.
31 8 06.

My darling old Luls —

I wonder if you have forgotten these three cousins of yours who are always talking about a certain little girl whose photograph sits on the wall and looks at them. Chad and I are writing our mail letters[1] here — and it is so hot that we wish we were both cosily tucked into the bath and writing on the back of a soap dish with the cold tap trickling down our heads.

Dear Aunt Phoeb was good & sweet to remember us with such long letters by the last Mail. We can't tell you how we appreciated them. I wonder if you can realise now — Luls dear — what a wonderfully brave Mother you have got. Tell her how we are all longing to come down to Park Street[2] and have a long talk. It is your birthday soon now dear — so this little note is [to] wish you all sorts of good things. My present — I shall give you myself when I get back — Doesn't it sound funny!

Do come down to the wharf to meet us, darling — but I'm afraid you will be dreadfully grown up — Will you?

Much love to Aunt Phoeb — Uncle Frank & your little self

From your loving old

Kass

MS McIntosh.

[1] At this time ships carried mail from England to Wellington two or three times a month.

[2] The Dyers lived at 5 Park Street, off Tinakori Road, Wellington. Lulu's mother, Phoebe Alicia Dyer, was the second daughter of Richard John Seddon (1845-1906), a Lancashire-man who was Liberal Prime Minister of New Zealand for the last 13 years of his life. Seddon, a close friend of Harold Beauchamp, had died on 10 June 1906.

∽

The Beauchamps sailed from Gravesend on the *Corinthic*, via Cape Town, on 18 October 1906 and arrived back in Wellington on 6 December. Until she again left for England 19 months later, KM's energies were directed to writing, music, an active social life, covert love affairs with both men and women, and a protracted battle with her father over her return to London. Her notebooks for these months are the most turbulent of any time in her life.

It was during this year and a half, when her first stories were accepted for publication in literary journals, that she determined to live as a writer.

∽

To Sylvia Payne, 8 January 1907

75 Tinakori Rd[1] [Wellington]
8.1.07.

My dearest Sylvia —

I have to thank you for really charming letters — Please believe that I appreciate your letters really more than I can say — And your life sounds so desirable — also you gave me a sudden illuminating glimpse of chrysanthemums at that moment you might have [been] R L S.[2] The New Year has come — I cannot really allow myself to think of it yet. I feel absolutely *ill* with grief and sadness — here — it is a nightmare — I feel that sooner or later I must wake up — & find myself in the heart of it all again — and look back upon the past months as — — — — cobwebs — a hideous dream. Life here's impossible — I can't see how it can drag on — I have not one friend —

and no prospect of one. My dear — I know nobody — and nobody cares to know me — There is nothing on earth to do — nothing to see — and my heart keeps flying off — Oxford Circus — Westminster Bridge at the Whistler hour[3] — London by hansom — my old room — the meetings of the Swans[4] — and a corner in the Library. It haunts me all so much — and I feel it must come back soon — How people ever wish to live here I cannot think —

Dear — I can't write anything — Tonight I feel too utterly hopelessly full of Heimweh. If you knew how I hunger for it all — and for my friends — this absence of companionship — this starvation — that is what it is — I had better stop — hadn't I — because I can think of nothing joyous. I have been living too — in the atmosphere of Death. My Grandmother died on New Year's Eve[5] — my first experience of a personal loss — it horrified me — the whole thing — Death never seemed revolting before — This place — steals your Youth — that is just what it does — I feel years and years older and sadder.

But I shall come back because here I should die —

Goodnight. It is almost frightening to say goodnight across such a waste of waters — but dear — please — think of me always — in silence — or when our letters speak as

Ever your loving friend
Kass.

MS ATL. Alpers 1953, 76.

[1] The large, handsome wooden house in Thorndon, close to Wellington city, which Harold Beauchamp had bought in 1898 when the Prime Minister, Richard Seddon (see p. 20, n.2), appointed him a director of the Bank of New Zealand.
[2] For a time, Robert Louis Stevenson was one of KM's favourite authors.
[3] Among the 'atmospheric' London paintings of James McNeill Whistler (1834-1903), the American artist and wit, was *The Last of Old Westminster*; however, KM probably had in mind his *Nocturne in Blue and Gold: Old Battersea Bridge*, in the Tate Gallery.
[4] The Swanwick Society was the literary club at Queen's College.
[5] Margaret Isabel Dyer, née Mansfield (1840-1907), is the grandmother in many of KM's stories, and is remembered with affection in the journal. Born in Sydney, she married Joseph Dyer at seventeen, spent her early married life in Tasmania, and in 1871 came to Wellington, where her husband was the first resident secretary of the Australian Mutual Provident Society. She is said to have died before KM got round to visiting her after the family's return to Wellington.

To Maata Mahupuku,[1] *[10 April 1907]*

[Wellington]

Birthday greetings to my sweetest Carlotta[2]   K

TC (telegram) Texas.

[1] Maata (or Martha Grace) Mahupuku (1890-1952) was from an important and wealthy Maori family in the Wairarapa, across the Rimutaka Range north of Wellington. She attended

Miss Swainson's School during KM's years as a pupil there, 1900–2, and they had met again in London in 1906.

² A TS copy of part of 'Carlotta's' journal reads very like KM's own journal at this time. On 10 Apr 1907 Maata wrote: 'I am 17 today. It is extraordinary how young I am in years and how old in body — ugh! I *am* miserable and oh! so bored . . . . I had letter from . . . K. this morning . . . . dearest K. writes "ducky" letters. I like this bit. "What did you mean by being so superlatively beautiful just as you went away? You witch; you are beauty incarnate." ' (Texas.)

A 1907 note of KM's considers: 'Do other people of my own age feel as I do I wonder — so absolutely powerful *licentious*, so almost physically ill . . . . I want Maata — I want her as have had her — terribly. This is unclean I know but true. What an extraordinary thing — I feel savagely crude — and almost powerfully enamoured of the child.' (Notebook 39, ATL.)

To Edith Bendall,¹ [before 22 July 1907]

[4 Fitzherbert Terrace,² Wellington]
Thursday Night

This afternoon on the Quay — I saw such a charming little group. A little girl with very red hair and a green frock sat on a doorstep — with oranges in her lap. And looking at her — with *more* than envy was a small boy in a red pair of knickers, and a tight holland bodice that buttoned down the back with three huge buttons — & his sister — a young lady vainly trying to appear out of an enormous pinafore — held his hand. She was distractingly pretty — and her hair was braided in one stiff aggressive little braid that stuck straight out behind — and was tied with an orange bow — They were all so delightful — I could have stood still & just rudely stared at them — Somehow they were so entirely picturesque — The shop behind them was full of coloured beads — do you see how nice that effect was? You would really have liked them — I know.

— — — — — — — — — — — — — — — — — — —

Do they — in New Zealand have a Childrens Thanksgiving Service? They do in the country in England — One year when I was staying with my Granny at the time — down in Kent — her German Grandchild of five³ was there so we took her — I shall never forget how beautiful it was — She wore the shortest little white embroidery frock — and white stockings & red shoes — And under her little white satin straw hat — with just a wreath of field daises round it — her curls tumbled round her — There was a hymn "All Things Bright & Beautiful", where the children had to hold their offerings as they sang. We lifted the German Baby right up on to the cushions in the pew — and she sang very gravely — holding her white basket full of coloured Easter Eggs — and flowers — and the sun streamed into the little old quaint church — and the children's voices — very thin and high — seemed to float in the air — and above them all I heard the

German Baby — exultant — joyful — her cheeks all rosy. Granny & I enjoyed ourselves so much that we both *cried* — to the Baby's horror and astonishment. She pulled my sleeve — "Kassie why are you lookin' so wistful" — I can hear her now — with a violent German accent. She *was* so precious.

— — — — — — — — — — — — — — — — — — — —

I'll see you on Saturday — dearest — won't I — At a quarter to three as usual? I'm so glad youre not going to read "In the Morning Glow"[4] — somehow. I longed to read that to you.

— — — — — — — — — — — — — — — — — — —

The Little Girl With the Fringe[5] is fascinating me — in fact all of them are wonderfully beautiful — I wish that I was as advanced in *my* Art as you in yours — but I'm far from it. Tomorrow I have Mr. Trowell[6] in the afternoon the idea is simply detestable tonight, but I expect I'll recover — — — One has to — you know — from everything.
Goodnight — darling —

Your devoted
K M B.

MS Leeming.

[1] Edith K. Bendall (b. 1879) had been to art school in Sydney; she became a close friend when KM returned home from London.
[2] In April 1907 Harold Beauchamp moved his family to a more impressive house, also in Thorndon but a little closer to the centre of the city.
[3] 'Granny' was not KM's grandmother, in fact, but her Aunt Louie Beauchamp (see p.8, n.3). The five-year-old was Felicitas von Arnim (see p. 15, n.3).
[4] This piece has not survived.
[5] One of a set of sentimental drawings illustrating KM's verses and stories, done by Edith Bendall for a book they were planning together.
[6] The father of her friend Tom Trowell, from whom KM was taking cello lessons.

To Martha Putnam,[1] 22 July 1907

4 Fitzherbert Terrace
22 VII 07.

Thank you very much indeed for the "Poor child" — Mattie. I am most grateful —

Yes — I quite agree that she was — to say the least — rather a morbid little individual — but to write — she was *most* fascinating. Never mind — soon I shall write some Poems full of cheerfulness — though to tell you a secret I prefer the others — the tragic pessimism of Youth — you see — it's as inevitable as measles!

I send you the sheet — it ought to read — "She & the Boy"[2] — and that is all —

It is so fine to see my children in such an abnormally healthy — clean — tidy condition —[3]

Thank you for that —

Yours sincerely
Kathleen Beauchamp.

MS ATL. Mantz, 271-2.

[1] Martha Putnam (1881-1945) was Harold Beauchamp's secretary when KM returned from London.

[2] An unpublished fairy story (Newberry).

[3] Miss Putnam was typing the poems KM was preparing for the proposed children's book (see preceding letter). Some of the poems appear as 'Child Verses: 1907' in *Poems of Katherine Mansfield*, ed. J.M. Murry (1923).

To [Thomas Trowell], 11 August 1907

[4 Fitzherbert Terrace]
Sunday 11.viii 07.

Beloved — tho' I do not see you know that I am yours — every thought — every feeling in me belongs to you — I wake in the morning and have been dreaming of you — and all through the day while my outer life is going on — steadily — monotonously — even drearily — my inner life — I live with you — in leaps and bounds — I go through with you every phase of emotion that is possible — loving you — To me you are man — lover — artist — husband friend — giving me all & I surrendering you all — everything — And so this lonliness is not so terrible to me — because in reality — my outer life is but a phantom life — a world of intangible — meaningless grey shadow — my inner life pulsates with sunshine and Music & Happiness — unlimited vast unfathomable wells of Happiness and *You.* One day we shall be together again and then — and then only — I shall realise myself shall come to my own. Because I feel — I have always felt — that you hold in your hands — just those closing final bars which leave my life song incomplete — because you are to me more necessary than anything else — Nothing matters — nothing *is* — while you usurp my life — O — let it remain as it is — do not suddenly crush out this one beautiful flower — I am afraid — even while I am rejoicing.[1]

But whatever happens — tho' you marry another — tho we never meet again — I belong to you — we belong to each other. And whenever you want me — with both my hands & say — unashamed — fiercely proud — exultant — triumphant — satisfied at last — — "take me". Each night I go to sleep with your letters under my pillow & in the darkness I stretch out my hands & clasp the thin envelope

close to my body — so that it lies there warmly — & I smile in the
darkness and sometimes — my body aches as though with fatigue —
but I understand —

Kãtherine Schõnfeld.[2]

MS (draft) ATL, Notebook 39. *Journal* 1954, 17-18.

[1] Two weeks after this was written, KM received a letter from Ida Baker telling her that
Tom's affections had been diverted to her former school friend, Gwen Rouse. A journal
entry for 28 Aug 1907 reads: 'Shall I say, Do as you please, live as you like, see life, have
experience, increase your outlook? Or shall I condemn it? This is how I think. It's a great
pity that artists do live so. But since they do — *well* . . . but I shall not.' (*Journal* 1954, 19.)
[2] At this time KM was usually called 'Kass', or Kathleen, by her family and friends. It
was in 1907 that she began to write under the name 'K. Mansfield', the first of a series of
noms-de-plume, nicknames, and variations on her own name which she used throughout
her life.

To [Thomas Trowell, sen.],[1] [September 1907]

[4 Fitzherbert Terrace]

My dear Mr Trowell —

I cannot let you leave without telling you how grateful I am and
must be all my life — for what you have done for me — and given me.
You have shown me that there is something so immeasurably higher
and greater than I had ever realised before in Music — and therefore,
too, in Life.

Do you know — so many times when you have been with me I
have felt that I must tell you that when I came from England friend-
less — and sorrowful — you changed all my life — — — And Music
which meant much to me before in a vague desultory fashion — is
now — fraught with inner meaning —

Please I want you to remember that all my life I am being grateful
& happy and proud to have known you —

Looking back I have been so stupid and you so patient — I think
of that little Canon of Cherubini's[2] as a gate — opened with so much
difficulty & leading to so wide a road —

I wish you — Everything with both hands — and all my heart, &
what I look forward to as the greatest joy I can imagine is to share a
program with you at a London concert.

MS (draft) ATL, Notebook 39. Mantz, 281-2.

[1] Thomas Trowell (1858-1945), violinist and conductor, was born in Birmingham, sailed
to New Zealand in 1880, and settled in Wellington. He was music master at St. Patrick's
College, and taught privately from his home at 18 Buller Street, where KM learned the
cello. He returned to England with his family in 1907, to be with his sons Tom and Garnet.
KM later parodied the tone of this letter in the note received by a musician in 'Mr Reginald
Peacock's Day', written in 1917.
[2] The Florentine composer Luigi Carlo Cherubini (1760-1842) wrote several canons;
those that survive are for voice, or voice and instruments, but KM must be referring to one
which had been arranged for cello.

To E.J. Brady,[1] 23 September 1907

4 Fitzherbert Terrace. | Wellington
23. ix. 07.

E.J. Brady Esq

Dear Sir —

Thank you for your letter — I liked the perempatory tone —

With regard to the 'Vignettes' I am sorry that [they] resemble their illustrious relatives to so marked an extent[2] — and assure you — they feel very much my own — This style of work absorbs me, at present — but — well — it *cannot* be said that anything you have of mine is "cribbed" — — — Frankly — I hate plagiarism.

I send you some more work — practically there is nothing local — except the 'Botanical Garden' Vignette — The reason is that for the last few years London has held me — very tightly indeed — and I've not yet escaped. You ask for some details as to myself. I am poor — obscure — just eighteen years of age[3] — with a rapacious appetite for everything and principles as light as my purse — —

If this pleases you — this MSS please know that there is a great deal more where this comes from —

I am very grateful to you and very interested in your Magazine.

Sincerely
K.M. Beauchamp.

MS Mitchell. Mantz, 274–5.

[1] Edwin James Brady (1869–1952), an Australian journalist, biographer, and from August to December 1907 editor of the Melbourne periodical, the *Native Companion*. Four pieces by KM were published in the monthly under Brady's editorship: 'Vignettes' on 1 Oct 1907, 'Silhouettes' on 1 Nov, and 'In a Café' and 'In the Botanical Gardens' on 1 Dec.

[2] Brady felt that the style of the three short 'Vignettes' owed too much to Oscar Wilde.

[3] The Australian editor had been doubtful of the identity and age of his would-be contributor, and on 10 Oct 1907 Harold Beauchamp wrote to assure him of both: 'She herself is, I think, a very original character, and writing — whether it be good or bad — comes to her quite naturally' (Mantz, 275).

To E.J. Brady, 11 October 1907

4 Fitzherbert Terrace. | Wellington.
11 X 07

Dear Mr. Brady

Thank you for your note — and the cheque too.

Encouragement has studiously passed me by for so long that I am very appreciative.

I like the name 'Silhouette' — If you do print more than one 'Vignette' in the November issue — please do not use the name K.M Beauchamp. I am anxious to be read only as K. Mansfield or K.M.[1]

Mr. Brady — I am afraid that so much kindness on your part may result in an inundation of MSS from me — but the kindness is very pleasant.

Sincerely
Kathleen M Beauchamp.

MS Mitchell. Mantz, 276-7.

[1] Only 'Silhouettes' appeared in the November *Native Companion*, and it — like 'Vignettes' and 'In a Café' — was signed 'K. Mansfield'. 'In the Botanical Gardens', KM's second contribution to the December issue, was signed 'Julian Mark'.

To Martha Putnam, [? 10] October 1907

4 Fitzherbert Terrace.
X 07

Am I asking too great a favour — when I say — 'Could you type this for me — my dear'.

I feel — *horrid* to do so — but really I will make it the last — and conquer my Fox machine[1] if I die in the effort! But my Editor wants something for a Summer Number — ∴ the haste — If it's impossible for you just send it back by Father — & I shall understand.

Are you better? I hope so — And here is a man that you will like[2] — will you — I wonder? Hm!

Yours, a little nervously
Kathleen.

MS ATL. Mantz, 273.

[1] The 'Fox Standard', the first of a series of models of the American Fox typewriter, was put on the market in 1906.
[2] The music student in KM's 'In a Café', published in the December (i.e. summer) issue of the *Native Companion*.

To Martha Putnam, [October 1907]

[4 Fitzherbert Terrace]
Friday.

Here is, written specially for you — a sort of continuation of the Café —[1] at least it is the same style — Could you — any time — type it for me — dear? And I do hope that you will like the man, because I think he is a dear. In one place you will see a sign (⌗) where I left out a sentence. I've just written it in on the back of that page.

What weather! Winter or Autumn I think.

I'd like to go with you to a Concert this afternoon — Mark Hamburg & Gerardy —[2] wouldn't it be *fine*!

Such is Life —[3]

Yours with love
K.

MS ATL. Mantz, 272.

[1] This 'continuation' of 'In a Café' — perhaps one of the pieces by KM which E.J. Brady had 'in hand and in type' when the *Native Companion* ceased publication at the end of 1907 (see Brady's *Life's Highway*, 1955) — has not survived.

[2] Mark Hambourg (1879–1960), a Russian-born pianist who became a British subject, and Jean Gérardy (1877–1929), a Belgian violoncellist, musicians KM particularly admired, had made concert tours of New Zealand in 1903 and 1902 respectively. It was Gérardy who encouraged the public appeal for the Trowell brothers to study in Europe (see p. 16, n.1).

[3] A phrase, then much used in Australia and New Zealand, purporting to be the last words of the famous bush-ranger Ned Kelly, hanged in Melbourne in 1880. The phrase is later given to Beryl in both *The Aloe* and *Prelude*.

To the Trowell family, 14 November [1907]

[4 Fitzherbert Terrace]
November 14th

My dearest Mr. Trowell, Mrs Trowell, & Dolly[1] —

By this time — though I can't yet realise it at all, you are nearly Home — You know I am sure, how very much I have missed you all, and how eagerly I am awaiting news — I pass 18 Buller Street, and just look at it out of the corner of my eye, and cannot feel that I shall not be able just to come in for three minutes — and eat a friendly pea nut with Dolly — over the dining room fire!

Do you know — what I have here, this evening, in my room. Well, the Graphophone!!! and I have had just a musical feast — including speeches from Birmingham — that I am sure it must have been a case of subconscious mind — and I am 11,500 miles nearer you than I feel I am. Miss Watson met me, the other evening at a 'social' (!) and then offered me the use of it —[2] So imagine me today carrying the Graphophone — three packets of records, and the cylinder home in the tram — It was worth the carrying though — when I heard the Beethoven Sérénade —

Oh! news — Selina is giving Miss Parker[3] some fiddle lessons — Rumour has it that she has already reached the intoxicating strains of "Nellie Bly" and "Lil is a Lady". Such is the incense we offer to

Fame. And last night Mr. Smith played the trombone in Mr. Parker's production — the Bride of Dunkerron. I hear, on competent authority, that his part teemed with triple cadenzas — though of course, *you* may not have come across them.[4]

The Parkers are all well, and we speak, constantly, of you all, and of how good it would be to pay you a little surprise visit — one of these days, soon — Today an English Mail came in, and I heard from a man at home that Arnold Trowell is teaching in London. Is that so? And what news is there about the boys? Do tell me a great deal. I get such very second hand information.

Mr Trowell — I am working for you very regularly, so that next year — if you will have me — I shall be a little better pupil than I have been, here. Dolly, dear, how is the French? Mrs Trowell, I want to ask you at least fifty things at once — which is horrid. By next year — they will have become hundreds. Kiss London for me — and tell it — that when I come back I shall live in a tent in Trafalgar Square — and only leave it for Bayreuth. I shall be with you soon, and Merry Xmas.

Ever your loving
Kass —

MS Richards.

[1] The Trowells' fourteen-year-old daughter.

[2] The Graphophone was the trade name for the Columbia gramophone. The records lent to KM by the unidentified Miss Watson apparently included speeches from the Birmingham Festival, held irregularly in that city 1768-1912.

[3] Margaret ('Millie') Parker, daughter of a Wellington chemist, was a friend of KM's and had been a neighbour of the Trowells in Buller Street.

[4] Mr R. Smith is listed as bass trombonist in the programme for *The Bride of Dunkerron*, a dramatic cantata with verses by Frederick Enoch and music by Henry Smart, performed by the Wellington Musical Union at the Town Hall on 12 Nov 1907. The Union's musical director was Robert Parker (1846-1937), who as a young man in London had been assistant organist at St. Matthias, Stoke Newington, to Dr W.H. Monk, compiler of *Hymns Ancient and Modern* (1861). In 1869 Parker went out to New Zealand, where he contributed greatly to the colony's musical life. Organist and choirmaster at St. Paul's Anglican Church, he was also music master at Miss Swainson's School, and for two years taught KM piano. Her memory of him survives as Mr Bullen in 'The Wind Blows', written in 1915.

To [Charlotte Beauchamp],[1] [18 November 1907]

Petane Valley.[2]
Monday morning —

Bon jour — Marie dearest. Your humble servant is seated on the very top of I know not how much luggage — so excuse the writing. This is a most extraordinary experience —

Our journey was charming. A great many Maoris on the train — in fact I lunched next to a great brown fellow at Woodville[3] — That was a memorable meal — We were both starving — with that dreadful silent hunger — Picture to yourself a great barn of a place — full of pink papered chandeliers and long tables — decorated with paper flowers, and humanity most painfully en évidence. You could cut the atmosphere with a knife,

MS (draft) ATL, Notebook 2. Mantz, 288.

[1] Charlotte Mary ('Chaddie') Beauchamp (1887-1966), second of the Beauchamp daughters, was also known as 'Marie' because of her likeness to the actress Marie Tempest.

[2] KM had been invited by her friend Millie Parker (see preceding letter) to join a camping holiday with Millie's cousin George Ebbett, a Hastings solicitor, his wife, and another couple, the H.J. Webbers. The trip, with the party travelling by two horse-drawn wagons, lasted almost a month, and covered a large area of the central North Island. Petane Valley is six miles north-west of Napier, on the east coast of the North Island.

[3] KM and Millie Parker had travelled the 200 miles from Wellington to Hastings by train. As there was no dining car, meals were bought at stations *en route*. Woodville is a small town in the Wairarapa, at the eastern end of the Manawatu Gorge.

To [Annie Burnell Beauchamp],[1] [20 November 1907]

Waipunga Riverside.[2]
Wednesday

Dear my Mother —

I wrote you my last letter on Monday — and posted it at Pohui[3] in the afternoon. I continue my doings. We drove on through sheep country — to Pohui that night — past Maori 'pahs'[4] and nothing else — and pitched our camp at the top of a bare hill above the Pohui Accommodation House — kept by a certain Mr. Bodley — a *great* pa-man[5] with 14 daughters who sit & shell peas all day! Below the hill there was a great valley — and the bush I cannot describe. It is the entrance to the Ahurakura Station[6] — and though we were tired & hungry Millie, Mrs. Webber & I dived down a bridle track — and followed the bush. The tuis really sounded like rivers running — everywhere the trees hung wreathed with clematis and rata and mistletoe. It was very cool & we washed in a creek — the sides all smothered in daisies — the ferns everywhere, and eventually came to the homestead. It is a queer spot — ramshackle & hideous, but the garden is gorgeous — A Maori girl with her hair in two long braids, sat at the doorstep — shelling peas — & while we were talking to her — the owner came & offered to show us the shearing sheds. You know the sheep sound like a wave of the sea — you can hardly hear yourself speak. He took us through it all — they had only two white men working — and the Maoris have a most strange bird like call as they hustle the sheep — When we came home it was quite dark & *how* I slept.

Next morning at five we were up & working — and really looking back at yesterday I cannot believe that I have not been to a prodigious biograph[7] show. We drove down the Titi-o 'Kura[8] — and the road is one series of turns — a great abyss each side of you — and ruts so deep that you rise three feet in the air — scream & descend as though learning to trot. It poured with rain early — but then the weather was very clear & light — with a fierce wind in the mountains. We got great sprays of clematis — and konini,[9] and drove first through a bush path — But the greatest sight I have seen was the view from the top of Taranga-kuma. You draw rein at the top of the mountains & round you everywhere are other mountains — bush covered — & far below in the valley little Tarawera[10] & a silver ribbon of river — I could do nothing but laugh — it must have been the air — & the danger.

We reached the Tarawera Hotel in the evening — & camped in a little bush hollow.

Grubby, my dear — I felt dreadful — my clothes were white with dust — we had accomplished 8 miles of hill climbing — so after dinner (broad beans cooked over a camp fire and tongue & cake and tea,) we prowled round and found an "agèd aged man"[11] who had the key of the mineral baths. I wrapt clean clothes in my towel — & the old man rushed home to seize a candle in a tin — He guided us through the bush track by the river — & my dear I've never met such a cure — I don't think he ever had possessed a tooth & he never ceased talking — you know the effect?

The Bath House is a shed — three of us bathed in a great pool — waist high — and we of course — in our nakeds — The water was very hot — & like oil — most delicious. We swam — & soaped & swam & soaked & floated — & when we came out each drank a great mug of mineral water — luke warm & tasting like Miss Wood's eggs[12] at their worst stage — But you feel — inwardly & outwardly like velvet — This morning we walked most of the journey — and in one place met a most fascinating Maori — an old splendid man. He took Mrs. Webber & me to see his 'wahine' & child — It is a tropical day — the woman squatted in front of the whare — she, too, was very beautiful — strongly Maori — & when we had shaken hands she unwrapped her offspring from under two mats — & held it on her knee. The child wore a little red frock & a tight bonnet — such a darling thing — I wanted it for a doll — but in a perfect bath of perspiration. Mother couldn't speak a word of English & I had a great pantomime.

Kathleen — pointing to her own teeth & then to the baby's — *"Ah!"*

Mother — very appreciative — *"Ai!"*
Kathleen — pointing to the baby's long curling eyelashes *"Oh!"*
Mother — most delighted *"Aii!"*
And so on.

I jumped the baby up & down in the air — and it crowed with laughter — & the Mother & Father — beaming — shook hands with me again — Then we drove off — waving until out of sight — all the Maoris do that — Just before pulling up for lunch we came to the Waipunga Falls — my first experience of great waterfalls. They are indescribably beautiful — three — one beside the other — & a ravine of bush either side. The noise is like thunder & the sun shone full on the water. I am sitting now, on the bank of the river — just a few bends away — the water is flowing past — and the manuka flax & fern line the banks.

Must go on. Goodbye, dear — Tell Jeanne I saw families of wild pigs *&* horses here — & that we have five horses — such dear old things. They nearly ate my head through the tent last night.

I am still bitten & burnt, but oil of camper, Solomon solution,[13] glycerine & cucumber, rose water — are curing me, & I keep wrapt in a motor veil. This is *the* way to travel — it is so slow & so absolutely free, and I'm quite fond of all the people — they are ultra-Colonial but thoroughly kind & good hearted & generous — and always more than good to me. We sleep tonight at the Rangitaiki[14] & then the plains & the back blocks.

Love to everybody. I am *very* happy —

Your daughter
Kathleen.

Later. Posting at country shed. Can't buy envelopes. Had wonderful dinner of tomatoes — Ah! he's found me an hotel envelope.   K.[15]

MS (draft) ATL, Notebook 2. O'Sullivan, 63-6; *UN*, 42-6.

[1] Annie Burnell Beauchamp, née Dyer (1864-1918), KM's mother, married Harold Beauchamp in 1884.

[2] Near the Waipunga Falls, delicately spectacular waterfalls on the Waipunga River.

[3] Te Pohue, a settlement with fewer than half a dozen European families, 26 miles north-west of Napier, serviced at the time by one coach a week.

[4] A fortified camp or village. KM's notebook of the trip contained a list of Maori phrases and the words she learned during this time.

[5] Henry Bodley was the owner of Whaka Station. 'Pa-man' was a Beauchamp family expression for a typical paterfamilias, a person of strong personality and quirky individuality. In *Katherine Mansfield and Other Literary Portraits* (1948), Murry defined the term (27) as meaning 'an oldish man who was a character, set in ways which were a trifle eccentric, but charming; old fashioned, courteous, and above all reliable. And behind all this it meant a man who belonged to the childhood world — a man whom a child could trust.'

[6] Another large sheep run a few miles along the road north.

[7] Trade name for an early form of cinema projector.

[8] Titiokura Saddle (2,289 ft.), and Turangakuma (2,625 ft. — see below), were the two highest points in the mountain ranges that the party crossed.

[9] Maori name for *fuchsia excortica.*

[10] Another settlement, of about a dozen Europeans, 50 miles from Napier.

[11] Cf. Lewis Carroll's poem 'Upon the Lonely Moor', which begins: 'I met an aged aged man.'

[12] A memory of the Queen's College hostel run by Clara Wood (see p. 5, n.4).

[13] A cure-all distributed from Melbourne, with the claim: 'Cures the Man of rheumatick, / The horse of sores and sprains / The cow of ulcerated udder / And the dog of mange.'

[14] A small settlement on the southern edge of the Kaiangoroa Plateau, at that time a vast tract of tussock and scrub.

[15] A few days later, on 25 Nov 1907, KM began another letter to her mother from Te Whaiti, a Maori settlement in the remote Kawhenua Range, but deleted the following lines in Notebook 2 (ATL): 'Monday   Well Mother I posted your letter at the Rangitaiki Hotel — and on the way out I saw the land-lord's wife — and thinking she was a happy woman questioned her as to her offspring'.

To [Annie Burnell Beauchamp], [29 November 1907]

Rotorua
Friday

Mother dearest

Thank you for your wire which I received today and for Chaddie's lovely letter — So Vera has definitely left;[1] I can hardly realise it. What a strange household you must be feeling.

You sound most gay at home — I am so glad.

I wrote to Chaddie on Wednesday. Yesterday was very hot indeed — A party of us went a Round Trip to the Hamurana Spring — the Okere Falls across Lake Rotoiti to Tikitere,[2] and then back here by coach — I confess, frankly, that I hate going trips with a party of tourists — they spoil half my pleasure — don't they yours? You know one lady who is the wit of the day, and is 'flirty', and the inevitable old man who becomes disgusted with everything, and the honeymoon couples — Rotorua is a happy hunting ground for these — We came back in the evening grey with dust — hair and eyes and clothing, so I went and soaked in the Rachael bath[3] — The tub is very large — it is a wise plan to always use the public one — and there one meets one sex very much "in their nakeds" — Women are so apt to become communicate on these occasions that I carefully avoid them — I came home, *dined*, and went into town with Mrs Ebett — We ended with a Priest Bath — another pleasant thing, but most curious — At first one feels attacked by Deepa's[4] friends — the humble worms — The bath is of aerated water, very hot, and you sit in the spring — But afterwards you[5]

MS (draft) ATL, Notebook 2. Mantz, 295-6.

[1] KM's eldest sister was staying in Sydney with the Lassetters, relatives of Aunt Louie

Beauchamp. According to KM's youngest sister Jeanne (now Mrs Renshaw), Vera was sent to Australia as a distraction from James Mackintosh Bell (see p. 52, n. 4), whom she later married.

[2] All tourist sites close to Rotorua.

[3] The Rachel and Priest Baths (see below) are mineral springs in Rotorua.

[4] 'Deepa' was the family nickname for KM's great-uncle, Henry Herron Beauchamp (see p. 8, n.1), in England.

[5] There is another opening to this letter, heavily scored through, in Notebook 2 (ATL):

Rotorua
Friday

Mother dearest —
Thank you for the wire which I received today and for Chaddie's lovely letter. So Vera has definitely gone I can hardly realise it! What a strange household you must be feeling — As to me: — I have been bathing twice a day — the Rachael and the Priest Bath they are delightful, but take it out of you to a very

(*UN*, 69)

To [R. B. T. Miller],[1] [1 December 1907]

Sunday
Nowhere.[2]

Dear Mr Millar —

I have to thank you for keeping my none too small amount of correspondence — I went to the Bank yesterday afternoon, foolishly forgetting that it was closing day. Would you kindly address any letters that may arrive for me c/o Bank of New Zealand, Hastings — I shall be there on Saturday —

This paper is vile, but I am once more on the march.

Once more thank you —

Sincerely yours
K.M. Beauchamp

MS (draft) ATL, Notebook 2. Mantz, 285.

[1] Robert B.T. Miller was the manager of the Bank of New Zealand in Rotorua.

[2] On the Sunday morning the party set out for Atiamuri, a camp site 24 miles to the south-west, on the Waikato River. Presumably KM wrote this on the way.

To [Jeanne Beauchamp],[1] [2 December 1907]

[Huka Falls][2]
Monday Night | *In Bed.*

Dearest Baby —

This will, I think, be my last letter to you — before I reach home — I wrote last to Chaddie from Rotorua — I must say I hated that town[3] — it did not suit me at all — I never felt so ill or depressed — It was, I

MS (draft) ATL, Notebook 2. Mantz, 300.

¹ Jeanne Worthington Beauchamp (b. 1892), youngest of KM's three sisters.
² Impressive falls where the Waikato River narrows into a shallow canyon.
³ KM recorded of Rotorua, 'the nearer they get to the town the more she hates it —
perhaps it is the smell . . . . Thursday the loathsome trip — Friday so tired that she sits in
the sanatorium grounds all the morning.' (Notebook 2, ATL.)

To [? Thomas Trowell],¹ [2 December 1907]

[Huka Falls]
Monday Night

<Dear Man —>
I am a vagrant — a Wanderer, a Gypsy tonight booming sound² —
it rises half a tone about each minute but that is all — it never ceases
— — — & where the water catches the light there is a rainbow pink,
blue and white — But it is all too short —

MS (draft) ATL, Notebook 2. Mantz, 300.

¹ Ian Gordon in *UN* (78) reads the cancelled salutation of this letter as 'Dear Marie'
and assumes the notebook entry is a draft letter to KM's sister Chaddie. But the second
word is plainly 'Man' in the MS, and the musical allusion suggests the draft may have been
addressed to Tom Trowell.
² Of the near-by falls.

To Martha Putnam, [? December 1907]

[4 Fitzherbert Terrace, Wellington]
Sunday Night.

My dear —
Here is the work — it is written, really in a 'faire hande' & will — I
hope — not be too much of a bother — I'm afraid you won't like
'Leves Amores'¹ — — — I can't think how I wrote it — it's partly a
sort of dream —
Castles have been tumbling about my ears since Father came
home. Do not mention — I pray you — my London prospects to
him² — he feels very sensitive — but — willy nilly — I GO — I'm
determined.
I wish that you were not always so busy — I always feel when I
am with you that there's so *much* I want to say — Oh, delightful
sensation — *and so rare* —

Well — I must go to bed — Shall I build a castle with a spare room
for you — Yes I will — so *please* return the compliment.

                                        Thanking You in Anticipation.

                                                                  K.

MS ATL. Mantz, 272-3.

¹ An unpublished story (ATL) about a lesbian encounter in the Thistle Hotel, Wellington.
² Harold Beauchamp, with whom KM was battling over her return to London, had
apparently been away on business.

To Martha Putnam, [January 1908]

                                        [4 Fitzherbert Terrace]
                                                       Thursday.

Thank you, indeed for 'Audrey'¹ — It was most good of you to
bother about her at all — And you have typed it so beautifully for
me —

Is your room a success? I do hope so — Of course you have been
busy lately — and so have I in a very pleasant sort of way — writing —
I mean —

Am just off to Island Bay² for a long day & maybe an evening —
I am going to write — and have to go to the sea for 'Copy' — *Do*
bring a book and come — too — dear — and we shall 'paddle' and
'bake'. Don't you *love* the two processes?

I wonder if you have read 'Luke Delmege' by Father Sheehan —
Father Macdonald lent it me — some days ago — and it is very
good.³

Oh, what a *beautiful* day — Thank you again — dear — I feel most
horrid to have bothered you so persistently about my annoying
children — — — — — You have indeed been a Godmother to them
— and they — too — are grateful —

                                                    Lovingly yours
                                                                  K.

MS ATL. Mantz, 273.

¹ 'The Education of Audrey', a story which appeared in the *Evening Post*, Wellington,
30 Jan 1909.
² A wild piece of coast on Cook Strait, a few miles south of Wellington; KM describes
(*Journal* 1954, 9-10) a visit to Island Bay.
³ *Luke Delmege* (1901) was a novel by an American priest, P.A. Sheehan. Alexander
McDonald, SM, a curate at the near-by Basilica of the Sacred Heart, attended musical
evenings at the Beauchamps.

To Vera Beauchamp,[1] *17 January 1908*

[4 Fitzherbert Terrace]
17 I 08.

My dearest sister – Thank you a great deal for your letter – Do you think of remaining until April – I think that so extremely wise – and Life sounds full of interest for you – Gaston La Touche[2] is worth a 1000 miles of 'mal de mer' to visit – I am sure – Oh, my dear – how absurd this plan is about my leaving in March – and of course I feel, undyingly certain that I shall leave in March and the diet of Hope and Assurance is eminently comfortable – So I am waiting for Guardie's[3] cable before I become involved in any definite occupation here – Meanwhile my days are full of work – as you know. Miss Isitt[4] was quite interesting – pardon the remark, she has a distinctly provincial trend of mind – but the gist of the matter with her was: Miss I: "With your genius and future I would go home steerage." That is very gratifying – but not feasible. Give me two years of your life – Vera – I pray you. I shall certainly read Keir Hardie's Serfdom & Socialism – he is progressive and sincere.[5] For a brilliant book read Mrs Henry Dudeney's latest: – 'The Orchard Thief' – it is clever from start to close – It is a book alive with epigrams written in a fluent, fascinating style – Like most feminine productions – there is much introspection – in fact the book is mainly introspection – and the plot is the inevitable two men and a capricious incorrigibly dimpled girl. Now you are saying: Not for *me* danke schön – but you would like it. She catches the very quintessence of the suburban atmosphere – where the middle class deck their minds with neat little rows of sham chippendale furniture (I am rather proud of that sentence) but do try & read the book – Honey – and give me your impressions.[6] I have just written a sketch "The Education of Audrey" which I think you might like – Of course it is London – but it is actually happy, and ends to begin – you understand?

L'autre jour, I meet Dr Tudor Jones[7] – and he asked me to spend an afternoon with him. I did so – but he is so eternally the same – He has one string to his bow – And he persists in twanging it a violent forte from the moment of meeting – I showed him some of my work, and he has promised me several very influential letters of introduction – He only wishes he had known me before – hein? we could have spent so much time reading together – What was Life but this: – a continual feeling for knowledge – summing up the result & feeling as fresh — — — — Do you know the Doctor in that mood — He illustrated that simple fact in at least two dozen ways — it formed the conversational basis — Oh, what a bore!

Last night Dr Crosby et femme — that is not French — I know — Aunt Li and Burney dined with us[8] — It was very pleasant — The Dr sat on my right — and I am exceedingly fond of him — He is lending me the precious Kennedy[9] while he goes away — and sending me Arnold Trowell's Reverie de soir — Oh, Vera, Tom has had the most magically successful concert — you know a packed hall — and glowing notices even from the Times — I am so glad — He played this Reverie then — and also at Queen's Hall — where the Duke of Connaught was present.[10] (Very very choice indeed my dear.) Chaddie, Mother & I saw 3 Little Maids the other night. It is so incomprehensibly feeble that I felt quite hysterical with laughter — Oh, the men, the costumes — the women — the *lady* opening a golf course, attired in purple velvet — Pompadour period — Bo-peep crook — uncovered bosom 1906. They all held up their skirts like the N.Z. football lady on the Eastbourne Pier.[11] Everybody *loves* it here — and the song "Aunty Found the Needle in the Haystack" (needless to remark she finds it by sitting on it) has become the rage of Wellington — especially by Dr Milsom & Webster & Reid — you know? . . .[12]

I could continue chatting like this for a week. You know that mood. But its mail day — so au revoir. Write me if you have time — dear — I think of you so often — Your sister

K.

MS ATL. Cited Meyers, 30.

[1] Vera Margaret Beauchamp (1885-1977), KM's eldest sister. She remained in Sydney until after KM left for England.

[2] A painting, *The First Born* (1883), by the French sculptor, painter, and engraver Gaston La Touch (1854-1913), was in the Art Gallery of New South Wales in Sydney.

[3] Henry Beauchamp (see p. 15, n.1).

[4] Possibly a Miss Isett who had taught elocution at Miss Swainson's School.

[5] James Keir Hardie (1856-1915), first Parliamentary leader of the British Labour Party, had left Wellington, after a tour of New Zealand, ten days before this letter was written. His *From Serfdom to Socialism* was published in 1907.

[6] *The Orchard Thief* by Alice Dudeney (pen name Mrs Henry Dudeney) appeared in 1907.

[7] This extravagant Welsh cleric, ordained a Presbyterian minister but converted to Unitarianism, lived in Wellington 1906-10. He claimed to be the first to introduce English readers to the work of Rudolf Eucken, who won the Nobel Prize for Literature in 1908. There is the beginning of a letter to him in Notebook 1 (ATL): 'Dear Dr. Tudor-Jones, I want to write you a few words only — of thanks'

[8] Arthur Crosby was an English doctor practising in Wellington. The other guests were Eliza Trapp, Annie Burnell Beauchamp's eldest sister, and her husband Burney Trapp.

[9] Possibly an arrangement of a traditional air by the Scottish folk-song collector and editor, Majorie Kennedy-Fraser (1857-1930).

[10] 'Reverie de soir' may be the 'Reverie', No. 3 in Arnold (Tom) Trowell's *Six Morceaux pour Violoncelle*, Op. 51 (1908), the published score of which was 'Dedicated to my dear friend Kathleen Beauchamp'. Arnold Trowell gave three concerts in London in 1907 at the Bechstein Hall, two in July and one in November; at two of these he performed 'Reverie du Soir'. There is no record of the Duke of Connaught attending the Queen's Hall in 1907.

[11] The J.C. Williamson Company's production that season at the Wellington Opera House of *Three Little Maids*, a musical by Paul Rubens, was advertised as 'Another Delightful Gaiety Success'. She is probably referring to a character at Eastbourne, the English seaside resort, at the time of the All Blacks Rugby tour of Britain in 1905.

[12] The song was introduced into *Three Little Maids* from another musical, *The School Girl*, by Henry Hamilton, Paul Potter, and Leslie Stuart. Edward Milsom, an Englishman, and Charles Webster, an Australian, were two young Wellington doctors. Jim Reid was another young Beauchamp family friend.

To [Thomas Trowell], 23 January [1908]

Outside the Town Hall, [Wellington]
January 23rd

Mein lieber Freund —

Die letze woche hat Dr Crosby mir — Ihre "Reverie du Soir" — mitgebrocken — So muss ich etwas schreiben — Ich finde diese Werk so wunderbar schön — so träumerisch — und auch so sehnsuchtsvoll. Hoffenlich, diese Jahre — höre ich Ihr die Reverie du Soir in einer Konzert spielen! Meine gute Freundin Ida Baker hat mir mehrerere Blätter von den Zeitunge gegeben — Was für eine succès merveille. Oftenmals in meinen Gedanken habe ich Ihnen kongratuliert. Ich komme nach England früh in March — Ich hasse Wellington — und — naturlich sehne ich nach London — Haben sie mehrere Journaux von mir gehabt?[1] Und was denken sie von dieser? Warum haben sie mir nicht erzählt! Wie geht Ihren Vater — und auch die Mutter und auch Ihren liebe würdige Schwesterchen? Das Haus — achtzehn Buller Strasse — steht so einsam aus! Mit vielen Grüssen fur diese Jahre 1908.

Ihre Freundin
K.

Muss aber Deutsch schreiben. Es giebt so vielen Leuten — der gar nicht diese Sprache kennen![2]

MS (draft) ATL, Notebook 2.

[1] Perhaps the issues of the *Native Companion* (see p. 26, n.1) in which her pieces had appeared.

[2] (Translation)

My dear friend —

Last week Dr Crosby brought me — your "Reverie du Soir" — So I have to write something — I find this work so wonderfully beautiful — so dreamy — and so full of longing too. I hope I shall hear you play the Reverie du Soir in a concert this year! My good friend Ida Baker has given me several pages from the newspapers — What a *succès merveille*. Often in my thoughts I have congratulated you. I am coming to England in early March — I hate Wellington — and — of course I long for London — Have you had several *journaux* from me? And what do you think of them? Why haven't you told me? How is your father — and your mother too, and also your dear worthy little sister? The house — 18 Buller Street — stands [? *for* looks] so lonely! With many greetings for this year 1908.

Your friend
K.

But must write German. There are so many people — who don't know this language at all!

To Sylvia Payne, 4 March [1908]

By the Sea[1] [Days Bay]
March 4th

My dear Cousin —

I am — you see, at last writing you a letter — because I must tell you — here tonight Sylvia — that I love you — far more than I loved you in England — that I would [like] — such an immeasurable great deal — to open wide this door — and welcome you in to the fire — and to the raging sea which breaks & foams against the yard fence.

Summer is over with us — there are briar berries in a green jar on the table — and an autumn storm is raging — The sea has never seemed so high — so fierce — It dashes against the rocks with a sound like thunder. Last night I was lying in my bunk. I could not sleep — I was thinking of you. Do you realise — I wonder — Cousin — how your voice charmed me at the Swanick meetings. I cannot exactly define what I mean — but it always made me feel I was very near you indeed — When I slept I dreamed that I came back to visit College — the only girl I knew in the Library was Marjory — she was not at all surprised to see me — I see her now — pushing back the ribbon in her hair — you know the way she had — and I asked for you — She said you were with Tudge[2] — and then I saw you standing by the window in the Waiting room — My dear — I felt I must run and put my arms round you and just say *"Sylvia"* but you nodded & then walked away — and I did not move —

It was a terrible dream.

How much has happened since we two walked together to the New Barnet Station.[3] My life has been so strange — full of either *sorrow* — or excitement — or disgust or happiness. In a year to have lived so much! And I have not made a friend. It is no good   I can have men friends — they persist in asking for something else. Do you know Sylvia *five* men has asked me to marry them. And now you will put down this letter and say "Kass is a second Sylvia Gifford",[4] but it is the stupid truth — I have been reading — French & English — writing and lately have seen a great many Balls — and loved them — and dinners and receptions. They have such a different meaning for me now — and here. I have finished My First Book.[5] If it never gets published — you shall laugh with me over its absurdities. Also I hope to leave for London next month — It is not unwise of me — it is the only thing to be done. I cannot live with Father — and I must get back because I know I shall be successful — look at the splendid tragic optimism of youth! One day — you must please know my brother[6]. He knows you very well indeed — and he and I mean to live together — later on. I have never dreamed of loving a child as I love this boy. Do not laugh at me when I tell you I feel so maternal towards him. He is intensely affectionate and sensitive — he reads a great deal — draws with the most delicate sympathetic touch — and yet is a thoroughly brave healthy boy. Do not let me write of him — he is away at school — and if I go back next month we may not meet for years —

I hear, constantly, from Ida. You know I love her very much indeed — I am — Sylvia — the most completely unsatisfactory disappointing — *dull* friend it is possible to conceive — and when we meet again you will think — that is enough — cela suffit — Chaddie & I — with our maid — are living alone at this little cottage built on the rocks. It has only three rooms — two bedrooms fitted with bunks — and a wide living room — We had both been feeling wretchedly ill — and bored with Wellington — oh, the tedium vitae of 19 years! so have come here — where we bathe and row and walk in the bush or by the sea — and read — and I write — while she pursues the gentle art of fashioning camisoles. One could not be lonesome here — I seem to love it more each day — and the sea is a continually new sensation with me. Our life is absolutely free — absolutely happy — and our maid is — Sylvia — we just die laughing — She is reading Marie Corelli[7] now — needless to remark Miss Corelli is her Messiah — and she treats Chaddie and me like slightly troublesome babies — Oh, do come — my Friend & spend a week with me — Have you received one tenth of my wireless messages? I do not feel that I have been away from you one day. Now I can feel your hand clasping mine — but the *wasted* years when we might have been friends. But I was always afraid then — & I am now — that you do not know me — & when you do — you will hate me.

Still — Sylvia — I love you — very dearly —and I shall do so always.
Kass

MS ATL. Cited Meyers, 119-20; cited Alpers 1980, 60.

[1] At the 'ideal little "cottage by the sea" ', referred to above, p. 18.

² For Marjorie Wilensky, see p. 19, n.5. Ethel Tudge was a girl a year senior to KM at Queen's College.

³ After retiring from his medical practice, Frank Payne moved from Wimpole Street, London, to New Barnet.

⁴ A fellow student at Queen's College.

⁵ KM had begun a novel, *Juliet*, in May 1907, but abandoned it soon after her return to New Zealand. She is probably referring here to the proposed book with Edith Bendall (see p. 23, n.1), which did not find a publisher.

⁶ Leslie 'Chummie' Beauchamp (see p. 198, n.1) was some five years younger than KM.

⁷ The sensational and extremely popular novelist Marie Corelli, pen name of Mary Mackay (1855-1924).

To Vera Beauchamp, [late March 1908]

[4 Fitzherbert Terrace]

Dear Vera —

You see that my Mrs Weston plan¹ has also fallen through. Now I am not conquered yet — and I know that I ought to get to London to work & study. I have been writing a great deal here but I can't do all that I know is in me — etc etc. You know that, situated as I am — I shall never make all that I mean to make of my life — Also — were I not convinced that I have a real *call* a duty which I owe to myself I'd give the project up. Now I do think that we are all sent into the world to develop ourselves to the very fullest extent — of course you do — too — and here there is really no scope for development — no intellectual society — no hope of finding any. You know exactly what this life is like and what life means here. Mother has the plan of sending us to London to live together — we three in a flat on £300 a year which is amply sufficient — of course knowing that the separation from her & from Father is purely temporary. Now what do you think. Do you think that your duty lies with them now — but if you married you would have to leave home — living here you certainly will not marry — You with music & painting — Chaddie singing etc — I literature — This plan refuses to be discussed on paper — so I shall give it up — I know you can argue it all out — & I waste words & state deep feelings so superficially. But to tell you the absolute truth — I can't stand this life much longer — I have tried to get work but I only can get work which helps my literature — & there's none to be got — I feel I am crying my own wares all the time — do you I wonder — understand. Mother (this is between you & me) informed me the other day — that it was your firm belief that nothing but a great trouble would ever *'put me right'*. I can't really let that pass — Vera without saying it shows how little you know of my life. I was almost amused — deeply hurt — and not a little surprised. It does not sound like one who has read Maeterlinck & Meredith. That rather cheap and distinctly simple philosophy of the ennobling power of sorrow does not surely belong to you — It is true in a very few cases but there is more strength required for permanent happiness in man than for sorrow. My dear girl — do you believe in drugging children for their ultimate good instead of administering happy thoughts. It is true that some people must go through fire before realising that others suffer from the heat — but that is a distinctly brute creation idea — This is a digression. Don't go laying down laws for other peoples natures tho', to a woman like Mother. I am convinced times without number that in the future that silly statement "she *ought* to have a real sorrow" — will be as unintelligible as a book of "Elizabethan simples for the stomach ache".

Your life sounds quite charming — and I am indeed glad to feel that you are there. Unless this last English plan matures — don't dream of returning here until it is necessary — Yesterday morning I spent with Trix[2] — she is one of the best. When I go to her house & she hugs me & says — "Bless you — dearest old girl — pretty nice to see you" & puts cushions at my back — and flowers in my soul — I do verily think that a woman is one of the most delightful creations possible — I feel — here is a breath of my own life —

The voice of the chrysanthemum is heard in the land.[3] Two blossoms — so full of colour that I feel they are lighting the dead summer on her journey — greet you from my table. Flowers like Tom's music seem to create in me a divine unrest — They revive strangely — dream memories — I know not what — They show me strange mystic paths — where perhaps I shall one day walk — To lean over a flower — as to hear any of his music is to suddenly [have] every veil torn aside — to commune soul with soul — This is like the hysteria of 17   it's the conviction of experience — Sister —

K.

MS ATL.

[1] One of several proposed plans for KM's return to England. Mrs. Weston was the wife of Captain T.S. Weston, a friend of Harold Beauchamp's, and the captain of the *Papanui* on which KM eventually sailed to England.

[2] This Wellington friend is unidentified.

[3] A fragment of a play (Newberry), probably from this time, is called *The Yellow Chrysanthemum*. It draws heavily on Oscar Wilde's *The Duchess of Padua*.

To Vera Beauchamp, [? April–May 1908]

[4 Fitzherbert Terrace]
Friday.

To the Apostle of the Blue Green Aura[1]
All Hail —
This is only to say that I have not forgotten you — Sister Mine — and
will write you good measure pressed down & running over next week —
At present I am cable waiting — which is you know — horrible — Do
— an' I pray you — read Le Morgan's book 'Alice-For-Short' — So
delightful — He — Le Morgan — was very much in with the P.R.B.
and a devoted ami of William Morris. He is also a designer — & wrote
his *first* book 'Joseph Vance' at *60* years of age[2] — I have 10,000
things which I am saying silently — My love to you — Cherie
Your
Mark.[3]

MS ATL.

[1] At this time KM was an enthusiastic admirer of the Pre-Raphaelite Brotherhood and
its successors. Earlier, at Island Bay, she had written: 'you know that peacock shade of
water. Blue — with the blueness of Rossetti; green — with the greenness of William Morris.'
(*Journal* 1954, 9-10).
[2] William Frend de Morgan (1834-1907), a professional artist who specialized in stained
glass and ceramics, published *Joseph Vance: An Ill-written Autobiography* in 1906, and
Alice for Short the following year.
[3] Cf. 'Julian Mark', the *nom de plume* with which 'In the Botanical Gardens' (see p. 27,
n.1) was signed.

To Vera Beauchamp, [? April–May 1908]

[4 Fitzherbert Terrace]
I am ashamed of young New Zealand, but what is to be done. All
the firm fat framework of their brains must be demolished before
they can begin to learn. They want a purifying influence — a mad
wave of pre-Raphaelitism, of super-aestheticism, should intoxicate
the country. They must go to excess in the direction of culture, become almost decadent in their tendencies for a year or two and
then find balance and proportion. We want two or three persons
gathered together to discuss line and form and atmosphere and sit
at the street corners, in the shops, in the houses, at the Teas. People
who would quote William Morris and Catulle Mendès,[1] George
Meredith and Maurice Maeterlinck, Ruskin and Rodenbach,[2] Le

Gallienne and Symons,[3] D'Annunzio and Shaw, Granville Barker and Sebastian Melmouth,[4] Whitman, Tolstoi, Carpenter,[5] Lamb, Hazlitt, Hawthorne, and the Brontës. These people have not learned their alphabet yet.

MS lacking. Berkman, 24-5.

[1] Catulle Mendès (1842-1909), French *Parnassien* poet, novelist, and playwright.
[2] Georges Rodenbach (1855-1898), Belgian *symboliste* poet and novelist.
[3] The poet and essayist Richard Le Gallienne (1866-1947) enjoyed a brief popularity in the 1890s; Arthur Symons (1865-1945), poet and critic, author of the influential study *The Symbolist Movement in Modern Literature* (1899).
[4] Harley Granville-Barker (1877-1946) was an actor, dramatist, and theatrical producer. 'Sebastian Melmouth' was the name assumed by Oscar Wilde after leaving prison in 1898, derived from the martyred saint and from the hero of Charles Robert Maturin's gothic novel, *Melmoth the Wanderer* (1820).
[5] Edward Carpenter (1844-1929), socialist and essayist, whose discussion of sexual behaviour, *Love's Coming of Age* (1896), won him contemporary notoriety.

To Vera Beauchamp, [? May–June 1908]

[4 Fitzherbert Terrace]
Friday.

You know — you have not answered my last rather nice & particularly long letter — Oh, Lady of the Blue-Green Aura — and I am a little surprised to find myself writing again — Send me a letter soon — will you —

Vera — I wonder how you felt when awaiting the Sydney cable — did you have one tenth of my suspense and rapturous assurance? I feel so confident that every moment the 'phone bell rings — & Father says IT HAS COME. Today Tom Mills comes from Feilding[1] — I believe that we carrol together cette après-midi. I am not at all keen — he has written me too many letters — told me too much of himself — and likes me far too much — to make it anything but a trying ordeal — It is a little ridiculous. I cannot keep the men I know *friends.* They persist in drifting into some other ridiculous attitude — I let them drift, and then suddenly see what a big big log we have both bumped against — so I say to myself "dear me, how inadvisable, but it is certainly copy." I wonder if you have seen Mrs Glyn's new book — "Three Weeks."[2] No — don't tell me that I am Marie Corelli with her feet on a muddy road — I don't say read it — but the frontispiece holds a portrait — and the tout ensemble delineates more nearly that indescribable *"call"* of the feminine — that subtle sex attraction — which began with the foolish affair of the apple — than anything I remember having seen for years. It is a pity that Elinor Glyn wastes a pretty talent and a decided charm in catering for the foolish. You are always expecting her very décolleté gown to slip right off her shoulders — it does not — but on the strength of the reputation she 'amasseth a seemlie fortune' —

I have been reading a good deal of Balzac — with such interest — He is colossal — As I read I always see him — sitting in his room — how many stories high? — in the white dressing gown — writing writing feverishly — with Paris like a little clock work toy whirring at his feet. "La passion est toute l'humanité"[3] yet — and this keeps him from being much read by young people — he deals with the senses *through* the intellect — n'est-ce pas?

And have you — I wonder read Guy de Maupassant's Pierre et Jean. It is really a most fascinating book — but I liked best his article in the front on the Novel[4] — and there is positively no difficulty with the language — the French seems to translate itself — or rather — it does not translate at all — I have had too, quite a mania for Walter Pater — and Nathaniel Hawthorne — and also Robert Browning — and Flaubert — Oh, many others — I have been spending days at the Library reading and writing a novel — entitled The Youth of Rewa — it is very much in embryo just at present[5] — I have posted your letter to Eileen — She is spending eight days at Nelson — she and I have become very good friends — she is clever — uncommon refreshing — and very satisfying. Our friends [hip] is based upon milk & soda at the D.I.C. so the foundation is deliciously insecure —[6]

Seen a good deal of Miss Isitt lately — she is charmed with you — "Oh isn't your sister quite delightful — Miss Beauchamp" — "I have never seen anyone more charming than your sister" — She does not like me at all — but I interest her.

Chaddie has been quite seedy with Dr Milsom in attendance — His sister you would like — She is wholesome — and clever — and womanly — I like her exceedingly.

By the way — I received a telepathic message from you that you had received a letter from Mr. Trowell — Now can that be so? The message was most vivid —

Well — well — well — that's how I feel — I wonder if we shall ever see each other again — & cry ourselves purple at your bedroom window. Isn't life strange — Vera
My love to you —

                                                                    Julian.

Of course you know Mark Hambourg is the father of a little daughter. Is Music resolving itself into an aggressive Maternity & Paternity — He is photographed with the baby already — I can so see Vere Bartrick-Bakers[7] face — with half shut eyes — & raised brows she stares at it through the smoke of Egyptian cigarets — — — — —

MS ATL.

[1] During the previous year, KM's father had consulted Thomas Lewis Mills, a Wellington journalist, about his daughter's ambition to become a writer. Mills was shocked by what he considered the 'sex-problem' element in her work, but did suggest that she send stories to the *Native Companion*. Mills was now a partner in the *Feilding Star*, in a rural town a hundred miles north of Wellington.

[2] *Three Weeks*, by the popular novelist Elinor Glyn, was published in 1907.

[3] The phrase is from Honoré de Balzac's 1842 *avant-propos* to *La Comédie humaine*.

[4] Guy de Maupassant's preface to *Pierre et Jean* (1888) describes the discipline of the writer's life.

[5] All that survives of the novel is a one-and-a-half-page fragment (ATL) in manuscript.

[6] Eileen Ward was the daughter of Sir Joseph Ward (1856–1932), Liberal Prime Minister of New Zealand 1906–12, 1928–30. The D.I.C. — Direct Importing Company — was a large department store on Lambton Quay, Wellington.

[7] Evelyn (Vere) Bartrick-Baker was a close friend of KM's at Queen's College.

To Vera Beauchamp, [12 June 1908]

[4 Fitzherbert Terrace]
Friday.

My dearest Sister —

It is long since I have written you but every correspondence of mine has been far more summarily treated; I am so busy day & evening —

July — you can imagine how I wait for the news[1] — my dear — surely the Fates have given me a very just share of anticipation — and Beauchamp Lodge[2] (which, dear, like most of the pleasant things in my life — I owe to you) sounds quite ideal.

My plans — Vera — they are Work — and struggle and learn and try and lead a full life — and get this great heap of MSS. off my hands and write yet more.

Après tout — I do not think that the dice is thrown hap hazard — I was not *ready* for London or for an independent life — when the Trowells went — so it is better to have waited and *thought* —

Culture — do you remember hearing, as we sat among the Cowslip Jelly — is reflecting upon knowledge — the power to do so — keenly — fully — How wonderfully true!

You know I go to the Technical School every day — Library until five in the afternoon[3] — then a walk — and in the evenings I read & write — by the way, read R L.S's Mother's letters from Samoa[4] some day — and *do* read 'Come and Find Me' by Elizabeth Robins[5] — that woman has genuis — and I like to think she is only the first of a great never ending procession of splendid, strong woman writers — All this suffragist movement is *excellent* for our sex — kicked policemen or not kicked policemen. Everybody amongst your kin is well and, I think, happy — Mother absorbed in cooking, dear Chaddie just the same — Jeanne — very plump and pink — she will make an adorable woman some day — riding, and Chummie with Erik Cruik-shank.[6] He is all that can be desired — except I find him greedy at table — I don't like to write that — no doubt he suffers from some mental atavism — but you know how that offends our taste.

All the florists windows are full of the blue light of violets. And I can't resist them — tight posies tied with yellow flax — *Do* you feel flowers like this — a sense of complete magic — I am spell bound — entranced[7] — One day, ma chère, I pray you share my little Roman villa and I mean to have a blossoming almond tree quivering against a blue sky — and wide, cool rooms lit with daffodils opening their gilded doors to the sunshine which drips through the window vines. Also my scheme includes a boatman with a pomegranate behind his ear!

Have you lately read Hans Andersen's Fairy Tales? If you have a copy in the house do look up the Fir Tree. The last sentence is so astonishingly Chopin I read it over & over — and the simple un-earthly words flood your soul like the dying phrase of a Majorca nocturne.[8]

It is sweet of you to come home before I leave — but don't unless you *wish* — to — you know — dear — I'd love to see you — but I would not like you to leave for that reason — Don't, at any rate — dream of it — until my passage is literally booked — And more I think than any two other people in the world — we don't *need* to see each other.

Here is a little news — don't call me conceited — I think I am [more] popular than almost any girl here at dances — Isn't it funny — It makes me glad — in a way — but it's a little trying — Shall I tell you the men who like me — too much — Well Bert Rawson — Arthur Duncan — Mr [?] Chafery — Ken Duncan[9] — etc. — this is all very much by the way — but I tell you for this reason — It's so unwise not to *desire* to *please* — & it is so amusing to find these men talking quite brilliantly about Amiel's Journal —

Dearest Sister — I love and admire you — I would give so much to hold your hand again — Since you have left I have *begun* to know you

Your devoted

K.

MS ATL. Cited *UN*, 23, 25.

[1] i.e., that she was to sail in July.
[2] The Paddington hostel for young women in which KM was to stay when she returned to London; see p. 59, n.1.
[3] In May 1908 KM enrolled for 'Commercial Subjects' at the Wellington Technical School. The General Assembly Library was close to where she lived, and she worked there in the large reading room provided for Members of Parliament.
[4] M.I. Stevenson, *Letters from Samoa 1891-1895*, ed. Marie Clothilde Balfour (1906).

[5] *Come and Find Me!*, by the American actress Elizabeth Robins (1862-1952), was published in 1908.

[6] A neighbourhood friend of KM's brother Leslie.

[7] On Friday, 19 June 1908, KM attended a 'violet tea', at which flowers, décor, and even sweets were violet. She won a prize for her impromptu verse:

> The Cupid child, tired of the winter day,
> Wept and lamented for the skies of blue:
> Till, foolish child! he cried his eyes away,
> And violets grew.

The poem, with details of the party, was published in the social column of the *New Zealand Free Lance*, 27 June 1908.

[8] 'The Fir Tree' by Hans Christian Andersen (1805-75) concludes: 'Past and gone, past and gone! — it's the same with all stories.' When Frédéric Chopin (1810-49) went to Majorca with the novelist George Sand, he wrote, among other pieces, the Nocturnes in G minor, Op.37 No.1, and in G major, Op.37 No.2.

[9] The four men named were all young friends of the Beauchamp family.

To Vera Beauchamp, 19 June [1908]

[4 Fitzherbert Terrace] In the Smoking Room
June 19th

Liebe Schwesterchen —

I was so exceedingly glad to receive a special letter from you by the last mail; I love your Family letters — you know, but they do not breathe of the Inner You, which I prise and delight in — as you know —

So, after all, the cable came, and I sail today fortnight — incredibly delightful Thought! The Papanui leaves from Lyttelton on July 4th. I leave here by the Maori July 2nd[1] — the cable came on Wednesday morning — I was at The Technical School & when I came home the family were all out — laying in large and varied stocks of machine needles! Nelly told me the news — I rang up Trix — who declared "God bless my soul — pretty nice — dear — *come* & see me" — and then popped round to Fan. Do you know before I saw her I did not feel one ounce of excitement — but when she heard the whistle of Carennos Staccatto Etudes — she came to the door — and we literally fell into each other's arms — I know I had tears of joy.[2] We sat in Fan's little room — and talked it all over again — the joy — the freedom — the bonhomie — the cheapness of the laundry — the Beauchamp Lodge knock — which is the two opening bars of Lohengrin's Wedding March — then I came home and descended unto vests and stockings —

Vera, it is really hard to realise — I am so afraid that I shall wake up and hear the bath tap running — why are we always so much more chary to recognise grief than joy — isn't it absurd — and distinctly shows a great lack of that mental fineness of poise — which will one day be the joyful lot of every one of us — (Here I am going to digress & describe clothes, because I want your opinion.)

I've nothing fashionable *at all* — simplicity and art shades reign supreme — A black flop hat with a wide wreath of mauve chrysanthemums round the crown — a little evening frock of satin — soft satin — made exactly after the pattern of Grandmother Dyer's wedding dress — a green straw Home Journal travelling hat with wide black wings — and everything in like manner — Chad & Mother have been yearning, I know to blossom into empire frocks and créations de la moment — but I haven't one — Clothes ought to be a joy to the artistic eye — a silent reflex of the soul — so I'm training my amenable little soul accordingly — Do you like it — — — — — — —

Digression *no 2* — I had to leave this letter — go into the kitchen & cut myself an entire round of bread & bloater paste — tin loaf — because the body refuses to consider itself dined on one piece of flounder & an orange — I didn't know that Life held anything so ineffably delicious as this bread — was für Warheit! Simple pleasures are the refuge of the complex, nicht?

Oh, Vera, and while I am on the subject of eating — for I am convinced E.F. Benson wrote the book on an empty, healthy tummy, do please read 'Sheaves' — It is delightful — and also it is, in parts Simpson Hayward incarnate. If you asked me for Benson in a nutshell I would quote: — "Ah, I *must* speak", said Hughie, taking fish and bacon on his plate at the same time, and eating very fast, . . .[3] The book is by no means a menu, don't think that — Oh, in a way it is — it creates a wonderful appetite — but *do* ménus do that — for many things. If you read it — *do* talk to me about it.

They have been making havoc of our pine avenue — cutting down some of the trees — sawing the branches off others — a horrible, crashing, tearing sound, then the clinging roots scattered on the yellow clay — The whole sight — the men in their rough clothes — the toiling horses — patches of sunshine lacing through the silver point boughs — on to the emerald grass — makes me think of a modern Belgian painting — do you see it — full of suggested sound — and strangely — death!

Chaddie has gone to a Ball at the Masonic Hall — — — to what base uses! It is after twelve o'clock so I shall sit up for her — as I feel — Eastbourne like — fresher than ever — I am glad that you will see Aunt Lil. She is really, what Mac would call "one of the best", and, between you & me, she worships you, my dear — endows you with all the virtues — respects you, and loves you very whole heartedly.[4] Writing to you, I live again, very vividly, certain charming experiences. Giggleamus et Viandem — the 'Admiral's Broom' — at Macs — and hair soup & raisins on the wild sea. Now I know I am going on to a ship — I feel almost hypernautical; the shipboard life — which is such an utterly different existence — another plane of existence — suddenly predominates. I can hear & smell & feel and see — nothing but ships — do you know that?

I pray you — marry an Englishman & come live in London — and take your Poor Relation to an Art Gallery with an Entrance Fee once a month — Ida & May have been down at Ridge Cap. Easter time & heavy snow — Will you ever forget that time & Cousin Lou, and our poor little shocked souls when Aunt Belle & Uncle Harry performed a charade in kimonos![5] Have you forgotten Ralph's Easter egg, or his nice, Grecian mouth — how often the Gods endow a man with a perfect profile and no brains to live up to it![6] Now *you* live up to your eyebrows — do you realise that fact — Talking about you I inst[inct]ively think of enamal work — perhaps — You know that charming remark of Dante Gabriel Rossetti: — "I am trying to live up to my blue china"[7] — that is by no means absurd — To whom shall I send your love, my dear? And of course you know if ever you want anything from a Watts Original to a Dying Pig — I am yours to command — Oh, Vera — the first time I stand on those College steps — dear sister — I shall send you a wireless of the most pregnant order — & when Henry Wood stands in his place & lifts his hand — silently — for one moment[8] — I['ll] send you another.

Do write to me — I feel I never can stop — Oh, that — face to face — we two could talk, I wonder when and how she [for we] shall again — and what will have happened in the meantime —

Do you know Theodore Watts Duntan's work — in the main, intensely artistic critical essays — but it was he brought into being that constantly recurring expression: — the renascence of wonder — I admire the man very much indeed; he lives with Swinburne, was a friend of George Borrow, William Morris — all that 'set'[9] — Isn't it extraordinary how one can never tire of these people — they are my very good friends — and I know them immeasurably better than the people I meet here — There is a fascination almost unequalled in collecting all the detail's of a man's life — studying his portrait — his work — bringing him, splendidly willing, to one's own fireside — I have R.L.S. and Dante Gabriel Richard Wagner & Jimmy Whistler — *all* the Brontës — countless others — haven't you? One day let us give a dream party — invite those in the flesh who are attune to meet those in the spirit. "Oh, Alice, allow me to introduce you to Mr Stuart Mill" — — —

It is bitterly cold; I hope that you are wrapped in a nice piece of dog — and have a fire in your bedroom — that is the epitome of quiet, fastidious, charming luxury — Aunt Li is giving me pour souvenir an opal ring — Do you know a large, uncut opal [*drawing of oval stone, with* 'natural size' *written beside it*] — which she possesses — and she is having it set in a thin wide silver setting — I am so pleased because — as you know *opals* are my aura, & any jewellry which I do possess is mounted in silver. I don't wish for gold — It is to fit the second finger — Doesn't it sound beautiful — My black box is up in my bedroom — there is a vast amount of sorting to be done — steamer clothes & otherwise. Clara is giving me a red leather manuscript book stamped with a black tiki & my name[10] — I'm taking only half a dozen books and my photographs and the W.F.C.A.[11] green candlestick — Your jewel case sticketh unto me more closely than a brother — thank you again for it.

My dear — this is all — Write me *reams*, please. I do want to have you again — before I sail — Vera — It is a lovely moonlight morning —

Bon Jour — Yours as ever

K.

'Meine Seele sucht nach Dir.'[12]

MS ATL.

[1] KM sailed to England from Lyttelton, a port near Christchurch, in the South Island, on the *Papanui*. The *Maori* was a ship on the Wellington-Lyttelton run.

[2] Fanny Sealey, a music teacher and friend in near-by May Street, was later music mistress at Samuel Marsden Collegiate (the successor to Miss Swainson's Terrace School) 1913-38. Miss Sealey had herself been a resident at Beauchamp Lodge, although it was on cousin Harry Beauchamp's advice that KM's father decided his daughter could live there. The Etude in C major, Op. 23, the 'Staccato Etude', by Anton Rubinstein, was frequently performed by the Venezuelan pianist Teresa Carreño (1853-1917), who had toured New Zealand in 1907.

[3] KM is remembering loosely a scene from ch. 3 of E.F. Benson's *Sheaves* (1908), in which Hugh Grainger carries on a conversation 'eating fish very fast'. G.H. Simpson-Hayward was a cricketer who toured New Zealand with the MCC in 1906-7; the side travelled from England on the same sailing of the *Corinthic* as the Beauchamp girls.

[4] 'Aunt Lil' was presumably an Australian relative, perhaps one of the Sydney Lassetters (see p. 33, n.1). 'Mac' was James Mackintosh Bell (1877-1934), whom Vera Beauchamp married in 1909. A Canadian, graduate of Queen's College, Kingston, Ontario, and Harvard, in 1905 he was appointed director of the geological survey of New Zealand.

[5] Aunt Belle Dyer, after a short period as Clara Wood's assistant at Queen's College (see p. 5, n.4), married Harry Trinder, a wealthy shipowner.

[6] Ralph (Rally) Beauchamp was the oldest of Henry Herron Beauchamp's children.

[7] The remark is usually attributed to Oscar Wilde.

[8] KM frequently attended the Promenade Concerts conducted at the Queen's Hall, London, by Henry J. Wood (1869-1944).

[9] Theodore Watts-Dunton (1832-1914), remembered as Swinburne's 'guardian' at Putney from 1879 until the poet's death, was influential as a critic in the *Athenaeum* in the last quarter of the nineteenth century. The phrase 'the renascence of wonder', which Watts-Dunton applied in 1880 to Thomas Chatterton, became the title of his introductory essay, 'The Renascence of Wonder in English Poetry', in vol. III of Chambers's *Cyclopaedia of English Literature* (1901). Watts-Dunton shared with the novelist and linguistic scholar George Borrow (1803-81) an avid interest in Romany and gypsies.

[10] Clara Palmer was a Wellington music teacher. A tiki, a carved Maori pendant in the shape of a stylised human figure, is often regarded as a good-luck charm.

[11] Wairarapa Farmers' Co-op Association, a general merchants on Lambton Quay.

[12] 'My heart longs for thee' — the quotation is unidentified.

To Vera Beauchamp, 26 June [1908]

[4 Fitzherbert Terrace]
June 26.

Dearest Sister —

This is going to be only an apology for a letter — I could not allow your last charming Brief to remain entirely unanswered. And firstly — yes — the dedication[1] belongs to you — please accept it. Thank you immeasurably for your 'Fat' re my work; it is so scarce — I think these are surely the seven lean years of appreciation.

This time next week I am gone — So much is taking place — farewell teas — & Bridges, and parties — that there is almost a glamour — But seeing the people now so much I realise even more fully — is that possible? — how glad I am to go —

I do hope that you remain in Sydney as long as seems possible — Mother & Father are so happy to know that you are in congenial, appropriate surroundings, and Chaddie won't miss me a great deal — with the male Home Journals arriving in such good measure pressed down & running over in Auckland —[2]

Jeanne is developing into a charming girl — of course she is no taller — & I'm afraid a little less sylph like — but her disposition is delightful — she is artistic — and — a family trait — keenly receptive & sensitive — I think Jeanne, properly guided — should be a truly remarkable woman — essentially womanly, lovable & capable. But she needs an unlimited display of Affection and *your* influence — ma chère. She is — du verstehst? — a child who requires *kissing*.

The days are full of rain — I want to say so much — but really dear there is not a moment — except I shall indeed treasure the tidy — on the boat & at B. Lodge — & write as often as you can — I love your letters.

I embrace you in the spirit — | Your sister
K.

MS ATL.

[1] To some story, or projected publication, which does not survive.
[2] Clearly a private joke, to do with letters from some admirer of Chaddie's in the north. The *Home Journal*, published in Auckland 1907-8, was a sentimental, folksy magazine dedicated to the cause of Prohibition.

II
ENGLAND AND BAVARIA
1908–1909

KM left New Zealand on 6 July 1908, sailing from Lyttelton on the *Papanui*, via Cape Horn, and arrived in London on 24 August. She stayed with Ida Baker for some days before going to the hostel in Paddington where her father had arranged for her to live. 'Maata', part of a projected novel she began in 1913 (*Turnbull Library Record*, vol. XII, no. 1 [May 1979], 10-28), gives an account of her arrival back in England. Her plans seem to have been vague, but her father allowed her £100 a year to pursue her 'career'. Within a few weeks of her arrival, her involvement with Garnet Trowell dominated her life.

To Garnet Trowell,[1] [? 10 September 1908]

[52 Carlton Hill,[2] St. John's Wood]

My dearest —

I feel I must just write you a little note — Fate has been so unkind to you both today. Dearest — I've wanted you ever since I saw you yesterday — I have been wretched — I don't know *why* exactly — but I feel we have so much to say and so little time to say it in before you go away.

Dearest — I love you so intensely that I feel I could téll you so now until we both are old — and then you wouldn't understand — You are my life, now; I feel as though your kisses had absorbed my very soul into yours — that even when I am with others the real life — our life — must go on together — all the same. Last night I went to Queens Hall[3] — do you understand me when I say the hall was full of emptiness. I feel I was all the time searching for you — through the music — through everything. Everybody I saw seemed to give me some faint resemblance — you know? I love you — I love you. I shall see you tomorrow. Get up & wake me early and let's go for a walk before breakfast — you & I.

Après tout — I am afraid. I'll have to run away with you & live on a farthing a week down in Cornwall.

I have nothing to say because I am feeling so much. Do you think you will be home before me tonight? Pour la première fois we sleep in the same house. I shall surely dream.

Your

Kass

I can't see you until tomorrow — quelque chose d'expliquer.   K

MS Windsor. Alpers 1980, 69.

[1] Garnet Trowell (1889–1947), twin brother of Tom, to whom KM transferred her affections soon after she returned to London in 1908. When he completed his musical studies in Brussels, he became a violinist (playing under the name of 'Carrington Garnett') with the Moody–Manners Company; the company toured England presenting grand opera in English-language productions, with Fanny Moody and Charles Manners as principals and Romualdo Sapio as conductor. Garnet continued to earn his living with orchestras until he married in 1923. Six years later he and his Canadian wife returned to her home in Windsor, Ontario, where he taught music until the Second World War, and thereafter worked for the Ford Motor Company until 1945.

[2] The address at which Thomas Trowell sen. and his family went to live on their return to England. KM was a frequent guest.

[3] The concert at the Queen's Hall on 9 Sept 1908, given by the resident orchestra under Henry Wood, included a performance of Beethoven's 'Leonora No. 3' Overture, as well as other nineteenth-century works.

To Garnet Trowell, [16 September 1908]

[Beauchamp Lodge,[1] 2 Warwick Crescent, Paddington]
Wednesday Night.

I have just come back from Carlton Hill, dearest, where I spent the afternoon — and stayed on to dinner. It was so delightful — they were really happy and merry, and I feel, very often — you understand me? I can bring happiness to that house — You see, my beloved — you have taught me so much of the joy of life — that the world is a glorious thing — and to be alive in it a tremendous delight — that I feel I must communicate it wherever I go. And when Mr. and Mrs. Trowell do not look on the bright side of things — I talk Beethoven to the one — and play with the other — and kiss Doll — so it goes better — du verstehst?

Dearest of all the world — you are never out of my thoughts. I love you — I love you eternally. With you I am secure and rested & content — and *only* with you — Oh, with you, I could conquer the world — Oh, with you I could catch hold of the moon like a little silver sixpence — & play ball in the garden with Dolly — with any one of the planets.

Garnet — take me — hold me — kiss me. Let me lose myself in you — for I am yours. When I think of you I feel that a flame leaps up in my body.

Words are so restricting and writing to you I feel they are but pebbles thrown into a bottomless sea — they create ripples on the surface of a *great depth*.

I saw today such a fine picture of Beethoven. It would have appealed to you — I know — the wind seemed to be in his hair, and he seemed to *hear* with his eyes — comprends tu? — frowning so. There is a sublime simplicity in Beethoven, not in accord with the spirit of our times. He loved the universe and God and love and virtue with a great, abiding natural love — never realised the subtle joy in pain — which is the supreme ecstacy of modern music. He was like a giant child walking over the earth. Flying out of houses which poisoned him into the open air — lying on his back in a field with his face turned to the sky — and writing village band music and the morning stars singing together in one vast elemental surge. How absurd! I to write to you about music — — — —

My darling, my dearest — while you are you I must needs be happy, and our Future seems to me such glorious happiness — such a perfect outlook that I feel I must *run* forward. Lying in my bed at night — I feel your kisses burn my mouth — I long inexpressibly for you — I love you love you *love you*

Kass.

Dearest, do send little Doll a note, she is waiting for a letter from you — anxiously. Find time to; I know you are terribly busy,[2] and you remember Mrs Trowell's birthday on the 20th? Thought I might remind you.

Goodnight.

MS Windsor. Cited Meyers, 40.

[1] Beauchamp Lodge, a hostel for between 30 and 40 girls, most of them students at the Royal Academy of Music, was a five-storey Regency building situated on a bridge over the Grand Canal at Paddington Basin. Administered by two women who were themselves professional musicians, the hostel's rules were liberal; the charge for a bed-sitting room, service, and all meals was 25/- a week.

[2] Garnet was now in Birmingham, on tour with the Moody–Manners Company.

To Garnet Trowell, [17 September 1908]

[Beauchamp Lodge, Warwick Crescent]
Thursday Night. Midnight

My dearest, I opened your letter just now and the three photographs fell into my thrilled and happy hands — Now you are framed on my writing table — you are on a little low shelf by my bed — and even against my candlestick; so your face shall be the last thing I see when

I blow out the light, and go to sleep. I think they are splendid — they are you. I've been trying to tell you which one I like best, but each one I look at is so precious that I really cannot. I've said: — "Now Kathleen, suppose you had to part with one — which two would you keep", but that's no use — I could never give up any. Thank you, darling for these — I must send you one next month of myself — I want to do so very much indeed, but funds won't permit until October. Ever since early this morning I have been at work, and this evening I ended with going to report on a Suffrage Meeting at 8 o'clock in Baker Street. It was my first experience. Immediately I entered the hall two women who looked like very badly upholstered chairs pounced upon me, and begged me to become a voluntary worker. There were over two hundred present — all strange looking, in deadly earnest — all looking, especially the older ones, particularly "run to seed". And they got up and talked and argued until they were hoarse, and thumped on the floor and applauded — The room grew hot and in the air some spirit of agitation of revolt, stirred & grew. It was over at 10.30.[1] I ran into the street — cool air and starlight — I had not eaten any dinner, so bought a 2d sandwitch at a fearful looking café, jumped into a hansom, & drove home here, eating my sandwitch all the way — it was a tremendous two pen'north — almost too big to hold with both hands — & decided I could not be a suffragette — the world was too full of laughter. Oh, I feel that I could remedy the evils of this world so much more easily — don't you? Starlight and a glad heart and hunger and beef in hansoms, and the complexities of life vanish like cobwebs before a giant's broom. But I must needs look at life differently to others — wonderful and life giving miracle — *you are alive* — nothing else matters.

Beloved, do you know what beautiful, satisfying letters you write? I kiss the pages where your hand has rested, and isn't this a strange fact. This day I wake, and think I could not love him more — and yet each night, before sleeping I think "Well, I *do* love him more" — So it is every day. Dearest, always after I post a letter to you I feel I have said so little. You must read between the lines, and then you will understand that I live for you —

Tomorrow night I am going away to spend until Sunday night with some relations. I shall write to you from there, but your letters must wait until I get back on Monday — I don't feel that I could live through the days — but I must. Husband — you are all I have in the world, and you are the whole world — *I love you*. Oh, *words*, and my heart is almost breaking with joy and love — I worship you.

Kiss me — take me — I am yours — How are we going to wait for Xmas?
Goodnight — darling —
[*Across top*]
I shall send you what work I have; it's very little just now.   K.X.

MS Windsor. Cited Alpers 1980, 73.

[1] There is no record of the publication for which KM may have been reporting, nor of the meeting she attended. It may have been in preparation for the gathering the following morning outside Holloway Prison to mark the release of May Philips, who had served a three-month sentence for demonstrating in Parliament Square. Speeches and a procession were arranged by the National Women's Social and Political Union.

To Garnet Trowell, [23 September 1908]

[Beauchamp Lodge, Warwick Cresent]
Wednesday Night.

Heart's Dearest —
I dreamed last night, most vividly, that I was with you. It was so sweet that I trembled to wake, and yet *when* I woke there was a letter from you — So reality was as good as dreaming. All that you say to me seems almost curiously familiar, for beloved — I feel it so strongly — Know that I shall love you eternally. When I think for one moment of what the Future holds for us together, what days, and oh, my Husband, *what nights*, I feel really that I do not belong to this earth — it's too small to hold so much. You and I we are surely universal. Other husbands and wives seem to me to be sitting in corners, you and I — *we* are exploring the whole house — from cellar to garret — nicht? If *all* the world left me and you remained then Life would be full — if *all* the world came to me and you were not here, in my soul, then Life would be empty . . . Oh, I could lock you in a prison of my arms and hold you there — until you killed me. Then, perhaps, I would be satisfied. I love you, Garnet, I love you. There is one comfort — every moment that we are parted brings us a moment nearer.
This afternoon I went to the Palace Music Hall & saw Maud Allen, the danseuse[1] — she was wonderful. As she dances, under the changing lights, coming and going to the sound of a thin, heady music which marks the rhythm of her movements like a kind of clinging drapery, she seems to sum up the appeal of everything that is passing, and coloured and to be enjoyed. Dance music is wonderfully fascinating in its way. The rhythm of a walze, slow, insinuating,

gathering impetus which is held back, creeping into the blood; and it is possession and abandonment, the very symbol of love — tu comprends?

It is a clear, still night. I think I shall go down to the Victoria Hall[2] & wait for the Opera to be over, then walk home with you, arm-in-arm. Are you tired, dearest. Would you like me to cut you some sandwitches, and I promise not to forget the mustard!

Above me a woman is practising the drum — not an inspiring instrument. It sounds like the growling of some colossal dog, and I know I shall have dreadful nightmares. She is working to play next year at Westgate in a chef d'oeuvre called "The Policeman's Chorus". Bien, mon cher, there is surely nothing like aiming high — I wish her success! Oh, the people here would make you laugh. Three months ago I would have rather scoffed at them, now I feel that I can't help loving them all — Beloved, I do so feel I can afford to be generous. Oh, dear, next door someone has started scales on the trombone — curiously like a Strauss Tone Poem of Domestic Snoring.[3]

I read & reread your precious letters — I'm still terribly busy, but over and above everything there is *you — you — you*.

I am yours for ever. You know that — yet I can't help but tell you over & over.

Goodnight darling

Kass.

MS Windsor. Cited Meyers, 40; cited Alpers 1980, 73.

[1] Maud Allen (1883-1956), the Canadian dancer and actress, was performing in what advertisements called 'her wonderful classical dances'. She attempted to revive Greek classic dance, usually performing barefoot in a loose Greek gown.

[2] The Victoria Hall, Halifax, where the Moody-Manners Company was engaged for the week.

[3] Cf. *Symphonia Domestica* of Richard Strauss.

To Garnet Trowell, [2 October 1908]

[Beauchamp Lodge, Warwick Crescent]
Friday Night.

My beloved — I am sitting, curled up in a big armchair — a red arm-chair which has just been put into my room — my writing case on my knee — and I bridge over the miles that separate us — I bridge them over with a thousand loving thoughts — and fly into your arms — Do you know, Garnet, I feel so curiously that you are the complement of me — that ours will be the Perfect Union — why I feel, my darling, that together, we could hold the world in the hollow of our hands, and watch it revolving — Apart from you Garnet — as I am, now, each separate thing in the world is a miracle, a revelation — because I seem to see all with *double force* — You and I — together — what will happen? . . . My wonderful Husband — teach me — Yes, I feel that, too — Since I have lived through you — I am so happy — so ready to laugh with sheer joy — I had lost my way in a forest — seeing terror in shadows, bogeys in trees — you, you found me — — — — — — I think, Garnet, of us meeting again — being together and alone — a sensation creeps over me as though the very spirit of life itself within me, quivered and woke — Do you know exactly what I mean? So curious it is, and so tremendously intense — I love you — I love you — How can one speak of anything so vast as this happiness — I, too, feel that words will not express it —

Today I had my photograph taken for you — but the proofs do not come until next week, and I shall send you copies the week after.

How very overweight these envelopes must be! Oh, I wonder that mine do not really burst their bonds in that stuffy red pillar box — Letters, letters, they say so little, but they mean so much.

It makes me happy, Darling, that you have *our* cigarettes. We must smoke those on our honeymoon — nicht? I shall take a box with me — and we shall lean out of the window, and look up at the mystical — night sky — which always fascinates and *calls* me — verstehst du — and the smoke of our Abdullah cigarettes, mingling together, shall wreathe itself into a fragrant incense upon the altar of — — — *Love Love Love.* I went into your room today — beautiful sunshine streamed through the window — touched your books with my hands — stood where we had stood — so closely together, and *still*, my dearest, the hot air vibrated with the passion of our kisses — the silence seemed to sing. I must go to bed — Goodnight, darling — Folded closely to you — I kiss you — I am yours for ever

Kass.

MS Windsor. Cited Meyers, 40.

To Garnet Trowell, [3 October 1908]

[Beauchamp Lodge, Warwick Crescent]
Saturday Night.

Dearest — now if we were in our own home — we would be lying on a sofa before an open window — watching the moon gild the autumn trees in *our* garden — happy with the long night before us — and the days and nights of — how many years — to spend together. I am sure we would both be smoking, and I rather feel that we would have some coffee — not a good idea at this late hour — you know! And the warm night wind would be blowing the window curtains languidly, to and fro. We would lie still, whispering or silent, until, suddenly — — mon dieu, *I* know — do you?

My poor boy! What a long journey before you tomorrow.[1] I hope it is not so stiflingly hot as it is in London. I am afraid you will be very tired; do take care of your precious self.

I had a letter from Gwen [Rouse] today. She really can't explain what happened. It was a weak letter — you know, Garnet, lacked stability. I feel that Vivian Kidd[2] could sway her in the same way time and again. Really it is difficult to know what to think. However Tom seems satisfied. She spoke of you and me in a way that made me exceedingly angry. She cannot understand what we mean to each other, and I — stupidly perhaps — feel that I would rather she did not mention us — I feel she has *no right* to — verstehst du?

Well, darling, our Godmother[3] is well and happy. A strange girl, you know, Garnet. She is more than good to me, and we have both brought into her life all the happiness it contains. That's a strange fact, but I have to realise it. She never, by any chance, takes the initiative — must be shown everything — never thinks for herself, and is content, yes, radiantly content, to have a little sparc room in our life, and, presumably, sew on buttons.

Today I took little Doll to hear Madame Carreño. We became so enthusiastic, but of course, you were there. Didn't you feel me slip my hand into yours, dear? What a tremendous genius! I am staggered by her playing, by her tone, which is the last word in tonal beauty and intensity and vitality — No other pianist can so sway me. After the Concert we went & saw her. She kissed me and held my hands, and said in her fascinating voice: — "My dear child, I must see *much* of you. I am your friend, remember, and I hope you know I played the Erl könig quite for you".[4] She wore a long green silk shawl over her dress, and her strange face, half tragedy and half laughter, looked brilliantly beautiful. There is, indeed, a woman after my own heart.

This evening I had my New Zealand letters; they always strangely depress me. I think the shadow of the old life creeps over me, and I feel so out of touch with them — they hurt me bitterly. However Vera says "We have never been such a happy united family", so I *ought* to rejoice, I suppose.

Beloved, it is only you that I want. Thinking of you I could almost weep for longing for the shelter of your arms. I love you — I love you, and no one else in the world matters — and I cannot help feeling the necessity of you, my darling, more each day. I so *need* you. I want to come to you, I want you to come to me. You must come home in six weeks' time. When can you know for certain? Christmas is too far off, dearest. If my Patience had to stretch so far it would surely break. Yet that is nonsense, I could wait fifty years for you.

Well, dearest, it is so late, you had better lock the windows and doors. I shall go to bed — come soon. I feel lonely tonight, and yet almost savagely passionate. Let us go up the stairs, together and look in at little Doll's room — she is sleeping. And, lying in your arms, I fancy the world is beating to the beating of our hearts. I love you — I love you, passionately, with my whole soul and body.

Goodnight darling

Kass

MS Windsor. Cited Meyers, 40; cited Alpers 1980, 73.

[1] After a week in Liverpool, the Moody-Manners Company was travelling to Newcastle upon Tyne.

[2] Unidentified.

[3] Another of KM's names for Ida Baker.

[4] The Venezuelan pianist's (see p. 52, n.2) recital at the Bechstein Hall on 3 Oct 1908 included a performance of Liszt's transcription of Schubert's *Der Erlkönig*, as well as Beethoven's Waldstein Sonata and compositions by Chopin, Schubert, and MacDowell.

To Garnet Trowell, [5 October 1908]

[Beauchamp Lodge, Warwick Crescent]

[First two pages missing]

I know it is absurd, dearest, but there is a strong wind blowing this morning, & I cannot help but feel the old days back again — I mean I get that frightful sensation of grief that used to come over me in Wellington. You alone could take it from me. It is like suddenly finding myself face to face with this ghost which terrifies me.

Garnet — I want you. I need you. I love you. I shall write to you again tonight, beloved, when I feel better.

Yesterday Carreño wrote to me — such a charming loving letter, and asked me to spend next Sunday afternoon with her. Of course I go. It is just after breakfast — I will go to Carlton Hill and be 'cheered up'. This morning it is too strong for me to fight — the restless longing and love & passion that I feel for you —

Come soon.

I am yours for ever

Kass.

MS Windsor. Cited Alpers 1980, 70.

To Garnet Trowell, [6 October 1908]

[Beauchamp Lodge, Warwick Crescent]
Tuesday Night.
The long day over, beloved, I turn to you, seeking from you what I know I shall always find — Yes, and more — rest & Divine Happiness.

Today I was lunching with some old people up in Hampstead; after lunch they let me wander alone in their garden. Such green lawns and hedges — I was standing watching a plant in the shadow, small, bare, not beautiful. And then, suddenly the sunshine streamed over it — a radiance. Ah, I thought — so my soul must always feel, knowing his love — worshipping him. I love you, my Husband. Your voice, your touch, fills me with the spirit of Eternal Youth and Joy. I feel that we two, husband and wife, would be irresistible, would conquer the universe. Love is supreme over everything. I love you with every part of my soul, with every pulse of my body. This evening, Dolly and I walked in the garden, and the sound of the falling leaves at our feet was like the sea breaking upon sand and shell — a strange, shivering sweetness of sound — And, almost like a Debussy thème, stars shone through the barren boughs of the trees. The air was very still; a little fog wreathing itself about the garden. And, you came, Life of my Heart, and walked with me — I felt that strong, beautiful sensation of rest and support that I feel only with you. My life has resolved itself into you; I care only for you — I feel for you, do you know, beloved, a consuming passion. Ah, the opal on your finger[1] is full of the fires of my heart. I feel that jewel has drawn from me the passionate fires of my soul — that you, wearing it, have really become part of me — I consume & burn in your arms — You, you are life itself.

I love you — I love you.

My darling, when we two are married, and go away together — more alone I feel than any other two people have ever been in the world — my heart will break into a thousand pieces of laughter and of joy — — — — — verstehst du? The past, you know, like a ruined city — ivy-grown towers & minaret — lies behind us — the future — still vague — but the present is ours — you & mine — to love each other in. I do not think that any man has ever been loved so strongly.

It is very late — I want to go out and post this letter tonight before I go to bed. With you I welcome all the vissicitudes of the world — welcome them — Yes, with both hands — for surely at *our* touch they would change — glorify become *turned into gold*.

Hold me — kiss me — never let me go for I am all yours for ever. Goodnight — my best beloved —

Kass.

MS Windsor.

[1] Garnet was apparently wearing the opal ring KM had been given by her Aunt Li (see p. 51-2) on leaving New Zealand.

To Garnet Trowell, [7 October 1908]

[Beauchamp Lodge, Warwick Crescent]
Wednesday morning

I must begin the day with you, my darling — Good morning — Here the city is smothered in fog, and the sun hangs like a gold ball in the half leafless trees — a raw, Winter morning.

Your two letters, my beloved, lie beside me on the table — I read them over and over. Oh, Garnet, I feel what you feel — I understand you completely & fully. Your letters seem to grip me and hold me — Isn't it terrible to have to translate ones passion into *words* — such agitating, bitter sweet words which yet are only ripples on the surface — of a boundless, untried ocean. Yesterday I heard two women speaking — One said a friend of hers — though she had been married two years, yet wrote to her husband every day when he was away. They commented upon the absurdity of the fact — the lack of news — the necessary dull routine — & I listened & smiled. Wondered what they could say if they knew that I wake in the morning with your name on my lips — think of you — mentally write to you all day, and do not end my letter until as I go to sleep — I say — I am *yours*. It is not ended even then — for — happily, I dream.

Last night I dreamed we were together in the country — *happy*, my dear, laughing like children — and at this moment I see myself slipping a carnation into your coat for a buttonhole — I can smell that strange carnation perfume — mystic and passionately sweet. I think, beloved, that were we two together in the most deserted — god forsaken desert it would surely blossom as a rose — — I never knew before what Passion meant — this complete absorption of the one into the other — I love you, I love you *boundlessly*. You will have my photographs next week. My birthday is on Wednesday and I mean you to have one on that day. I hope the proofs will come today.

Dear, I can picture your landladies — there must be something fatal about us. People always persist in confiding in me the most intimate facts of their domestic relations — in the first breath — So when we are together, j'ai peur that we will never get the landladies out of the room!!

You have transformed me utterly — I am a different person — or rather — pour la première fois — I feel so much myself. In the early morning, Garnet, still half awake, I feel more curiously your nearness than at any other time. I try not to quite wake to reality — for half-dreaming — you are really beside me — I bury my head in the pillow & whisper your name over & over.

I must begin work. I *love* you — I kiss you — I belong to you for ever

Kass.

Little Doll sent you a X yesterday.

MS Windsor. Cited Meyers, 40; cited Alpers, 70.

To Garnet Trowell, [12 October 1908]

'52' [Carlton Hill, St. John's Wood]
Monday.

My dearest One —

This morning I got your letter[1] — oh-so gladly. But you do indeed raise my curiosity. What is the rumour? Do tell me even [if] it does not eventuate — it is such a wonderfully, beautiful thought. Can't I understand the surprise of those fellows at hearing you play! I wish indeed that I had been there also, darling — Dolly and I went out this morning on business. I had no time in which to write to you — I thought of you *all* yesterday especially in the afternoon when I went to see Madame Carreño and spent two hours with her — talking in the half dark — in a fascinating room full of flowers and photographs — fine pictures of her famous friends, and Russian cigarets — and books and music and cushioned couches — you know the type of room — We talked, I think in the main — of Music in Relation to Life — of the splendid artist calling — of all her journeys — a great deal besides. Truly she is one woman in a thousand. Beloved, today I feel, I am ashamed to say, tired to death — I want you and you and you. Feel restless, needing you, and no one else in the whole world. Oh, Garnett, know how much I love you. I feel my love for you is like the whole sea — as deep and as boundless — as restlessly passionate. I feel I want to shut my eyes — to be deaf to all that is happening in the world — to fly to your arms — to pillow my head on your shoulder — Beloved — your arms round me — then would I have fresh strength to begin the world with again. Garnet, what is

Love. Ah, there is a question I have asked myself all my life and the answer is *you you & you*. On Wednesday evening I leave London to go and stay in Surrey until the following Monday. So, dearest, will you address my letters

> c/o Mrs Trinder
> Melrose
> Upper Warlingham
> Surrey.

I do not want to go — your letters will be my only joy — and writing to you. The house is quiet. Mrs Trowell is asleep in here — Doll reading — Tom upstairs. Beloved this silent, clockfilled room is waiting for you to come in. I shall see you pass the window & run and open the door for you — Still the weeks are surely passing. Histed[2] is sending you one of my photographs to arrive on my birthday. Après tout, my darling, my birthdays belong to you. So I send this remembrance. My wonderful, splendid Husband, you alone I love. And I am yours for ever. Oh, how much better I feel for having written to you. So rested — so happy again

> Your
> Kass.

MS Windsor.

[1] From Glasgow, where the Moody–Manners Company was now performing.
[2] The photographers Histed & Co., 42 Baker Street.

To Garnet Trowell, [13 October 1908]

> [Beauchamp Lodge, Warwick Crescent]
> Tuesday Morning

Beloved — though I do not see you, *know* that I am yours. Every thought, every feeling in me belongs to you — I wake in the morning and have been dreaming of you — and all through the day, while my outer life goes on steadily, my inner life, I live with you, in leaps and bounds. I go through with you every phase of emotion that is possible — *loving* you — *that* life pulsates with sunshine and Happiness, unlimited, vast unfathomable wells of Happiness — and *you*. Oh, would that I could once express in words all the passionate, heavenly thoughts that break in tumultuous waves over my heart at the thought of you.

I wonder if you have ever swum in a very rough sea. I have — You plunge into the breakers — the waves break right over you — but you shake the water out of your eyes and hair — and there is a sensation of extraordinary strength. Something gigantic has you in its power — you are laughing, intoxicated — half wild with laughter and excitement. So I feel when I am tossed upon the very sea of passionate bliss. I love you — I *love* you.

Today London is muffled in a wrapper of grey fog. It is cold and raw. There is a heavy, rumbling sound of carts passing . . . You know such a day in a city?

Last night I went to the theatre — with some New Zealand people — and came right back here from Trafalgar Square in a hansom. It was close upon twelve o'clock. The sky was flushed with faint fires — hollowed into a perfect pearl. Dim men and women were clustering in broken groups round the doors of the public houses. From some of the bars came the sound of horrible laughter. And all the streets stretching out on every side like the black web of some monstrous spider. In the Edgeware Road we passed a great procession of the unemployed.[1] They carried a scarlet banner. You cannot think how horrible and sinister they looked — tramping along — hundreds of them — monotonously, insistently — like a grey procession of dead hours.

I came back into my room here and made some tea — & drank it, sitting curled up in my chair — a little heap of your letters on my lap. I read them slowly, my darling, and seemed to be living with you as I read — your wonderful satisfying letters. Were you, I wonder in bed and asleep, while I sat, still, and thought of you so vividly that I feel you would have been waked from the deepest slumber.

Garnet, this is the last day of my nineteenth year. Just think when we are both *over thirty*. I think we will be very young indeed. I must work.

My Beloved — dearest of all the World I kiss you. I kiss you — I am so happy today that I would like to wave a flag out of my window — you know that feeling? Ah, dearest — *I love you*
I am yours for ever —

Kass.

MS Windsor. Cited Meyers 41; cited Alpers 1980, 74.

[1] There were as many as 800,000 unemployed in Britain during the financial recession of 1908.

To Garnet Trowell, 15 October 1908

MELROSE[1] | UPPER WARLINGHAM | SURREY
Thursday. 15 X 08

My dearest,

It seems so strange to be sitting in the sunshine, and outside, instead of Paddington Station, long vistas of garden and trees, and spreading far and away the sweet green English country. Only one regret have I this morning, which is that your letter has to arrive later than it does in London, but I woke with your name in my heart on my lips — I kissed *our* ring,[2] my darling — and sent you, for this day, my *loving* loving greetings.

It seems that Love grows like a magic flower — Oh, Beloved, I am thinking of you *all* the time, seeing everything with you. I went to Carlton Hill yesterday; they were so splendidly happy, and you can think how pleased the little Mother was with my ring — also Doll also Tom — they thought it perfect.

Then I caught the 4.50 train and arrived at the country station in the middle of a sunset . . . tu comprends? Oh, Garnet, such a perfect drive to the house. I was all alone — and I felt that I must almost cry out at everything — at the green lawns, shadowed & sweet — the valley below all wreathed in fairy mist, and the sky full of pink rose leaves . . . You see? This house, too, has furniture and indeed whole fireplaces that I feel I would like to steal for *us* in the Future — such a beautiful gate table, and brass carved Flemish buckets for coal, and old oak chests. My room looks out over the garden. When I woke I jumped out of bed, and leaned out of one of the little lead paned windows. The gardener was digging below, and the sun shone on the warm red earth — a breeze shook the lilac trees. Beloved, you are so near me today — that I am radiantly happy. Oh, how much do I love you. "To him that hath shall be given"[3] — don't you understand that phrase?

Do let us bicycle away into the country today. Here is perfect summer weather & country — but I want you & you & you. My darling — I kiss you — I *love* you. We have never been out of London together — do you realise that — for I don't. I feel we have lived our lives together — I *know* how you feel about Nature. Garnet — what is ahead of us both — Oh, we shall seek out the heart of the world. Après tout — I have found it.

Such a fascinating baby of two[4] here! She's a darling, and you would have loved her in her bath last night — squeezing the sponge over her curls — She's like a little dimpled Cupid-ess. (What's the feminine.) She is staggering in here now, with a white fur monkey as big as herself in her arms, and says: — "*Is* you busy, Auntie Kassleen?"

I feel I could write to you forever — today. My darling, know that I belong to you — absolutely. Thinking of you I am in your arms — You give me Life. Your

Kass

MS Windsor. Cited Alpers 1980, 74.

[1] Melrose was one of the properties belonging to Aunt Belle Dyer's husband, the ship-owner W. Harry Trinder.

² Garnet seems to have sent KM a ring for her birthday, probably as a 'secret' engagement ring.

³ Cf. the parable of the Talents, Matthew 25:29.

⁴ Aunt Belle's daughter and KM's first cousin, Madge Trinder.

To Garnet Trowell, [16 October 1908]

[Melrose, Upper Warlingham, Surrey]
Friday evening —

I am in my room, dearest, sitting and watching the valley so smothered in blue mist that I cannot see where land ends and where sky begins — it is like a great, blue, motionless wave covering the land . . . .

Garnet, I have had such a perfect day. Quite early this morning I motored with two women to a place called Ashdown Forest — a perfect sunshiny day. The hedges, like green ribbons fringing the white road — and the sweet Surrey woods powdered with gold, splashed with crimson lined our route. We passed through villages such as you and I love — the quaint towered church, the old inn, the cottages with tiny flowered filled windows. And commons ringed about with young oaktrees, and a pond in the middle, and happy English village never was young — has existed always in an old, they will be how many years hence — — — I always feel that an English village never was young — has excited always in an old, quiet way. That the ivy crept over the church while it was being built — that the quaint worn stone steps of the houses were never new and hideously white!

At Ashdown Park the women played golf all day, so I wandered by myself to a little village called Forest Row where I posted your cards — and then, through some fields I discovered a *fascinating* castle — Brambletye Castle — old and ivy grown.¹ There was no one to be seen — it stood in a meadow — and I could see, all about, fragments of the wall — an old Gothic gate etc. Garnet, I spoke to you, beloved all the time and then I walked through a forest and a park. Sunlight was drenching the trees, but the road was in shadow. I was so happy that I felt I must fling myself down on the warm grass — feel *one* with the whole great scheme of things. You know the sun filled world seemed a revelation — I felt as tho' Nature said to me "now that you have found your true self — now that you are at peace with the world accepting instead of doubting — now that you love — you can see". Beloved half the world is blind, as you say — I cannot understand how they pass their days, but, since you have held and dominated my life, I feel the last veil between me and the heart of things has been swept away —

We came back here in the twilight — I sat in the front of the car — the cold air blew upon my face — We seemed like a dragon, so fast we sped, eating up the road — tu comprends? And in my heart a fire raged and burned fiercely — I felt so close to you that I trembled with joy — — — and almost — — — fear. My darling, in my room your letter welcomed me. What inexpressible happiness! But in a way I'm worried. Don't get over tired, dear Boy. Please take care of your precious self for this poor little girl who cannot take care of you — I think — yes, I'm rather afraid, Beloved — you'll have a very tyrannical wife!

It is quite dark now — a train passes — and fussily tears its way into the country — the sound excites me curiously. Don't you like travelling at night — peering out of the window at the dark stations — & then half sleeping and waking and arriving at a quite strange new place. Not alone — Oh, that would be horrible, but together — Garnet — what *fun*! I could write to you for ever. I *love* you — I *love* you. Dearest of all the world — take me and hold me — I am yours for ever

Kass.

MS Windsor. Cited Meyers, 40; cited Alpers 1980, 70.

¹ The ruins of the Jacobean mansion, Brambletye House.

To Garnet Trowell, [19 October 1908]

[Beauchamp Lodge, Warwick Crescent]
Monday Night. | In My Room.

Best Beloved and Dearest One —

It's so fine to be back here even tho' I love the country — I feel so wonderfully happy tonight that were you with me I really don't know *what* would happen. Your letter is beside me. Would that I had heard 'Die Meistersinger';¹ it must have been a fine performance. And you are coming home on November 23rd — that is the best news I could ever have — Not such a long way off, at all — Think when the train comes into the station. I'll be meeting you this time, just reversing it — Oh, Husband — I *love* you — I *love* you.

I came back this morning, lunched with our Godmother — Found her rather miserable, but I soon made her laugh and she became very merry indeed. We went up to Carlton Hill — I took Doll some sweets & bought some cigarets at Dicky's (Ethel² was there, to my disgust.)

They were all so gay — Garnet we laughed together. Oh, I felt I could make them so happy through you — it was all through you, Beloved — We went down to the kitchen and sat on the table and talked. Little Mother was simply like a girl — you know when she is much younger than even Doll. They heard nothing from Tom — rather naughty not to have sent them a p.c. but perhaps they will have a letter tomorrow. Then Ida and I walked home — past the Warrington Hotel[3] — *our* walk — you know — even the lights trailing in the canal did not look so haunted tonight — and I came gladly to this room which seemed

[*Letter incomplete*]

MS (fragment) Windsor.

[1] Wagner's opera was part of the Moody-Manners repertoire, which also included *Tannhäuser, Aida, Madame Butterfly, Cavalleria Rusticana, Pagliacci,* and *Maritana.*
[2] Unidentified.
[3] In Warrington Crescent, off Maida Vale.

To [Garnet Trowell], [21 October 1908]

[Paris]
Wednesday 21st   *20 after three.*
Well, after a day of most turbulent packing Margaret and I drove off to Victoria[1] 20 after seven. London looked garish, festive, alluring, only in the Park there were vague [*illegible*] crowds huddled together at the Marble Arch — a body of Police waited by their horses. Victoria — the huge station seemed alive with police and passengers. Already by the Continental train strange foreign types of people gathered — a Pole, tall, thin, smoking a long narrow cigar, a Turk, scarlet fez topping his sombre face. We four filled a compartment. There were wide fat English seats with a neat little white antimacassar buttoned across the top. And the doors were slammed — a last view of the wide platform and we had rushed our way into the country. I read a little and then huddled up in the corner, half sleeping, half waking. I thought of you. To open my eyes and find you beside me — if it was *we* two together going abroad. I felt, mainly, wrapped in a great cloak of thought. And so on and on. Every now and then, out of the window pane, I saw a signal box loom up in the darkness. We shattered through the tunnels — then a halt at Lewes, ten minutes off Newhaven. Packets of corn beef sandwiches were produced and black grapes in frilled white paper — we have one of those extraordinary little meals that English people indulge in travelling. And then Newhaven: all change. Tired sleepy people, children crying

fretfully, the Pole again — and again the cigar — the Turk weighed down with huge white wicker baskets, stream along the platform up the dark gangway to the darker boat. I have a confused impression of rain and [? dancing] lights and sailors in great coats & boots like Flying Dutchman mariners. We go aft to the Ladies Cabin where a little French woman is in attendance, her white face peering curiously at us over billows and billows of apron. Such wide blue velvet couches, such hard bolsters for tired heads. We slip off boots and skirts & coats, wash, and wrapped round in my big coat & a rug tucked round my toes I settled down for the night. It was amusing, you know, all round these same huddled figures, in the same little brown rugs, like patients in a hospital ward. And the little French woman sits in the middle knitting a stocking. Beside her on a red table a lamp throws a fantastic wavering light. All through the hours, half sleeping, half waking I would open my eyes and see this little bowed figure & the wavering light seemed to play fantastic tricks with her & the stocking in my fancy grew — gigantic — enormous. It seemed almost symbolical — the sleeping figures and in the light the little quiet woman knitting an eternal stocking. At last I really slept only to be wakened — deux heures et demi. My shoulder & hip ached, my hand had gone to sleep. I stretched wearily — still the strong thudding vibration of the boat, the swishing of the water. Then suddenly — how can I describe it, beloved — it was as though I lay in your arms. For a moment I turned my face to the wall, could not look at people feeling as I did. I was strong, refreshed, waked to such full life that I got up laughing, plunged my face into the glad cold water, & booted & spurred, ran up on deck to find Dieppe — the landing stage like the mouth of some giant monster, and a little crowd of officials groaning a gangway on board. We disembark, hustle up the sanded stairs to the luggage room where the play posters on the walls — Normandy, Bretagne, Paris, Luxembourg — are like magic hands stretched out in invitation. See what I hold — come here. In the buffet we have rolls and strong coffee out of thick white cups. In the centre of the table there is a little flat strong peasantware bowl of berries. I think — dear me, he wouldn't believe that. Next table to me a honeymoon couple — she with a new wedding ring and all [? certainly] new luggage. I look at them and think, dear me, how *much* happier we would be, how at ease we would feel, where these two only look nervy, ashamed & apologetic to the waiters. And again into the high padded carriage. A porter runs along the platform shaking up the darkness with a jangly bell, shrill whistles sound, & now we are finally to Paris. At first on one side the street of rain washed cobblestones, on the other the harbour full of lights — the darkness. I slept but woke at Rouen — it was bitterly cold. An official with a bell about the size of a 3d bit dashed along the platform. Opposite in a buffet 2 gendarmes were drinking. We started again and next I remember blue light flooding the windows of the carriage. I rubbed one — a little peephole for myself — and saw green trees white with frost. Then little by little dawn, a sky like steel — on both sides of us quaint small grey blue villages, houses, fields girt with Noah's Ark trees. And now and again the moon, like steel, slipped through the strees. At last Dawn came — in the sky hung a pink banner of cloud. It grew and widened until at last it touched the houses & fields — peered into the mirror. Dawn sat up in bed with a pink fascinator round her head. At the station sleepy officials shouted French French French, & then St. Lazare at last — a great platform — cold with the coldness of more than Winter.

MS (draft) ATL, Notebook 8.

[1] Margaret Wishart, a music student also living at Beauchamp Lodge, was the daughter of an admiral; KM was travelling with the Wisharts to France for a brief holiday, and to attend a naval wedding in Paris.

To Garnet Trowell, [24 October 1908]

[Paris]
Saturday Night.

My dearest Boy —

Your letter last night did so enchant me but I feel so strongly, too — the stupidity of our separation. Do you know I feel indeed, curiously, married to you — that I shall go back to London on Sunday and find you at the Station — Oh, my darling, could that be so — we would I think — truly set the thames ablaze with our passion of love and joy — For indeed, dearest I love you so much now — see that foolish last word but I have always loved you — I love you so entirely that I feel — and especially in the evenings and at night — that I cannot rest without you. Oh, Garnet — my splendid Wonderful husband, each day, it seems, do I take the blossoms from the tree of Love, and each day new and more wonderful flowers burst into bloom in their place — I feel that you and I are bound together by a thousand thousand things. Oh, but when you come *home*. Indeed I feel that my love for you has so grown since you left that I can give you so much more — I did not think it could grow but it has, and does — comprends tu? Darling, mere words and a French pen can never express all this I mean — but I *love* and *love* you. How fine the Forth Bridge[1] must be — I'm glad you didn't walk back ten miles — You have the descriptive faculty in letter writing — One day I'll come to you, for assistance — and we will write a book together — a Book of Love, nicht?

Yesterday we spent the day at Versailles — starting by tram quite early in the morning — through Paris — by the riverside — through the gates — past St. Cloud — and into the beautiful French country and then to the Palace & Gardens. Looking back upon it all I feel I must have dreamed so much beauty — the pictures — the rooms which Louis XV gilded with the very blood of the people — the chapel built by Madame de Maintenon to "purify the Palace"! the theatre where Madame de Pompadour sat with Louis XV — the statuary — the ballrooms — and above everything — the marvellous gardens and fountains — Avenues of chestnut trees, darling, burning a red bronze with the fires of Autumn — and among them these marvellous marble figures — Apollo — Venus — the four Seasons — Cupid — etc etc. Then the fountain of Apollo — the fountain of Neptune — the fountain where Latona is seen beautiful as a flower — turning the inhabitants of a village into frogs & lizards & turtles — the grotto of Apollo set about with trees — and a lake where yellow leaves flooded like sunlight — the green lawns — and always the marvellous distance effects — one feels it is an eternal magic world — that Versailles is indeed the hunting ground of Gods & Godesses. It was full of ghosts in the day, what would *they* be at night!! We left the garden in the evening — outside there was a great Fair. Long, brilliantly lighted booths which made me feel like a child — especially the toys and gingerbread frogs — and kites and cakes and books and sweets. I bought you a little packet of most fascinating things which I will send you from London — Felt we two were buying them together — and the queer little old Frenchman seemed to be so pleased with my delight that he made me a present tied with ribbon of confiserie fearful and wonderful — We got back here dined, and went to a Reception where I sat on a sofa & talked to an English Naval Lieutenant until after eleven, and this poor child was so tired & ennuyée, that I almost 'saw double' — you know that degree of fatigue? I came home, my darling, and went to bed, thinking of you — dreaming of you all the night through. Today I have been to the Arc de Triomphe and the very top of Notre Dame — and the Tomb of Napoleon and the Luxembourg — I feel very tired with so much beauty and fascinating new thoughts & conceptions.

Life seems to me each day, my husband, fuller & more worth living. I feel I have such a vivid sense of existence — loving you. My next letter will be from London — again. I am more than sorry to leave Paris. Indeed it is easy to realise what Paris means — And she is a city for — — — — you & I. The picturesque aspect of it all — the people — and at night from the top of a tram — the lighted interiors of the houses — you know the effect — people gathered round a lamp lighted table — a little, homely café — a laundry — a china shop — or at the corners the old chestnut sellers — the Italians selling statuettes of the Venus de Milo — & Napoléon encore Napoléon. I picture us with perhaps two small rooms high in the Quartier Latin — setting out at night — arm in arm — and seeing it all and because we were together — a thousand times more. I picture us coming home at night — and sitting over a wood fire — coffee and cigarets — the shutters closed — the lamp on the open table — like the sun on a green world — & *you* & *I* — the world shut out — and yet the world in our power — I love you too much to dare to fully realise all this —

It is late. High over the roofs — we are on the fifth floor — floats the sound of bells — very strange at this hour — haunted — like bells heard in deserted churches under the sea — — — — verstehst du? I must go to bed — We leave tomorrow so I must get up early & pack. Darling — you too will be travelling tomorrow[2] — bon voyage — Ah, when will you surely come to London November 23rd or before — — — — J'attends.

Goodnight — dearest-of-all-the-world. I kiss you — Oh, thank God for letters — they are my one grande consolation — Think of it — I love you for ever with all the strength I possess — Beloved — I am yours. I can never belong to you more than I do now — it's impossible — yet, how one longs for the bond to be sealed. Ah, I *love* you.

Kass

MS Windsor. Meyers, 41-2.

[1] The Moody-Manners Company was now in Edinburgh.
[2] With the Company to Middlesbrough.

To Garnet Trowell, [25 October 1908]

[Beauchamp Lodge, Warwick Crescent]
Sunday Night. In My Room.

Dearest,

I am back in London again, and tho' it is really Monday morning already I am stealing a night off and start a letter to you. We left Paris by an early train this morning, and travelled through the lovely French country — such woods all ruddy with Autumn colouring — and villages — and Rouen — where I should like to have spent at least a week — and finally Dieppe . . . a rough sea journey is a strange conglomeration of sensations — I, in a moment, seem caught in a web of a thousand memories — am a child again, sitting on the deck in my Grandmother's lap, & me in a red riding hood cloak! And then going over to Picton & Nelson,[1] to England for the first time and the second time. . . It was frightfully rough today. I lay still, perished with cold and felt dreadful — the few hours seemed an eternity of time. What joy to reach Newhaven — to come into the air and see the pale, grey town — the lights shivering in the cold harbour, *and* a gangway leading to land. Observe me a few moments later, dearest, on the Newhaven platform, wrapped in two coats and woollen gloves and furs, eating a sugared bun nearly as big as myself and laughing with sheer joie de vivre.[2] Sorry tho' I am to leave Paris — it is good to be here again. And in my room a glowing fire welcomed me and white chrysanthemums again. Do you know a mood when you unpack, and even change the position of the furniture — make minute accounts of the money you have spent — undress — arrange your books and pictures — that's what I have been doing — & now my little reading lamp and this faint flutter of the fire — have lured me to stay up and write and read. Also, my darling, you have been in my thoughts so constantly and so strongly all day long, that I had to speak to you. Outside a cold wind shivers the branches of the leafless trees — but in this warm, lighted room, I feel alone with you. My darling my heart is so full of love — emotions seem to clamour for expression — all the time I feel on the verge of being able to express to you just what I do truly feel — but impossible. I can only say that I love you and love you. That our love for me lights the world — has made of life something infinitely precious that now I can never be sad for long — or even tired for long — I am indeed, my dearest, so wrapped up in you — Yes, just as I was that night — both of us — you remember under the big fur coat. Tonight, our ring on my finger shines with a strange radiance and brightness. Garnet, I think of you, and all the rest of the world dwindles and fades. You and I are together, alone, upon a strange new planet, whose wonders we two explore — — — — — How *passionately* do I love you — surely, my darling — you know — But the separation — doesn't it seem ridiculous? Absurd, and meaningless. . . Dear, I think you'd better have your fur coat posted to Middleborough — don't you — or will you wait till you come home? Don't get cold just at the beginning of the Winter — it would be quite simple to post. . . What do you think. Are you warm enough leaving the theatre at night now — & the trains are the coldest places. Remember to tell me. I kiss you — my most precious one — I kiss you & I am yours forever

Kass

MS Windsor.

[1] Two towns at the top of the South Island, across Cook Strait from Wellington. KM's paternal grand-parents lived in Picton.

² Another version of this passage survives in draft:
Observe me then dearest on the Newhaven platform wrapped in two coats and woolly gloves & furs, and eating a sugar bun as big as myself almost with the joy of the world. A rough sea journey is a strange conglomeration of sensations. I, in a moment seem caught by a thousand memories — am a child again sitting on the deck in my Grandmother's lap — and me in a red riding cloak going over to Nelson or Picton — [?bangled] for the first time & the last — — It was frightfully rough. I lay still, perished with cold and felt dreadful. Eventually Margaret & I succumbed to the fearful agonies of mal de mer & the few hours seemed an eternity of time. What joy to reach Newhaven, to come up into the air & see the pale shadowed town — the lights shivering in the cold harbour — the gangway leading to land. I began to laugh & observe (ATL, Notebook 8.)

To Garnet Trowell, [29 October 1908]

[Beauchamp Lodge, Warwick Crescent]
Wednesday Night. 1 AM.

My most Beloved One —

I feel that I must write you a long letter tonight and try and say what never can be said between us — only felt and expressed — never written —

My soul is full of love for you. Your letter this morning did so satisfy me — that — oh, I had strength to conquer the world — and I wrote four poems which I send you tonight. They are to be set to music — so you will understand just what music I want — I know. Can't you imagine it. For instance that one "In the Church" almost recitative at the beginning with a strange organ like passage — then the ivy, rough, cruel, horrible, and then the first verse in a dream — you hear it? And then "By the Sea Shore", with strange Macdowell, Debussy chords — and the lilac tree, full or [*for* of] a rythmic grace — I wrote them for you — truly — and to suit Tom's composition.¹ Take them with a thousand kisses. I wish that you could come in — home from the theatre — and this our room — I sit at the table — wrapped up in my kimono — a little reading by me — and a glass of hot milk — (which I detest) I am not at all inclined to sleep. Oh, what delight to lie in your arms and talk and talk. No, I wouldn't do it — as it happens, my darling — as I'd make you go to sleep quickly — you would be so tired —

I pause here and sip a little hot milk — it's detestable — but excellent for the complexion — mon cher — so I suffer in silence —

I ran up to '52' for dinner tonight: they were all so gay. And as we sat by the fire — your letter to Doll and the little Mother arrived. Dearest I wish you could have seen their faces — heard their happy voices — heard Mother's "Bless that darling child", seen Doll, radiant. Oh, dear, I felt rather worried because I hate to think of you being cold and shut up in that theatre. Are you warm enough at night.

Does Mrs Lyon provide you with plenty of blankets? *Do* keep warm
— it's the secret of keeping well this weather — Darling — I feel as
though I'd been married to you for years — as though I ought to be
looking after you — I'm afraid you will be thoroughly spoiled from
the 22nd to the 30th.

I put up little Doll's hair tonight; she looked beautiful — and very
like a Greuze girl[2] — and the child was so excited — and begged me
to let her go and meet you at the station in a long skirt — and her
hair on top — but I said *"no"* — what a horrible shock you would
have had! When I think of you — Garnet — I am almost wild with
love and joy and passion — Oh, that the days would fly past —
Think of us going home — together & knowing that is for a week —
I am jealous for you — I am hungry for you — I *love* & LOVE &
LOVE you. I am glad that you arrive late — there is a certain almost
intoxicating glamour over London then — that holds me always, and
with *you* — — — Beloved — I must copy out those poems — & then
start work. Goodnight — What a journal we shall write in that week.
Tom and Gwen declare that they possess the dining room — so we
shall be in your room — I had much rather — I feel, to tell you the
truth — a little curiously about Gwen — very out of sympathy with
her — I do hope that the sensation will pass — — — — Goodnight —
Husband — dearest

I am forever your devoted wife

                                                    Kass. *Kiss* me

[*Enclosures*]

In the Church

> In the church, with folded hands she sits
> Watching the ivy beat upon the pane
> Of a stained glass window, until she is fain
> To shut her eyes — — — Yet ever hears it tapping —
>
> > "Come out," says the ivy
> > I spring from the mound
> > Where your husband lies buried
> > You, too, in the ground —
> > (The hour is at hand)
> > You must lie down beside him.
>
> In the church, with folded hands she sits
> Seeing a bride and bridegroom hand in hand
> Stand at the altar, but no wedding band
> Crowns the young bride — save a chaplet of ivy leaves.

On the Sea Shore —

Deafening roar of the ocean
The wild waves thunder and beat
Sea weed, fragments of wreckage
They fling them up to her feet.

She, her pale face worn with waiting
Stands alone in the shuddering day
And watches the flight of a sea gull
Wearily winging its way.

"Why do you scream — Oh, sea bird
And why do you fly to me?"
"I am the soul of your lover
Who lies drowned far out at sea."

The Lilac Tree

The branches of the lilac tree
Are bent with blossom — in the air
They sway and languish dreamily,
And we, pressed close, are kissing, there
The blossoms falling on her hair —
Oh, lilac tree, Oh, lilac tree
Shelter us, cover us, secretly —

         . . . .

The branches of the lilac tree
All withered in the winter air
Shiver — a skeleton minstrelsy.
Soon must the tree stand stripped and bare
And I shall never find her there
Oh, lilac tree, Oh lilac tree
Shower down thy leaves and cover me.

A Sad Truth[3]

We were so hungry, he and I
We knew not what to do
And so we bought a sugar cake
Oh, quite enough for two —

We ate it slowly, bit by bit
And not a crumb was wasted
It was the very best, we said
That we had ever tasted —

But all this happened years ago
Now we are rich and old
Yet we cannot buy such sugar cake
With our united gold.

[K. Mansfield 1908][4]

Letter MS Windsor; enclosures MS Newberry. Letter cited Meyers,
41. Enclosures publish'ed *Adam* 370-375, 72-3.

[1] The 'poetical' compositions of the American composer Edward Alexander MacDowell
(1861-1908), a student of Teresa Carreño, were in vogue at this time, particularly in Germany. No setting by Tom Trowell of any of KM's poems has survived.
[2] The French painter Jean-Baptiste Greuze (1725-1805) was admired for his domestic
scenes, and his portraits of adolescent girls.
[3] Published in *Adam* 370-375 under the title 'A Song with a Moral'.
[4] In the hand of Garnet Trowell.

To Garnet Trowell, [2 November 1908]

[Beauchamp Lodge, Warwick Crescent]
Monday Evening

My Best Beloved One —
I have just come in from such a fine afternoon with our little Doll.
She is truly a dear child — and I like to take her about — and make
her see things as we see them — our point of view — tu comprends?
We wandered about in the British Museum — among the beautiful
china & Venetian glass — and curios and precious books — a prodigal
wealth of loveliness on every side — almost a fantastic glory of
colour. Then I took her to the Vienna Cafe[1] — and she had some of
their famose chocolate, and then we walked up to Baker Street —
fog in the air — but lamps lighted everywhere — and Doll and I
talking & talking — — — do you know of whom? Now — seriously,
my darling — how much do I love you — I pause and think — but
that's manifestly absurd for the thought feeds on itself — becomes
stronger and more passionate each time I pause — Oh, you and I,
we stand on the shore of an ocean — boundless — untried — Over
the horizon how many magic isles — lie hidden in clouds of rose
colour? But we stand, hearing only that marvellous, symphonic rush
of sound — together. It seems, to me, that the world is ours — alone
— we are the one — now — here — Garnet — when I say your name —
I almost *tremble* — I love you & you & you — — — —
I have been writing some words for two songs of Tom's so I send
you a copy. The one called a 'Song of Summer' — I thought of you
and me — waking in the morning — with the sun in our room in the
country — so you will understand it. The other had to exactly fit

the music — which it does — he's delighted and says I have caught his thought exactly — but it's a morbid thought and not at all as I feel — — — — And here is another poem after the style of the Newspaper Girl — realism — you know — it's a little cruel —[2] I have a strange ambition — I've had it for years — and now, suddenly here it is revived — in a different way — and coming hammering at my door — It is to write — and recite what I write — in a very fine way — you know what I mean. Do you know exactly what I mean. Revolutionise and revive the art of elocution — — — take it to its proper plane — Nothing offends me so much as the conventional reciter — stiff — affected — awkward — but there is another side to it — the side of *art*. A darkened stage — a great — high backed oak chair — flowers — shaded lights — a low table filled with curious books — and to wear a simple, beautifully coloured dress — You see what I mean. Then to study *tone* effects in the voice — never rely on gesture — though gesture is another art and should be linked irrevocably with it — and express in the voice and face and atmosphere all that you say. *Tone* should be my secret — each word a variety of tone — — — — — I remember once hearing a Danish woman with a violinist at the Eolian Hall give a recital but it was conventional & not on these lines[3] — Even then it was fine — Well, I should like to do this — and this is in my power because I know I possess the power of holding people. I would like to be the Maud Allen of this Art — what do you think. Write me about this — will you? You see — I could then write just what I felt would suit me — and could popularise my work — and also I feel there's a big opening for something sensational and new in this direction — — — — —

It is a cold evening — how is it with you. My darling how I love — & love you. Oh, to feel your kisses once more thrill me with an anguish of joy — for you alone I love with all my soul — Garnet — it is certainly stronger every day — now. What will we do & say in the first few moments when we are together? Do you know? I cannot & yet can picture them.

Take care of yourself — my darling — Don't work too much[4] — Oh, to be with you for five minutes even — to see you — to feel you with me —

I love and love you — I belong to you

Kass.

[*Enclosures*]

A Song of Summer

At break of day the Summer sun
Shines through our windows one by one
He takes us by his great, warm hand
And the world is changed to Fairyland.

He gives us fairy bread to eat
And fairy nectar, strange and sweet
While a magic bird, the whole day long
Sings in our hearts his mating song.

The Winter Fire

Winter without, but in the curtained room
Flushed into beauty by a fluttering fire
Shuttered and blinded from the ugly street
A woman sits — her hands locked round her knees
And bending forward . . . O'er her loosened hair
The firelight spins a web of shining gold
Sears her pale mouth with kisses passionate
Wraps her tired body in a hot embrace . .
Propped by the fender her rain sodden boots
Steam, and suspended from the iron bed
Her coat and skirt — her wilted, draggled hat.
But she is happy. Huddled by the fire
All recollections of the dim grey day
Dwindle to nothingness, and she forgets
That in the street outside the rain which falls
Muddies the pavement to a greasy brown.
That, in the morning she must start again
And search again for that which will not come —
She does not feel the sickening despair
That creeps into her bones throughout the day.
In her great eyes — dear Christ — the light of dreams
Lingered and shone. And she, a child again
Saw pictures in the fire. Those other days
The rambling house, the cool sweet scented rooms
The portraits on the walls, and China bowls
Filled with 'pot pourri'. On her rocking chair
Her sofa pillow broidered with her name —
She saw again her bedroom, very bare
The blue quilt worked with daisies white and gold
Where she slept, dreamlessly . . . .
. . . Opening her window, from the new mown lawn
The fragrant, fragrant scent of perfumed grass
The lilac tossing in the shining air
Its purple plumes. The laurustinus bush
Its blossoms like pale hands among the leaves
Quivered and swayed. And, Oh, the sun
That kisses her to life and warmth again
So she is young, and stretches out her arms . . . .

The woman, huddled by the fire, restlessly stirs
Sighing a little, like a sleepy child
While the red ashes crumble into grey . . . .

Suddenly, from the street, a burst of sound
A barrel organ, turned and jarred & wheezed
The drunken, bestial, hiccoughing voice of London.

[1908.] [5]

Letter MS Windsor; enclosures MS Newberry. Letter cited Meyers, 37, 40–41.

[1] A restaurant at 24–28 New Oxford Street.
[2] Only two of the three poems, 'A Song of Summer' and the 'realist' poem, 'The Winter Fire', have survived.
[3] No such recital was given in these years by a Danish woman; KM may have been thinking, however, of a dramatic recital by Blanche Theeman, given at the Aeolian Hall on 2 June 1906.
[4] Garnet was now with the Moody-Manners Company in Hull.
[5] In the hand of Garnet Trowell.

To Garnet Trowell, [4 November 1908]

[Beauchamp Lodge, Warwick Crescent]
Wednesday Night.

My darling little Boy —

Just a note to say 'goodnight' before I get into bed — I'm sitting curled up on my eiderdown in a frilled nightdress which I'm sure you could not but admire — and I feel so very wide awake — — — you know the sensation. Margaret (my Paris friend) and I have just finished a little supper — cooked over my fire — and eaten with horn spoons, out of little French bowls de mariage — of boiled onions — of all things on earth! And we have laughed so much at nothing and been so gay that I feel it is senseless to go to bed. You must meet Margaret. She is really a fine girl — full of joie de vivre — I was so glad of your letter tonight dearest — Oh, what a waste to turn the gas off at the meter when you were alone — I love you I love you I *love* you.

I am yours for ever

Kass

MS Windsor.

To Vera and Jeanne Beauchamp, 5 November 1908

Beauchamp Lodge [Warwick Crescent]
5 Nov 1908

My dearest V and J.

Just a joint note to say 'Fröhliche Weinacht' and joy to you both in the year that is coming. May you both find those Beautiful Things that the world is so full of. I have been looking at the little Nelson photograph — it is so good — so characteristic — I love to think of you two together. Oh, Jeanne, I am so glad you have Vera. Oh, Vera, isn't it joy to have Jeanne — I get hungry for her sometimes — and your thoughts — as she & I walked round the Esplanade[1] together — & Life walked between us — didn't he, Jeanne? Your letters do so satisfy me. I thank & kiss you both for them. All my news is in the family letter — I just popped in here to say "good night & Bless you both". Chummie, too is included here — He is surely the brother of brothers. Dear me! Do you ever sing "Too proud to beg, too honest to steal?"[2]

I hug you, all three

Your devoted
Sister K

MS ATL.

[1] The long waterfront in Thorndon, at the end of Tinakori Road.
[2] From the Victorian song 'Shabby Genteel', by Harry Clifton:
Too proud to beg, too honest to steal,
I know what it is to be wanting a meal;
My tatters and rags I try to conceal,
I'm one of the Shabby Genteel.

To Garnet Trowell, [8 November 1908]

44, KEYHAM TERRACE, | H.M. DOCKYARD, | DEVONPORT.
Sunday Morning.

My dearest —

I am alone in the house; a cold day & everybody has gone to church — but here there is a brilliant fire and I am far happier.

Since writing to you yesterday — a great deal seems to have happened — that is always the case — — — — Yesterday afternoon I saw the launching of a great battle-ship — one of the most splendid, impressive sights possible, I think. There were thousands of people — from the ultra smart to the poorest workmen and their wives — all gathered together — And the ship was held in place by iron girders and supports. She towered above everybody. On a flag enveloped platform — Mrs Asquith — a very large section of the Naval world — and a chaplain and choir assembled.[1] We were all you see down below. It was a brilliant day, but a fierce wind rushed down and about. The crowd was silent, while the choir & sailors sang a hymn. You see the dramatic effect — it caught me. Strange visions of the victories and defeats — death — storms — their voices seemed crying in the wind. And all the builders of the ships — the rough men who had toiled at her — stood silently on her deck, waiting for the moment to come — — — And all the time we heard inside the ship a terrible — knocking — they were breaking down the supports, but it seemed to me almost symbolical as tho' the great heart of the creature pulsated — And suddenly a silence so tremendous that the very wind seemed to cease — then a sharp, wrenching sound, and all the great bulk of her swept down its inclined plank into the sun — and the sky was full of gold — into the sea — which waited for her. The crowd cheered, screamed — the men on board, their rough faces — their windblown hair — cheered back — In front of me an old woman and a young girl — the little old woman, whose grand uncle had been in the fighting Temeraire[2] — trembled & shook and cried — but the girl — her flushed face lifted — was laughing, and I seemed to read in her tense, young body, anticipation, realisation — comprends tu? . . .

Oh, Garnet, why is it we so love the strong emotions? I think because they give us such a keen sense of *Life* — a violent belief in our Existence. One thing I cannot bear and that is the mediocre — I like always to have a great grip of Life, so that I intensify the so-called small things — so that truly everything is significant. In Winter — to look out over a silent garden — I like first, to get that sense of loneliness, so [*for* ? that] simplicity of barrenness — and *then* always — I like to be able to see the flowers pushing their way up through the brown earth. It is the superficial attitude which kills Art, always. Give Life a little attention, a little enthusiasm — and "Fair Exchange is no robbery", she says, & heaps out arms with treasures. Why, it is the same with Love. The more you give me, the more I feel that you enrich my nature so I can give you more.

I dreamed last night that we were at a Tchaikovsky concert together last night. And in a violin passage, swift & terrible — I saw to my horror, a great flock of black, wide winged birds — fly screaming over the orchestra — it's rather strange — waking I can see that — too, in much of his music — can't you? Oh, Music, Music — Oh, my Beloved — the *worlds* that are ours — the *universes* that we have to explore — we two, my dearest, shall find the heart of Life hidden under its wrappings — like the gold seeds of a rose under a thousand

crimson petals. I love you. I love you. It is like this. I have been wandering through a castle with barred windows, locked doors, helplessly. At last I come to the gates — and you have unlocked them and you are there. I give you the keys — and you say "It is so simple, it is like this." Unlocking one door of my castle — all the others fly open to you. Keep my keys. What use are they to me — they are yours. I belong to you.
Loving you

Kass.

MS Windsor. Cited Meyers, 41, 43; cited Alpers 1980, 75–76.

[1] HMS *Collingwood,* a battleship of the Dreadnought class, was launched at Devonport on 7 Nov 1908, with the wife of the Prime Minister officiating at the ceremony. KM attended as a guest of Margaret Wishart's naval family.
[2] A famous battleship of Nelson's fleet.

☙☙☙☙

Towards the end of 1908 Garnet Trowell's parents put an end to their son's romance with KM. Shortly afterwards, through a friend at Beauchamp Lodge, she met the thirty-one-year-old George Bowden, who had held a choral scholarship at King's College, Cambridge, and was now a professional singer. They married at Paddington Register Office on 2 March 1909, and KM left her husband the evening of the same day. A week later she returned to Garnet, staying with him in Glasgow and Liverpool. In April she took a flat in Maida Vale, and at the end of the month, knowing by now that she was pregnant, she spent a few days alone in Brussels.

Annie Burnell Beauchamp sailed from Wellington as soon as she heard of KM's marriage. At the end of May 1909 she installed her daughter at Bad Wörishofen, a spa in the Bavarian Alps 50 miles west of Munich, then returned to New Zealand where she at once cut her daughter from her will. At Wörishofen KM suffered a miscarriage, probably in late June. She stayed on at the spa to recuperate, living for the next six months at various addresses, under the names of Käthe Beauchamp-Bowden and Käthi Bowden.

℘

To [? Ida Baker],[1] [? before April] 1909

[London]
Did you ever read the life of Oscar Wilde — not only read it but think of Wilde — picture his exact decadence? And wherein lay his extraordinary weakness and failure? In New Zealand Wilde acted so

strongly and terribly upon me that I was constantly subject to exactly the same fits of madness as those which caused his ruin and his mental decay.[2] When I am miserable now — these recur. Sometimes I forget all about it — then with awful recurrence it bursts upon me again and I am quite powerless to prevent it — This is my secret from the world and from you — Another shares it with me, and that other is [Kitty Mackenzie[3]] for she, too is afflicted with the same terror — We used to talk of it knowing that it wd eventually kill us, render us insane or paralytic — all to no purpose —

It's funny that you and I have never shared this — and I know you will understand why. Nobody can help — it has been going on now since I was 18 and it was the reason for Rudolf's death.

I read it in his face today.[4]

I think my mind is morally unhinged and that is the reason — I know it is a degradation so unspeakable that — — one perceives the dignity in pistols.

Your
Katie Mansfield '09

MS lacking. Alpers 1980, 91.

[1] Ida Baker (1888–1978), called 'Lesley Moore' or 'LM', was KM's closest woman friend from her time at Queen's College until her death. This letter was among papers left by KM at George Bowden's flat. On either side of the paper wrapped round it she wrote, 'Never to be read, on your honour as my friend, while I am still alive. K. Mansfield.'

[2] KM's early notebooks, as well as several of her early stories, are drenched in Wildean influences. In June 1907 she recorded her feelings for a female friend, and asked, 'O Oscar! am I peculiarly susceptible to sexual impulse?' (*Journal* 1954, 14).

[3] A doctor's daughter in Wellington; she went to England in 1908.

[4] 'Rudolf' was a friend of the Trowell twins whom KM met in Brussels at Easter 1906, and who later committed suicide. 'Today' suggests she had kept a photograph of him.

To [Garnet Trowell], [28–30 April 1909]

[Travelling, and in Brussels]
In the train to Harwich. I am afraid I really am not at all myself — so here I am — I took a drug this afternoon & slept until after five — then Ida [Baker] woke me — Still half asleep & terribly tired I packed — had some supper — M. [Margaret Wishart] most excited at the prospect of me going away again & still on the spur of the moment, I take the train to Liv. S. S. [Liverpool Street Station] bought a 2nd class ticket & here I am — tired out still but unable to sleep. The carriage is full — but Garnie I feel that I am going home. To escape England it is my great desire — I loathe England — It is a

dark night full of rain. There is a little child opposite me in a red cloak sleeping. She shakes her hair much as Dolly did when I was a girl in Brussels so many years ago[1] — Everybody sleeps but I — The train shatters through the darkness. I wear a green silk scarf & a dark brown hat with a burst of dull pink velvet. I travel under the name of Mrs K. Bendall[2] —

Morning in the Bruxelles — I have slept splendidly — taken a small brandy & soda before turning in, and now feel almost better, though I have still that intolerable headache which has haunted me — I sit in the ladies cabin on my hat box washed & dressed & very evidently amused — at everybody — I have just washed & brushed my hair. The *people*. Oh the fat lady in pink wool — ye Gods — & the other pious old English governess — who intends staying at a convent just outside Brussels — Everybody thinks I am French — I must go to Cooks & see about everything.

29th April — In this room. Almost before this is written I shall read it from another room and such is Life. Packed again I leave for London. Shall I ever be a happy woman again. Je ne pense pas, je ne veux pas. Oh to be in New York. Hear me, I can't rest — that's the agonizing part.
    'Tis a sweet day, Brother,[3] but I see it not. My *body* is so self conscious — Je pense of all the frightful things possible — "all this filthiness" — Sick at heart till I am physically sick — with no home — no place in which I can hang up my hat — & say here I belong — for there is no such place in the wide world for me. But attendez — you must not eat, & you had better not sleep! No good *looking* 'fit' and *feeling* dead.

In the train to Anvers. I love Belgium for I love green & mauve. I wonder when I shall sit & read aloud to my little son.

MS (draft) ATL, Notebook 2. *Journal* 1954, 40–41.

[1] KM and her sisters, chaperoned by Aunt Belle Dyer, had visited Brussels at Easter 1906, when the Trowell twins were students at the Conservatorium there.
[2] KM had assumed the name of her Wellington friend, Edith Bendall, while travelling. She again used the surname in the novel of which she planned and wrote two chapters in 1913 (see p. 57): Ida Baker is there cast as 'Rhoda Bendall'.
[3] Cf. George Borrow's *Lavengro* (1851), and his other Romany tales, where this form of address is common. At different times KM affected the role of a vagrant, and much later, telling Virginia Woolf of this period of her life with Garnet, she fabricated 'wandering about with traveling circuses over the moors of Scotland' (*LVW* II. 248).

To [Garnet Trowell], [June 1909]

[Pension Müller, Türkheimer Strasse 2] [1]
Worishofen | Bavaria

A.C.F. Letter.   Night

It is at last over — this wearisome day, and dusk is beginning to sift in among the branches of the drenched chestnut tree. I think I must have caught cold in my beautiful exultant walk yesterday, for today I am ill. After I wrote to you I began to work but could not — *and* so cold. Fancy wearing 2 pairs of stockings and 2 coats — & a hot water bottle in June and shivering. . . I think it is the pain that makes me shiver and feel dizzy. To be alone all day, ill, in a house whose every sound seems foreign to you — and to feel a terrible confusion in your body which affects you mentally, suddenly pictures for you detestable incidents — revolting personalities — which you only shake off — to find recurring again as the pain seems to diminish & grow worse — Alas! I shall not walk with bare feet in wild woods again. Not until I have grown accustomed to the climate. . . The only adorable thing I can imagine is for my Grandmother to put me to bed — & bring me a bowl of hot bread & milk & standing, her hands folded — the left thumb over the right — and say in her adorable voice: — "There darling — isn't that nice." — Oh, what a miracle of happiness that would be. To wake later to find her turning down the bedclothes to see if your feet were cold — & wrapping them up in a little pink singlet softer than a cat's fur. . . Alas!

Some day when I am asked — "Mother, where was I born". and I answer — "In Bavaria, dear", I shall feel again I think this coldness — physical, mental — heart coldness — hand coldness — soul coldness. Beloved — I am not so sad tonight — it is only that I feel desperately the need of speech — the conviction that you are *present*. . . that is all.

Sunday morning. Yet another Sunday. What has this day not brought us both. For me it is full of sweetness and anguish. Glasgow — Liverpool — Carlton Hill — *Our Home*. It is raining again today — just a steady, persistent rain that seems to drift one from one memory to the other. When I had finished my letter to you I went down to supper — drank a little soup, and the old Doctor next me — suddenly said — "Please go to bed *now*" & I went like a lamb & drank some hot milk. It was a night of agony — When I felt morning was at last come I lighted a candle — looked at the watch & found it was just a quarter to twelve! Now I know what it is to fight a drug — Veronal was on the table by my bed — oblivion — deep sleep — think of it! But I did not take any. Now I am up and dressed — propping

MS (?draft) ATL, loose papers. *Journal* 1954, 41.

¹ After a brief stay with her mother at the expensive Hotel Kreuzer, in the Bavarian spa of Bad Wörishofen, KM moved, alone, to the Pension Müller on 12 June 1909. It provided her with the setting for her stories *In a German Pension* (1911), where it retains its name.

To Annie Burnell Beauchamp, 24 August 1909

Wörishofen

The Church & a little white tower of the convent you can see, Janey¹ dear. The large building opposite is the Kurhaus.

Wörishofen
24 August 1909

And here the statue of Pfarrer Kneipp, & the fountain of Wörishofen water. That's the Kinderasyl behind and the Kneippianum.²

MS (2 picture postcards) Newberry.

¹ A family nickname for KM's mother. At the end of 1920 KM used the name in 'The Stranger', a story based on her parents.
² The postcards both show views of Wörishofen, famous for the curative properties of its waters, publicized in the late nineteenth century by Father Sebastian Kneipp. The buildings mentioned were associated with the *Wasserkur*.

To Jeanne Beauchamp, 10 November 1909

[c/o John Brechenmacher,¹ Kaufbeuher-strasse 9]
Worishofen   Bayern.
10 xi 09 | Snowed In!

My Sister;

This is just to greet you this Xmas, to wish you for the next year — knowing you as I do — your heart's desire and for every day of the year and every 'Aunt Charlotte golden minute'² blessings and Happy Realities. Will you take all this in your sweet hands and hug it close against your heart?

Your birthday gift, little Sister is here beside me on the table — it is a fat Polish dictionary with a green leather binding, and an air, already, of great weariness with life — in fact it goes about with me every day, and is such good company too, for the brass pig³ now is attempting to learn the new language which is manifestly absurd at his age and bristle losing condition. But thank you! Last night, sitting working here, the great jug of scarlet blackberry vine threw a twisted shadow on the wall — rather, my lamplight, more than a little fascinated, stencilled for me the trailing garlands with a wizard finger, and so I thought of you. Did you get the thought. Did you find it hanging on to the edge of your skirt ("Good gracious, is that a cotton. . . Where *can* I have picked it up". . .) "My dear, allow me to present you with a Bavarian mind wave!" Will Chummie take this share here of Xmas love and greetings. Give it him your sweet self and I know he will then understand.

Bless you, my darling, and remember you are always in the heart — oh tucked so close there is no chance of escape — of your sister

Kathleen Bowden.

MS Newberry.

¹ KM appropriated the name of the family with whom she was lodging for one of her sharpest German stories, 'Frau Brechenmacher Attends a Wedding', published in the *New Age,* 21 July 1910.

² A reference to the rhyme KM later used in her story 'The Voyage' in 1921:

Lost! One Golden Hour
Set with Sixty Diamond Minutes.
No Reward Is Offered
For It Is GONE FOR EVER!

³ An ornamental nib-wiper, a present from her father on leaving New Zealand.

To an unidentified recipient, [1909]

[Wörishofen, Bavaria]

Do you know my dear, joking apart, and very seriously speaking I do not think that I shall live a very long time — Heaven knows I *look* well enough — like a Wienerin people say here and they could not say more — but I am not at all well — my heart is all wrong — and I have the most horrible attacks of *too* much heart — or far too little. Sometimes my heart hardly goes at all — and then sometimes it — does the opposite —

So that is the reason why I want to get so much into a short time. And that is the reason that when I am alone the böse or gute Geist jogs my elbow and says — "You'll have so much of this sort of thing later on — Make use of a short daylight."

PC of MS (Bowden) Alpers. Cited Alpers 1980, 101.

III
ENGLAND: 1910–1913

KM returned to England early in 1910, asked George Bowden to take her back, and for several weeks lived with him at 62 Gloucester Place, Marylebone.

After an operation for 'peritonitis' in March 1910, KM spent several months with Ida Baker in Rottingdean on the Sussex coast. There KM suffered the first attack of what she then believed was rheumatic fever; not until 1918 was the illness diagnosed as a venereal infection.

KM later destroyed what she called 'the long and complaining notebooks' from this period. Nine of her Bavarian stories were published, between February and August 1910, in the *New Age*, the Fabian weekly edited by A.R. Orage (1873-1934). Apart from a few uncollected pieces, all of KM's published writing for the next two years appeared in that magazine; and Beatrice Hastings (1879-1943), a South African journalist who was Orage's mistress and a formidably aggressive and witty woman, became a close friend.

To the Editor, The New Age, *[11 August 1910]*

[n. a.] [1]

Sir,

A rabbit nibbling a lettuce leaf one moment before it becomes a python's dinner is hardly a spectacle for universal and ironic laughter — whatever crimes the rabbit may have committed, whatever just hunger the python may feel. And yet if we are to believe the Little Fathers of Fleet Street the whole world has been bursting its sides over Crippen stroking a newly-grown beard and Miss Le Neve with her trousers safety-pinned on confronted by the Inspector from Scotland Yard and six good men and true snapped into a carefully prepared trap with that quiet air of triumph which doubtless distinguishes the true British sportsman.[2] This nation of fair play seems satiated with small game, and in the desire to outdo "Teddy" is on the warpath for human heads. Captain Kendall, supported by his Kermit of a first officer,[3] has become the latest national hero, and I have no doubt but that he will be publicly presented with Miss Le Neve's outfit of boy's clothing to grace his pretty little country home in the vicinity of Pinner.

Perhaps we have underestimated the peculiar subtlety of the methods employed by Scotland Yard — perhaps full to the brim of that entente cordiale syrup which flowed at the funeral of our late lamented Peace Maker,[4] they have banded all the nations of the world together as brothers — invited them down into the cellar to have a look on their own account and chase after the little man with bulging eyes and false teeth and his typist who proved her guilt by wearing another lady's dresses. I believe that the English nation has the reputation of not being particular with regard to its food — quantity, never mind quality, being the axiom. Certainly the stomach for which the Press caters is a mighty affair indeed, and now the staple joint of the Crippen menu being "off", demands the scrapings of prison plates which the "Daily Mail" so obligingly heats up for breakfast each morning.

There can be no question of judging Crippen. He can be bought outright, with a photograph and a book of words, by any street gamin possessed of a halfpenny.

Surely we owe a debt of gratitude to all concerned who have shepherded us in this personally conducted tour into the hidden chambers of that machine which separates the wheat from the tares with all the impartiality and infallibility of our Courts of Law.

KATHERINE MANSFIELD

Printed letter, The *New Age*, 11 August 1910.

[1] At the time of writing this letter KM was staying with Orage and Beatrice Hastings at 39 Abingdon Mansions, Pater Street, Kensington.

[2] The pursuit of the murderer Dr Hawley Harvey Crippen, and his capture through a marconigram sent by Captain Henry Kendall from the liner *Montrose*, received enormous public attention during July 1910. The boy's dress of Ethel le Neve, Crippen's mistress, on the Atlantic crossing provoked the captain's suspicions, and he even sent in his wireless the detail of safety pins securing Miss le Neve's trousers. The couple were arrested by Inspector Dew of Scotland Yard, whose ship, the *Laurentic*, had overtaken the *Montrose* off Quebec. After a sensational trial, Crippen was hanged on 23 Nov 1910.

[3] Theodore ('Teddy') Roosevelt, President of the United States 1901-9, was a noted big-game hunter whose *African Game Trails* was published in 1910. Kermit Roosevelt, his twenty-year-old son, accompanied the hunting expedition, and provided photographs for his father's book.

[4] King Edward VII had died on 6 May 1910 and was buried in St. George's Chapel, Windsor, a fortnight later.

To the Editor, The New Age, *[25 August 1910]*

[n. a.]

Sir,

As a respectable citizeness of pagan England I cannot fail to be thrilled by R. M. Kerr's letter justifying the claims of Canada's seven millions to a literature pioneered by the "two boldest novelists of our time", Grant Allen and Elinor Glyn.[1] Far be it from me to repudiate Mr. Allen's statement in declaring his own novels rubbish, but Elinor Glyn doubtless "because she is a woman", and "even more admirable" has not yet spat upon her inspiration or condemned her feminine fancies as unfit reading for our hardy Colonial children. Am I to understand as a result of this very natural and praiseworthy modesty she is to accept the precious ointment of the reading public — she is to be provided with a little bower of laurel wreaths sacredly set apart for the production of yet another "Three Weeks"?

But I think it is "hardly fair" to speak of that exquisite creature in purple draperies who ate so many strawberries and cooed like a dove,[2] and was obviously the slave of her sexual passions, as a "real free woman".

If Elinor Glyn is the prophetic woman's voice crying out of the wilderness of Canadian literature, let her European sister novelists lift shekelled hands in prayer that the "great gulf" may ever yawn more widely.

As regards the United States it would seem that the only course open to the entire literary world is to make a pilgrimage into those pregnant fastnesses where stories "too true to life and too vivid in imagination to be printed in any country" are "handed round in the form of typewritten manuscripts" (did ever creation take on so novel a disguise) — "among a very few select persons".

Mr. Kerr has touched America with the wand of romance. Fascinating thought! That your companion on the Elevated Railway may be hiding under a striped chewing-gum wrapper the quivering first fruits of his soul.

KATHERINE MANSFIELD

Printed letter, The *New Age,* 25 August 1910.

[1] Kerr's letter, in the *New Age* on 18 Aug 1910, had attacked an article by 'S. Verdad' — pen name of the journalist John McFarland Kennedy — denying that there was any literary life in North America. Elinor Glyn (1864-1943), author of *Three Weeks* (1907) and other best-selling novels, was born in Canada, and Grant Allen (1848-99), a prolific author of popular scientific and travel books as well as novels had lived there.

[2] All attributes of the royal heroine in *Three Weeks.*

To William Orton,[1] *[late summer 1910]*

[132 Cheyne Walk,[2] Chelsea]

Dear —

The windows are wide open and the river so beautiful that I shall stay here watching it for one thousand years.

You know, Michael,[3] this river.

And there is not one star in the sky. The sky is like a shell —

I have red and white tulips growing in the centre of the praying mat. The red ones look as though they have fed on brackish blood. But I like the white ones best. They are dying — each petal ever so faintly distorted — and yet such dainty grace. I wish you were here.

The barge outside my window is called the Lizzie Rochester. I think she has only got one mate and one sailor. She is showing a green light now.

A man is singing outside the Cremorne Arms[4]

> 'Somebody loves me
> How do I know
> Somebody's eyes 'ave told me so-o'

Do you know that tree of mine believes every word of it — and is wide awake — with excitement.

MS lacking. Orton, 276-7.

[1] William Orton (1889-1952), a teacher whom KM met at a tennis party in Hampstead in the summer of 1910, shared her interests in literature and music. Over the next year a close friendship developed, of which Orton gives an account in his autobiographical novel, *The Last Romantic* (1937). The work, so Orton confirmed to Alpers, accurately reproduces extracts from KM's letters to him, which have not survived.

[2] The flat overlooking the Thames which KM rented for six months from the painter Henry Bishop, whom she had met through Orage.

[3] 'Michael' is the name Orton gives himself in his novel.

[4] A public house then standing near the junction of Cheyne Walk and Cremorne Road, Chelsea.

To William Orton, [autumn 1910]

[132 Cheyne Walk]

. . . Dear, there is a wreath of vine about the brows of the skull.[1] I made it myself, pricking my fingers. — Little Lais[2] came. I met her and brought her home. I think she was happy: she made me feel eighteen. What very pretty hair! I expect I shall see her quite often and take her to concerts and I am sure I shall take her to the National Gallery. *Now* you understand.

Yes, I own it — I was just as I said I should be — but time and again I was a little confused — recognized the you in me and the me in you — a most married sensation (here we both pause, look at each other and laugh) . . .

A man is coming to spend the evening with me.[3] I don't feel entirely responsible for my actions. I want to smile mysteriously and to run away and work that sewing machine all by myself in the little house at Strand-on-Green.

There! I knew that would happen. My soul has just opened the door — come in wrapt up in its fur coat and declares it is about to fly off to Tanford Hills.[4]

'Please don't be so inconsiderate. You must stay with me tonight.'

'No, I refuse. You are too ridiculous. You are behaving like a baby.'

'Very well. Give Michael my love — please — and take him — a little of this lavender perfume. When will you come home?'

(with reserve) 'M'm. That depends.' —

Please greet my soul kindly. It is very fond of music!

Katharina.

MS lacking. Orton, 275-6.

[1] A feature of KM's flat was a skull in which she burned candles.

[2] Orton's name in the novel for a young friend, Edna Smith; see p. 108, n.1.

[3] Probably Francis Heinemann, with whom KM was having an affair (see Alpers 1980, 119). A glimpse of him survives in 'A Dill Pickle', a story she wrote after accidentally meeting him again in 1917.

[4] Orton's fictitious name for the grammar school he then taught at.

To Sylvia Payne, 3 December 1910

132 CHEYNE WALK, | CHELSEA. S.W.
3 XII 10

Dearest Cousin,

The Bakers were away when your letter arrived, and therefore a delay in forwarding it to me —

I wish I could convey to you through the all too slight medium of a letter the sorrow I feel for you and the sympathy and love I would like to give you in your loss.[1] I had no idea that Cousin Frank had been ill for so long — Sylvia, darling —

Come and see me whenever you feel inclined — just let me know with a card — I am always here —

Your loving Cousin
Kathleen.

MS ATL.

[1] Frank Payne had died on 16 Nov 1910.

To William Orton, [15 April 1911]

[69 Clovelly Mansions,[1] Gray's Inn Road]

Dear: the evening is slipping away and away like the river. Dark it is and warm.

My life has been sad lately — unreal and turbulent. You know the absurd unreality of reality and the sense of chaotic grief that overpowers us when we attempt to fuse ourselves. . . . So — blind I have been lately and deaf and frightened. But now I am utterly happy. I am at home again here — my rooms yield me their secrets and their uttermost shadows. I wander alone in them smiling, a silk shawl wrapped round my body, sandals on my feet. I lie on the floor smoking and *listening*. I look through the windows sometimes — and at night and sunset I watch the sky. Everything is a wonder. Flowers are my joy and water and my Russian village, and Buddha and the toys.[2] Then I read poetry and study and begin to write again. Then the spring is coming and from my windows I can see the rich buds of the trees. Ah, how lovely. Beauty is solitude for me — and I am growing in her ways.

Yes, the poems — I cannot forget them, and I understand them far better. Many other poems I know — especially poems about rain and fitful winds and stars in dark pools of water. I think of you more often than you think of me. You are always in my heart — even when my heart — my beloved and my dear — has been most like the sand castle and nearest the waves — you have been safe and secret and treasured. I shall always love you. One day perhaps we shall smile again to each other and I shall take your head in my hands and kiss you tenderly. Perhaps and perhaps. Good night. It is Easter Eve. Christ be with you.

Catherine.[3]

MS lacking. Orton, 285–6.

[1] A three-room flat which KM rented from January 1911.

[2] The toy Russian village was a present from Francis Heinemann, who shared KM's Slavic enthusiasm. Also impressed by the Japanese–British Exhibition at Shepherd's Bush the year before, she had decorated her flat in Eastern style, with a stone Buddha from Burma contributed by Ida Baker.

[3] KM's spelling her name with a 'C' at this time had, as Orton reported, a religious significance for her.

To the Editor, The New Age, [25 May 1911]

[n. a.]

A P.S.A. [A Pleasant Sunday Afternoon]

Sir,

Finding ourselves on Sunday in Ditchling-on-Sea, without any literature, we were driven to rely upon memories of our favourite authors.[1] We forward our summaries for the benefit of your readers who may sometime find themselves in a similar situation.

K.M. and B[eatrice] H[astings]

MR. BART KENNEDY

A grim day. Too full and pregnant swelled the sky. I looked out of the window. In at my room. Struck a match — and kindled my pipe. With a sort of bloody anger — fist clenched over knotted hand bones, dreamed of the world. The world as it is. This place. This stewpot of Fine Endeavour, this melting-pot of Rancid Waste and Fever. Ants. On the floor I observed the greenish whiteness of my Sunday newspaper. Like black ants the letters swarming. I looked deeper. I saw buildings where these ants fashioned this greenish whiteness. I saw the sweat pour from their wizened bodies into the oily maw of the machines. I heard in the clanging crying of these automatic monsters — hand-fed by them — the crying clangour of the inarticulate. Then deeper. And all over the world. Little figures — ants again — yes, strangely ants — sinking their contorted vision — pen-digging in public offal. I plunged. And this greenish whiteness became significant — flew like the flag of England — with a dry crackling over my red thoughts. I looked out of the window. I opened it. I was passionately sick.

MR. G. K. CHESTERTON

There is a broom-stick in my garden. The bristles shining yellow as ripe corn, and observing from the wadded chair of my Sunday musings the long, pure, unbroken line of the handle, I appreciate, for the first time, most fully and completely, the charm of the witches' progress — the fascination of broomsticks. Magic in this clean and intimate weapon by day, those yellow bristles turn a dull gold at evening time and change at nightfall to a thick, mysterious darkness. I find myself regretting my complete abandon to my English dinner, and I long to leap from my wadded wrappings and straddle the broomstick for the one, great, simple adventure. For it seems to me that adventure can only be sought after in the near consciousness of very beautiful, homely things. Things which have felt the good grip of our hands, watching and guarding us as the crucifix the fingers of a little nun telling the shining length of her rosary. I want to combine, and call "sister" the broom sweeping the untroubled glory of my Bickens field hillsides with that plaintive swishing down the London area steps of my lighter — my very much lighter — so my friends tell me — youth. I protest that the one is as romantic as the other. . . .A new broom sweeps clean is fine enough to scroll the spring heavens and thrill the soul with rare, mysterious unity of thought as a barrel-organ grinding out a Catholic chant in a half-forgotten street at evening time.

MR. RICHARD LE GALLIENNE

Like country children in starched pinafores, soberly and a little tearfully gathered together at Sunday school, the pansies star my garden walks. There is long grass in the orchard, lush and thickly green. . . .it swings in sombre rhythm. And over the grass fall the frail, shattering petals of apple-blossom. . . .April Showers came into my study, with a blue ribbon dropped from the amber curls of Shining Feet. She said: "Darling, do I disturb you?" and as I kissed her, she drooped her fragrant bosom over my shoulder. I answered: "For your dear question, I shall read you my poem". April Showers clapped her hands.

> Lush and thickly green,
> Ah, why must I think of graves!
> Of lovers that might have been,
> Under these swinging waves.
> My sad soul could not rest
> Till April knocked my door,
> Leaning her delicate breast
> Over me — as of yore.
> She cried — "Beloved, see
> The apple-blossom fall
> Like angels' feathers a-free
> From winter's barren pall".

From the room above we heard Shining Feet cry out as though in pain. She put her finger to her lips, subtly smiling. . . . Little Feathers! Little Shining Feet!. . .

MR. ALFRED AUSTIN

Droop ye no more — ye stalwart oaken trees,
For mourning time is spent and put away —

Red, white and blue unfurls, the morning breeze
Bring leaves — strew leaves for Coronation Day.
And thrill along your mighty, crusted bark,
King George, our Sailor King, goes to be crowned,
Your limbs have nursed his navy — the long mark
Of his wide Empire by your arms is bound.
Bud roses! scatter at the matron feet
Of his proud consort, Mary, all your bloom.
Let Englishman the bronzed Colonial meet
In brotherhood — and weave upon the loom
Of this great Empire stronger, deeper ties —
Ties that shall hold 11,000 miles.
Perhaps in some far Heaven of the skies
Edward the Peace-maker looks down and smiles.

MR. EDEN PHILLPOTTS

As usual I was out and about the moor. It ran up misty to the sky-line, only the delicate morning petals glimmering between green blades, at the tip of each of which a dewdrop ready to flutter its opalescent upon my umbrous boots. . .and wave upon wave now rising, foaming away like the very sea to the empyrean. . .with a shadow where the signpost white and stark on the road below the red-roofed farm led the eye towards Burryzizzer, lying like a maid amid the heather. . .the meaning of the familiar and yet. . .I saw a gleam of rounded whiteness. . .nay, creamness, milkness. . .something — a sensation of approaching primevalness.

Then I saw that the woman was trying to feed a child which lay cooing and slapping her magnificent breasts. She made no movement though I approached as the crow flies. "Tell me your story", I cried. "Fear not; your history will be sacred to the public." Her great, round, deep, shining, hard eyes searched mine and I blinked, sorry for her. The woman always pays! Still she said nothing, but mechanically buttoned up her dress. "Ah, don't," I cried; "don't let a mere accident embitter thee so. Thee knows we'm all frail. Confide, poor toad, in me, a stranger, but almost a woman myself. Tell me the fellow's name and I'll write a book about him un he'll marry 'ee or thou'lt have his blood in the end." Still those luscious lips were sealed. She lifted the child and rose at last, and I saw my next story vanishing. However, one of the old ones with new names would serve (I know my hydropathic public). Suddenly she dealt me a sounding box on the ears. And I recognised her hand. She had done the same thing twice before. "Tha'll feel Tom's boot if thee stops here a minute," she murmured, and went towards the farm.

MR. ARNOLD BENNETT

In Pottinghame High Street, at seventeen minutes past three on a certain Sunday in the year of our Lord eighteen hundred and ninety-five, the fine dust was stirring. It was round, grey, piercing, sandy dust that rose and fell with precocious senility; for the month was June, and June is early for dust. Out of the vacant-looking, but actually swarming, two-storeyed houses that run monotonously up one side and down the other, a girl leaned. She threw out faded flowers, violets and a wallflower, and disappeared. Her bedroom expressed a character at once original and passive. The neatness of enforced non-conformity ruled her collars and shoes, but a bright blue petticoat, frilled with dyed lace, betokened a side of its owner's nature, perhaps unsuspected by Pottinghame, perhaps never to be suspected by Pottinghame, perhaps better never to be suspected by Pottinghame. For Pottinghame is a town whereof someone said somewhere that its influence and its decree were unique. Once a Pottinghammer, always a Pottinghammer. Let Pottinghame pronounce benediction, the Pottinghammer went blessed: but let Pottinghame pronounce malediction, the Pottinghammer went cursed. And the influence aforesaid of Pottinghame upon the Pottinghammer lasted just as long. Tinker, tailor, be you, gentleman or novelist, a Pottinghammer never gets away from Pottinghame.

The family of the Luke Pilders were below awaiting Susan's advent to pour out tea. The little parlour bore curiously that same distinctive touch as above signified by the output of stiff cuffs and dyed lace. No house in Pottinghame could be complete of course without. . . .

(To be continued until 1950.)

MR. H. G. WELLS[2]

So we stowed Biology and got to business.

"Why not?" she asked.

"Affairs," I replied laconically. She understood, and moaned a little. My heart-strings creaked — a man's heart-strings.

"Damn!" I burst out. "Do what you will with me."

So we stowed Biology and got to business.

"England!" I snarled. "Pah — England will have to do the best she can without me. You're my England now, curse you, bless you."

She fell at my knees, clinging, weeping, smiling: "God!" The epithet seemed to be torn out of her. I wondered. . . .

"You won't expect too much, Anthelesia?"

"Only three girls and three boys."

"Curse the expense," I said.

So we stowed Biology and got to business.

Printed letter, The *New Age*, 25 May 1911.

¹ As well as parodying certain established writers of the time — including the then Poet Laureate, Alfred Austin (1853-1913) — KM and Beatrice Hastings were here mocking Bart Kennedy (1861-1930), an American author of travel books and fiction who also wrote on social issues in *The Hunger Line* and *A Tramp's Philosophy* (both 1908); the Mauve Decade poet Richard Le Gallienne (see p. 45, n.3), author of numerous works now dated by their feyness and sentimentality; and the playwright and novelist Eden Phillpotts (1862-1960), an exponent of 'realism' whose fiction was often set on Dartmoor.

² The parody of Wells is directed specifically at his *Ann Veronica* (1909).

*To Edna Smith,*¹ [September 1911]

69, CLOVELLY MANSIONS, | GRAY'S INN ROAD, | W.C.

I came home again, Edna.² I grew 'homesick' — for my yellow pillows — for my rooms — above all for my complete and absolute privacy. The people hurt me all the time — They ruined everything. They *sprawled* over everything — & stared and remarked and would not let me be. I came home & danced for joy. It was sunset light. When I slipped the key in the door & closed the door — standing against it a moment — seeing a faint glow from the Buddha room — I felt as though the waters of sweetness and light had flowed over my aching heart. I told over everything and could not say often enough that I was happy. No, it is here only — in these rooms that I wish to live for the present and a long time to come. Are you coming soon? Are you coming one evening? Are we going to a concert together — you & I? Quite soon? Edna, dear?

Since I came home I have been wanting to write all the time — the desire drove me away and drove me here again. He is away from London³ for some time to come — so I am quite alone. But not yet do I know *what* it is that clamours for utterance at the gates of my heart — rather there are so many — with such richness of spoil in their hands (& the East! quite suddenly) that I still pause — deliberating — terribly grave. I cannot afford anything in the faintest touch unworthy — Edna to write like that! Suddenly stir the wings of a giant and all-powerful desire — one wing stretched over the Future — the other over the past — and the flight of those wings is rapture — Art! Art! Do you too exult in the very word and lift your proud head — It is not an anodyne: it is an elixir.

X   X   X

I want to talk to you about Zola & ask if you have read the 'joie de vivre'.⁴

Emile Zola.

Endless are our discoveries — ceaseless our battles — I want one day to write a whole book for you — I think and think about you — my dear and lovely friend. You are so near and vivid — Proschai, my darling. My hands in yours a moment — & the soft Russian word of farewell.

Your
Katya.

MS Weber.

[1] Edna Smith (1892–1975) — 'Lais' in *The Last Romantic* — later wrote biographies under the name of 'Edna Nixon'. She had a turbulent relationship with William Orton, writing to a friend in 1928: 'At nineteen my love affair came to an end for various reasons, one being Katherine Mansfield who rather took a fancy to my lover and myself. She played with us both for a little and then went on her way. She was a beautiful, wonderful creature and I never bore her any grudge.' (Quoted in a private letter from her daughter, June 1977.) At this time KM wrote in a journal which she shared with Orton: 'We are the three eternities — Michael and Lais and I. For Michael is darkness and light and Lais is flame and snow and I am sea and sky.' (*Journal* 1954, 47.)

[2] In August 1911 KM was ill with what she believed to be pleurisy, and had gone first to Bruges, then to Geneva.

[3] The absent 'he' is unidentified.

[4] Cf. Zola's *La Joie de vivre* (1884).

To the Editor, The New Age,[1] *[5 October 1911]*

[n.a.]

Along the Gray's Inn Road

Sir,

Over an opaque sky grey clouds moving heavily like the wings of tired birds. Wind blowing: in the naked light buildings and people appear suddenly grotesque — too sharply modelled, maliciously tweaked into being.

A little procession wending its way up the Gray's Inn Road. In front, a man between the shafts of a hand-barrow that creaks under the weight of a piano-organ and two bundles. The man is small and greenish brown, head lolling forward, face covered with sweat. The piano-organ is bright red, with a blue and gold "dancing picture" on either side. The big bundle is a woman. You see only a black mackintosh topped with a sailor hat; the little bundle she holds has chalk-white legs and yellow boots dangling from the loose ends of the shawl. Followed by two small boys, who walk with short steps, staring intensely at the ground, as though afraid of stumbling over their feet.

No word is spoken; they never raise their eyes. And this silence and pre-occupation gives to their progress a strange dignity.

They are like pilgrims straining forward to Nowhere, dragging, and holding to, and following after that bright red, triumphant thing with the blue and gold "dancing picture" on either side.

KATHERINE MANSFIELD

Printed letter, The *New Age*, 5 October 1911.

[1] Although printed in the *New Age* as a letter to the Editor, it seems obvious that this evocation of the Gray's Inn Road was submitted as a prose poem. KM's friendship with Orage and Beatrice Hastings had considerably cooled by this time, and the appearance of the sketch in the correspondence columns of the weekly may be read as a piece of editorial malice.

To J.B. Pinker,[1] 11 October 1911

69 CLOVELLY MANSIONS, | GRAY'S INN ROAD. | W.C.

11   X   1911

James Brand Pinker Esq

Dear Sir,

Would you grant me a little space of your valuable time in the near Future? I have a good deal of work that I am anxious to send you but I should much like to see you before doing so —

Thank you for the return of Hide & Seek[2] — yes, the creature was an abnormal size —

Faithfully yours
Katherine Mansfield

MS Newberry.

[1] James Brand Pinker (1864–1922), literary agent who represented the interests of, among others, Henry James and Joseph Conrad.
[2] A story, presumably, which has not survived.

In December 1911 John Middleton Murry, an undergraduate at Brasenose College, Oxford, began to correspond with KM about contributions she had sent him as editor of *Rhythm*, a quarterly magazine of the arts. The magazine, which had first appeared in the summer of 1911, was inspired by an enthusiasm for fauvist painting, the philosophy of Henri Bergson, and by discontent with English taste. KM and its editor met, through the novelist W. L. George (1882–1926), at the end of the year, and she encouraged Murry in his decision to come down from Oxford a few months short of his

Greats examinations, although he did return to sit his Schools. In April 1912 she became assistant editor of *Rhythm*, and contributed stories, sketches, and critical opinion. Goaded by considerable animosity from Orage, she ended her association with the *New Age*.

After Murry's inexperience had led him to print 3,000 copies of several issues of *Rhythm*, of which less than one sixth sold, Charles Granville ('Stephen Swift'), publisher the previous December of KM's *In a German Pension*, took over the financing of the journal as a monthly from June 1912. KM became Murry's co-editor, and Granville paid them £10 per month. A few months later, when Granville went bankrupt and fled the country, Murry found himself owing £150 to his printers, the St. Catherine Press. Edward Marsh guaranteed Murry's overdraft, the editors continued without pay, and KM pledged her own allowance of £100 per year. Martin Secker agreed to take over publication from November 1912. The last three issues of the magazine, May–July 1913, appeared under the new name of the *Blue Review*.

℘

To Jeanne Beauchamp, 1 January 1912

'69' [Clovelly Mansions, Grays Inn Road]
January 1st 1912

Dearest Jeanne:

Have you or has Leslie the copy of a book by Frank Harris called Macteague?[1] I do not think it was returned to me & it does not belong to me & is wanted immediately by its true and lawful owner. If you have it may I beg for return; if not for a card from you just telling me? I'll be so grateful, dear.

I had a letter from Father today: a very charming letter. Ida starts business this week. Do, of your kind heart, try and interest some of your "wealthy friends" in her hair-brushing. Wouldn't, for instance, Eileen Russel be keen — or her set? Ida has had cards printed and she was wondering if Jane [Annie Burnell Beauchamp][2] would take one or two.

I wonder if you saw the old year out & the New Year in? I became pious as the night waxed and went into the highways and byways to search for a church — but not finding one open I had to offer up my prayers to the Lord in the open street with nothing but the cold comfort of pavement for a Mother's knee.

Trouble with MacTeague is that I wanted to have news of him

before Wednesday noon — if possible. Time for my 'bye'. Bless you, dear — and may the New Year hold all manner of sweet treasure for you.

Ever your loving
K.M.

MS Newberry.

[1] The Beauchamp family were in England, having come over for the coronation of George V in June 1911, and stayed on for several months. The book in question was the novel *McTeague* (1899) by Frank Norris.

[2] Ida Baker (using KM's name for her, 'Lesley Moore') was trying to make a living by what an advertisement in *Rhythm* for July 1912 called 'Scientific Hair-Brushing' at Lesley Moore's Parma Rooms, South Moulton Street. Chaddie's friend Eileen Russel and her set are unidentified.

To Jeanne Beauchamp, [3 January 1912]

[69 Clovelly Mansions, Gray's Inn Road]
Wednesday

Dear Sister:

Many thanks for your letter: Macteague must be in hiding chez moi and I'll search him out this morning. Yes, I like those rose windows in The Abbey. Do you know the Guildhall Museum? There is some delicious roman glass there — coloured like the breasts of pigeons.[1] I heard from Father again last night: he sounds better. My miserable book[2] refuses to end itself at all: I begin to understand the Lord's delaying of the final trump!

God bless Everybody
K.M.

MS Newberry.

[1] The collection in the Guildhall Museum, Basinghall Street, London, relating to the history of the City of London includes Roman glass work.

[2] KM frequently referred to a story she was working on as a 'book'.

To William Orton, [February 1912]

c/- Madame Bieler | 8 rue St. Leger | Geneva.[1]

Tell E. [Edna Smith] where I am.

I have nothing at all to say but I think this card is very lovely.[2] And now all the red leaves are thick upon the ground and the mountains are white with snow.

I am quite alone.

+ Catherine.

TC (picture postcard) ATL.

[1] KM was briefly in Switzerland, again for health reasons.

[2] The card shows a view of Lake Geneva.

To J. M. Murry,[1] [12 April 1912]

[69 Clovelly Mansions, Gray's Inn Road]
This is your egg. You must boil it.   K.M.

MS lacking. *BTW*, 202.

[1] John Middleton Murry (1889-1957), who in April 1912 took up KM's invitation to become her lodger at Clovelly Mansions; this note was waiting for him on his first morning. Several weeks later they became lovers.

To George Bowden,[1] 23 May 1912

[69 Clovelly Mansions, Grays Inn Road]
23 May 1912

Dear G.

I called at the Bank of New Zealand this afternoon and saw Mr. Kay[2] who gave me your letter and told me of his interview with you. Thank you for your letter. I should very much like to see you if it can be arranged and discuss your project with reference to an American divorce. I think it is in every way the wisest plan for us both.[3] But arrange a time for us to meet, G. will you? I was sorry not to see you on Saturday afternoon.

Believe me, | Yours sincerely,

K.

TC ATL. Alpers 1953, 167-8.

[1] George C. Bowden (1877-1975), whom KM married on 2 Mar 1909.
[2] Alexander Kay (1854-1932) was manager of the London branch of the Bank of New Zealand 1910-21, during almost all of KM's adult life in England. He often acted as her adviser.
[3] Murry claimed of this time that 'Had Katherine been free, we would have married the next day. . . . Katherine's husband refused to take divorce proceedings against her. They were begun and dropped. It seemed to us monstrous that the caprice of a husband should thus prevent us; but it may be that there were excuses for his conduct of which we were ignorant.' (*BTW*, 215).
Bowden's account, given in two letters to Alpers, of 1 Nov 1949 and 1 Jan 1950 (both PC, ATL), is different. He was considering leaving for the United States and raised the possibility of an American divorce. But when he called at Clovelly Mansions to discuss it, and asked his wife if she and Murry planned to marry, 'She looked quizzically at him [Murry] and said something like, "Do we, J.M.?"' Bowden had the impression that 'the idea [of divorce] was distasteful to her, as indeed it was to me. . .and I might hazard that the irregularity of her position, in which she had taken the initiative, was less repugnant to her than the prospect of the passive experience of "being divorced". Hence it was not until I wished to remarry that the proceedings. . .were completed.'

To Frank Harris,[1] *[? mid-1912]*

[69 Clovelly Mansions, Gray's Inn Road]
Nighttime.

I want to write and thank you for the time we spent with you today, and to say how much we enjoyed ourselves — It is always so wonderful to be with you and hear you speak. Then everything is not only possible, but splendidly possible, and everything that happens is an adventure — something vivid and fine.

I count myself very privileged you have made "this art business" far more serious than ever before to me — and I thought it meant almost everything in the past years — but now I seem to realise for the first time what it may mean — and knowing you, and hearing you — I must needs go humbly. Ever since I have loved Tiger[2] we have spoken of you. You are our hero and our master — always.

Katherine Mansfield

MS Texas.

[1] Frank Harris (1856–1931), journalist, biographer, and fiction writer, whom KM met in June 1912. Harris published her uncollected story, 'The House', in his recently acquired magazine, *Hearth and Home,* 28 Nov 1912.

[2] 'The two Tigers' was a nickname given KM and JMM by the novelist Gilbert Cannan (see p. 119, n.1), because of an illustration by Margaret Thompson in the first number of *Rhythm* showing a tiger stepping on a monkey's tail. In the August 1912 number they signed a joint review, 'Jack and Jill attend the Theatre', with 'The Two Tigers'. 'Tig', and more frequently 'Wig' for KM, became a common form of address between them.

To Sylvia Payne, *[11 September 1912]*

Runcton Cottage | Runcton[1] | Near Chichester.
Dearest Cousin,

I *was* glad to hear from you. And we are quite near each other for Selsey is only about five miles from here. A train comes part of the way & then stops and a road leads to Runcton Cottage. Is there any way in which you could come over & spend the day? Id be more than happy, darling, to have you for longer than a few minutes. Do try! I want to talk over heaps of things with you. I want you to see our house — which is just 'settled' — for I don't know how many years . . . It charms me — perhaps because it feels so much like 'home' and there is a garden and trees that I am beginning to know . . . At present I dont care any more for cities. Theres no time to grow in them or to discover the dusk and feel the rain cloud and hear the wind rise and fall. I feel, in the country, sadly lacking in grace. But I feel that true happiness dwelleth not in cities — —

Please come if possible — & stay the night. Id like to ask you for a long visit but just now we are so frightfully busy trying to recover from the expense of moving that we're working too strenuously for time for even the people whom we love —

Yours always
Kathleen

MS ATL.

[1] In early September 1912 KM and JMM moved to a small house in a village on the Selsey side of Chichester.

To Edward Marsh,[1] [12 October 1912]

RUNCTON COTTAGE, | RUNCTON, | NEAR CHICHESTER.

Please dear Eddie Marsh will you try & lunch with us at the Moulin d'or[2] on *Monday* at 1.15. War has been proclaimed & Tiger & I are going into action against the High Courts of Justice.[3] We badly want the counsel of our friends.

Yours,
Tiger.

MS Rawlins.

[1] Edward Marsh (1872-1953), at this time Private Secretary to Winston Churchill at the Admiralty, was a patron of the arts and the editor of *Georgian Poetry*; he was a recent friend of the *Rhythm* editors.

[2] A restaurant in Romilly Street, Soho.

[3] Granville had absconded, and *Rhythm*'s editors were facing a court action over their debt to the printers.

To Martin Secker,[1] [late October 1912]

RUNCTON COTTAGE, | RUNCTON, | NEAR CHICHESTER

Dear Mr. Martin Secker.

Thank you for your letter this morning and for the specimens of paper & type and for your kind note in The P.M.G. It felt very funny to be a 'Thing that matters' but Filson Young really was a darling to do it.[2]

We shall be in London on Monday. May we see you in the afternoon & discuss this matter of printing? We'll bring the Trade list

from Stephen Swift & some back numbers. So may we say 3.30.
I should think we'd arrive with a rhythm painted hand barrow. But
not really.

Thank you again.

Sincerely yours
Katherine Mansfield.

MS Bemis.

[1] Martin Secker (1882-1978), bookseller and printer, started his long career as an
independent publisher in 1910.

[2] Filson Young in his regular column, 'The things that matter', in the *Pall Mall Gazette*
for 23 Oct 1912, explained Murry's recent financial setback, and encouraged the public to
support 'their beautiful little magazine'. Young was one of a group of friends and literary
men, including H.G. Wells, Lord Dunsany, Gilbert Cannan, Frank Swinnerton, and Ford
Madox Hueffer (later Ford), who helped keep *Rhythm* afloat.

To Compton Mackenzie,[1] *[November 1912]*

3, PEMBRIDGE CRESCENT, W.[2]

Dear Mr. MacKenzie

It is proposed to float as a Limited Liability Company the well-
known publication, "RHYTHM," which is the organ of the advanced
artists of this country and, to a certain extent of the Continent. We
are of opinion that, apart from its artistic chances, the property
appears to be capable of supporting itself and, eventually, of earning
profits. To this effect we wish to place it on a sound financial basis
by supplying it with working capital not exceeding £500. This sum
will, we believe, suffice to wipe out all the liabilities incident on the
foundation of the paper and leave in hand a balance which will be
used for advertising.

We are glad to be able to say that Mr. Martin Secker has agreed to
act as the publisher of "RHYTHM."

The shares will be of a nominal value of £5 or £10, as may be
decided at the meeting: it is understood that you are in no wise
committed by attendance. A certain amount of money has already
been subscribed, and this appeal goes out *to none save those who are
interested in the movement.*

We are not inviting immediate subscriptions: we wish to lay the
whole proposal and all the figures before you, and, to this effect,
beg to invite you to a meeting, which will be held at this address, on
Thursday, 7th November, at 3 p.m. If, however, the paper is already

known to you and you feel able to promise to take up shares, we shall be greatly obliged if you will communicate with W. L. George, at this address.

Faithfully yours,

GILBERT CANNAN, W.L. GEORGE,
KATHERINE MANSFIELD JOHN MIDDLETON MURRY.

R.S.V.P.

SHORT FINANCIAL STATEMENT.

The total liabilities to be met, incident upon the foundation of the paper and the early part of its career amount approximately
to   —   —   —   —   —   £118
Against this there is a credit to be collected of   —   £51

On the current circulation the publication shows a small monthly balance of profit, at present inadequate for the accumulation of funds for advertising and for the advance expenses of publication.

The money required should not, therefore, be looked upon as necessary for the support of the publication, but as working capital.

TS Texas.

[1] Compton (later Sir Compton) Mackenzie (1883-1972), Scottish novelist and auto-biographer.
[2] The address on this circular letter is that of W. L. George, although Mackenzie's name at the head of the typed sheet is in KM's hand. As George was the only one of the four signatories with business experience, it is likely that most of the wording is his. The scheme proposed came to nothing.

To John Drinkwater,[1] *[November 1912]*

RHYTHM | <16 KING STREET, COVENT GARDEN, LONDON, W.C.>

EDITORIAL [57 Chancery Lane][2]

Dear Mr. Drinkwater.

Thanks very much. We're glad to agree to your suggestion. We'll put you on the free list. And we hope you'll send us another poem. . . Rhythm is having a literary supplement in December.[3] It ought to be an interesting number altogether.

Of course we quite agree with you that poets ought to be paid for their poetry — all manner of fine and lordlie summes. If only

Rhythm will turn into a really big ship on a fair sea — we'll put our belief into action. . . But don't wait until then before you send us another poem — will you.

Sincerely
Katherine Mansfield (For J.M. Murry.)

MS Newberry.

[1] John Drinkwater (1882-1937), dramatist, actor, poet, and biographer, was then beginning to establish himself as a writer in London.

[2] Forced to give up Runcton Cottage, KM and Murry had taken a one-room flat in Chancery Lane, which doubled as office and home.

[3] *Rhythm's* 'literary supplement. did not appear until March 1913, but Drinkwater's long poem, 'Travel Talk', led off the issue for December 1912.

To John Drinkwater, 18 January 1913

RHYTHM | 57, CHANCERY LANE, LONDON, W.C.
January 18th 1913.

Dear Mr John Drinkwater,

Would you review the Georgian Poetry book[1] for us — or could you write something about your Theatre for our next number?[2] We'd be so delighted & grateful if you would do either of these things.

I am sorry that we did not see you when you were in London for the Poetry House occasion.[3] Perhaps next time you'll come & see us. We are nearly always at home.

Many people have told us how much they liked your fine poem.

Sincerely yours
Katherine Mansfield.

MS Newberry.

[1] Edward Marsh's first anthology of *Georgian Poetry* (1912) included some of Drinkwater's own verse. The volume in fact was warmly reviewed by D.H. Lawrence in *Rhythm*, March 1913.

[2] In February 1913 Drinkwater was to begin as manager of the new Birmingham Repertory Theatre. He contributed a long poem, 'Lines Spoken at the Opening of the Birmingham Repertory Theatre, February 15th, 1913', to the June 1913 issue of what was by then called the *Blue Review*.

[3] Harold Monro (1879-1932), whose *Poetry Review* had begun publication exactly one year before, had established his Poetry Bookshop at 35 Devonshire Street. It was officially opened by Henry Newbolt on 8 Jan 1913.

To John Drinkwater, [? late January 1913]

Rhythm, | 57 Chancery Lane.

Dear Mr John Drinkwater.

Forgive me for not answering your postcard sooner. I am ashamed, for you were prompt & it seems like ingratitude on my part. Which it wasnt.

We'd be delighted to have an article on the Theatre from you & copy is due on March 1st — long time ahead. All success to your Theatre. What fun — having a Theatre!

Sincerely yours
Katherine Mansfield.

MS Newberry.

To Edward Garnett,[1] 30 January [1913]

Rhythm, | 57 Chancery Lane, E.C.
30th January

Dear Mr Edward Garnett.

I had a letter from Mr Lawrence tonight in answer to one I'd sent him asking him for a story for Rhythm. Oh, I think the simplest thing is for me to send you his letter.[2] Here it is.

And we would be quite willing & glad to publish 'The Soiled Rose' simultaneously with the Forum.[3] If that isn't satisfactory may we trouble you to send us one of Mr Lawrence's stories?

Faithfully yours
Katherine Mansfield.

MS Texas.

[1] Edward Garnett (1868–1937), critic and dramatist, was a reader for several publishing houses, including Heinemann and Duckworth, both of whom published D.H. Lawrence. He also acted as Lawrence's general literary adviser.

[2] This was KM's first contact with D.H. Lawrence (see p. 150, n.1), who had replied to her letter requesting a story for *Rhythm*, with the instruction to ask Edward Garnett for 'The Soiled Rose' (*LDHL*, I. 507).

[3] By the time the story appeared in the *Blue Review*, May 1913, it had actually been published in the American magazine *Forum*, March 1913.

To Edward Garnett, *[early February 1913]*

[Rhythm, 57 Chancery Lane, E.C.]

Dear Sir

Here it is — Im sorry. I explained to Mr Lawrence that we dont pay: I made it quite clear —[1]

Sincerely
K.M.

MS Berg. *CLDHL* I. 181.

[1] Garnett seems to have written insisting on payment. Lawrence wrote to Garnett, 1 Feb 1913, 'Are you cross with me for telling Katherine Mansfield she could have a story for *Rhythm*, for nothing? I wanted to do it. But if you disapprove, then I won't promise anymore.' (*LDHL* I. 510).

To J. M. Murry, *[? April 1913]*

['The Gables',[1] Cholesbury, Bucks]

Dear Jack.

This is just 'good morning' — to you.

It has been a warm bright day here — very quiet. Immediately you had gone the house fell fast asleep, and it refuses to wake up or so much as smile in a dream until next Friday. I feel that I have been here a long time — and that its New Zealand. I'm very happy, darling. But when you come into my thoughts I refuse you, quickly, quickly. It would take me a long time away from you before I could bear to think of you. You see, when I am not with you every little bit of you puts out a flaming sword —

[Letter incomplete]

MS (fragment) ATL. *LJMM*, 2.

[1] In the spring of 1913, Gilbert Cannan (1884-1955), a contributor to *Rhythm* and a prolific novelist, and his wife Mary, who formerly had been married to J.M. Barrie, found KM and Murry a cottage on the edge of the common at Cholesbury. KM stayed in the cottage during the week, with Murry coming at weekends.

To J. M. Murry, [early May 1913]

['The Gables' Cholesbury]

Jack dear.

Yes Friday *will* be fun. I am beginning to 'pretend' that you are a sailor — trading with all sorts of savages from Monday until Friday — & that the Blue Review is your schooner & Secker the Fish Eyed Pilot. Couldnt you write a long-complicated-extremely-insulting-symbolical-serial round that idea with minute, obscene descriptions of the savage tribes. . . ? Thank you for Pa's letter. He was cheerful and poetic, a trifle puffed up but very loving. I feel towards my Pa man like a little girl. I want to jump and stamp on his chest and cry "youve *got* to love me". When he says he does, I feel quite confident that God is on my side.

It is raining again today, and last night the wind howled and I gloomed and shivered — and heard locks being filed and ladders balanced against windows & footsteps padding up-stairs — — — all the old properties jigged in the old way — Im a lion all day, darling, but with the last point of daylight I begin to turn into a lamb and by midnight — mon Dieu! by midnight the whole world has turned into a butcher!

Yes, I like Boulestin[1] very much. There's something very sympathetic about him.

Goodbye for today, darling

Tig.

MS ATL. *LKM* I. 1-2.

[1] X. Marcel Boulestin (1878–1943) discussed 'Recent French Novels' in the June 1913 issue of the *Blue Review*, and contributed a satirical drawing in July. A journalist and bon vivant, he later became famous as a restaurateur and published many books on food, as well as a volume of autobiography, *Myself, My Two Countries* (1936).

To John Campbell Perkins,[1] 5 or 6 May [1913]

[n.a.]
May 5th or 6th

Dear 'John',

Do not think me bold to address you in so informal a fashion but you are going to marry my sister & I cannot feel that her lover could be quite strange to me.

I want to send you my sincerest good wishes. And to say I think you are the most fortunate of men to marry so enchanting a woman as Marie — Marie and I were very close to each other when we were little girls — and whole pieces of my memory are planted with her sweet and charming flowers. In fact whenever I think of my sister I see her walking in our garden with a little smile on her lips and a great posy in her arms. I am sure that is how she walks over the world.

It is difficult for me to write to you because Im such a conceited and proud creature that I can hardly imagine a man "good enough" for Marie. Forgive my frankness, but I cant explain otherwise my difficulty. I hope that we shall meet one day. Bring her to England — soon.

Bless you both —
Katherine Mansfield.

MS Texas.

[1] Lieut.-Col. John Charles Campbell Perkins DSO (1866-1916), Controller of Military Accounts for the Western Circle, India, married Charlotte (Marie) Beauchamp in Wellington on 26 May 1913. He died three years later at Mhow, India.

To J. M. Murry, [? 12 May 1913]

['The Gables', Cholesbury]

Jack dearest.

. . . the postman knocked into my dream with your letter and the back door key. I had locked myself in 3 times 3 with Mrs Gom's[1] key but I am glad you sent me ours.

I have begun the story and mean to finish it this evening: it feels pretty good, to me.[2] Walpoles letter was a little too strenuous. (what is a beautiful picture?)[3] But I prefer that to Gilberts one remark 'Davies steeped in Bunyan'.[4] Oh, dear! Im afraid Walpole is having his birthday cake far too soon — like all our young men (except Jack & Tig.) What a surprise for them when we sit down at the heads of their tables — all among their cake crumbs and groaning little tummies — you, with a laurel wreath on your darling head, & me trailing a perfectly becoming cloud of glory.

Pride is a charming, sheltering tree: but don't think Im nesting in it. Im only standing underneath with my eyes turned up for a moment's grace.

Last night Mrs Gom and I had a glass of dandelion wine, and over it I heard how Mrs Brown's petticoat had dropped off in the hurdle race "King Edward's Coronation time." Such goings on!

Goodbye for today. I love you. "Not tomorrow, not the next day, but the next." Tell me what train you are coming by. I cannot quite believe that you are coming back here. I feel — — quite alone and as if I were writing to someone in the air — so strange.

MS ATL. *LKM* I. 2.

¹ The part-time servant at The Gables.
² Probably 'Millie', published in the *Blue Review* in June 1913.
³ The novelist Hugh Walpole (1884–1941) reviewed fiction for the *Blue Review*. Murry wrote to him on 18 May 1913, replying to what must have been Walpole's criticism of two drawings by Derwent Lees in the May issue: 'I agree with you about the Lees drawings, I think. They were not beautiful; and I am with you in exacting 1 beautiful picture each time.' (Texas.)
⁴ Gilbert Cannan's remark referred, apparently, to 'The Beggar's Hunt', a piece of short fiction in the May 1913 *Blue Review* by the Welsh poet and novelist, W.H. Davies (1871–1940).

To J. M. Murry, [13 May 1913]

['The Gables', Cholesbury]

Dear Jack.

Floryan¹ is taking this for me. Will you phone Ida [Baker] to come to Chancery Lane and see about his box, because some things of his are in the top of my box and he had better have them all. The story is really, rather what I'd thought. He has had false promises and believed them: it's no good discussing it. He promises to pay you back in little sums of £1 and £2.

About Banks and Gaudier² — I cant write. Gilbert will deal with Banks as she deserves. I am worried and anxious about you all the time. Gilbert will silence Banks. Mary says he's seldom angry & when he is hes dreadful — thats true. He'll believe nothing but truth of you. He is devoted to you. He said "I wish Jack would always come to me" . . . Mary said "Oh Id like to put my arms round him and hug him". Do not answer the door after office hours. During office hours don't answer yourself. Come tomorrow. My letter from G. [George Bowden] says divorce papers will be served in a day or two.³ No damages & no costs for us to pay.

Ive seen the farm & we all agree its perfect.

All these things to comfort you a little. But come here and I will tell you all. I wait for you until tomorrow. Phone Ida to come at 7

& Floryan will then call for his box. If impossible for her then make some arrangement. I am going to telegraph you now.

Yours
Tig.

MS ATL. *LJMM*, 7.

[1] Floryan Sobieniowski (1881-1964), who was to translate more than 40 of G.B. Shaw's plays into Polish, had met KM at Wörishofen after her pregnancy. He helped to develop her interest in Slavic life, and in Stanislaw Wyspianski, the Polish poet and dramatist, and contributed to *Rhythm* as its 'Polish Correspondent'. In England he became a great nuisance to both KM and Murry, inviting himself to live with them at Runcton, and scrounging money from them. He now turned up to claim a box of possessions he had left behind.

[2] In 1912 there had been a brief but intense friendship between KM and Murry and Henri Gaudier-Brzeska (1891-1915) and his companion Sophie Brzeska. *Rhythm* published several of his drawings, and Sophie would have moved into the Runcton cottage had Gaudier-Brzeska not overhead KM criticizing her. There was then a period of considerable bitterness, with the sculptor convinced that Murry had tried to cheat him. On 12 May 1913 he and Georges Banks, a woman artist who had also contributed to *Rhythm*, jointly attacked Murry in his office, and demanded he return any of their work he still held (see *BTW* 246-7).

[3] Bowden soon after this withdrew his petition for divorce.

To J. M. Murry, [14 May 1913]

['The Gables', Cholesbury]
Wednesday

Dear Jack.

No letter from you today. I am sending you the Banks drawings this evening. Enough string came with my parcel from Ida to make it possible. If you want any meat (and if — oh, well no — not necessarily) bring some down with you, please dear. *Meat* and *tea*. That is all we want. It is a very grey day again, here, half raining - and a loud roaring noise in the trees. This morning a robin flew into my room. I caught it. It did not seem at all frightened but lay still and very warm. I carried it to the window & I cannot tell you what a strange joyful feeling — when the little bird flew out of my hands. I am sorry you did not write to me. I count on your letters in the morning & always wake up early and listen for the postman. Without them the day is very silent.

Do you want to drive — tomorrow? Let me know in time.

Goodbye for today, my darling.

Tig.

MS ATL. *LKM* I. 3.

To J. M. Murry, [19 May 1913]

['The Gables', Cholesbury]

Dear Jack.

I've nursed the epilogue to no purpose.[1] Every time I pick it up and hear "youll keep it to six," I *cant* cut it. To my knowledge there aren't any superfluous words: I mean every line of it. I don't "just ramble on" you know, but this thing happened to just fit 6½ pages — you cant cut it without making an ugly mess somewhere. Im a powerful stickler for form in this style of work. I hate the sort of licence that English people give themselves — — to spread over and flop and roll about. I feel as fastidious as though I wrote with acid. All of which will seem, I suppose unconvincing and exaggeration. I can only express my sincerest distress (which I do truly feel) and send you the epilogue back. If you & Wilfred[2] feel more qualified for the job — — oh, do by all means — But I'd rather it wasn't there at all than sitting in the Blue Review with a broken nose and one ear as though it had jumped into an editorial dog fight. It's a queer day, with flickers of sun. The epilogue has worried me no end — and I can still hear — tossing about — the aftermath of that thunder. "Its not fair. Swinnerton can do it. . .you've got to cut it". . .etc etc. Can't you cut a slice off the D. Brown.[3] I really am more interesting than he is — modest though I be. . .

Tig

Dont think of this letter. I'm frightfully depressed today. I love you, darling. Do not let us forget that we love each other. Your sad beyond words   Tig.

MS ATL. *LKM* I. 2-3.

[1] KM contributed an 'Epilogue' — in fact a short story — to each number of the *Blue Review*. The one referred to here is 'Epilogue: II' for June, later collected as 'Violet'.

[2] The poet Wilfred Wilson Gibson (1878-1962) was Murry's assistant editor.

[3] Frank Swinnerton contributed an article on 'General Literature' to the June 1913 issue; W. Denis Browne was the magazine's music critic.

To J. M. Murry, [20 May 1913]

['The Gables', Cholesbury]
Tuesday.

My dearest.

I am sorry for my anxiety of yesterday. It was not to be silenced at all except by your wire. Dont know what came over me — but I don't feel very well — and I suppose that was the reason. Nothing much — headache — Your letter — thank you. And the news was good. Johnny is a darling — Floryan a rather dangerous fraud — Albert — "very sweet"[1] — I'm glad you saw Abercrombie.[2] Gilbert called here yesterday & I gave him his proof.[3] He brought back your baccy pouch & some French books. Mrs. Gom is here today & my room is very clean & bright with a fire. Its dull — grey — inclined to rain. I am sending you some reviews.

Take care of yourself — I'm better today — except that I'm all burning up inside with a raging fire — — but, my God, its good to be here —

On Thursday we'll see each other. Take my love.

Tig.

P.S. I dont know whether you will roar at me, darling for doing these books in this way. But they lent themselves to it & I thought if you read the review you would see that its almost silly to notice them singly & that they gain like this. If wrong — return the thing & I'll do you 2 little ones. . .   X

MS ATL. *LJMM*, 6-7.

[1] The Scottish painter John Duncan Fergusson (1874-1961), deeply influenced by the Fauves, had been a friend of Murry's since their meeting in Paris in 1910. A painting of Fergusson's called *Rhythm* had suggested the name of the magazine, and a line block of the design appeared on the cover of each issue. Albert Rothenstein was a friend who had written to Murry.

[2] Lascelles Abercrombie (1881-1938), poet, dramatist, critic, was a contributor to *Rhythm* and the *Blue Review*.

[3] Gilbert Cannan had written a theatre review for the June *Blue Review*.

To J. M. Murry, [? May–June 1913]

['The Gables', Cholesbury]

Am I such a tyrant — Jack dear — or do you say it mainly to tease me? I suppose Im a bad manager & the house seems to take up so much time if it isn't looked after with some sort of method. I mean. . .when I have to clean up twice over or wash up extra unnecessary things I get frightfully impatient and want to be working. So often, this week, Ive heard you and Gordon[1] talking while I washed dishes. Well, someone's got to wash dishes & get food. Otherwise — "there's nothing in the house but eggs to eat." Yes, I hate hate HATE doing these things that you accept just as all men accept of their women. I can only play the servant with very bad grace indeed. Its all very well for females who have nothing else to do. . . & then you say I am a tyrant & wonder because I get tired at night! The trouble with women like me is — they cant keep their nerves out of the job in hand — & Monday after you & Gordon & Lesley [Ida Baker] have gone I walk about with a mind full of ghosts of saucepans & primus stoveses & "will there be enough to go round". . .& you calling (whatever I am doing *Tig* — isn't there going to be tea. Its five o'clock.) As though I were a dilatory housemaid!

I loathe myself, today. I detest this woman who "superintends" you and rushes about, slamming doors & slopping water — all untidy with her blouse out & her nails grimed. I am disgusted & repelled by the creature who shouts at you "you might at least empty the pail & wash out the tea leaves!" Yes, no wonder you 'come over silent'.

Oh, Jack, I wish a miracle would happen — that you would take me in your arms & kiss my hands & my face & every bit of me & say "its alright — you darling thing. I quite understand."

All the fault of money, I suppose.

But I love you & I feel humiliated & proud at the same time. That you *dont* see — that you *dont* understand and yet love me puzzles me — — —

Will you meet me on Wednesday evening at the Café Royale[2] at about 10.30. If you cant be there let me know by Wednesday morning. . . Ill come back & sleep at '57' if I may even though I *don't* live there.

Jack — Jack — Jack.

Your wife
Tig.

[*Across top*]
3 reviews tomorrow.)

MS ATL. *LJMM*, 4-5.

[1] Charles Henry Gordon Campbell (1885-1963), later 2nd Baron Glenavy of Milltown, was a young Irish barrister whom KM met in 1911. His wife Beatrice (see p. 262, n.1) became a close friend of KM's.
[2] The café in Regent Street, a favourite rendezvous for KM and her friends.

To J. M. Murry, [June 1913]

['The Gables', Cholesbury]

Jack dearest —

I sent your glasses yesterday — packed — I hope — carefully enough. Thank you for the money:[1] Im going to start again keeping a strict account of every penny I spend & then we can see where the screw is loose or the shoe pinches — or whatever it is.

Last night as I got into bed the bed refused to have me & down I flew with my feet up in the air. I was terrified but I couldn't help laughing — & once started I kept on — It seemed no end of a joke to be all alone in what R.C.[2] would call the 'profound stillness of the June night' & to be served that age old trick!

"Mrs Walter" is here today and were having clean pinnies from head to foot. Such relief that Ive written my reviews again & started my epilogue.[3] I went in to see Baby Gomm this morning. He was sucking. Such a pretty sight as a rule. But Mrs Gom's sharp worn face above him somehow filled me with horror.

You poor darling! Having to write to me at such 'impossible hours'. Well, assert yourself & "be hanged if you will." Id rather wait for the afternoon post or until you feel 'I want to talk to Tig' — So treat me like that in future. Ill phone you when I get to London tomorrow, but I know Wednesday is your busy day & I dont want on any account to disturb you.

Things have straightened out in my mind & Im rather ashamed that I told you — what I did yesterday. It sings in my ears rather like the wail of the little girl left behind on the fence — — — more anger than anything else. I kiss your eyes and your soft furry ears and your darling, frightening mouth —

I am your
Tig.

Café Royal 10.30. if I don't hear from you tomorrow.

MS ATL. *LKM* I. 3-4.

[1] Murry had sent her a postal note for 35s.

[2] Richard Curle, a contributor to *Rhythm*, who later published studies of Meredith and Conrad.

[3] 'Epilogue III: Bains Turcs', for the July 1913 issue of the *Blue Review*. No reviews by KM appeared in the *Blue Review* at this time.

IV
ENGLAND AND FRANCE
1913–1915

After the demise of the *Blue Review* with its third issue, in July 1913, KM and Murry established themselves in London again, and Murry now wrote and reviewed for the *Daily News* as well as the *Westminster Gazette*. In June 1913, KM and Murry had met D.H. Lawrence and Frieda Weekley — the beginning of an intense and turbulent association — and Lawrence was now pressing his new friends to settle in Italy with him and Frieda.

At the end of 1913 Murry judged he could earn a living reviewing French books for the *Times Literary Supplement*, and that the novel he was planning might more easily be written in Paris. He and KM unwisely crossed to France, taking with them all their own furniture and some of Ida Baker's. In Paris, Murry's weekly income dropped from the £12 he could make in England to about 30 shillings. Then, early in 1914, as he was failing to meet the quarterly instalments on his debt to the printer of *Rhythm*, he was summoned to appear before the Bankruptcy Court in London.

During their months in Paris, KM wrote 'Something Childish But Very Natural', her longest story to date, which was not published until after her death.

To Jeanne Beauchamp, [11] October 1913

8 Chaucer Mansions[1] | Queen's Club Gardens | West Kensington.
October 1913

My darling sister J.

Thank you for the pink sachet. It is quite exquisite. I appreciate every stitch, dearest, and every little daintiness, and the initial looks most regal! Mother's jacket has not yet arrived but the sachet is kept apart for the purpose.

It is like winter already. This morning there was a fog & I am sitting by a fire with michaelmas daisies and chrysanthemums in the room. I have been rather seedy and not got over it, Im sorry to say. However by the time this reaches you I shall be alright again. It started with excema and then I got a small attack of flue and then — familiar ailment — a touch of congestion. It is this last which 'clings so fond'. But it's really 'very small beer' as Deepa [Henry Herron Beauchamp] would say.

I have had 3 birthday presents already. Marie sent me some indian work and John (my John) has given me an ivory shoe horn and a little ivory backed hand mirror — he picked them up in an antique shop — and Ida has given me two little button brooches. My birthday is not until next Tuesday. But I set great store by birthdays, still and count the days as though I were only a baby and not nearly a quarter of a century old.

My dear, I wrote a story called 'Old Tar' the other day, about Makra Hill, and sent it to the Westminster who accepted it.[2] I'll send you a copy as soon as it appears which will be next Saturday, I hope. Don't leave the paper on the Karori road or I shall be taken up for libel. They have asked for some more New Zealand work so I am going to write one on the Karori School.

The prospect of seeing Vera and our one and only nephew is quite exciting.[3] She will be here in a week or two; and Chaddie talks of England at the New Year or shortly after. I expect we shall all sit in Vera's house pull down the drawing blinds, turn the table upside down and start playing Coras and Evas.

Tell me about yourself. What are you doing? How do you spend your days and who do you know? Let me have a long letter one day, will you, sister — The sachet, when I opened it, still smelled of you — so sweet and fine.

My love to everybody.

I am always your devoted sister,

K.

MS Newberry.

[1] The large block of flats in Barons Court to which KM and Murry moved after the demise of the *Blue Review*.

[2] 'Old Tar: A Karori Story', published in the *Westminster Gazette* on 18 Oct 1913, was set on Makara Hill, above the Karori Valley where KM lived from the ages of five to ten.

[3] Vera Beauchamp, now Mrs Mackintosh Bell, was coming from Canada with her ten-months-old son, Andrew.

To Charlotte Beauchamp Perkins, 22 December 1913

Hotel de l'Univers | 9 Rue Gay-Lussac | Paris.

22. xii. 13.

My dearest Marie —

It seems a long time since I have written to you but indeed dear, I have been so busy and there have been such countless things to do before we were able to fold up our tents, and ever since we have been in Paris the days have flown. It was much more difficult to get a flat here than we anticipated and then the locality and manner of renting them was quite strange. Now, dear, my apologies & explanations over I want to thank you for the lovely rug. It arrived two days before we left and it is going to look lovely on the floor of my new room, I know. Jack and I were simply charmed with the colouring & design. If your John [Campbell Perkins] had, indeed, any part in the choosing of it — please convey to him my sincerest and most cordial thanks for the lovely gift.

Jack will be over in England every three months & I hope thus to have news first hand of Vera. That was my real reason for regretting that we should have come just at this time to Paris — I had wanted to be in the same city with V. when her baby came.[1] She was, poor darling, dreadfully upset last time I saw her at the sudden and inexplicable illness of Andrew, but thank goodness he seems quite himself again now. Ida is brushing V's hair for her twice a week. I am sure that will do her good. Indeed there seems some idea of Ida going to *Ontario* to start business there! I expect she'd do very well.

Jack & I had endless worries at the last moment, letting the flat, and having the furniture packed etc. and our journey was one of the real and oldfashioned horrors by sea. I was prostrate in five minutes & Jack — very nearly. It was bitterly cold this side in the train, too & we arrived to find there had been some mistake at the hotel & they had reserved us 2 tiny rooms on the *6th* floor. However life gradually swung to its new pendulum, and now that we have found a dwelling — 31 Rue de Tournon Paris VI — I think we will be very happy. We have to wait another week in the hotel while the present occupier moves away her Spanish furniture (!) and then our chairs & tables which Cooks are keeping will be set out and the flowers bought and the kettle on the gas stove & Jack & I will be happy. We are both *wretched* without a home & without our own particular creature comforts.

The weather is icy, but Paris looks beautiful. Everything is white & every morning the sun shines & shines all day until it finally disappears in a pink sky. The fountains are just a bubble in their basins of ice — And now the little green Xmas booths are lining the streets — I am going to enjoy life in Paris I know. It is so human and there is something noble in the city — Then the river is so much more a part of it than the Thames. It is a real city, old and fine and life plays in it for everybody to see. Jack and I are dropping into speaking French together and leaving English alone until we have really mastered the other. Once "at home" I shall study hard.

Marie, what a wonderful time you have had on your travels. I envy you all that you have seen of India, and you have seen it in such a splendid way. If you come home from India this year I suppose you will come via [*word missing*] and that will mean Paris won't it?

I have not really seen the shops yet at all. I have not yet had a moment to myself, because added to everything Jack has been prostrate with a chill. He begs me to thank you for your Xmas card & to send his love & greetings.

This is an unsatisfactory letter I feel, darling.

My best wishes to you & John for the New Year. And my fondest love to you now and always. Take care of your precious little self.

Always your devoted sister

K.

MS Newberry.

[1] Vera Beauchamp Bell's second son, John, was born in London the following month.

To J. M. Murry, [8 February 1914]

31 RUE DE TOURNON (6ème) [Paris]

Sunday morning.

Your letter this morning was a lovely surprise. I had not hoped to hear from you until tomorrow at earliest. Thank you, darling.

Everything is quite alright, here. Your room feels cold and it smells faintly of orange flower water or furniture polish — a little of both. I spent a great part of the day reading Theocritus and late last night, happening upon our only Saint Beuve I found the first essay was all about him.[1] What I admire so much in your criticism — your *courteous* manner: Saint Beuve has it to perfection.

Do not worry about me. Im not in the least frightened, but if Campbell abuses me too heartily tell him "I am not one of a malignant nature but have a quiet temper."[2]

Its a spring day. The femme de ménage is cleaning the windows and Ive had a bath —

Take every care of yourself

Tig.

MS ATL. *LJMM*, 9.

[1] The essay on Theocritus by the French poet and critic Charles-Augustin Sainte-Beuve (1804–69) was first published in 1846.

[2] Murry was staying in London with Gordon Campbell at 9 Selwood Terrace, South Kensington. KM is echoing Fragment 72 from *Sappho: A Memoir and Translation* by H.T. Wharton (1887).

To J. M. Murry, [9 February 1914]

31 RUE DE TOURNON (6ème)
Monday morning

Dear Jack.

I am glad that Campbell is looking after you well — glad, too, that you went to see W.L.G[eorge]. That was a good idea. Lesley writes me — the weather is beastly — and here it is so warm and sunny that I have sat with my window open yesterday and today. (Yes, dear, mentioned 'with intent'.) I wish you would buy a pair of shoes as well as the pepper & salt trousers. Try to. You want them so badly and Ive no faith in those cheap Boulevard beauties.

Everything, here, too 'is just the same'.[1] The femme de ménage is singing in the kitchen — a most improbable song. It runs along — very blithe and nice — for about five notes and then it *drops* — any distance you like, but a little deeper each time. If the 'aspects' were not good that song would frighten me no end. .*provided* that I was in a little house on the edge of the steppes with a mushroom shaped cloud over it & no smoke coming out of the chimney etc. etc. But things being what they are, my romantic mind imagines it a kind of 15th century French Provincial Ride-a-Cock-Horse — you know the business. .dashing off on someone's knee to get a pound of butter and being suddenly "tumbled into the gutter."[2] Which, after all, is a very pleasant place to fall. I wonder if Queens played this Disturbing Game with their youngest pages.

My door has been mended. I am told that a workman came at nine, wrenched out the remains of the old panel, tapped the wood with an iron hammer, clapped in a new panel, clattered over the hall — but I did not hear a sound. I slept until a quarter to ten.

You will tell me the exact time of your arrival. Won't you? If it is early morning I'll not meet you but at any other hour I would like to go to the station. You have all my love.

Tig.

No letters have come. I sent a 'bleu'[3] on Saturday for you —

MS ATL. *LKM* I. 4–5.

[1] Murry had written on 8 Feb 1914 (ATL) to say how the Campbells had received him, that he had lunched with W.L. George, and that 'Everybody's just the same'.
[2] An echo of the nursery rhyme, ending: 'And down goes y-o-u'.
[3] i.e. a telegram, from the French *pneumatique*, familiarly called a *petit bleu*.

To J. M. Murry, [10 February 1914]

31 RUE DE TOURNON (6ème)

Dear Jack.

If you are staying so long I had better send you this to answer. Do not worry about anything here. We are alright. Im afraid I am rather childish about people coming & going — and just, now, at this moment when the little boy has handed me your telegram[1] — the disappointment is hard to bear.

Your room is ready for you. It looks lovely — Do whatever is best, dear, but remember that all the people are very little and that really & truly we are awfully strong —

Very well, dear
Tig.

MS ATL. *LJMM*, 9.

[1] The telegram (ATL) read 'MUST SEE BANKRUPTCY FRIDAY BETTER STAY.' When Murry did appear before the Receiver, his creditor was reprimanded for pressing a debt that was not morally Murry's.

To J. M. Murry, [11 February 1914]

31 RUE DE TOURNON (6ème)
Wednesday.

Well, Jack dear.

I expect I did not understand your wire quite fully. Telegrams are always frightening. Now that Ive read your letter I am able to write to you more sensibly. You are right to stay until the matter of the bankruptcy is fixed up. I quite understand that, dear, and I am thankful they are more or less nice.[1] Don't rush and don't consider me. If you find it more convenient to stay longer, just wire me.

Now about the other and 'more important' affair. It is difficult to discuss by letter. I do not think that it is any good you staying anywhere if you are worried about money. A constant strain like that wears you out quicker than anything. If we cannot live over here on £10 a month (and we cant) theres an end of this place for the present. I *think* that you had better do what you think — I mean take the Westminster job for at least a year and feel the security of a regular £5 a week for that time. Your work needs freedom from these grinding fears. About exchanging flats I expect it would not be difficult. But it would take time, I am sure. What is at the back of your darling mind? Is it your idea to stay at Campbell's and me to stay here until the exchange is effected? Tell me quite plainly, won't you? Did you take a return ticket. Would you rather stay on now and save the money and manage things by letter? You know Jack darling, quite seriously speaking, I can be happy in any place where we are together, but without you all places alike are deserted for me. No more now.

Tig.

Don't send any more postcards — like you did today, please dear.[2]
[*Across top*]
excuse writing. Tired.

MS ATL. *LJMM*, 9–10.

[1] Murry wrote on 10 Feb 1914, explaining that he had called at the Bankruptcy Court and 'they were nice. They said they wouldn't make any attempt to touch my earnings, and that there wouldn't be any difficulty, if I filed a statement of my affairs immediately.' (ATL.)

[2] From what Murry said in his reply on 12 Feb 1917, he had been sealing his letter when Beatrice Campbell gave him an initialled postcard to enclose: 'It seemed so utterly foolish, considering what I was writing about. But couldn't help it.' (ATL).

To J. M. Murry, [12 February 1914]

31 RUE DE TOURNON (6ème)
Thursday

My dear one.

You are good to me. Two letters this morning and a telegram yesterday afternoon. I wished that I might have sent you one in return but I thought you would not expect it so I. . .guarded the money. It would be a great relief to talk over everything, but by the time you get this letter it will be Friday morning and unless your plans have changed you will have no time to reply to me except 'in person'. I talked over 'the business' with you yesterday as much as I could by letter and without you. Depend upon us — we're quite strong enough now to find a way out of our difficulties and we *will* and be happy, too, and do our work. (By being happy I mean happy together in the 'odd times', you know.) And if I can get a room in London that hasn't another opening out of it and isn't the logical end of a passage I can work there as well as anywhere — supposing we arrange to leave here at once.

I read the letter that you wrote me with Lesley and my breast ached, my dearest.[1]

Tig.

Can you let me know the *exact time* of your arrival. If you feel you'd rather keep the money, don't worry to, but I have been

very careful of my money here, & everything is paid up to date —
the two weeks laundry & the femme de ménage and I have 60 francs
left.

[*Across top*]
Cheque enclosed

MS ATL. *LKM* I.5; *LJMM* 10–11.

[1] Murry, writing on 11 Feb 1914 from Lyons tea shop in Oxford Street, where he met
Ida Baker, told KM he was thinking of early in the morning when 'my head flops down to
snuggle between your breasts' (ATL).

To Ida Baker, [24 February 1914]

31 RUE DE TOURNON (6ème)
Last moments.

Dear Ida —

Everything is packed of ours — the book packer is here now & we
are waiting for the man to come & take away the furniture. Grimy
and draughty and smelling of dust, tea leaves and senna leaves and
match ends in the sink — cigaret ash on the floor — you never saw
an uglier place — now, nor more desolate. The clock (sold, too) is
ticking desperately — & doesn't believe it's going yet & yet is hopeless. Jack, in a moment of desperation yesterday sold even the
bedding . . . Yes I *am* tired, my dear a little — but its mostly mental.
I'm tired of this disgusting atmosphere & of eating hardboiled eggs
out of my hand & drinking milk out of a bottle — Its a gay day
outside. What we shall do until the train goes I can't think — Very
little money and we both don't want cafés. Oh, how I love Jack.
There is something wonderfully sustaining & comforting to have
another person with you — who goes to bed when you do & is
there when you wake up — who turns to you & to whom you turn.
The dear little toilet set is on the same table with me — all packed
into the basin. I have been talking to the book packer. He is tall &
more graceful than anyone Ive ever seen. He wears light blue woollen
shoes & has never worn boots since he was 'tout petit' — that's why
he walks so — doesn't seem to put his feet *down* at all but he has a
delightful sort of swaying stride. I have given Carco a few souvenirs —
the egg timer which *charmed* him and some odd little pieces like
that.[1] The guitar has gone — & the candlesticks — except the dragons.
I have an idea I shall find the femme de ménage has taken something
really important before I go. She was a little too gushing and grateful

to be innocent, I'm afraid. (Katie, you are really revolting.) I wonder
they are [*illegible*] going down to Canterbury . . !

MS Murry. *BTW*, 277–8.

[1] When Murry returned to Paris, he and KM prepared to move back to London. The
furniture they had paid £25 to have shipped across three months before, they were now
obliged to sell for a fraction of its value. They moved out on Mardi Gras, the novelist Francis
Carco (see p. 148, n.1), who prided himself on his knowledge of the *demi-monde*, having
taken Murry round several brothels to sell off their possessions. Their concierge happened
to have died the same day, and the furniture was moved to cries of '*C'est dégoûtant*'.

The six months from March to September 1914 make up the longest
period of KM's adult life from which no letters survive. When she and
Murry returned to England in February, they lived first, and briefly,
at 119 Beaufort Mansions, Chelsea, then in disagreeable lodgings at
102 Edith Grove, before moving into a vermin-infested flat, again in
Chelsea, at 111 Arthur Street. Ida Baker had left in March for
Rhodesia, and the numerous letters written to her there over the
next two years were later burned at KM's insistence.

When war was declared in August 1914 Murry volunteered for
service with a bicycle battalion of the Middlesex Regiment, but
was rejected because of recent pleurisy. He and KM were on holiday
in Cornwall, and in Sussex, in September, and in October they
moved to a cottage near Great Missenden, Bucks, only a few miles
from the Lawrences, at whose wedding they had been witnesses in
July. Through them KM met, that autumn, the most loyal of her
male friends, S. S. Koteliansky.

For several months KM was extremely unhappy. Murry was self-
absorbed and remote, and she wrote at the end of August 1914, 'I do
not trust Jack. I'm old to-night. Ah, I wish I had a lover to nurse me,
love me, hold me, comfort me, to stop me thinking.' (*Journal* 1954,
61.) By the end of the year, she was considering leaving Murry.

To [Laura Kate Bright],[1] [21 September 1914]

[n.a.]
[. . .] Here in London, we are in the throes of this frightful war.
There are camps of soldiers in the parks and squares, in the streets
there is always the sound and the sight of soldiers marching by. The
big white trains painted with the red cross, swing into the railway
stations carrying their sad burdens and often at the same time other

trains leave crowded with boys in khaki, cheering and singing on their way to the front. At night London, usually so bright with lamps and electric signs, is darkened, and huge searchlights sweep the sky and the hundreds of London newspaper boys run up and down the streets like little black crows shouting: "War! Latest news of the War! War!!" Although in many ways these are dark and depressing days, still they are brightened by the display of real and splendid courage on the part of all the people. The fact that England is fighting for something beyond mere worldly gain and power seems to have a real moral effect upon the people, and they are become more brave and more generous than one could have believed in days of peace. Last week I saw some of the poor Belgian refugees arriving in London, one an old lady of 93, who had walked miles to escape the soldiers. Her house had been burned down and all her possessions were gone, but she stepped out of the train in a black dress and white muslin cap, calm, her hands folded as though she were walking into a friend's house. The little children were heartbreaking; they stared about them as if they were dreaming. One little girl had brought her kitten all the long journey with her; and a small boy, whose parents had both been shot, carried an old shawl knotted into a doll. People seem to think that this war cannot be over for two or three years, but perhaps that is pessimistic reckoning. It is hard to believe that men can go on killing for so long in these days. [. . .]

Printed letter, *Evening Post* (Wellington), 6 November 1914.

[1] Laura Kate Bright (1862-1941) was a close friend of Annie Beauchamp's in Wellington, whom KM and her sisters called 'Godmother'. She became Harold Beauchamp's second wife in January 1920. This unacknowledged excerpt from KM's private letter to her was published in the Wellington *Evening Post* under the note, 'Writing from London to a Wellington resident . . . a correspondent says . . .'

To Sylvia Payne, [23 September 1914]

[Udimore,[1] near Rye]
Dear Cousin,
    Dont bother to send me the book. Im coming home on Friday — & there is really no time for reading here. Neither is there even the *smell* of a cottage at 5/- a week! But the country is pretty — sheep

& willows & little streams — pretty, pious country — Come to tea on Sunday will you — if you're not busy —

Yours
Kathleen

MS (postcard) ATL.

[1] Having spent the first part of September 1914 in Cornwall, in a cottage arranged for them by the novelist J.D. Beresford, KM and Murry went in the latter part of the month to another cottage on the Sussex coast near Rye. They were back in Arthur Street, Chelsea, by the end of the month.

To Harold Beauchamp,[1] 15 December 1914

Rose Tree Cottage[2] | The Lee | Great Missenden.
December 15th 1914.

My dearest Father,

I have no words with which to thank you for your wonderful generosity. If only you were not so far away from me so that I could thank you as I long to — with my arms round your neck. Mr Kay summoned me by a mysterious note to the Bank and handed me your letter and when I had read it he chuckled and said 'What do you think of that. Bit of a surprise, eh?' and he rang the bell for the messenger — you know his manner. "Just bring me five sovereigns — will you". When they were handed him he put them in a row in front of me on the table. "There you are," he said. "Run away and buy yourself some fish and chips for your Christmas dinner." And he kept saying — "Thats wonderfully good of your Father — you know." I did not know what to answer. I felt quite what the French call 'bouleversé' by my sudden riches. Father darling, you have made me feel happy and free. I thank you with all my heart. The wheels of my life are going round beautifully in consequence and the check action the spring balance and the jewels in two holes are all intact. I hope that my small parcel to you arrives safely. The man in the shop was anxious for me to buy you a tie with the flags of the allies embroidered upon its breast *or* a bulldog with its forefeet on a flag, but I remained firm.

As you may imagine I have felt dreadfully anxious about Mother. Chaddie wrote to me by the last mail that she had received an answer to a cable and that 'Mother was better'. I had wished to cable myself. She has been in my thoughts and in my heart continually. I hope that by now she is up and out again. Mother's courage is a lesson to all her children; there is no one like her and she makes me feel ashamed of my little illnesses and weak moments. Forgive me for not having written as often as I should have to her and to you Father. I pledge you my solemn word that I will turn over a new leaf from this Christmas and send news regularly — whatever it is. Your two dear letters — I read them again in the tube from the Bank to Oxford Circus — the tube packed with people — city pa men and soldiers for the most part. I squeezed your letters inside my muff and had great difficulty in refraining from beaming at everybody like a little girl. out for the day with her Papa. When you write suddenly — "What a bother — isn't it?" I hear your voice so plainly that I cannot believe you are far away — and then, too, you convey so much of your personality in your handwriting. Do you remember those horses you used to draw on the back of envelopes with very over-developed ears and under-developed stomachs?

Nothing is talked of at present but the latest development of the german culture-war — namely the East Coast raid.[3] I am sure the Kaiser will not be satisfied until Zeppelin has flown over London and dropped a few bombs into the palaces and baby carriages there. I have ordered for you from the 'Times' a copy of the french 'yellow book' which I found awfully interesting giving their official account of the developments. It is a sister ship to the English 'white book' and almost more interesting, because the french people cant keep the human interest out of their government even.[4] Diplomacy seems to be a difficult trade to put a lad to in these days. A day or two ago I was talking to a young man who has just returned from the front wounded in the foot. He has been acting as interpreter and general rouse about. He says that in the trenches in France the most remarkable thing is the frightful boredom that the men feel. They don't feel excited or 'up guards and at 'em' they spend days and nights simply waiting — very cold, very wet and with nothing on earth to do. And he tells a story of a tommy wiping his bayonet with a wisp of grass and saying "Well, I suppose we'll 'ave ter give the blighters 'ome rule same as we did in Sarth Africa." This same young man got his foot wound while being reproved by his colonel for not having shaved that morning. "We were standing in the street," he said, and the old man was going for me. "Why haven't you shaved sir," he roared. When a shell whistled over our heads and exploded in the market square and caught me in the foot." (Whereupon I heard *you* saying — "I suppose that was about the closest shave you ever had in your life".)

I had hoped to get a small job not far from the fighting line last month, but now it has been postponed until January, when D.V. I shall go to France and write some human documents for a newspaper syndicate.[5] I am very keen to do so. At present I am working hard and 'cuddling my cards'. With the extra money I feel able to afford a servant to come in and light fires and do the hard work which is an immense saving of energy. It is very cold on the top of this hill, but we have chopped down a damson tree in the back garden and the side of the fireplace is stacked with logs. I have been doing a lot of digging in the garden, too, but the natural soil seems to my maiden efforts to be almost entirely concealed by large stones, primeval dog bones, ossified remains various, and pieces of broken soup tureens. Very little nourishment to be got out of *that*.

Goodnight, Father dear. A happy New Year to you, and all the love and grateful thanks of your devoted child

Kass.

MS ATL.

¹ Harold Beauchamp (1858–1938) left school at thirteen, married Annie Burnell in 1884, and pursued a highly successful business career in Wellington as importing merchant, company director, member of several boards, and a director of the Bank of New Zealand for 38 years. He was knighted in 1923.

² The small and damp cottage KM and Murry had taken, for 5s. a week, from October 1914. The Lee, Great Missenden, Bucks, was near the Lawrences at Chesham and the Cannans at Cholesbury.

³ On the morning of 15 Dec 1914 German cruisers shelled Scarborough, Hartlepool, and Whitby, killing more than 50 people.

⁴ *The French Yellow Book*, like *The British Blue Book* and *The German White Book*, was an official compilation of diplomatic correspondence previous to the outbreak of the Great War. Its intention, as a *Times* advertisement stated, was to show 'the efforts of the Allies to maintain peace, and the persistent endeavour of the German Government to thwart those efforts'.

⁵ This is a story KM also told her brother Leslie early in the next year, for on 11 Feb 1915, soon after arriving in England he wrote home: 'She is more in love than ever with J.M. Murry which is a thing to be grateful for and with a new contract with one of the Monthlies for a series of war sketches, they have prospects of a little money coming in. . .' (ATL).

To Annie Burnell Beauchamp, 15 December 1914

Rose Tree Cottage | The Lee | Great Missenden | Bucks.
December 15th 1914.

My darling little Mother,

How terrible that you should have been ill again, and so severely ill. Do you know I have had an extraordinary presentiment that something was happening to you. Every evening when my work was done and I sat down by the fire I felt your nearness and your dearness to me and such love for you in my heart and such a longing to hold you in my arms that I could have cried like a baby. The only way to cure my sadness was to talk about you to Jack and make him see you, too. I really believe (with all the 'going into the silence' nonsense aside) that you and I are curiously near to each other. I feel *through* you so much and I dream of you so vividly. Oh, my little precious brave Mother, if my love can help you to get strong you are better now. My heart yearns over you. I see you in bed with your pretty hands crossed and your springy hair on the pillow and I cannot bear to think that we are far away from each other, and that I cannot come in and ask you if you feel inclined for a little powwow. I am quite well and strong again, but I pray that you are better and that you are going to have a happy Xmas and a New Year full of the blessings that you deserve.

I have just written to Father thanking him for his munificent Christmas present to me. You can think what it means and how it oils the machinery. I feel very 'chirpy' and I have engaged a pleasant decent body to come and do the strenuous work of this cottage in consequence. I mean the *scrubbing*, my dear, and lighting fires, cleaning stove etc. Scrubbing when one runs it to earth really doesnt seem to me to be a human occupation at all. Id rather keep the floor moist and grow a crop of grass on it. It is the one thing that I really do jib at and yet my new woman Mrs Herne attacks it like a lamb and I sit very snug in my little sitting room and listen to her.

It is very cold. We have had several falls of snow and the ground is frozen hard, but I love such weather at Christmas time. We are having a Christmas party at our friends the Lawrences on Christmas Eve, and the Cannans are giving a dinner with charades to follow on Christmas day and some friends of *theirs* a party on Boxing Day. So Mary Cannan has asked us to go and stay with them from Christmas Eve until the festivities are over. It will be great fun, I expect.[1] Mary Cannan is a charming woman; I wish that you had met her. I feel sure that you and she would get on beautifully. Their house is rather like Aunt Chaddie's was at Eastbourne, just the same type and I shall enjoy the lap of luxury for a little, and not having to think about meals. Poor Mrs Lawrence was the daughter of a german baron and her position at the present crisis is a little delicate, but she has been making marzipan all the week and talking with extraordinary german cheerfulness about her cousins 'Otto and Franz' who are 'sure to be killed in this war — *if* not dead already' and it is only we who feel her position, I suppose. The Germans are a very curious people. I suppose this war is as hideous to them, poor souls, as it is to us. Its the fault of the Prussians and not those simple warm-hearted bavarians, after all. Of course I cannot understand why somebody doesn't shoot the Kaiser, but I suppose these deeds are more difficult than they appear to the female eye.

Christmas this year in London is a farce except from the military standpoint. Everything is given over to the soldiers. It is strange to see all those enormous windows in Oxford Street full of khaki and wool and pots of vaseline and marching socks. Wherever one goes women are knitting — the girls in the shops knit, the women in the buses and tubes. I can't help wondering what the results are like. I heard of one old concierge in Paris sending a beloved son a pale blue balaclava helmet with a tassel on the top!

I was talking the other day to Miss Royde Smith (a woman on the Westminster Gazette.)[2] Her sister has been helping in a house full of refugees, but she said her experience was unfortunate as nearly all the inmates were ladies and all of them had brought dogs, and nice little metal trays that one had to keep strewn with clean sand so that the dogs could pay their debts to nature without going into the street and getting their paws wet. She said she spent her whole day flying from one room to another to attend to these little creatures and her enthusiasm suffered a very severe temporary eclipse after a week of it. These were of course, wealthy refugees. I travelled the other day with a very different variety — a woman and her husband, quite 'poor class' people, but very neat and clean and pleasant looking. They could not speak a word of english, and they had been staying in the north of England in quarters improvised for them out of the public baths. They had not a penny between them but the woman said never — no never had she dreamed of such hospitality. All the people in the little town — none of whom could speak a word of french had asked them to tea in turn. Every day they had been out to tea — always in silence — and the only way to get over the lack of conversation was to press them to eat. The woman told me that "my poor husband, Madame, whose stomach has been very small from childhood is a changed man." "Pork pies, ham, tinned apricots, five sorts of jam, cakes, bread, puddings, Madame, at five o'clock in the afternoon." Can't you imagine the spread — and the silent expressive gestures of the hosts and guests and the horror of the poor little belgian pa man with an eye upon his waistcoat. I gathered from what she told me that the people in the town had looked upon them as a kind of circus — of course, all in the kindest way. But whenever life grew a little dull they were off in parties and "had a look at the Belgians." "Never alone for one moment, Madame", said the little belgian, turning up her eyes at me. "They sat round us [in] circles — from morning till night — smiling so beautifully, Madame, but *never* leaving us alone."

My dear darling. Here is a little handkerchief which looks like you, to me. Bless you always. I simply devoured your letters. I am always your own devoted child.

MS ATL.

¹ Two parties took place over Christmas 1914, one at the Lawrences' cottage at Chesham on 23 December, the second at Gilbert and Mary Cannan's in the evening of Christmas Day. Everyone had drunk a good deal when, prompted by S.S. Koteliansky (see p. 147), Murry devised an unscripted play closely based on his and KM's relationship, and on her desire to console a foreigner — probably Francis Carco (see p. 148, n. 1), in Murry's mind, but played by the painter Mark Gertler (1892-1939). He and KM threw themselves into their parts so enthusiastically that the Lawrences intervened, and Gertler 'ended the evening by weeping bitterly at having kissed another man's woman and everybody trying to console me' (letter to Lytton Strachey, 1 Jan 1915, *Mark Gertler: Selected Letters*, ed Noel Carrington [1965], 77.) For Murry's account of the party see *BTW*, 321-2.

² Naomi Royde Smith (d. 1964), novelist, playwright, and biographer, was literary editor of the *Westminster Gazette* 1912-22.

*To Douglas Clayton,*¹ *4 January 1915*

ROSE TREE COTTAGE, | THE LEE, | GT MISSENDEN
January 4th 1915

Dear Sir,

Would you kindly type me 2 copies of this short story² at your earliest convenience — My friend Mr. D H Lawrence advised me to write to you — Are you too busy to do some typing for me from time to time?

Yours very truly
Katherine Mansfield.

MS Newberry.

¹ Douglas Clayton (1894-1960), a nephew of Constance Garnett's who as well as being a professional typist ran a small printing business in South Croydon.

² The story is unidentified, although KM recorded finishing 'Brave Love' soon after this, on 12 Jan 1915 (*Journal* 1954, 68).

To Douglas Clayton, [1 February 1915]

Rose Tree Cottage | The Lee | Great Missenden

Dear Mr Clayton

I beg you to forgive my delay in acknowledging your parcel & settling your account. I've no excuse to offer except my own dilatoriness. The typing was beautifully done, thank you.

And now I cant find your account. It was seven & something so I'll send an order for 8/- and the extra pennies — if there are any — can come off my next account.

Yours truly
Katherine Mansfield.

MS Texas.

To S. S. Koteliansky,[1] *[1 February 1915]*

ROSE TREE COTTAGE | THE LEE | GT. MISSENDEN
Monday

Dear Kotilianski,

When I opened the parcel I found your presents — The cigarettes in the charming little box and the chocolates. Thank you very much indeed for them. I am smoking one of the cigarettes now and the russian skirt fits well — I like it.

Next Monday I am coming up to London for several days. I shall phone you and give you my address — That was a good idea of yours about Notting Hill; I am sure something will come of it. It is almost warm here today and there is at least threepenny worth of sun shining on my walls; in the field outside the window new grass lifts its myriad shining spears — We had a letter from Lawrence this morning. He sounds really very happy — and full of hopes — So there is one person at least for whom the war is over.
Goodbye,

My love to you
Katherine

MS BL. Dickinson, 81.

[1] Samuel Solomonovitch Koteliansky (1882-1955) was a Ukrainian Jew who had come to England on a grant from Kiev University about four years before 1915, and remained in England for the rest of his life. On 29 Jan 1915 KM wrote, 'Saw Koteliansky at the station. He was very nice. I rather cling to him. He brought me a skirt and some cigarettes and some chocolates.' (*Journal* 1954, 72.)

To S. S. Koteliansky, [4 February 1915]

[Rose Tree Cottage, The Lee, Great Missenden]

Will you be at the Bureau[1] next Monday afternoon at about 4?

Katherine

MS (postcard) BL.

[1] The Russian Law Bureau, a small office at 212 High Holborn which translated and certified Russian documents.

To S. S. Koteliansky, [5 February 1915]

[Rose Tree Cottage, The Lee, Great Missenden]

Kotiliansky

No, it is next Monday that I shall be in London — next Monday morning. I am sorry there has been a misunderstanding. Did I say so or did I *write* so — I don't remember. Anyhow next week you can tell me yourself.

I know I shall find good rooms next week with flowers growing on the window sills.

Katherine.

[*On back of envelope*]
If you care to come down for the weekend — come, and we can go back to town together on Monday morning.

MS BL.

∽

KM's unhappiness with Murry was exacerbated by her correspondence with Murry's friend, the French novelist Francis Carco, and her belief that she was in love with him. When Leslie Beauchamp arrived in England in February 1915, he gave his sister the money to visit France, and Murry made no effort to dissuade her. She left London on 15 February, travelling to Gray, in the Zone des Armées, where Carco was serving with the French army. Accounts of the visit, which lasted only a few days, survive in the *Journal* 1954, (75–9), and in the closely autobiographical but undated story 'An Indiscreet Journey', unpublished in her lifetime.

The brief affair was a disappointment, and KM's restlessness continued. Although she was reconciled with Murry, she returned to Paris twice in the next few months, before settling at 5 Acacia Road, St. John's Wood, in June 1915.

∽

To Francis Carco,[1] [mid-February 1915]

[Paris]

Darling, je pense dans quelques jours venir vous voir à Besançon et quitter Paris pour vous. Je suis dans le petit café en bas sur le quai. Il faut un temps délicieuse et je suis près de toi. Je vous donner un baiser. Je vous demande comment est votre bras et s'il est bien que je viens vers vous.[2]

MS lacking. Carco 1916, 198.

[1] The poet and novelist Francis Carco (1886–1958), born Francis Carcopino-Tusoli in New Caledonia, of Corsican descent, published his first novel, *Jésus-la-caille*, in 1914. He had known Murry since his student days, and became friendly with KM during her time in Paris in the winter of 1913–14.

In *Montmartre à vingt ans* (1938), Carco recalled (187): 'Katherine Mansfield m'écrivait en français. Elle m'affirmait que Londres, en 1914, "est comme une soupe aux larmes" et se moquait des "ridicules cocottes des music-halls avec les cocardes belges à leurs chapeaux'."

In *Les Innocents*, a novel published in 1916 in which KM appears as 'Winnie Campbell', Carco included short extracts from her letters, now lost.

[2] (Translation)

Darling, I intend in a few days to leave Paris and come to you at Besançon. I am in the little café downstairs on the quai. The weather is delightful and I feel close to you. I kiss you. How is your arm? Do you want me to come to you?

To Francis Carco, [mid-February 1915]

[Paris]

Je suis venue ici à cause de vous.[1] Je me suis promenée jusqu'à la nuit. Voici les étoiles déjà et le petit vent qui vient toujours avec elles.[2] Dans la salle prochaine, on joue du billard. J'entends le clic! clac! des balles. La femme qui vend les cigarettes ici porte un chapeau. Pourquoi? Chéri, j'ai commencé à pleurer et pleurer. . .Dans l'après-midi j'ai trouvé un petit banc dans un jardin et je restais là, disant: Courage. Il ne faut pas . . . Courage! Mais tout était inutile. . .[3]

MS lacking. Carco 1916, 199–200.

[1] Carco noted in *Les Innocents* (199), 'un soir, à bout de courage, elle lui avait écrit du café de la place Blanche.'

[2] The word 'elles' was added to the text as it had appeared in *Les Innocents* when Carco used the letter again in *Bohème d'artiste* (1940), 261. In *Montmartre à vingt ans*, where he also quotes from the letter, he says that from 'j'ai commencé' to the end of the quotation appeared 'un paragraphe plus haut'.

[3] (Translation)

I came here because of you. I walked about until nightfall. Already there were stars and the slight wind that comes with them. In the next room people are playing billiards. I hear the click-clack of the balls. The woman who sells cigarettes here wears a hat. Why? Dear, I have begun to weep and weep. . . In the afternoon I found a little bench in the garden and I stayed there, saying: Courage. I must not. Courage! But it was all in vain. . .

To [J. M. Murry], [c. 20 February 1915]

[Gray,[1] Haute-Saône, France]

I seem to have just escaped the prison cell, Jaggle dearest, because I find this place is in the zone of the armies and therefore forbidden to women. However, my Aunt's illness[2] pulled me through. I had some really awful moments. Outside the station he was waiting. He merely *sang* (so typical) "Follow me but not as though you were doing so" until we came to a tiny toll house by the river against which leant a faded cab. But once fed with my suitcase and our two selves it dashed off like the wind — the door opening and shutting to his horror as he is not allowed in cabs. We drove to a village near by, to a large white house where he had taken a room for me — a most extraordinary room furnished with a bed, a wax apple and an immense flowery clock. It's very hot. The sun streams through the blind. The garden outside is full of wallflowers and blue enamel saucepans. It would make you laugh, too.

MS (draft) ATL, Notebook 4. *Journal* 1927, 24-5.

[1] The town in eastern France, on the Saône between Dijon and Besançon, where Carco was stationed.
[2] KM's fabricated excuse for travelling into the Zone des Armées.

To [Frieda Lawrence],[1] [20 February 1915]

[Gray, Haute-Saône]

England is like a dream. I am sitting at the window of a little square room furnished with a bed, a wax apple and an immense flowery clock. Outside the window there is a garden full of wall flowers and blue enamel saucepans. The clocks are striking five and the last rays of sun pour under the swinging blind. It is very hot — the kind of heat that makes one cheek burn in infancy. But I am so happy I must just send you a word on a spare page of my diary, dear.

I have had some dreadful adventures on my way here because the place is within the zone of the armies and not allowed to women. The last old pa-man who saw my passport, 'M le Colonel' — very grand with a black tea cosy and gold tassel on his head and smoking what lady novelists call a 'heavy Egyptian cigarette' nearly sent me back. But Frieda, its such wonderful country — all rivers and woods and large birds that look blue in the sunlight. I keep thinking of you and Lawrence. The French soldiers are 'pour rire.' Even when they are wounded they seem to lean out of their sheds and wave their bandages at the train. But I saw some prisoners today — not at all funny — Oh I have so much to tell you. I had better not begin. We shall see each other again some day, won't we, darling.

'Voila le petit soldat joyeux et jeune' he has been delivering letters.[2] It is hot as summer — one only sits and laughs.

Your loving
Katherine.

MS (draft) ATL, Notebook 4. *Journal* 1927, 23-4; *Journal* 1954, 74.

[1] Frieda Lawrence (1879-1956), born Frieda von Richthofen, grew up among the Prussian nobility. In 1898 she had married Ernest Weekley, bore him three children, and lived with him in Nottingham when he was appointed to the University as a Professor of French. She eloped with D.H. Lawrence (1885-1930), who had been a student of Weekley's, three weeks after meeting him in April 1912.
[2] Carco, who had enlisted in the French Army at the beginning of the war, was serving as a postman with a bakery unit.

To S. S. Koteliansky, [26 February 1915][1]

[Rose Tree Cottage, The Lee, Great Missenden]
Friday

I shall not be in town until Monday. I have got such severe rheumatism that I can hardly move. What a stupid creature! Last night
I wore my dress. You cannot think how much I like it. It is very
lovely and there is something almost fairy in it. It makes me feel
that wonderful adventures might happen if only one is dressed
and ready.

I did not realise until I reached home how many cigarettes you
had given me. Kotiliansky, it is my turn to give presents, I am
beginning to feel. Tell me — what shall I give? One thing if you want
it is yours to keep. Don't forget, among your many employers your
loving friend

Kissienka.

MS BL. Dickinson, 82.

[1] KM returned to England from France on 25 Feb 1915.

To S. S. Koteliansky, [1 March 1915]

[Rose Tree Cottage, The Lee, Great Missenden]
Monday

My dear Kotiliansky I hope you are not waiting for me today — for
I am unable to come to London. My rheumatism still makes walking
an impossibility — and I suffer very much. However I am in hopes
that it will leave me suddenly and then I shall come. We are going
to shut up this house and live in London until the summer. Jack has
seen some rooms (rather, they were my idea) in Fitzroy Street & as
soon as I am able to move I am going to see them. So we shall be in
London quite soon & more or less permanently. This cottage is too
cold & too depressing. Will you post the enclosed letter to Beatrice
Hastings[1] for me? And will you buy a postal order for 2 francs 50
for me and put it in the letter to Madame Masquelier[2] — I will pay
you when next we meet, but I can't get foreign money orders here
& this money *must* be paid. I hope I am not worrying my very
busy friend.

When we are settled in London we must have some good times

together. Make up a little basket of dreams — will you — and I will, too, and we shall be ready, then. I feel about 800, Kotiliansky, for I can hardly walk at all, nor turn in my bed without crying out against my bones.

Kissienka.

MS BL. *LKM* I. 6.

[1] Beatrice Hastings, who had left Orage in 1914, was now living in Paris.
[2] Mme Masquelier was Francis Carco's concierge on the quai aux Fleurs, Paris, where he had kept a flat.

To S. S. Koteliansky, [early March 1915]

[Rose Tree Cottage, The Lee, Great Missenden]

Koteliansky

I can't find the english address of the Smart Set — so would you look it up in a telephone book or literary year book (there is one in the Holborn Library) and send this story for me as soon as possible.[1] I have enclosed an addressed envelope — Stick a stamp on it for me — will you?

I hope you don't mind this fractious invalid — but I will do the same for you when we're in Russia.

K.

Read the story if you care to.

MS BL. Dickinson, 81.

[1] The *Smart Set*, subtitled 'A magazine of cleverness, was published in New York. An English edition, with additional English material, was edited by H.J. Gillespie from 30 Norfolk Street, The Strand. KM's story, apparently 'The Little Governess' (see p. 154, n.1), did not appear there.

To S. S. Koteliansky, [8 March 1915]

[Rose Tree Cottage, The Lee, Great Missenden]
Monday.

My dear Kotiliansky.

I have wanted to write to you; you have been in my mind several days. Thank you for doing those things for me — the english money does not really matter. I am in bed. I am not at all well. Some mysterious pains seem to like me so well that they will not leave me.[1] All the same I am grateful to your Ancestral Grandfathers —

for — for some curious reason I can work. Im writing quite quickly — and its good. Send me a little letter when you have the time. I have an idea that Lawrence will be in London today.[2] It is very cold here. It is winter and the sky from my window looks like ashes. I hear my little maid go thumping about in the kitchen and when she is quiet I listen to the wind. My God, what poverty! So I write about hot weather and happy love and broad bands of sunlight and cafés — all the things that make life to me. Yes, you are quite right. I *am* wicked. Would it be very rude if I asked you to send me a few cigarettes? If it would — do not send them.

Today I had a most lovely postcard sent me from my concierge in Paris — hand painted roses as big as cabbages — and so many of them they simply fall out of the vase!

Always your friend
Kissienka.

MS BL. *LKM* I. 6-7.

[1] These recurring pains, which KM believed were rheumatic, were the result of a gonorrheal infection contracted several years before.

[2] The Lawrences had planned to spend the weekend with Lady Ottoline Morrell (see p. 245, n.1) at Garsington, but were prevented by their both suffering from influenza.

To S. S. Koteliansky, [10 March 1915]

[Rose Tree Cottage, The Lee, Great Missenden]
Wednesday late afternoon.

Your parcel came at midday. You cannot think in what dramatic circumstances. I was 'up' for the first time and downstairs and be-cause of my hideous wickedness I had begun to cry dreadfully — that is quite true — when in walked the cigarettes — the chocolates and the thrice blessed little bottle of whisky. So I drank some whisky & smoked a cigarette and dried my eyes & sent you a very superior form of blessing — which I hope you caught safely.

I have asked Frieda if she can put me up this weekend. I am coming to London on Friday, mon cher ami, and I will come then and see you a moment. But if you go to the Lawrences on Saturday and if Frieda will have me it will be — to quote Kotiliansky, a russian friend of mine — "very very nice."

I am glad that you liked the Little Governess[1] — but wait. Ive written such different things just lately — much much better — and I am going on writing them.

Jack sends you his kindest regards. He also is coming to see you on Friday but he is not going down to the Lawrences. Yes, I have a special disease. Pray your Ancestors for my heart.

Till Friday
Kissienka.

MS BL. *LKM* I. 7.

¹ 'The Little Governess', sent to Kot for him to forward to the *Smart Set*, was not published until the autumn, when it appeared under the name of 'Matilda Berry' in *The Signature*, 18 Oct and 1 Nov 1915.

To J. M. Murry, [13 March 1915]

[Greatham,¹ Pulborough, Sussex]

My darling Bogey,²

I came here by a fly with a man with a black patch on his eye. It was a most complicated journey — I kept thinking of my 'wandering boy' & the journey in the dark that you told me of, & when we took the 10th turning my hand flew out to you. It is a very nice cottage & I feel like you that ours is sordid in comparison. This bathroom, this thick white distemper & a fire in ones bedroom all dancy in the dark.

I gave Lawrence your love — and he sends his & so does Frieda. They love you both of them. I have talked a good deal of your book.³ Lawrence wants to review it for some paper: its a good idea, I think.

Brother sent me a letter today asking me to spend a weekend with him in London — so I had to wire him.⁴ I have seen Mrs Saleeby — she called me 'Katherine' — I don't know why that touched me. I like her but she seems to me unhappy — she appeals to me — Mary keeps your letter but you said you were coming here soon & Mrs Saleeby says if the promise is not kept "there will be no holding Mary".[5]

The country is lovely — sand and pine trees — daffodils in flower — violets and primroses in plenty, and on the marshes this morning there were almost as many seagulls as we saw in Rye.

I am sitting writing to you & Frieda & Kotiliansky are talking. My brain is wispy a little — my precious dear. I hope you & Goodyear[6] are alright in the cottage.

I shall be in London tomorrow & I will take that 6.25 train from Marylebone — send Collins for me — will you please?

My work is snapping at my heels but I have to down rover it, so far. Bogey *did* you see a book here called Irene Iddesley.[7] It is such a treat. I shall have to give you a copy — it is the ideal book to read in bed. My boy, I am very near you and I feel very free in my love. I do love you, you know dearly — dearly. I want to talk to you.

The downs so free are lovely — but I cannot walk quite there. I am *much* better — the air is so good, and the hot baths with sea salt — very sumptuous!

If I were quite alone & writing to you I should say something different — I want to tell you something about myself — but I hardly know what it is — against the others talking. I expect you know better than I do — I have a notion that your intuitions are almost angelic.

I hope Campbell was decent.[8] I feel that I dislike him utterly — that he is a fool & no end of a beggar — However — — —

Thats all Bogey. Two little quick kisses. Your

Tig.

MS ATL. *BTW*, 342.

[1] Between January and August 1915 the Lawrences lived at Greatham, in a cottage owned by Viola Meynell (1885-1956) daughter of the poet Alice Meynell (1847-1922).

[2] 'Bogey' had been a nickname in New Zealand for KM's brother Leslie.

[3] The novel *Still Life* (1916), on which Murry was at work; in *BTW* he described it (319) as 'analysing my own inward life to immobility'.

[4] Leslie Beauchamp was on an Officers' Training Course at Balliol College, Oxford.

[5] Monica Saleeby, the eldest of Alice Meynell's daughters, had known KM in 1908-9. Mary Saleeby was Monica's 10-year-old daughter.

[6] Frederick Goodyear (see p. 250, n.1), a close friend of Murry's from their undergraduate years at Brasenose College, Oxford.

[7] *Irene Iddesleigh* (1897), a novel by Amanda M'Kittrick Ros.

[8] At the end of 1914 there had been a disruption in the closeness between Murry and Gordon Campbell, although the friendship survived.

To J. M. Murry, [19 March 1915]

Paris.[1]
1st morning.

My dearest darling,

I have just had dejeunér — a large bowl of hot milk and a small rather inferior orange — but still not dressed or washed or at all a nice girl I want to write to you. The sun is very warm today and lazy — the kind of sun that loves to make patterns out of shadows and puts freckles on sleeping babies — a pleasant creature.

Bogey, I had a vile and loathsome journey. We trailed out of London in a fog that thickened all the way — A hideous little french women in a mackintosh with a little girl in a dirty face and a sailor suit filled and overflowed my carriage. The child combed its hair with a lump of brown bread, spat apple in our faces — made the Ultimate impossible noises — ugh! how vile. Only one thing rather struck me. It pointed out of the window and peeped its eternal "qu'est ce?" "C'est de la *terre*, ma petite", said the mother, in-different as a cabbage.

Folkstone looked like a picture painted on a coffin lid and Boulogne looked like one painted on a sardine tin — Between them rocked an oily sea — I stayed on deck and felt nothing when the destroyer signalled our ship — We were 2 hours late arriving and then the train to Paris did not even trot once — sauntered — meandered — Happily an old Scotchman, one time captain of the California, that big ship that went down in the fog off Tory Island[2] — sat opposite to me and we 'got chatting.' He was a scotchman, with a pretty soft accent. When he laughed he put his hand over his eyes & his face never changed — only his belly shook — but he was "extremely nice" — quite as good as 1/- worth of Conrad — At Amiens he found a tea wagon and bought ham and fresh rolls and oranges and wine and would not be paid so I ate hearty — Paris looked exactly like anywhere else — it smelled faintly of lavatories. The trees appeared to have shed their buds. So I took a room (the same room) and piled up coats and shawls on my bed to 'sleep and forget'. It was all merely dull beyond words and stupid and meaningless.

But today the sun is out. I must dress and follow him. Bless you, my dearest dear — I love you *utterly — utterly* — beyond words — & I will not be sad. I will not take our staying in our own rooms for a little as anything serious — How are you? What are you doing?

Address my letters to the post until I give you another address —

This is a silly old letter — like eating ashes with a fish fork — but it is not meant to be. I rather wanted to tell you the truth. I read

last night in the *Figaro* that the 16ᵉ Section (Carco's) are to be sent
to TURKEY.[3] Alas! the day —

Jaggle Bogey, love tell me about you, your book, your rooms —
Everything

Your
Tig.

MS ATL. *LKM* I. 8-9; *LJMM*, 15-16.

[1] Although reconciled with Murry, KM felt unable to work in England, and returned to
Paris on 18 Mar 1915. She spent the first two nights there at a hotel, possibly the same
Hôtel de l'Univers (see p. 132) at which she and Murry had stayed in December 1913.
[2] The liner *California*, on a voyage from New York to Glasgow with 1,000 passengers,
ran on the rocks at Tory Island, off Co. Donegal, on 27 June 1914. There were no casualties.
[3] Carco avoided service in Turkey by training as an aviator.

To J. M. Murry, [19–20 March 1915]

[Paris]

Darling

I went to Chartier[1] to lunch and had a maquereau grillé et epinards
à la creme. It was very strange to be there alone — I felt that I was a
tiny little girl and standing on a chair looking into an aquarium. It
was not a sad feeling, only strange and a bit 'femme seuleish' — As I
came out it began to snow. A wind like a carving knife cut through
the streets — and everybody began to run — so did I into a café and
there I sat and drank a cup of hot black coffee. Then for the first
time I felt in Paris. It was a little cafe & hideous — with a black
marble top to the counter garni with lozenges of white and orange.
Chauffeurs and their wives & fat men with immense photographic
apparatus sat in it — and a white fox terrier bitch — thin and eager
ran among the tables. Against the window beat a dirty french flag,
fraying out in the wind and then flapping on the glass. Does black
coffee make you drunk — do you think? I felt quite enivrée (Oh Jack
I *wont* do this. It's like George Moore.[2] Don't be cross) and could
have sat there years, smoking & sipping and thinking and watching
the flakes of snow. And then you know the strange silence that falls
upon your heart — the same silence that comes just one minute
before the curtain rises. I felt that and knew that I should write
here. I wish that you would write a poem about that silence sometime, my bogey. It is so *peculiar* — even one's whole physical being
seems arrested. It is a kind of dying before the new breath is blown
into you. As I write I can almost see the poem you will make — I
see the Lord alighting upon the breast of the man and He is very

fierce. (Are you laughing at me?) So after this intense emotion I dashed out of the café bought some oranges and a packet of rusks and went back to the hotel. Me voici. The garcon has just polished the handles of the door. They are winking and smelling somethink horrible. The sky is still full of snow — but everything is clear to see — the trees against the tall houses — so rich and so fine and on the grey streets the shiny black hats of the cabmen are like blobs of Lawrence's paint. Its very quiet. A bird chirrups — a man in wooden shoes goes by. Now I shall start working. Goodbye, my dear one.

The same night. Very strange is my love for you tonight — don't have it psychoanalysed — I saw you suddenly lying in a hot bath, blinking up at me — your charming beautiful body half under the water. I sat on the edge of the bath in my vest waiting to come in. Everything in the room was wet with steam and it was night time and you were rather languid. "Tig chuck over that sponge." No, Ill *not* think of you like that — Ill shut my teeth and not listen to my heart. It begins to cry as if it were a child in an empty room & to beat on the door and say Jack — Jack — Jack and Tig — Ill be better when Ive had a letter. Ah my God, how can I love him like this. Do I love you so much more than you love me or do you too — — feel like this?

Tig.

Saturday morning. Just off to see if there are any letters. Im alright, dearest.

MS ATL. *LKM* I. 9–10; *LJMM*, 16–17.

[1] Chartier was a chain of inexpensive restaurants in various parts of Paris.
[2] George Moore's *Confessions of a Young Man* (1886) recounts the *frissons* of an artist's living in Paris.

To J. M. Murry, [21 March 1915]

[13 quai aux Fleurs,[1] Paris IVe]
Sunday early afternoon.

My darling one,

Still no letter — perhaps I can be certain of one tomorrow. I walked to the post this morning and then finding neither light nor murmur there I went to the Luxemburg gardens. About 3 of the biggest chestnut trees are really in leaf today — you never saw anything lovelier with pigeons & babies adoring. I walked and walked until at last I came to a green plot with the back view of the head and shoulders of a pa-man rising out of an enormous stone urn — d'une forme d'une carotte. Laughing with my muff as is my solitary habit I sped to see his face & found that it was a statue of Verlaine.[2] What

extraordinary irony! The head seemed to me to be very lovely in its
way bashed in but dignified as I always imagine Verlaine. I stayed a
long time looking at that & then sunned myself off on a prowl.
Every soul carried a newspaper — L'Information came out on orange
sails — La Patrie lifted up its voice at the metro stations. Nothing
was talked of but the raid last night.[3] (Im dying to tell you about
this raid but Im sure I shant be able to.) Oh, Jaggle, it was really
rather fine. I came home late — I had been dining with B. [Beatrice
Hastings] at the Lilas.[4] It was a lovely night. I came in, made some
tea — put out the lamp and opened the shutters for a while to watch
the river. Then I worked until about one. I had just got into bed and
was reading Kipling's "Simple Contes des Collines,"[5] Bogey, when
there was a sharp quick sound of running and then the trumpets
from all sides flaring "garde à vous". This went on — accompanied by
the heavy groaning noise of the shutters opening and then a chirrup
of voices. I jumped up & did likewise. In a minute every light went
out except one point on the bridges. The night was bright with stars.
If you had seen the house stretching up & the people leaning out — —
& then there came a loud noise like doo-da-doo-da repeated hundreds
of times. I never thought of zeppelins until I saw the rush of heads &
bodies turning upwards as the Ultimate Fish (see *The Critic in
Judgement*)[6] passed by, flying high with fins of silky grey. It is
absurd to say that romance is dead when things like this happen — &
the noise it made — almost soothing you know — steady — and clear
doo-da-doo-da — like a horn. I longed to go out & follow it but
instead I waited and still the trumpets blared — and finally when it
was over I made some more tea & felt that a great danger was past —
& longed to throw my arms round someone — it gave one a feeling
of boundless physical relief like the aftermath of an earthquake.
Beatrice's flat is really very jolly. She only takes it by the quarter
at 900 francs a year — four rooms & a kitchen — a big hall a cabinet
and a conversatory. Two rooms open on to the garden. A big china
stove in the salle à manger heats the place. All her furniture is second
hand & rather nice. The faithful Max Jacobs conducts her shopping.[7]
Her own room with a grey self colour carpet — lamps in bowls with
Chinese shades — a piano — 2 divans 2 armchairs — books — flowers
a bright fire was very unlike Paris — really very charming. But the
house I think detestable — one *creeps* up and down the stairs. She
has dismissed Dado & transferred her virgin heart to Picasso — who
lives close by.[8] Strange and really beautiful though she is still with
the fairy air about her & her pretty little head still so fine — she is
ruined. There is no doubt of it — I love her, but I take an intense,
cold interest in noting the signs. She says — "it's no good me having
a crowd of people. If there are more than four I go to the cupboard &

nip cognacs until its all over for me, my dear." — or "Last Sunday I had a fearful crise — I got drunk on rhum by myself at the Rotonde & ran up & down this street crying and ringing the bells & saying "save me from this man". There wasn't anybody there at all." And then she says with a fairish show of importance — "of course the people here simply love me for it. There hasn't been a real woman of feeling here — since the war — but now I am going to be careful — "

Myself, I am dead off drink — I mean the idea of being drunk revolts me horribly. Last time I was drunk was with Beatrice here[9] and the memory stays and shames me even now. We were drunk with the wrong people. Not that I committed any sottise but I hate to think of their faces and — ugh! no — I shall not drink again — like that — never — never. As I write to you the concierge is doing the flat and she will persist in talking. Do I like flowers? Cold or heat? Birds or beasts? She is one of those women who can't lift or replace a thing without giving it its *ticket* — but she's a good soul and looks after me and fills the lamp without being told. Of course everybody she ever knew has died a grisly death in this war — & the fact that Carco is going to Turkey seems to delight her beyond measure. Il ne reviendra jamais!

Today everywhere they are crying voici les jolies violettes de Parme & the day is like that. Under the bridges floats a purple shadow — I must start working. (I believe now she is dusting simply to spite me — & to keep me off my work. What a bore these women are —) How are you managing? dearest? Does the house-keeper come up — oh, Jack write often. I am *lost lost* without letters from you — things haven't got their real flavour — Keep me very close to your heart in my own place. Dearest of all I love you utterly —

I am your

Tig.

MS ATL. *LKM* I. 10–12; *LJMM*, 19–21.

[1] Francis Carco's flat near Notre-Dame on the Ile de la Cité, overlooking the Seine, which he had made available to KM in his absence.

[2] The bust of the poet Paul Verlaine in the Jardin du Luxembourg is by Auguste de Niederhäusern, called Niederhäusern-Rodo (1863–1913).

[3] Two Zeppelins had flown over Paris the previous night, dropping incendiary bombs on the rue Dulong and the rue des Dames, in the 17[e] arrondissement, near the railway yards.

[4] The Closerie des Lilas, on the boulevard du Montparnasse.

[5] Rudyard Kipling's *Plain Tales from the Hills* (1888) was translated into French in 1906.

[6] In October 1913 Murry had completed a long poem, published by the Hogarth Press in 1919, called *The Critic in Judgment*. KM seems to be confusing its title with Byron's *The Vision of Judgment* (1822), and her memory of stanza LVII:

Upon the verge of space, about the size
   Of half-a-crown, a little speck appear'd
(I've seen a something like it in the skies
   In the Aegean, ere a squall); it near'd,
And, growing bigger, took another guise;
   Like an aerial ship it tack'd, and steer'd; . . .

[7] Beatrice Hastings was living in Montmartre, at 13 rue Norvins, 18[e]. The modernist poet Max Jacob (1876-1944) was close to her and her artist friends.

[8] The Italian painter Amedeo Modigliani (1884-1920), whom she called 'Dedo', had until recently been Beatrice Hastings's lover. Pierre Sichel argued in his 1967 biography, *Modigliani* (287), that the painter's successor with Hastings could not have been Picasso, who was then living at 5 rue Schoelcher in Montparnasse and thus was not 'close by', but was, rather, an Italian sculptor, Alfredo Pina. In *LJMM* (20), Murry printed the name simply as 'P'.

[9] Perhaps while KM was staying in Paris the previous month, on her way to visit Carco at Gray.

To Francis Carco, [c. 21 March 1915][1]

[13 quai aux Fleurs]

C'était très curieux. J'ai entendu les pas qui courent vite sur le quai, puis la sonnerie de *Garde à vous!* Un peu de temps ensuite, on entendait les moteurs des zeppelins qui semblent dire: do-do, do-do, mille fois, comme pour vous rassurer et vous mentir au même moment. Mais, ce qui me plaisait surtout, c'était la nuit dans toutes les maisons quand on a ouvert les persiennes et la vue de toutes les personnes par la fenêtre. C'était comme un rêve. J'ai pensé que toutes ces personnes ont, subite, l'idée de voler.[2]

MS lacking. Carco 1938, 198-9.

[1] Although KM assured Murry that Carco no longer interested her, she continued to correspond amicably with him. A reply to this letter, dated 26 Mar 1915 (ATL) and signed 'Marguerite Bombard', as Carco continued the game of false stories and *noms-de-plume*, urged her again, 'Venez donc nous voir. Maman en serait enchantée.'

[2] (Translation)
It was very curious. I heard steps running on the quai, then the alarm blaring *Take cover*! A little while later we could hear the motors of the zeppelins which seemed to say: do-do, do-do, a thousand times, as if at once to reassure you and to deceive you. But what pleased me most was the darkness in all the houses when they opened the shades and the sight of all the people at the windows. It was like a dream. I thought that everyone, quite suddenly, was going to fly.

To J. M. Murry, [22 March 1915]

[13 quai aux Fleurs]
monday afternoon.

D. Bogey

I have just had your first letter — But won't you have a little more money this week from the Westminster? And if you simply haven't enough to buy the necessities can't you go to Lawrence until a cheque comes — or is that impossible — I am frightfully sorry about all this and the curtains — what misery! Has Beatrice [Campbell] got a pair she could *lend* you for the time being? I suppose all my suggestions sound silly and beside the mark, darling — of course the thing to do would be to have a band of the green lining material put down the outside of each curtain — Make Beatrice find you a little machinist. She would do it for almost nothing. The green stuff is ordinary casement cloth from Warings.[1] About the gas stove — they always take 8 to 10 days. I suppose you can buy *fish* & cook it on the primus alright — can't you? *Dont live* on sardines.

My precious, how hideous it all sounds. I read your letter and a very sweet big dropping rain fell on the pages all the while — I wonder if things are better — I wish I knew how much the furniture had cost to come to Elgin Crescent.[2] Perhaps it would be a good plan to get Rose to send by Collins another chair or two & the round table as an *odd table*. I do not know exactly what else to suggest. Keep me posted with whatever news you can — Your letter has dried me up — Nothing has happened here that will fit in with it at all — it all sounds "silly" — my news and of no earthly importance.

Ive read a book by Rachilde. 'L'Heure Sexuelle' — She is a fascinating creature far more interesting than *Colette* the *master*.[3] She started me off with a leap this morning. Now I am on my way to tea with Beatrice — a pain d'epice (only half one at 40) under my arm. But oh, what a horrible state of things in London with you — No, Ill recover from it and I would a million times rather that you told me than that you remained silent.[4]

Did you get a letter from me posted at Victoria? Perhaps the gas man took it.

No, I stop writing. All my nerves are up in arms. Damn this bloody money! I wont even say that I kiss you — you don't want me to —

Tig.

MS ATL. *LJMM*, 21-2.

[1] Waring & Gillow, decorators and furnishers, 8-11 Pall Mall East.

[2] i.e. from Rose Tree Cottage to the flat Murry was preparing for them at 95 Elgin Crescent, Notting Hill.

[3] Rachilde was the pen name of Marguerite Vallette (1860-1953), a prolific writer who, with her husband, established *Le Mercure de France*, a literary review associated with the Symbolist movement. Her *L'Heure sexuelle* was published in 1898. The novelist and autobiographer Sidonie-Gabrielle Colette (1873-1954), first woman president of the Académie Goncourt, began to publish her 'Claudine' books in 1900.

[4] A letter from Murry on 20 Mar 1915 (ATL) had complained about buying furniture, and how much it cost.

To S. S. Koteliansky, 22 March 1915

my address
{
Katy Mansfield
13 Quai aux Fleurs
La Cité
Paris
}

22 iii 1915

Dear Kotilianski,

Write me a letter when you feel inclined to — will you? I am staying here for a while instead of at the rooms in London. I understood you that weekend at the Lawrences for I have been like that myself. It is a kind of paralysis that comes of living alone + to oneself and it is really painful. I was silly and unsympathetic for Lawrence could not understand it because he has never felt it and I should have been wiser. But come quite alive again this spring — will you? I do not know how it is in London just now but here the very fact of walking about in the air makes one feel that flowers and leaves are dropping from your hair and from your fingers. I would write you a long letter but I am afraid you cannot read my handwriting. Tell me if you can and then I will. Yes, write to me here —

The nights are full of stars and little moons and big zeppelins — very exciting. But England feels far far away — just a little island with a cloud resting on it. Is it still there?

With love to you
Kissienka.

MS BL. *LKM* I. 12-13.

To J. M. Murry, [22 March 1915]

[13 quai aux Fleurs]
Monday night.

Dear Bogey,

When I wrote to you this afternoon I was not a nice girl — I know — Now, sitting writing to you by the light of a candil — with the whole house so quiet & closed and all the people in the cellars — I am sorry. The trumpets sounded about an hour ago. All the lights are out — except one on the bridge — very far and one by the police station at the corner. I have been standing at the open window — search lights sweep the sky. They are very lovely, lighting up one by one the white clouds. Now and then someone passes, or a cart all

dark gallops by. When the alarm sounded the sirens & fire whistles
& motors all answered. I was in the street — and in a moment or two
it was almost pitch dark — just here and there a flicker as someone
lighted a cigarette. When I arrived at the Quai aux Fleurs & saw all
the people grouped in the doorways and when people cried out
"n'allez pas comme ca dans la rue" I was really rather thrilled. The
concierge, all the house and an obscure little old man who is always
on the scene on every occasion asked me if I would 'descendre' but
I hate the idea & I came up — of course all the gas was turned off
and hung out of the window. It was extremely terrifying suddenly —
in fact (prosaic!) I was nearly sick! But after that the wonderful
things happening & especially a conversation between a man at a
fifth floor window and a thin man on the quai got me over my
mal d'estomac — Those two men talking — their voices in the dark
and the things they said are unforgettable — also — a fool who came
along the quai whistling his hands in his pockets and as big drops of
rain fell shouted with a laugh — "Mais ils seraient mouillés — ces
oiseaux des canailles." The rain — the dark, the silence & the voices
of the 2 men — the beauty of the river and the houses that seemed
to be floating on the water — Ah, Jack!

As I wrote that more bugles sounded. Again I ran into the bedroom with the lamp, again opened the window. A big motor passed
— a man in front blowing a trumpet — you heard from far & near
the voices raised. "C est fini?" "Fini, alors?" The few people in the
street ran blindly after the motor & then stopped — I went on the
landing with my big rusty key to put on the gas again, because its
cold and I wanted a fire. The little man came up the stairs & of
course I couldn't find the letter or the number and of course he
knew all about it. "Attendez — attendez. Voulez-vous allez voir si
le gaz prend". He was far greater fool than I — but I mercied him
bien & managed it myself. These raids after all are *not* funny. They
are extremely terrifying and one feels such a horror of the whole
idea of the thing. It seems so cruel and senseless — and then, to glide
over the sky like that and hurl a bomb — n'importe où — is diabolic
— and doesn't bear thinking about. (There go the trumpets again &
the sirens & the whistles. Another scare!) All over again. At B's
[Beatrice Hastings's] this afternoon there arrived "du monde"
including a very lovely young woman — married & *curious* — blonde
— passionate — We danced together. I was still so angry about the
horrid state of things.

(Oh God — its all off again!) I opened the shutters — the motors
flew by sounding the alarm — I cant talk about the tea party tonight.
At any rate it isn't worth it really. It ended in a great row. I enjoyed
it in a way, but Beatrice was very impossible — she must have drunk

nearly a bottle of brandy & when at 9 o'clock I left & refused either
to stay any longer or to spend the night [t]here she flared up in a
fury & we parted for life again — It seemed *so* utter rubbish in the
face of all this — now. A very decent and pleasant man saw me home
happily. Otherwise I think I might have been sitting in a Y.M.C.A.
until this moment — it was so very dark. But a lovely evening — very
soft with rain falling. B. makes me sad tonight. I never touched
anything but soda water & so I really realised how the other people
played on her drunkenness & she was so half charming and such an
utter fool.

It is raining fast now on the shutters — a sound I love to hear —
England feels so far away at this moment — oh very far — and I am
quite suddenly sad for you. I want you as I write — and my love
rises, my darling & fills my breast. Perhaps tomorrow in your letter
you may sound happier. Oh, my little lover, my dear dearest I shall
write no more now — I must go to bed & drink some hot milk pour
me faire dormir tout de suite.

Goodnight, my heart's treasure
Tig.

MS ATL. *LKM* I. 13-15; *LJMM*, 22-4.

To J. M. Murry, [22–24 March 1915]

[13 quai aux Fleurs]

I don't know what you think of yourself but *I* think youre a little
pig of a sneak. Not a letter — not a sign — not a copy of the Saturday
Westminster [Gazette] — plainly nothing. Why are you so horrid —
or is it the post? Ill put it down to the post & forgive you, darling.
A baby in arms could play with me today — The weather is so warm
Im sitting with the windows wide open & nothing but a thin blouse
on (in a way of speaking.) All the trees are popping and the air
smells of mignonette. Big open barges full of stones are being towed
by black & red beetles up the river — the steering men lean idly —
legs crossed — you know their way — and the water froths against
the bows. The carts passing make a merry jingle and the concierge
has put a pink hyacinth in her window. Bogey, (Im a fool when I'm
alone. I turn into a little child again) There is a woman on the opposite side of the river. She sits with her back against a tree her legs
stretched out in front of her, combing her long brown hair. To this
side and to that she bends and then with that charming, weary
gesture she throws her head back and draws the comb all the length

of it. If I were near enough I am sure I would hear her singing. The idle time of the year is coming, Jaggle, when you can sit outside with a piece of bread & butter on your knee and watch it frisle. (How do you spell that?) I felt very flat when I bought La Patrie at midday & found that no zeppelins had arrived after all. Unfortunately I had already posted your letter[1] so you can laugh at me. This afternoon Im going to write about last night. Ill send it to you. Do what you will with it. Send it somewhere — will you please? I don't want *anything* about Paris to go to the New Age — I must not make daisy chains in Biggy B's meadows.[2]

I dreamed last night about Bowden — I was at an opera with you sitting on a converted railway carriage seat & I heard Bowden talking of his wife to an american lady. Then he saw me & I went up and spoke to him. Just as I was saying I never had and never could love him *etc.* Mrs Saleeby appeared & seeing us together she came up to me and kissed my hands and said "Oh Katherine I always felt such love for you — & now I know why" — & she pressed me to her & said "Caleb is at home digging in the garden"[3] This so touched me that I nearly sacrifiged myself on the spot but I knew you were waiting for me in a little house in South Kensington   the opera had disappeared & I was sitting on the stump of a cut tree & Bowden leant against it toying with a top hat — so I pressed his hand awfully kindly, picked up a very large rabbit that was watching us, with twitching ears and walked away, saying to Bowden over my shoulder — "there is always a beginning and an ending George." But he burst into tears and called — "Ah, my dear — *dont dont* be so wonderful" "If that is the case" thought I, "Im wasting myself. I shall take some inexpensive but good dancing lessons." Then I woke up.

Next day. After all I never wrote a thing. Yesterday I began reading & read on until past midnight. There are so many books of the "young men" here & I glanced through a number to get an impression. Heavens! What a set of lollipops! Really I did not come across *one* that counted. Upon the same stage with the same scenery the same properties, to the same feeble little tune one after one pipes his piece and the audience being composed of a number of young men and females exactly like himself, with precisely the same burning desire to feel the limelight on their faces, applaud and flatter and cherish. You can't believe they were not all littered at a breath. Funny if it weren't so damned ugly — and the trouble is that nobody will even kick their little derrières for them because they have[n't] got em to kick — seulement "deux globes d'ivoire"! Afterwards I began to read Stendhal's '*Rouge et le Noir.*' You can imagine how severe and noble it seemed and does still by morning seem to me. But what I feel most deeply is — how *tragic* a great work of art appears —

all these young 'nez-au-ventisists' have their place and their meaning
in this world but I seemed to see Stendahl with his ugly face & pot
belly and little pig's legs confined within a solitary tower, writing his
book and gazing through the window chink at a few lonely stars.
(Dont whistle!)

I must go off to the post. I could write to you all day. It is raining
fast and my lung hates the weather. I press your hand very hard
Jaggle — I believe in you and I love you profoundly today.

Goodbye for now, my darling

Tig.

MS ATL. *LKM* I. 15–17.

[1] Presumably that of 'Monday night', 22 March.

[2] Beatrice Hastings's impressions of Paris, strongly pro-war in their tone, were appearing
regularly in the *New Age* under the name of 'Alice Morning'.

[3] It was at the home of the popular-science writer, Dr. Caleb Saleeby, and his wife
Monica (see p. 155, n.5) that KM met George Bowden in the winter of 1908-9.

To J. M. Murry, [25 March 1915]

[13 quai aux Fleurs]
Thursday morning.

My own Bogey —

Yesterday I had your letters at last. But first I *never* got a cross
postcard about the sofa: you never mentioned it until this letter.
Here are the directions. Take a bus to Blandford Street which is off
Baker Street. Walk down it and turn into South Street. King has got
a filthy little shop with a sewing machine in the window and some
fly blown cards which say "Loose Covers". More than that I can't
tell you myself. Have you written to him and enclosed a stamped
envelope? If not, I would do that *at once*.

You seem to have done perfect wonders with the rooms — the
carpentering job I saw and heard as plain as if Id been there — to
the very sand papering. All the things are floating in my brain on a
sea of blue ripolin.[1] I feel those rooms will be lovely. If Frieda is
there ask her about the curtains. She can sew even though I don't
think shed have ideas. I saw such jolly low stools yesterday — very
firm with rush seats 1.75. I wish I could send you 2 or 3. They
are nice.

I had a great day yesterday. The Muses descended in a ring like
the angels on the Botticelli Nativity roof — or so it seemed to
"humble" little Tig and I fell into the open arms of my first novel.[2] I
have finished a huge chunk but I shall have to copy it on thin paper

for you. I expect you will think I am a dotty when you read it — but — tell me what you think — won't you? Its queer stuff. Its the spring makes me write like this. Yesterday I had a fair wallow in it and then I shut up shop & went for a long walk along the quai — very far. It was dusk when I started — but dark when I got home. The lights came out as I walked — & the boats danced by. Leaning over the bridge I suddenly discovered that one of those boats was exactly what I want my novel to be — Not big, almost 'grotesque' in shape I mean perhaps *heavy* — — with people rather dark and seen strangely as they move in the sharp light and shadow and I want bright shivering lights in it and the sound of water. (This, my lad, by way of uplift) But I *think* the novel will be alright. Of course it is not what you could call serious — but then I cant be just at this time of year & Ive always felt a spring novel would be lovely to write.

Today I must go to Cooks with my last goldin sovereign in my hand to be changed — I am getting on alright as regards money & being very careful. Cooked vegetables for supper at 20 the demi livre are a great find and I drink trois sous de lait a day. This place is perfect for working.

I read your letter yesterday in the Luxembourg gardens. An old gentleman seeing my tender smiles offered me half his umbrella & I found that it was raining but as he had on a pair of tangerine coloured eye glasses I declined. I thought he was a Conrad spy. My own dear darling — what are you doing about a bed? Surely not that vile sofa all these nights!

I have adopted Stendhal. Every night I read him now & first thing in the morning. This is a vague letter but it carries love and love and kisses from your

Tig.

MS ATL. *LKM* I. 17-18; *LJMM*, 25-7.

[1] A proprietary name for a make of enamel paint.
[2] KM had begun writing her long story *The Aloe*, which she eventually revised and altered to become *Prelude*. The *Mystic Nativity* by Sandro Botticelli is in the National Gallery, London.

To J. M. Murry, [26 March 1915]

[13 quai aux Fleurs]
Friday evening.

Dearest darling,

I am in such a state of worry and suspense that I can't write to you tonight or send you anything. When I came back from the fruit-less search for letters the concierge began a long story about an

Alsatian in the house who had received yesterday a four page letter for the name of Bowden. Another came today, said she: I gave it back to the postman. I literally screamed — I have *written* this name for her & she'd utterly forgotten it thinking of me only as Mansfield — Since then Ive simply rushed from post office to office — The Alsatian is out: Im waiting for her & the postman now. My heart dies in my breast with terror at the thought of a letter of yours being lost — I simply don't exist. I suppose I exaggerate — but Id plunge into the Seine — or lie on a railway line rather than lose a letter. You know Bogey, my heart is simply crying all the time and I am frightened, desolate, useless for anything.

Oh, my precious — my beloved little Jag, forgive Tig such a silly scrawl — But Life ought not to do such things to you & to me — I could *kill* the concierge — yes, with pleasure — "Une lettre d'Angleterre dans un couvert bleu" —

Courage! But at this moment I am simply running as fast as I can and crying my loudest into your arms —

I will write you properly tomorrow. This is just to say that I love you and that you are the breath of life to me

Tig.

MS ATL. *LJMM*, 27.

To J. M. Murry, [27 March 1915]

[13 quai aux Fleurs]
Saturday.

My Bogey, my little King,

Im doing the unpardonable thing — writing in pencil, but Im in bed still and having breakfast, so please forgive. I kept my eye upon the hole of the door until 12 oclock last night when the Alsatian deigned to ascend. As she did *not* know this flat was occupied she had a pretty fright at sight of me in the inky darkness — but after a long disappearance when I decided to hit her if she had not got it she appeared. V'la! At the same time — carrying her little lamp and all wrapped up in a shawl & wonderfully beautiful I thought — she put her hand on my arm — "Attandez!" she said — & disappeared & brought me back a pink hyacinth growing in a pot — "Ca sant de la vraie fleur" said she — Then I came in and read your Monday night letter — I read it and then I read it again — Then I dropped it into my heart and it made ever bigger circles of love — flowing over and over until I was quite healed of that torment of waiting. I love you —

you know. I love you with every inch of me — You are wonderful — you are my perfect lover. There is nobody but you. Hold me, Bogey, when I write those words, for I am in your arms, your darling head in my hands & I am kissing — kissing —

The rooms sound lovely. I hope by now the sofa is there. I hope another cheque has come. The moment Kay sends my money I will send some to you.

I think Orage wants kicking.[1] Just that — Of course what is so peculiarly detestable is his habit of lying *so* charmingly — his "I should be delighted, Katherina," rings in my ears. Beatrice I have not seen since her famous party. Its an ugly memory. I am glad it happened so soon — I think next morning she must have felt horribly ashamed of herself for she was drunk and jealous and everybody knew it. I am thankful that I stood firm — I feel so utterly superior to her now —

To tell you the truth, both of them are bitter because they have nearly known love and broken and we know love and are happy — Bogey, *really* and *truly* how happy we are. Now I am giving you all sorts of little hugs and kisses and now big ones and long long kisses — —

No — I really *must* get up. What a farce it is to be alone in bed in the spring when you are alive —

Tig.

MS ATL. *LJMM*, 28.

[1] In a letter of 22 Mar 1915 (ATL) Murry had complained of how badly he was sleeping, and that Orage, of the *New Age*, had been rude to him.

To J. M. Murry, [28 March 1915]

[13 quai aux Fleurs]
Saturday.

Dearest one,

I am really worried about money for you. Will you have got another cheque by now? I do hope to heaven that you have. I always feel you become wicked and don't spend enough on food if you're hard up & you are really rather dependent on good meals — if you only knew it. I shall be eating chestnut buds if Kay doesn't send me my money sometime next week. I don't know how money goes — I keep a strict account (one of those amazing fourfold affairs in which we are so expert) and every penny is reckoned — and yet, Bogey, it seems to fly. A franc in Paris is really 8d in England just now. But don't think I am complaining, because I am not — merely stating my case — & I know my money *will* come next week. I have asked Kay to send it through Cooks. It is the simplest way and really the post offices are merely a collection of stools and stamp paper. Yesterday, after I had nearly cried through a grating about my lost letter, the man suggested brightly, cleaning his nails on an old nib, 'perhaps the postman *threw it away*'. . .

I wanted to tell you about a nice time I had on Thursday night. At about seven I left the house buttoned up in my black & white coat & went for a walk behind the Hotel de Ville. I found most curious places — and I found at last a little market where every third body was either frying or eating polish pancakes. The air smelled of them and of 'petits gris' — tiny snails which you bought by the shovelful. It began to rain — Under an old stone arch 3 hags wrapped in black shawls were standing — their hands crossed over their bellies. At their feet there lay three little baskets of herbs — Dry twigs — withered bundles and tiny packets. Their heads were raised, watching the drizzle and the green light from a lantern fell on their faces. All of them were talking — whether to each other or to themselves you could not tell, for their voices did not pause. It sounded like a song. It was one of the most ancient things I have ever seen or heard. Having a besoin to faire mon service I went into one of those little 10c places. In the passage stood an immense fat and rosy old market woman, her skirts breast high, tucking her chemise into her flannel drawers and talking to an equally fat old ouvrier — who began to help her arrange her affairs, saying as he tugged and buttoned 'mais tu sais, *ma petite* tu ne peux pas sortir comme ça.' I went on much further, then down an alley on to a quai — There was a bird shop there. The window was flying with canaries and java sparrows and green love birds and white doves and parrots. Outside the shop two little girls were standing, their arms round each others necks. One had rings in her ears and the other wore a bangle — They were watching the birds and eating an orange between them quarter by quarter — The birdseller was a dark young man with long black moustaches and narrow eyes . . . I don't know why but I had a curious sensation that I was in a dream and that I had seen all this years and ages ago.

Finally it poured so with rain that I hunted and I hollered and found a café — very poor — the people eating — chauffeurs and ragbags of people. But a woman came in — skinny, enceinte, but very alive — and a curious enough boy followed her. They were so wet that the woman said "faut danser". And they danced — As far as I could make out this is what they sang as they turned round and round — the people who ate banged with the bread on the table and the plates clattered —

Si'l en reste un bout ce sera pour la servante
Si'l en reste pas d'tout elle se tapera sur l'ventre
Et zon zon zon Lisette, ma Lisette
Et zon zon zon Lisette, ma Lison.

All the while my hat dripped over the table. I kept taking if off and shaking it on the floor but when the boy was greeted by a very smart young friend who came to my table and said 'je veux manger une belle fricassée avec vous, ma fleur,' I paid and ran away.

The concierge has brought me another letter, written on Wednesday night. My darling, if you write me letters like that Ill not be able to bear my love. I simply adore you. But that old *beast* upstairs must be poisoned, Jaggle. Don't give him another crumb. I *implore* you. I think you were very brave all the same. Im glad about the curtains & glad Kot came. Floryan is rather a hateful idea.[1] No, you won't find anything of mine in the New Age because I won't send them a line. I think Orage is too ugly. No, *don't send me any money* — I haven't the need of it.

Heres a confession. I cannot write if all is not well with us — not a line. I do write in my own way through you. After all it is love of you now that makes me write & absolutely deep down when I write well it is love of you that makes me see and feel. You darling — you darling. Je te veux.

Tig.

MS ATL. *LJMM*, 29-31.

[1] In his letter of 24 Mar 1915 (ATL), Murry described an old man who lived upstairs in Elgin Crescent, who kept coming down and bothering him, asking him for fuel, and was curtly dealt with. The same letter mentions that he had met Floryan Sobieniowski accidentally, and given him their new address — 'I felt that it was no use having a grudge against him.'

To J. M. Murry, [28 March 1915]

[13 quai aux Fleurs]
Sunday

Jack, I shant hide what I feel today. I woke up with you in my breast and on my lips — Jack I love you terribly today — the whole world is gone — there is only you — I walk about, dress, eat, write but all the while I am *breathing* you. Time and again I have been on the point of telegraphing you that I am coming home as soon as Kay sends my money. It is still possible that I shall.

> Jack Jack I want to come back
> And to hear the little ducks go
> Quack! Quack! Quack!

Life is too short for our love even though we stayed together every moment of all the years. I cannot think of you. Our life — our darling life — you, my treasure — everything about you —
No, no — no — Take me quickly into your arms. Tig is a tired girl and she is crying.
I want you — I want you. Without you life is nothing.

Your woman
Tig.

MS ATL. *LJMM*, 31.

To S. S. Koteliansky, [29 March 1915]

[13 quai aux Fleurs]
Monday.

Kotiliansky, dear friend

I am extremely fond of you this afternoon. I wish you would walk into this café now and sit opposite me and say — "do not look at these people; they are extremely foolish." But no, you will not; you are dancing on the downs with the fair Barbara[1] and Kissienka is forgotten. No, I won't come to any of your weddings. You will marry some woman who will show me the door — because I come and sing in the street you live in my beautiful russian dress (given me by my anonymous friend) and you dare to look out of the window. I have just finished Two Frightful Hours trying to buy a corset — not really a corset but a kind of belt — I have spent every penny that I haven't got upon an affair of violet silk which is so exquisite that I lament my lonely life. .Now Frieda would say that I was being *very* wicked, but you understand — don't you? All the while I write I am looking at you and laughing a little and you are saying to me, "really, you are a *deplorable* creature!"

Your letter was given to me and I read it while I was half awake — when in bed — and after I had read it I lay smoking and watching the sun dance on the ceiling — and I wondered why on earth I *had* fled away and could not find any answer. At any rate I can tell you frankly that the illness that I had in England and longed to be cured of — is quite gone for ever — — I believe it was my "heart" after all, you know, but not the kind of heart that Dr. Eder[2] punches. Shut your eyes a minute. Do you feel frightfully happy — just now — just at this minute. I do — I should like to lie in the grass beside a big river and look up at the sun until the sun went down — and then go slowly home to a little house hidden in a ring of poplar trees — carrying a large bunch of daisies. Do you see this house? It is a new one — just built at this moment — it is in some place very far away and there are woods near, and this river. A tiny little balcony has a table on it with a red and white cloth and a jar of clovers — and we sit there in the evenings, smoke and drink tea. Now *you* can build a little of it.

To tell you the absolute truth a friend of mine is coming to London at the end of this week. (Do not tell anybody.) Her name is Katherine Mansfield and if she should ring up the Bureau on Friday — answer her. Will you?

Yes, Kotiliansky, you are really one of my people — we can afford to be quite free with each other — I know.

My dear, it is so hot in this café that if Mrs Eder were here she would have taken half a dozen sun baths! Yours with love

Kissienka.

MS BL. *LKM* I. 20-1.

¹ Barbara Low (1877-1955), an early Freudian psychoanalyst in England, author of *Psycho-Analysis: A Brief Outline of the Freudian Theory* (1920).
² Montagu David Eder (1865-1936), also a Freudian, was married to Barbara Low's sister Edith. A frequent contributor to the *New Age*, he later became a leader in the Zionist movement.

To S. S. Koteliansky, [4 May 1915]

[95 Elgin Crescent,¹ Notting Hill]

Kotiliansky, my dear,

I did not tell you all the truth last night. When you asked me if I was writing and I said 'yes' it was not quite true. I *cannot* write my book living in these two rooms. It is impossible — and if I do not write this book I shall die. So I am going away tomorrow to finish it. Then I promise to come back shorn of all my wickedness, dear friend. It is agony to go, but I must go. Jack wonderfully understands. Write to me, will you? You can address the letters to 'Mansfield' — the concierge knows that name — Tell me about your eyes; tell me you are not so depressed; let me hear any more news that you have of Olga.² I will write to you often — write to me *often often* — for I shall be very lonely I know. Goodbye, just for now. I press your hands *tightly*. Goodbye. You are so dear to me.

Kissienka

MS BL. *LKM* I. 7.

¹ The new flat Murry had taken for them, to which KM returned on the last day of March 1915.
² Koteliansky's friend or relative Olga is unidentified.

To J. M. Murry, [6–7 May 1915]

[13 quai aux Fleurs, Paris IVe] [1]

Jeudi.

I cannot tell you how beautiful this place is by daylight. The trees on the island are in full leaf. I had quite forgotten the life that goes on *within* a tree — how it flutters and almost plumes itself and how the topmost branches tremble and the lowest branches of all swing lazy.

It is very warm today. All the windows are wide open. From early morning people have passed along the quai carrying lilac . . little stout men, the bunch upside down, looped to a finger by a knotted string — young girls carrying it along the arm — little children with their faces quite buried — and old fat women clasping the branches — just a frill of flower showing above their bosoms. I ran out at seven to buy some oranges. Already the shops were open. Already the sausages were looped round a lilac jar — the tailoress bent over the machine had a piece in her bodice — (I shant tell you any more because you won't believe me. Its everywhere.) Ill tell you where I saw it first yesterday.

Jag: Oh, Tig, don't *harp* so!

Tig: Just this, and then I wont. But we drew up alongside a hospital train. From my window I could see into the saloon. There were pallet beds round the walls — the men covered to the chin never moved an inch. They were just white faces with a streak of hair on top. A doctor, stout and ruddy with a fine blond beard stood at the window drying his hands and whistling. All round the walls of the car kind female hands had placed big bunches of purple and white lilac. What lovely lilac! said the people in the train with me. "Look! Look how fine it is!" The wounded men did not matter a rap. (Then came a cry from the étage above. Fermez vos persiennes s'il vous plait! But I wasn't in time. Whether the lady sheared a sheep outside her window or merely shook her bedroom mat I do not know. A little of both. Damn her.)

And now there comes a little handcart with 3 babies in it and a quantity of newspapers. It is dragged by two other infants — men of about 8 or nine. They stopped outside here, let down a kind of false leg which steadied the cart and strolled over to the lavatory — talking — unbuttoning their breeches and shouting to the babies to keep tranquille. But alas! No sooner had they disappeared than the infants with screams of rage began throwing the papers into the wet gutter. Back rushed their lords and now they are picking up the muddy papers and the culprits hang their heads over the side of the wagon like people about to be guillotined — — terribly chastened.

Next morning. I went out to lunch yesterday at a very good little brasserie — overlooking Place du Chatelet — *and* cheap — quite as cheap as Chartier and frequented only by old men and a priest or two. Afterwards, like a fool I took the métro to the Palais Royale & went to look for Smiths to see if they had the Golden Bowl.[2] Oh, that walk — it stretched for miles — and each moment I thought it was going to end. My leg finally trailed after me like a tired child and they had not got the Golden Bowl — so I came home and worked and did not go out again. We had the thunder last night and today it is silvery and now and then some rain falls. I had a horrible dream about Lesley Moore last night & then I dreamed that you came up here to see me dressed in khaki — very handsome and happy.

Tomorrow I will send you some work, darling —

I don't want to complain, Bogey, but I do think my leg is a bit off, don't you? It hurts like billy-o today — Goodbye for now, my dearest dear

Tig.

MS ATL. *LKM* I. 22-3; *LJMM*, 31-3.

[1] KM returned to Paris, for the third time this year, on 5 May 1915.
[2] W.H. Smith & Son, booksellers, had a shop at 248 rue de Rivoli. Henry James's *The Golden Bowl* was published in 1904.

To J. M. Murry, [? 7 May 1915]

[13 quai aux Fleurs]

If you lean over the Pont St. Louis you look down on to a little court which is called Port de L'hotel de ville. It is a pleasant cobbled square with poplars and lime trees growing against the wall. Where it slopes down to the river there are 2 upturned boats. An old man in a straw hat sat by one of them today tapping it over with a hammer and over the other two little boys wriggled, dabbling their hands in the water. There were some mattresses propped against the wall in the sun and a wooden frame set up covered with a square of red linen. An old woman in a lilac print dress with a white band over her head and under her chin was tossing grey flock and feathers on the red linen square. An immense heap of them beside her was lifted and shaken and gathered up for her by a younger woman in black wearing a cotton bonnet. It was very warm in the sun and the flock and feathers were so dusty the two women coughed and sneezed as they worked, but they seemed very happy. I watched until the mattress was filled and folded over like a pie crust. Then the younger woman took a little camp stool and sat down with a needle and thread, stitching and the old one replaced the "buttons" in the cover with a long long needle like a skewer. Now and again the two little boys ran up to have their noses blown, or the old man sang out something and they sang back — — —

Whose fault is it that we are so isolated — that we have no real life — that everything apart from writing and reading is "felt" to be a waste of time.

I walked on today and came to a garden behind Notre Dame. The pink and white flowering trees were so lovely that I sat down on a bench. In the middle of the garden there was a grass plot and a marble basin. Sparrows taking their baths turned the basin into a fountain and pigeons walked through the velvety grass pluming their feathers. Every bench and every chair was occupied by a mother or a nurse or a grandfather and little staggering babies with spades and buckets made mud pies or filled their buckets with fallen chestnut flowers or threw their grandfathers caps on to the forbidden grass plot. And then there came a chinese nurse trailing 2 babies. Oh, she was a funny little thing in her green trousers and black tunic, a small turban clamped to her head. She sat down with her darning and she kept up a long bird like chatter all the time, blinking at the children and running the darning needle through her turban. But after I had watched a long time I realised I was in the middle of a dream. Why haven't I got a real "home", a real life — Why haven't I got a chinese nurse with green trousers and two babies who rush at me and clasp my knees — Im not a girl — Im a woman. I *want* things. Shall I ever have them? To write all the morning and then to get lunch over quickly and to write again in the afternoon & have supper and *one* cigarette together and then to be alone again until bed-time — and all this love and joy that fights for outlet — and all this life drying up, like milk, in an old breast. Oh, I want life — I want friends and people and a house. I want to give and to spend (the P.O. savings bank apart, darling.)[1]

Tig.

MS ATL. *LKM* I. 25-6.

[1] Murry's recent letters had referred often to money and the expenses of furnishing their new flat. On 5 May 1915 he told her, 'I can stick £2.10 in the bank almost immediately' (ATL).

To J. M. Murry, [8 May 1915]

[Café Biard, rue de Rivoli, Paris]
Saturday afternoon.

Boge darling

I shall write you my letter today in this Café Biard whither Ive come for shelter out of a terrific storm rain & thunder. Im soaked and my bones are in dismay already. It is the most absurd *rot* to have to think like an old pusson every time the rain falls — this is rheumatiz for a dead spit for me — But Im not sad dearest of all — I am only surprised at God — —

I am writing my book. Ca marche, ça va, ça se dessine — its good. Your letter this morning. Thank you my Bogey. Letters really arrive very quickly — I hope you had one from me today. I was glad to hear of the good cheque. How much does that mean for the Bank seven quid I make it — Get your Sickerts[1] framed when you can to show yourself what a good & rich boy you are. Besides I'd love to turn up my eyes at them when I come home.

The conscription scare is only a false alarm — isn't it? Of course the Daily Mail shrieks it each day — but I don't like the idea of even a tentative Times leader. Tell me all you know — the idea is hideous. I wish to God I hadn't dreamed of you in khaki — but perhaps you were thinking & your thoughts reached me. But they would never make you go would they! Ill say no more Betsy until I hear.[2]

Last night I woke to hear torrential rain. I got up with a candle & made the shutters firm — and that awful line of Geo. Meredith's sang in my head "And Welcome Water Spouts that Bring Fresh Rain".[3] Then I dreamed that I went to stay with the sisters Bronte who kept a boarding house called the Bronte Institut — *pain*fully far from the railway station and all the way there through heather. It was a sober place with linoleum on the stairs. Charlotte met me at the door & said "Emily is lying down" — Kot, I found was also there taking supper. He broke an orange into a bowl of bread and milk. "Russian fashion" said he, "try it. Its very good —" But I refrained. Then the bell tinkled and the concierge gave me your letter. How can all these people afford cabs. Even girls in pinafores without hats are jumping into fiacres. I cannot afford even the principle — I found a photograph of Willy [W.L. George] today — he looked like Edward VII in spirits of wine — an awful fat-head — Of course he has got *some*thing but he's terribly small beer, I'm afraid — *And* a snob *and* heartless. So I feel. Frank Harris is writing Pro Germanics in the Continental Times. He is roaring down England and roaring up Germany.[4] I feel very disgusted. "And you?" (As they are always singing in Wagner's operas for a kick off.)

There goes Eve Balfour.[5] Yes, it is. No, it isn't. Yes, it is. No, it isn't. Alas, another case of mistaken identity, like the darkey who was asked why he stole the old lady's parrot & said "AAW Boss, Ah took it for a lark."

Jag: Tig, What a *fool* you are today.

Wig: But it wont stop raining & Im stuck, dearest & wondering if the waiter will flick me away next time he comes.

Tell me about your dinner party.

I shall have to face this music and "plunge" after all. It is extremely hot and muggy and airless.

Goodbye for now, my darling.

I am always your
Tig.

MS ATL. *LKM* I. 18-19; *LJMM*, 33-4.

[1] Etchings given to Murry by the artist Walter Sickert (1860-1942), who approved of his art criticism in the *Westminster Gazette*.

[2] Murry had written on 5 May 1915: 'I see from a "Times" leader today that there's a very good chance of conscription after all. I don't want to go very much; but if we all go — well, I won't grumble so much. But it's probably a false alarm. I do feel inclined to damn this silly old war.' (ATL.) Conscription by 'attesting', a method by which men declared their willingness to serve when called, was introduced in October 1915. Full conscription for all men of military age came in April of the following year. ('Betsy' was an affectionate and teasing term KM used with Murry, and also with Frederick Goodyear.)

[3] Cf. George Meredith, 'Earth and a Wedded Woman': 'And welcome waterspouts of blessed rain!'

[4] Frank Harris's war articles made him extremely unpopular, especially when his pieces from the New York *Sun* were published as a book, *England or Germany?*, in January 1915. The *Continental Times* was an English-language newspaper published in Berlin.

[5] Lady Eve Balfour, niece of the Conservative politician and former Prime Minister, A. J. Balfour.

To J. M. Murry, [8–9 May 1915]

[13 quai aux Fleurs]

Dear Bogey

The lamplighter is just going his rounds, but I am sitting in the dusk still — I have just come in from a small walk. I returned to the garden of Notre Dame — It was dusky already and the smell of the flowering trees a wonder to enjoy. I sat again on a bench. Hardly anybody was there; an old man on the other end of my bench kept up a buzzing in his beard and a few extremely wicked babies without any hope of bed played ball — just their heads and knees and flying hands to be seen. How black the tree stems were and how fine the leaves. They were like a tune given out in the bass with a wonderful running treble — and above the trees uprose Notre Dame in all its venerable beauty. Little birds flew among the towers — you know the little birds that always fly about ruins — Looking at them I wanted to write a sonnet — using as an image of old age & the thoughts of old age flying out and returning — the tower and the birds. I shall write it one day —

I have been writing my book all the afternoon. How good the fatigue is that follows after! Lovers are idling along the quai. They lean over the parapet and look at the dancing water and then they turn and kiss each other — and walk a few steps further arm in arm and then stop again and again kiss. It *is* rather the night for it, I must say.

The rain stopped after I had posted your letter today but it is still un temps très lourd — I bought a litre of white wine today for 45 (very good) and it is lying in a basin of water in the kitchen zinc. The butter and the milk sit on a brick outside the kitchen window. "*Some* summer" as a fool at the music hall would say.

Write to me as often as you can, my dear love. Of course no human being could compete with my effugions and well I knows it but alone in furrin parts is not the same as being even as alone as I realise you are in England — I wonder if Beatrice Hastings has maxed her jacob yet or if she flew to Italy with her Dado [Modigliani]. I am not really curious and I'll *never* seek to know.
Sunday morning.

I have just had your summer letter ± the D[*aily*] N[*ews*]. London does sound good, & the idea of drinking cider & then sitting in my special little garden[1] was very alluring. I know that garden better than any other in the world. I see it now as I write. But, for some strange reason I have always gone there to cry. I well remember one dreadful new years eve when I went there & sat on one of the benches crying into a little black velvet muff with blue ribbons (Lesley had it after) and an awful old woman with a jet bonnet watched a long time & then she sighed & said "well, that's 'ow it is, my dear."

No, dearest darling, the Lawrences of course do not understand.[2] I HOPE you posted the letter to them I gave you. What became of your dinner party? I mean with Muirhead Bone[3] — F[rancis] C[arco] as you know simply doesn't exist for me —

I found last night in the letter rack a copy of that song 'Dodo' — It is called "Idylle Rouge" — I send you a verse and the refrain. I had got it all wrong. My work I'll send when its copied out — A high, strange wind blows today, but the sun shines. I dream — oh, I dream so strangely here — There is half past 9 o'clock. I am still in my sprigged nighty. I must get up.

(Yes, I want you, too. I want to lean against you and laugh and forget Time and his jangling bell. Yes, I want to be your lover. Darling.

Tig.

(This goes on for verses of *Horrid Tragedy* — I'll sing it for you one day — It is really very 'pa' when sung.

> Quand on l'voyait
> On n'aurait pas dit
> A son air peu *bra va che*
> Que c'etait un dangereux bandit
> Un vrai chef d'*apach*es.
> C'est pour sa maitresse
> Qu cambriolait
> Pour n'pas qu'ell'fass la *no-ce*,
> Elle tremblait pour lui
> Car ell'l'adorait
> Et disait l'berçant comme un gos-se.

Refrain.

> Dodo, mon homm'
> Fais vit' dodo
> Tout pres d'ta mai-tresse
> Blotti dans mes bras
> T'oubliras bientôt
> Tes pensées mauvais's
> Bercé par ma tendr*esse*
> Serr' toi bien pres
> De moi — j'ai peur
> Qu'un jour. Tes caresses
> Ne vienn'nt a m' manquer
> J's'rais foll' de douleur
> Car je t'aime de tout mon coeur![4]

MS ATL. *LKM* I. 23-5; *LJMM*, 34-6.

[1] The Friday before Murry and Kot had drunk cider and then sat in Leicester Square.
[2] Lawrence and Frieda were convinced KM had returned to Paris to be with Carco.
[3] Muirhead Bone (1876-1953), a Scottish painter commissioned as a war artist.
[4] 'Idylle Rouge', words by Saint Gilles and Paul Gay, music by Georges Picquet. KM quotes from the song in the second part of 'An Indiscreet Journey'.

To Francis Carco, [c. 8 May 1915]

[13 quai aux Fleurs]

L'homme qui éclaire les lampes est venu avec sa petite étoile au bout d'une grande canne. Quand je vois ça, mon cœur tremble toujours, pour tous les soirs, dans toutes les grandes cités. [. . .] Deux jeune gens sont arrêtés sur le quai et, malgré le froid, en face du vent, un long oh! un tres long baiser . . . Et puis, ils sont disparu . . . oui . . . aussi vite que possible, comme si la maison brûle chez eux.[1]

MS lacking. Carco 1938, 185, 187.

[1] (Translation)
The man who lights the lamps has come with his little star at the end of a long road. When I see it my heart always trembles, for all the evenings, in all the great cities. [. . .] Two young people have stopped on the quai and, in spite of the cold, in the face of the wind, a long, oh! a very long kiss. . .And then, they are gone. . .yes. . .as quickly as possible, as if their house were burning down.

To J. M. Murry, [9–10 May 1915]

[13 quai aux Fleurs]
Sunday evening

Instead of having dinner today I ate some bread & drank some wine at home & went to a cinéma. It was almost too good. A detective drama, so well acted and so sharp and cruel with a horrible decor — the environs of Calais — Wickedness triumphed to everyone's great relief, for the hero, an apache called L'Fantôme was an admirable actor. And there was a girl there, mistress of 'Bébé' and 'le faux curé' two other apaches.[1] I wish you could have seen that girl act. She was very still and then her gestures *sprang* from her — Pale, you know. A little round head and a black dress. All the while the orchestra played a tango that we have heard before, a very 'troubling' tune. Before going in I walked up to the Luxembourg gardens — but the Sunday crowd, you know, the women mincing in their high boots like fowls in the wet and the shop walker men and the "Ah c'est beau" "dis — c'est joli" — c'est *très très* joli — "tout à fait beau." I felt exactly as though I were dead. It is very beautiful outside the window this afternoon. The wind shakes the trees so. There was a great excitement a few minutes ago. I saw the policeman before the station below suddenly stiffen & then at the bottom of the steps that lead on to the quai — you know where I mean — below here? — there came a grey little frog squirming in the grip of two gendarmes. They were evidently hurting him but my policeman flew to their aid. He got behind the man & suddenly thrust his hand

between the man's legs. You should have heard the yell he gave &
you should have seen the jerk that sent him forward — Life is a
funny business.

Now there are birds wheeling and flying in the air and the sky is
pink. It is evening — I have not spoken to anyone since Wednesday
except to say comment ça fait? or to say "oui, c'est bien terrible" to
the concierge — It is curious for one who has been much alone —
this *sinking back* into silence.

Monday. Oh, Bogey I haven't got a letter. The Daily News came & I
even looked for a little message on the inside of the wrapper. It is
ten o'clock. I shall start work and drown my disappointment. That
means no news of you until tomorrow and I love you. I love you

Tig.

I went out on the landing just now to get some water. The concierge was sweeping the stairs & the woman below me came out to
talk to her. "The little lady upstairs came in very late last night,"
said she. "Who". "La maitresse de Francis Carco," bawled the voice.
"No, she was not out at all — Ce n'est pas son habitude de sortir le
soir," said the concierge. I am still trembling with fury. I wanted to
pack up and go that moment. I suppose people do not matter — but
they certainly *can* hurt. And Ive no letter from you all day, dear
darling.

MS ATL. *LKM* I. 31-2; *LJMM*, 36-7.

---

[1] The film was probably an instalment of Louis Feuillade's serial thriller, *Les Vampires*
(1915), though the setting of the film is Paris, not Calais. The actress was Musidora.

To J. M. Murry, [11 May 1915]

[13 quai aux Fleurs]
Tuesday morning.

My dearest of all

I have just got your Saturday evening letter and you can imagine
what I feel about the supper party & about Frieda. I could *murder*
her. Everything you told me made me boil and made my heart fly
out for my Bogey — What a great fat *sod* she is — I should like to
send a pig to kill her — a real filthy pig. . Lawrence has got queer
blind places, hasn't he?[1]

Poor Arthur — the beginning of the day sounded very like a
little you.[2] But I envied him being on the Serpentine with you.
Lesley and I used to go in the old days but Ive never been since.
Its a lovely thing to do.

Yesterday was simply hellish for me. My work went very well, but all the same — I suffered abominably. I felt so alien and so far away — & everybody cheated me — everybody was ugly — and beyond words cruel. I finally got to such a state that I could go nowhere to eat because of the people and I could hardly speak. At half past ten I shut up shop & went to bed, but not to sleep. The three apaches of the cinema, L'Fantome, Bébé, & le faux Curé tried the key of the door all night & tiptoed on the landing. Finally through the shutters there came two chinks of day. Do I sound foolish and cowardly? Oh, but yesterday was simply Hell. In the evening (Id gone out to get a lamp glass. The concierge with relish, had smashed mine) I sat in a little garden by a laburnum tree — I felt the dark dropping over me and the shadows enfolding and I died and came to life again "time & time again" as Mrs C. used to say. I went to buy bread at a funny shop. The woman hadn't got a nose and her mouth had been sewn up and then opened again at the side of her face. She had a wall eye. When she came into the lamp light with the bread I nearly screamed, but she clapped her poor hand to her head & smiled at me. I cannot forget it. This morning things are better. It is such a fine day, but I could not stand a month of yesterdays. I'd come home in a coffin, Jaggle.

My darling, my dearest — your letter written so beautifully is on the table. It expresses you so. I love you with every bit of me — I am your own woman your

Wig

Shut your eyes a minute. Hold me very hard — Now I am giving you little kisses & now a big big kiss.

PS. I have opened your letter again to say that your Sunday one is just come, so I am rich today with *2* letters. Don't cast your clouts before May is out — in other words, keep your pants on, Boge. (How absurd it sounds.) I should like to have seen the sewing — but I shall, shant I? Found another BUG in the kitchen today (did I tell you about the first which nearly bit off my hand?) and also a large black louse with white spots on it. I am being so careful — careful of money. You'd be surprised — Every sou is counted out and put down in my book. I detest money — Isn't it a long time since Ive heard from Lesley?

Im sorry the sylph is cold to you,[3] my dear love — and I hope the Lawrences were nicer. The concierge has just refused to get me some milk. Its ½ past 11 & Ive had no breakfast. She *is* a swine.

Tig.

[*Across top of letter*]
A letter from you.
MS ATL. *LJMM*, 38–9.

¹ Murry had written on 8 May 1915 that Lawrence, Frieda, and an invited guest came to dinner. 'I was hurt that they were late, seeing that they knew I had to get it all myself, but to find Frieda fatuously laughing on the doorstep, as though it were so very Bohemian to be an hour and a half late — no, that was a little too much. After an hour of it, she decided that I was dull, and to prove to me what a party should be began to sing German continental songs in that idiotic voice of hers.' (ATL.) She also ate more than her share.

² Murry had arranged to meet his young brother for his birthday, but the boy was late arriving.

³ A woman in a near-by tobacconist's, of whom Murry wrote on 9 May 1915 'She's very cold to me, not cold — I don't mind that — but she despises me profoundly' (ATL).

To J. M. Murry, [12 May 1915]

Cafe Biard, Rue de Rivoli
Midi

Dearest Boge darling —

Heres the history of my lunch. I decided I could never go to the brasserie again — because there was a black cat that frightened me there so today I sought pastures new — All were *impudently* full so I fell back on Chartier. I wanted something cheap so I ordered pied de veau. My strike! I got the exact contents of Magginalli's stomach as described by doctor Spilsbury¹ — hairs feathers and all — and a hoof thrown in for 'make weight' I suppose — I had that removed, but still hungry I ordered risotto milanais & got a lump of rice originally covered in tomato sauce, but the sauce had run on to someone's creme d'Isigny in transit. Then I ordered compote de rhubarbe. C'est fini. & looking down at that moment I saw on my thumb an immense BUG — dining in all possible comfort & half full already. That was the limit. I fled here — and this coffee is just like squeezed wet flannel. I wonder if it is the war that has made the people here so hideous or if I am out of joint. They appear to me a nation of concierges. And the women look such drabs in their ugly mourning. I wish I had some new shoes and a straw hat. My head & my feet are always hot — but these are minor things. It is a brilliant fine day — Everything shines.

The *fool* of a concierge has written to F.C. & said I am here — Consequence was a despairing letter at midday. If I will not write will I at least see his friend Réné Bizet² "très charmant avec beaucoup de talent," so that he can tell F.C. how I am. How absurd! Of course I won't.

How terrible it is that waiters must have flat feet — these are shuffling about — sweaty — ugly — If they were turned out of their cafés whatever would they do? Plainly nothing.

My book *marche bien* — I feel I could write it anywhere — it goes so easily — and I know it so well.[3] It will be a funny book — Now Ive finished my coffee — I am going. Goodbye my precious

Wig.

MS ATL. *LKM* I. 32–3; *LJMM*, 39–40.

[1] The body of a girl called Maggie Nally was found at Aldersgate Street Underground, London, early in April 1915. The analysis of the contents of her stomach, by the eminent pathologist Bernard Spilsbury, revealed giblets and hair.

[2] Réné Bizet (1887–1947), French poet, novelist, and short-story writer.

[3] *The Aloe* was based very firmly on KM's own childhood in Wellington, and set in the two houses she had lived in as a child in Tinakori Road and Karori.

To [J. M. Murry], [c. 13 May 1915]

[13 quai aux Fleurs]

I did not tell you that I dreamed all night of Rupert Brooke.[1] And today as I left the house he was standing at the door, with a rucksack on his back & his broad hat shading his face. So after I had posted your letter I did not go home. I went a long very idle sort of amble along the quais. It was exquisitely hot — white clouds lay upon the sky like sheets spread out to dry. In the big sandheaps down by the river children had hollowed out tunnels and caverns. They sat in them stolid and content, their hair glistening in the sun. Now and then a man lay stretched on his face, his head in his arms. The river was full of big silver stars, the trees shook faintly — glistening with light — and I found delightful places: little squares with white square houses — quite hollow they looked with the windows gaping open, narrow streets arched over with chestnut boughs & perhaps quite deserted with a clock tower showing over the roofs. The sun put a spell on everything. I crossed and recrossed the river & leaned over the bridges & kept thinking we were coming to a Park when we weren't. You cannot think what pleasure my invisible, imaginary companion gave me. If he had been alive it would never have possibly occurred, but — it's a game I like to play — to walk and to talk with the dead who smile and are silent, and *free*, quite finally free. When I lived alone I would often come home, put my key in the door & find someone there, waiting for me. 'Hullo! Have you been here long?' I suppose that sounds dreadful rubbish to you. I am sitting on a broad bench in the sun hard by Notre Dame. In front of me there's a hedge of ivy. An old man walks along with a basket on his arm, picking off the withered leaves. In the priests' garden they are cutting the grass. I love this big cathedral.

The little view I have of it now is of pointed narrow spires, fretted against the blue, and one or two squatting stone parrots balanced on a little balcony. It is like a pen drawing by a Bogey. And I like the saints with their crowns in their collars and their heads in their hands.

Like the old saints in some cathedral, découpé but with their crowns hanging over their collars.

MS (draft) ATL, loose papers. *Journal* 1927, 27-9.

[1] The poet Rupert Brooke (1887-1915), an acquaintance of both Murry and KM, died at Skyros on 23 Apr 1915

To J. M. Murry, [14 May 1915]

[13 quai aux Fleurs]

Dear Boge,
    This is about the 4th letter I have written and torn up (the others I mean. This I will send) The others were nothing. My rheumatism is simply dreadful. I am very tired with it — *dead* tired and sick of it, but my work goes 'alright'.
    Fancy GIVING YOURSELF UP to LOVING someone for a fortnight, as you say you will do for Lawrence in the summer.[1] My strike! I think you are quite right, but it does surprise me as an idea.
    You *are* seeing a lot of people, Bogey. You always do when I am away — I wish I knew where [Frank] Harris was in Paris. Ive a perfect mania to see him — & to hear his bitter laugh.
    Quelle vie.
    I send back this letter. I dont know what to say — *Why* do the fowls come in? I am ill and alone voilà tout.

Tig.

MS ATL. *LJMM*, 40.

[1] Murry had written on 11 May 1915, after spending an evening with the Lawrences during their brief visit to London from Greatham, Pulborough: 'Poor devil he is so lonely, with that bitch of a Frieda, always playing traitor, and hurting him in every secret and intimate part of his soul . . . . But I think I shall ask him to come away with me for a fortnight's holiday during this summer to see if I can urge him to the point of leaving her. Not that I think I can do very much directly; but I have an idea that he might be happy were he away with me for a bit, because he would know that I was loving him.' (ATL.)

To J. M. Murry, [14 May 1915]

[13 quai aux Fleurs]
Friday afternoon.

My dearest darling —

I am determined to come home on Wednesday; Ill arrive at Victoria at 9 oclock — My work is finished my freedom gained. If I stay they will ① cut the gas off ② arrest me as a spy ③ F[rancis] C[arco] is coming to Paris at the end of next week. Voila des beaux raisons! Besides which I have only to polish my work now; its all really accompli. I am simply bursting to come. If this throws you into a fury do not attend me à la gare — or come & dont recognise me or something.

Ah, Bogey be glad — Such a *good* Wig is coming back with money in her pocket, too — for I have lived MOST CAREFULLY —

But what with Bugs and no gas and a heart full of love and fun — I cannot cannot cannot stay alone. So there you are — Do my letters arrive all safely — I write every day — I am very silly ce soir — drunk on a black coffee — dearest — I believe — But Life is fun — and I'll take up my leg and walk. What perhaps is the source of my amusement is that I was marched off to the police station today — as I was here without papiers de séjour I thought it was all up $\pm$ the cheek of those police — where was my husband — how many children have you — None — "Pourquoi pas" said the inspector. I was a frozen Union Jackess — There is a darling baby in this café with me. She is drowning her brioche in a cup of weak coffee — drowning it *deliberately* holding it down with a spoon!

Dearest darling —

I am hanging up the curtain in the little house today[1] — Ah, I do simply love you — you funny boy — Anoint your derrière, love with Zinc ointment.[2] Buy steak for Wednesday — They are selling huge asparagras here — so big that it looks like the first sentence of a Willy [W.L. George] novel. I love love love you — will this letter arrive on Monday — then start the week with my arms tight round you a moment — for I adore you Bogey and I am only yours. Wednesday then, dearest Heart. I shall see your old grey hat at Victoria. But come on the platform — this time — & I will lean out of the Kerridge and wave.

Always your
Wig

MS ATL. *BTW*, 345; *LJMM*, 40-1.

[1] The house in St. John's Wood to which they were to move on KM's return.
[2] Murry had written on 12 May 1915 (ATL) of 'a funny and most uncomfortable swelling'.

To J. M. Murry, [15 May 1915]

[13 quai aux Fleurs]
Saturday afternoon.

I got very sane after I had written to you yesterday — I wish something in you didn't make me feel a 'silly' when I want to write at full tilt. Its because you never do; you're such a guarded and careful little Bogey — and so frightened I shall 'make a scene'. I won't, dear. I promise you. Im not *at* all sure this afternoon whether Ill come on Wednesday or whether Ill wait a week. Perhaps Id better wait a week. If I *do* come I *won't* wire if I *dont* come I *will* wire. Its a fair toss up.[1] Yesterday evening I sat in a little parc and played with the idea with a *sou*. The sou said every time "Yes, go —" but that was yesterday. And this morning again your calm letter as though we were "seule pour la vie" shook up against the apple cart.

You sent me a letter from Lesley — which was simply marvellous. She wrote, as she can, you know of all sorts of things, grass and birds and little animals and herself and our friendship with that kind of careless, very intimate joy — There is something quite absolute in Lesley — She said at the end of a page — "Katie, dearie — what is *Eternity*?" She's about the nearest thing to 'eternal' that I could ever imagine. I wish she were not so far away.[2] Things are so changed now. You and I still love each other, but you haven't the need of me you had then and somehow I do always have to be *"needed"* to be happy. Ive expressed that abominably — and its not even quite true, for what I call your need of me was more or less an illusion on my part. Youre an amazing person in the way you can accept just so much and no more — No, Im beating about the bush and not really saying what I want to — *and* it really doesn't matter — But I do wish my tall, pale friend were here to walk with and sit with. Youre not the slightest use — for it doesn't come natural for you to desire to do such things with me. Its I who plead like "une petite pensionnaire" to be taken out on a Saturday afternoon or to a music hall —

A lovely woman sits in here with me. She's got a fool of a man with her that she hates beyond words. So would I. She wears a big rose under her chin — her eyes are lovely but very shadowed with a purple ring. She is not *only* bored: she is trying not to cry. Three fat jossers at a table nearby are vastly amused. Two dirty little froggies smoking pipes 'a l'anglaise' & ragging each other are next to me. They occasionally sing at me — or snap their fingers. They are the most hideous little touts — Blast them! Now, I might have known it, my lovely woman is playing a game of cards with her cavalier — Mon dieu! She does look lovely with the fan of cards in her hand, the other hand hovering over and her lips just pouting. I must go. This is a fool of a letter. What makes you disgruntled?[3] Is your book worrying you? No, I cant send any of mine because Im too dependent on it as a whole under my hand. The BUGS are still flourishing in the kitchen. One violated me last night.

Pretty business this german chasing — and a pity they have to photograph such decent, honest looking wretches as the belles proies.[4] Its a filthy. trick; there's no difference between England and Germany when the mob gets a hand in things — No difference between any nation on earth — They are all equally loathsome.

Goodbye for now, my dear. *Hanged* if I know whether I'll see you on Wednesday or not — If I do wire that I am not coming you might send me that £1; just to reassure me — will you — Oh, Bogey — dearest —

Tig.

MS ATL. *LKM* I. 20; *BTW*, 345-6; *LJMM*, 41-3.

[1] KM returned from France to Elgin Crescent on 19 May 1915.

[2] Ida Baker was with her family in Rhodesia between April 1914 and September 1916.

[3] Murry had begun his letter on 13 May 1915: 'Yesterday I was in a bad mood and did nothing. Today I wasn't in a bad mood and did nothing. . . .' (ATL.)

[4] In the same letter Murry had enclosed a photograph from the *Daily News* 'showing four policemen *just looking on* while some poor unfortunate German's whole house is plundered'.

To [J. M. Murry], [15 May 1915][1]

[Paris]

Wednesday Victoria impossible Monday because consulate wire if alright.[2]

Bowden.

MS (draft) ATL.

[1] On the morning of 15 May 1915, Murry had wired 'COME BACK DARLING. MURRY' (ATL). KM drafted her reply that afternoon across the bottom of Murry's telegram.

[2] Murry's reply, sent on 17 May 1915, was 'COME WEDNESDAY DARLING MEET LOVE. MURRY' (ATL).

To S. S. Koteliansky, [17 May 1915]

[13 quai aux Fleurs]
Monday Night.

Kotiliansky, dear friend, I will not wait any longer for a letter from you. Jack tells me about you, but that is not enough; it is too remote. I had wanted a letter from you to say that you 'understood' — not to reassure me, you understand, but just because — I always want you to understand. It is a rainy evening — not at all cold, rather warm, but rainy, rainy. Everything is wet; the river is sopping, and if you stand still a moment you hear the myriad little voices of the rain. As you walk the air lifts just enough to blow on your cheeks. Ah! How delicious that is! It is not only leaves you smell when you stand under the trees today; you smell the black wet boughs and stems — the 'forest' smell. This evening I went walking in a park. Big drops splashed from the leaves and on the paths there lay a drift of pink and white chestnut flowers. In the fountain basin there was a great deal of mixed bathing going on among some sparrows. A little boy stood just outside the park. He thrust one hand through the railing among the ivy leaves and pulled out some tiny snails, arranging them in a neat row on the stone wall. "V'la! Mes escargots!" But *I* was rather frightened, that, being french, he'd take a pin out of his jacket and begin eating them! And then they locked the park up. An old caretaker in a black cape with a hood to it locked it up with a whole bunch of keys. There is a wharf not far from here where the sand barges unload. Do you know the smell of wet sand? Does it make you think of going down to the beach in the evening light after a rainy day and gathering the damp drift wood (it will dry on top of the stove) and picking up for a moment the long branches of sea-weed that the waves have tossed and listening to the gulls who stand reflected in the gleaming sand, and just fly a little way off as you come and then — settle again.

This evening a mist rose up from the river and everything looks far away. Down below, two nuns went by, their ample skirts gathered in one hand, the other holding an umbrella over their white hoods. And *just below* — there is a court where the market men take their barrows for the night — their palms, and their rose trees and china blue hydrangea bushes. You see the barrows with waving shining leaves float by like miraculous islands. Very few people are out. Two lovers came and hid behind a tree and put up an umbrella. Then they walked away, pressed against each other. It made me think of a poem that our german professor used to read us in class.

Ja, das war zum letzenmal
Das, wir beide, arm in arme
Unter einem Schirm gebogen. — —
Alles war zum letzenmal.

And I heard again his 'sad' voice (so beautiful it seemed, you know) and I saw again his white hand with a ring on it, press open the page![1] But *now* I know the perfect thing to do on a night like this. It is to ride in a little closed cab. You may have the windows open but you cannot keep out the smell of leather and the smell of *upholstered buttons*. The horse makes an idle klipperty klopperting. When we arrive at the house there is a big bush of lilac in flower growing over the gate and it is so dark that you do not stoop low enough and drops and petals fall on you. The light from the hall streams down the steps.

Scene II

K: "Tell me frankly. Does it *not* feel damp to you?"

Visionary Caretaker: "Ive had fires in all the rooms, m'm. Beautiful fires they were too. It seemed a pity to let them out; they burned that lovely."

M. or N: "It feels as dry as bone to me, I *must* say."

The Visionary Caretaker beams at 'M or N'. Her little girl puts her head round the door. In her pinafore she has rather a wet kitten.

Visionary C: "And if you *should* like a chicken at any time, m'm, or a few greens I'm sure my husband and I would be only too pleased etc etc etc etc. . .

I am laughing, are you? The queer thing is that, dreaming like that I can't help living it all, down to the smallest details — down to the very dampness of the salt at supper that night and the way it came out on your plate, the exact shape of the salt spoon. . .

Do you, too feel an infinite delight and value in *detail* — not for the sake of detail but for the life *in* the life of it. I never can express myself (and you can laugh as much as you please.) But do you ever feel as though the Lord threw you into eternity — into the very exact centre of eternity, and even as you plunged you felt every ripple that flowed out from your plunging — every single ripple floating away and touching and drawing into its circle every slightest thing it touched. No, I shan't write any more. I see you, my wise one, putting down this letter and saying — "no. I must go to Barbara to explain this. . ."

I feel a little bit drunk. Its the air, and the noise the real waves make as the boats, with long fans of light, go dancing by.

We shall see each other again soon. But I can't deny that I feel a little neglected. I had *counted* on a reply to my letter, after all.

Don't forget me — don't go far away. As I write I hear your voice and I see you swing out into the hall of the bureau as though you were going to beat to death the person who had dared to come in.

With this letter I send you big handfuls of very 'good' love.

Kissienka.

MS BL. *LKM* I. 26-9; Dickinson, 82.

[1] A recollection of Walter Rippmann at Queen's College. The lines quoted are from 'Erinnerung—an C.N.' by the German poet Eduard Mörike (1804-75).

V

FRANCE

1915–1916

The death of KM's brother in early October 1915 was the most severe emotional crisis of her life. At first she turned from both Murry and England, and between mid-November and the beginning of April 1916, she lived in the South of France. Murry had travelled out with her, and after a fortnight in Cassis, returned to England on 7 December 1915, leaving KM at Bandol. When he rejoined her there at the end of the year, they enjoyed the happiest months of their eleven years together. KM worked again on *The Aloe*, and more and more turned to her memories of Wellington for her writing. She wrote on 22 January 1916: 'Now — now I want to write recollections of my own country. Yes I want to write about my own country until I simply exhaust my store. Not only because it is a "sacred debt" that I pay to my country because my brother & I were born there, but also because in my thoughts I range with him over all the remembered places. I am never far away from them. I long to renew them in writing.' (*Journal* 1954, 93-4.)

To Leslie Beauchamp,[1] [25 August 1915]

SELFRIDGE & CO. LTD. | OXFORD STREET, | LONDON - W.
THE LOUNGE, READING AND WRITING ROOMS,
Wednesday 1915

Dearest,

I have an odd moment to spare & I'll use it in sending you a line — Ever since last Sunday you are close in my thoughts. It meant a tremendous lot, seeing you and being with you again and I was so frightfully proud of you — you know that — but I like saying it. But the worst of it is I want always to be far *more* with you and for a long enough time for us to get over the 'preliminaries' and live together a little.

I heard from Mother this mail. She was very cheerful & says she has such happy letters from you. Again she wanted first hand news of you so I have written this mail & told her just what I would want to hear if I were she. She is a darling and her personality simply enchants me in her letters.

Do you know a day when your heart feels much too big? Today if I see a flag or a little child or an old beggar my heart expands and I would cry for joy. Very absurd — Im 26 you know — This is not a letter. It is only my arms round you for a quick minute.

Your
Katie.

MS ATL.

[1] Leslie Heron Beauchamp (1894-1915), KM's only brother, and the youngest in the family; having completed an Officers' Training Course (see p. 155, n.4), he had been commissioned as a lieutenant in the South Lancashire Regiment — 'The Prince of Wales's Volunteers'. He saw KM intermittently during his months of training, and in the third week of August 1915 he stayed with her at Acacia Road, while on a bombing instructors' course at Clapham Common. He crossed to France in late September, and was killed in a hand-grenade accident at Ploegsteert Wood, near Armentières, on 7 Oct 1915.

To Mary Hutchinson,[1] [11 November 1915]

5 Acacia Road[2] [St. John's Wood]
Thursday.

Dear Mrs Hutchinson,

Thank you for your kind note — I should like very much to come to dinner on Monday evening at ¼ to 8. It is awfully nice of you to say that you liked the sketches in the Signature.[3] I am busy with a book of them & its so pleasant to think that they've given you pleasure —

Im rather ashamed to have mentioned the Café Royale business[4] — If I think people don't see me I expect the worst — — Very silly — Until Monday

Yours very sincerely
Katherine Mansfield

MS Texas.

[1] The socially prominent Mary Hutchinson, née Barnes (1889-1977), whose mother was Winifred Strachey, a cousin of Lytton Strachey. She was married to the barrister St. John Hutchinson.

[2] The 'little house' (see p. 188, n.1) into which KM and Murry had moved in June 1915, on her return from Paris.

[3] A prospectus for *The Signature*, a magazine planned by Lawrence and Murry, had promised 'a series of six papers on social and personal freedom by D.H. Lawrence and J.M. Murry, and a set of satirical sketches by Matilda Berry'. In the event the magazine ran for only three issues, 4 Oct, 18 Oct, and 1 Nov 1915. KM contributed three stories under the name of 'Matilda Berry': 'Autumns' I and II (later collected as 'Apple Tree Story' and 'The Wind Blows' respectively) on 4 October, and 'The Little Governess' in the next two issues (see p. 154, n.1).

[4] The 'Café Royale business' is unexplained; KM had only recently met Mrs Hutchinson, probably at the party on 5 Nov 1915 given by the Hon. Dorothy Brett (see p. 321, n.1) at which she met other members of the Bloomsbury set for the first time.

To Mary Hutchinson, [15 November 1915]

[5 Acacia Road, St. Johns Wood]

VERY MUCH REGRET THAT I CANNOT DINE WITH YOU TONIGHT LEAVING
ENGLAND SUDDENLY A DAY EARLIER[1] AND SIMPLY IN CHAOS PLEASE
FORGIVE ME.

KATHERINE MANSFIELD.

Telegram Texas.

[1] KM and Murry left for the South of France on or about 16 Nov 1915.

To S. S. Koteliansky, 19 November 1915

GRAND BAR DE LA SAMARITAINE
1, RUE DE LA REPUBLIQUE, 1 | & QUAI DU PORT, 2 | MARSEILLE
19ième Novembre 1915

Koteliansky dear,

I have been on the point of writing to you several times but —
just not had the time or the place or something. *Business first.* I
left one of my brother's caps in a drawer upstairs in his room.
Would you get it and keep it safely for me. Also, I meant to give you
for your room the *fur rug* in my sitting room — you know the one.
I don't want the Farbmans to use it and I do want you to keep it for
me. Put it on your bed. It is so warm and it looks and feels so lovely.
Tell Sarah that I have written to you and asked you to send it to
me — PLEASE do this.[1] That is all — except that our address is c/o
Thomas Cook + Sons, Tourist Agency, Rue de Noailles, Marseille —
We shall call there for letters under the name of *either* Bowden
(when Ill get them) or Murry, for Jack. If I started to tell you about
all that has happened I never would end. Indeed, I have been gathering
a big bouquet for you, but it has become too big to hold and it has
dropped out of my arms. You will have to believe me, darling, that
the flowers *were* there and *were* for you — I am glad that I came.
Many times I have realised that Acacia Road and all that it implied
is over — for ever.

This is a confused and extraordinary place — It is full of troops —
french, african, indian, english — In fact there are 'types' from all
over the world and all walking together down narrow streets choked
with tiny carriages painted yellow, white mules with red fringes over
their eyes — — — All those kinds of things you know. The port is
extremely beautiful. But Ive really nothing to say about the place
until I write to you for weeks, for all my observation is so *detailed*

as it always is when I get to France. On the mantelpiece in my room stands my brother's photograph. I never see anything that I like, or hear anything, without the longing that he should see and hear, too — I had a letter from his friend again. He told me that after it happened[2] he said over and over — "God forgive me for all I have done" and just before he died he said "Lift my head, Katy I can't breathe —"

To tell you the truth these things that I have heard about him blind me to all that is happening here — All this is like a long uneasy ripple — nothing else — and below — in the still pool there is my little brother.

So I shall not write any more just now, darling. But I think of you often and always with love.

Katy.

MS BL. *LKM* I. 34; Dickinson, 82-3.

[1] The Russian journalist and political commentator Michael Farbman (?1880–1933), a friend of Kot's from the Russian Law Bureau, with his wife Sophie took over the lease of 5 Acacia Road. Kot rented a room from them, and continued to live in the house until his death in 1955. 'Sarah' may have been a servant who looked after the house.

[2] i.e. the grenade accident at Ploogsteert Wood; see p. 198, n.1. The friend's letter has not survived.

To S. S. Koteliansky, [28 November 1915]

[Hôtel Firano, Cassis (Bouches-du-Rhône)]
Sunday

My darling friend

Today, for the first time since leaving England I had news of you. I am glad you have taken the fur. Thank you for sending the letters: Jack talks 'business' but I need not — So I will not. Is everything 'just the same'? It feels to me far away. Not that I long for it or anything like that but all that rather false life of the last few months seemed to dissolve utterly when I left it. I don't even think of it. But *you* remain and you are still with me here. I am glad to be away from Marseilles. Murry does not like this place but in many ways I do. For one thing, and its awfully important, the sea is here — very clear and very blue. The sound of it after such a long silence is almost unbearable — a sweet agony, you know — — — like moonlight is sometimes. And then there are high mountains covered with bright green pine trees. Tufts of rosemary grow among the rocks and a tall flower with pink bells which is very lovely. Yesterday, in the middle of a forest, I found the hut on chicken legs.[1] Two white pigeons sat on the roof and on the doorstep a tiny cat slept in the sun. But I did not hear the spinning wheel.

I shall be able to write here in a day or two. My room is nice, darling. The walls are blue, with small flowers standing on their feet at the bottom of the wall and the same flowers standing on their heads at the top. Outside the window there are trees. Jack has just read to me what he wrote to you — Dont believe the conjugal 'we' — Its not worth protesting but its not really true of me — never.

In my *heart* I am happy — because I feel that I have come into my own. You understand me?

> Goodbye for now
> I am always lovingly yours.
> [*No signature*]

MS BL. Dickinson, 83.

[1] According to Russian folklore, the hut on chicken's legs is the dwelling of the evil witch Babayaga. Cf. the movement entitled 'The Hut on Fowl's Legs' in Mussorgsky's *Pictures at an Exhibition* (1874). KM may well have known the painting on the subject by V.M. Vasnetsov.

To J. M. Murry, [8 December 1915]

> [Hôtel Beau Rivage, Bandol]
> Wednesday morning.

My darling Bogey,

The 'comfortable party' brought me your letter this morning on my breakfast tray. I read it & kissed it. It was wicked of you to send me the 5 francs & awfully sweet of you. Doesn't the Havre Southampton route mean a longer sea journey? I am thankful you got a corner seat from Marseilles to Paris. I keep thinking about you, my Bogey. You were quite right to go back.[1] Yesterday after you had gone I bought some biscuits & oranges & after putting them in my room & entering the fact of them in my Account Book (!) I went for a walk. It was hot and sunny with big reine-claude waves breaking on the rocks. When I came back I picked my geraniums — toujours in a state of lively terror. I wanted to tell ① the proprietor ② the gardener ③ the girls hanging out washing ④ anyone in and out of sight that I had permission. I even suspected that the white dog had been taught to hurle when the pensionnaires touched the flowers. But there they are in the lovely jug you gave me — un joli petit bouquet.

The crepuscule descended just as it did the day before. At six I took Jules Laforgues rather cynical arm[2] & descended to the salon &

read until dinner time. A New Lady appeared in bright purple velvet, low neck & short sleeves, tiny waist, large pear shaped derrière, big fat shoulders, marabout scarf, little round head with curls like escargots on the forehead. I was *quite overwhelmed.* After a chaste repast (your serviette, my precious, was still there — I got awfully sentimental over it) the man that we said was english,[3] made me a leg and offered me two copies of the Times. I took about 2 hours reading them — picked them absolutely clean & decided that the english newspapers were the finest *etc* & that no other nation etc could possibly etc. But they were packed with meat. An attack on Lunn's father as a pro german — attempted suicide of Miss Annesley Kenealy — Sir John Simon's attack on the Times — the King's first excursion in a Bath chair (Note the capital *B*. Heavens! What a dignity it gave!)[4] After I had returned them the englishman's lady opened a rapid fire. But I kept under cover & she changed her tactics & told me a lot of interesting things. For instance: November is the very bad month of the year for the South of France. 'Parisians' never come then. December is early spring. The flowers begin — the jonquils & the oranges. The villas open & the parisians arrive. The mistral *never* blows here — *never.* This place abounds in charming walks & one can buy a map of the forest paths for 50 centimes. (But shall I 'enter those enchanted woods'[5] do you think Boge, even with a map of the paths. Courage! I must!) They are expecting 25 people at this hotel for Christmas. This was told to encourage me, I think — and so on until bed time. I woke early and for a long time forgot you were not with me but felt you beside me & only when I wanted to tell you my Extraordinary Dream I remembered.

It is a lovely day again — very bright & warm. They are still digging up the garden & prizing up little rock borders with disused railway lines & telegraph poles. The boats with red sails are sailing on the sea & your ship is quite close in. Yesterday afternoon they lowered a boat & the exhausted crew 'tumbled' (see the Lancet)[6] into it & were rowed to shore.

That is all for just now, my darling heart. Here's your tooth pick that you left & you also forgot to take your face rag. But that I wont send. You can buy one (a wash glove) for 4¾ anywhere.

You know I love you. I love you simply tremendously. I put my arms round you & kiss you —

Tig.

MS ATL. *LKM* I. 35-7; *LJMM*, 44-5.

[1] After an uncomfortable fortnight in Cassis, KM and Murry had moved to Bandol, where he stayed with her for two nights before returning to London.

² The ironic self-deprecation, and use of free verse, of the French poet Jules Laforgue (1860–87) later strongly influenced English poetry.

³ This was F. Newland-Pedley FRCS (1854–1944), one of the founders in 1889 of the dental school at Guy's Hospital, London. Murry gives a chapter, 'Portrait of a Pa-Man', to this gifted and eccentric man in his *Katherine Mansfield and Other Literary Portraits* (1949).

⁴ *The Times* on 30 Nov 1915 printed a letter claiming that Sir Henry Lunn, the father of Murry's friend, the biographer and critic Hugh Kingsmill (1889–1949), harboured pro-German sympathies. Founder of a prosperous travel business and an unsuccessful Liberal candidate for Parliament, Sir Henry had recently tried to organize a manifesto, signed by Oxford dons, denouncing the competence of *The Times*.

In the same issue of the paper was a report on the police court hearing on the novelist Annesley Kenealey's attempted suicide by morphine. Sir John Simon, a member of Asquith's Cabinet, had the week before attacked *The Times* over its handling of war news, and the use the Germans made of this in their own press. King George V was recovering from an accident on 28 Oct 1915 when his horse reared and fell on him during an Army inspection in France.

⁵ Cf. George Meredith, 'The Woods of Westermain', whose opening lines, 'Enter these enchanted woods, / You who dare', are repeated at the end of each of the poem's four sections.

⁶ It is likely that Newland-Pedley (see n. 3) was plying KM with copies of the *Lancet*, the weekly 'Journal of British and Foreign Medicine', for which he was an enthusiast. He had written to the journal three times in 1915, even arguing on 16 Jan 1915 that in the Army 'Extra pay should be given for good teeth'.

To Anne Estelle Drey,[1] *8 December [1915]*

address: Mme Bowden | Hotel Beau Rivage | Bandol | (Var)
VIII XII

Darling Anne,

I have been wanting to write to you for days, but this morning is really my first free time and the first time that I have been anything like 'settled' since leaving England. My little John Bull Murry went back to London yesterday — Perhaps that will tell you a little what kind of a time we have had. I could write books about it until I died and then not finish the telling. It has been so funny and so tragic and so utterly unlike what we had expected and imagined. Marseilles became colder and colder — I got really very ill there with fever & spent my time drinking hot milk with sugar & orange flower water in the cafés & then keeping up my strength! with little glasses of brandy. Both of us got poisoned, I think from eating mussels and pistachio ices at the same time — The old stone floors started my rheumatism again & everybody cheated Murry *at sight* — Even before he bought anything they put up the price — So we decided to go to Cassis-sur-Mer for *at least* a couple of months. We found there a very comfortable looking hotel kept by a fat woman called 'Tante' & two nieces. We had a huge room with four windows to get the lovely sun & read with great satisfaction in every single guide book that Cassis was the first station d'hiver sur la côte d'azur —

The day we arrived the mistral was blowing. I put my head out of the train window & it blew the trimming off my hat.
[*Letter incomplete*]

MS (fragment) ATL. *LKM* I. 34-5.

¹ Anne Estelle Drey, née Rice (1879-1959), was born near Philadelphia and worked as a magazine illustrator in the United States before she settled in Paris in 1906 and began to paint seriously. She met Murry through their mutual friend J.D. Fergusson, contributed regularly to *Rhythm*, and became one of KM's closest friends. In 1913 she married the journalist O. Raymond Drey (1885-1976), who had written art and theatre criticism for *Rhythm* and the *Blue Review*.

To J. M. Murry, [9 December 1915]

[Hôtel Beau Rivage, Bandol]
Thursday morning. A little before ten.

My Bogey,

I expect you are in London. I have just washed & dressed & put on my white broderie anglaise jacket (I really *do* look rather a pretty girl) & now I'm sitting in the sun by the open window smoking the first cigarette. The air is like silk today & there is a sheen upon the world like the sheen on a bird's wing. Its very quiet except for the gardener and his spade and warm as fine wool. Yesterday afternoon I walked to Sanary — which is the next bay to this — on the road that follows past the palm avenue. Really it was very hot — You walked along with your eyes & nose screwed up & breathed Hail Maries that you wouldn't freckle or be violated by a black soldier. But I wish you could have been there & seen that bay. There is a long beach there too and on the other side of the road fields of jonquils in flower. Two women one in grey & one in yellow with black straw hats were picking them. As I passed they stood up & held the big nodding bunches before their eyes to see who was passing. There is a tiny villa there, too — with a glass verandah and a small garden. It could not have more than 2 rooms — It looks right over the bay to the open sea. Behind it rears up an old rock covered with that pink heath & rosemary. A board on the gate said 'à louer'. I confess to hanging over the fence for a long time & dreaming . . Coming home in the evening with driftwood to burn − − the lamp on the round table − the jar of wild flowers on the mantelpiece. Sitting on the verandah in canvas chairs after supper & smoking & listening to the idle sea. But don't be frightened, dear one, you were not there. It was my Brother who sat on the verandah step stroking a kitten that curled on his knee.

Bogey, I think the Oxford Book of English Verse is *very* poor.

I read it for hours this morning in bed. I turned over pages & pages & pages. But except for Shakespeare & Marvell & just a handful of others it seems to me to be a mass of falsity. Musically speaking, hardly anyone seems to *even understand* what the middle of the note is — what that sound is like. Its not perhaps that they are even 'sharp' or 'flat' — its something much more subtle — they are not playing on the *very note itself.* But when, in despair I took up the French Book I nearly sautéd from the fenêtre with rage. Its like an endless gallery of French salon furniture sicklied oer with bed canopies, candelabra, and porcelain cupids all bow and bottom. Of course there *are* exceptions.[1] Victor Hugo, by the way reminded me very much of our white bull taking a railway ticket — to Parnassus — And I wasn't a bit 'surprised'.

Am I being a bit of a bore? Ill stop, my darling. You can think how I am longing to hear from you — you know what your letters mean.

My dear darling I am always your little mate

Tig.

MS ATL. *LKM* I. 37-8; *LJMM*, 45-6.

[1] *The Oxford Book of English Verse* (1900) was chosen and edited by A.T. Quiller-Couch. *The Oxford Book of French Verse* (1907) was chosen by St. John Lucas.

To J. M. Murry, [10 December 1915]

[Hôtel Beau Rivage, Bandol]
Friday.

Jag-Bog,

I don't know whether you expect me to write to you every day but I shall do so (D.V.) & you will too, won't you? Once a day really isn't too often & its my only dear signal that you are well. Today came your Paris letter with the swindle from Cooks (which made me furious!) & the lady with the Dates.[1] "Net gain 4d" re baggage was very *pa* of you. I heard you saying that. Darling, what a frightful adventure with O Hara San. What a Minx to take off her head like that[2] — but you ought to have known, Bogey. You are always accusing me of the same thing. I hope you do see De la Mare — thank you for sending me his note.[3]

Yesterday I went for a long walk round by the sea towards St. Cyr (which is very beautiful & wild & like my NZ.) & then I struck inland & came home by little lanes & crooked ways bordered with olive trees — past the flower farms — I thought I should never get home again. I got quite lost & though I kept hearing voices the walls were always in the way & when I peered through the gates there was never a soul to be seen except jonquils & daffodils & big blue violets & white roses. The sun went down — I passed a little villa called 'Allons-y' and coo-ed but a Fearful White Dog happily attached to a pump answered me so effectually that I decided to strike into a wood & have done with it. But at that moment a far too agile malignant looking goat appeared — vaulted over a wall just ahead of me — I rushed in the opposite direction and got found at last.

My work is shaping for the first time today — I feel nearer it. I can see the people walking on the shore & the flowery clusters hanging on the trees — — if you know what I mean. It has only been a dim coast & a glint of foam before — The days go by quickly.

My precious one, I long for your first London letter. I expect it will arrive on Sunday or Monday — so I *must* be patient. Take care of yourself, my darling boy. Buy something for your hair & use it. Do keep warm. Buy yourself another pair of those pants. Do keep happy. Eat good food. Don't call this 'swank' on my part. It is not — Perhaps it *is* partly that I love to frown at you & give your tie a perfectly unnecessary little tug. Even though you do say 'for God's sake woman, let me alone.'

I kiss you on your eyes & your lips & the top curl of your hair.

Tig.

MS ATL. *LKM* I. 38-9; *LJMM*, 46-7.

[1] Murry wrote (8 Dec 1915, ATL) that he had been given a false rate of exchange when he changed money on his way home, and that a woman from Algiers had given him some dates on the train.

[2] KM's Japanese doll, lent to Murry as a mascot; its head had come off on the journey to England.

[3] The poet and editor Walter de la Mare (1873-1950) had become a friend during the days of *Rhythm*. His note has not survived.

To J. M. Murry, [11 December 1915]

[Hôtel Beau Rivâge, Bandol]
Saturday.

My dear one,

No letters today. I cannot hope to hear from you before Monday, I think. So I am not disappointed. The weather has changed. Last night a wind sprang up — one of the lesser winds — a forlorn, piping creature that I don't remember having heard on land before — a wind I always connect with the open sea & night in the cabin — and a hollow dread that the land has gone for ever. I dreamed that I had a baby (Virtue always rewards me with this elfin child) and Grandmother was alive. I had been to sleep after it was born & when I woke it was night & I saw all the people in the house lying on their backs asleep too. And I was sure my baby was dead. For a long time I was too frightened to call anyone — but finally called to Grandmother & she came in and said nonsense, child he's getting on beautifully (as though 'he' were a cake in the oven.) She brought him in to reassure me — a charming little creature in a flannel gown with a tuft of hair.[1] So I got up and kissed Grandmother who handed me the baby and I went downstairs & met you in the street. The moon was shining — you looked lovely; it shone particularly on your grey felt hat which you wore à l'espagnole — But we were very poor; we lived in a tenement & you had put a banana box across 2 chairs for the baby. "The only *brick* is," you said, "how the hell can we go to a music hall?" Then I woke up, switched on the light & began to read Venus & Adonis. It's pretty stuff — rather like the Death of Procris.[2]

Yesterday I had de la veine & wrote in the afternoon & then went for a short walk along that bar that encloses the harbour. It was sunsct. Its a good place to walk — the sea on either side rushes up & the town — just showing a glimmer of light here and there looked marvellous. I sat on a stone & began thinking "I believe it is perfectly necessary to one's *spiritual balance* to be somewhere where you can see the sun both rise & set" etc etc — & such like nonsense — très serieuse — when I remarked a gazelle like military form approaching — in blue with a braided cap. This ensemble, thought I, is exactly like the cover of a 95 centimes novel. Myself on a rock — a red sunset behind — this graceful form approaching — — — It came near — & then a blithe, cheerful dead sure voice positively *hailed* me. Vous promenez seule, Madame? I had a good look at the upstart — olive skin, silky eyebrows & silky moustache — *Vain* — there is no word for it. I said 'oui, Monsieur seule.' Vous demeurez à l'hotel Beau Rivage, n'est-ce pas? Silence. Je vous ai déja remarqué plusieurs fois. (His French was right — Mine isn't.) Then I looked at him like Frank Harris would look at Dan Ryder quoting Shakespeare[3] & he drew himself up, saluted, said 'Ah, pardon je suis très indiscret.' I said *exactly* like Harris — *très* indiscret Monsieur, & walked home. Scarcely had I gained the road when a gentleman in a cape approached. Vous promenez seule, Madame? But that was a bit too steep I said "Non Monsieur, avec une canne —" What a race! They're like german commercial travellers! Send me a bulldog in your next letter, sweetheart. The sea is very choppy today. Far

as you can see the waves break — like a school of fishes — I love you
— I am your own girl

Wig.

MS ATL. *LKM* I. 39-40; *LJMM*, 48-9.

[1] *The Journal* 1954 recollects (101) a very similar occurrence in KM's childhood, when her grandmother showed her Gwen, her baby sister, in January 1891. The baby died at three months.

[2] KM is comparing Shakespeare's poem with the painting by Piero di Cosimo in the National Gallery.   .

[3] When KM first met Harris he had recently published *The Man Shakespeare* (1909), and *The Women in Shakespeare* (1911), and considered himself the ultimate authority. For the bookseller Daniel Rider, see p. 334, n.1.

To J. M. Murry, [12 December 1915]

[Hôtel Beau Rivage, Bandol]
A windy Sunday.

Dearest and only one,

I really do think I may expect your first London letter tomorrow & I ought to hear from Kay, too. Ive not had a sign so far.

For some unaccountable reason, chéri, Ive got our Marseilles fever again with all its symptoms — loss of appetite, shivering fits, dysentery. What on earth can it be? I really think it is a noisome fever from some black man in a cafe near to The Vieux Port. At any rate its horrid & I am a ragged creature today. If I hadn't got William Shakespeare I should be in the ultimate cart, but he reads well to a touch of fever. However, I expect I shall be a better girl by the time you get this, so don't go and worry, darling of my heart. I bought a most superior exercise book yesterday for 4 sous *but* at about five oclock the eternal silence was broken by a rap at my door & a pretty creature with gold rings in her ears, spanish boots like Bogey's & flashing eyes & teeth brought in a basket — My laundry. I only send a *morsel* — the veriest fragmint & Lord! there was a bill for 3.15. *How* the rings the teeth eyes & boots vanished — counting the precious money into her hand I paid for them, every one. I shall have to cut myself a little pair of football shorts out of the Radical.[1] I can see that — How are you? Where are you? What are you doing now?. . .

The salon my dear has become impossible ground while the wife of that englishman remains in this hotel. Did you remark her — she is a Belgian — I never met her like — she out belgians anything imaginable. However Ill be even with her and put her to paper and have done with her. I shall creep to the post and back but that's

my limit today. Otherwise I'll keep my room & try & write & read.
Send me a book, precious when you can. Take care of yourself — I
kiss you, Bogey — I am

                                                              Tig.

MS ATL. *LKM* I. 40-1; *LJMM*, 49-50.

¹ *Le Radical,* a republican daily paper published in Marseilles.

To J. M. Murry, [12–13 December 1915]

                                    [Hôtel Beau Rivage, Bandol]
                                    Sunday night before dinner.

My darling one
    I have just put on my *spencer* an extra *pair* of *stockings* and
another shawlet & Im still frozen. I rang for Mary Anne to make me
a fire but she is evidently gone a junketing for I cant find her. The
only minion I did find said they could not mont any bois until
demain. Which seemed to me absurd. Suppose I were in convulsions
& had to be wrapped in blankets & laid on an hearth. (Would that I
were!) Also I am as empty as the little french boy's tirelire & there's
nothing to eat here. And the salon is full of travellers a sitting round
the fire a toasting of their unworthy toes — Oh, what a wretched
little swinging-on-a-bare-twig of a goblin you have got tonight — &
her maladies have been sich that she has been forcéd to guarder her
chambre all day except for to post my letter. At about five I nearly
swallowed the tea spoon and had done with it. For I have added a
sore throat to my fever & I am trying to gargle every 2 hours with 3
sous worth of borax & it tasted awful. Just when I wrote in my
diary adieu chère terre, a nice little boy who belongs to the hotel
brought me a letter from you — it was a gift from heaven. Darling
love, never was a letter more welcome. It was indeed one of my
great aunt Charlottes 'direct answers' to prayers.¹ I read it once &
then twice and then I absorbed it, you know. If you are not careful
and less sweet to me I shall say TOUJOURS, too, & then you'll be
finally caught out. I do hope they give you a bed among the pottery,
dear love. Can you choose your jug and basin from the stock? *I* saw
that shop the day Munro flouted me & nearly entered in² (Forgive
me; I am all sticky with eating so much and such continuous, continent, Shakespeare.) You told me very little of Kot. *Didn't* he fall
down dead when he saw I wasn't there? And where did you sleep
that first night, sirrah?
    Ah, but I wanted you today. Today I have longed for you. Have

you known that? Can I long for you so and you not know? It's a terrible thing to wonder over. But I am so bound up in you that *'us'* is become a kind of separate & loving being that I can scarcely bear to part with & cannot understand why it should ever really leave me — Only pretend & then come back laughing into my arms — Dearest — dearest —

After lunch today a kind gentleman lent me an Historical Roman (Je vous remercie, maman. Bon soir, chèr Père) but I also saw the last 2 numbers of La Vie Parisienne left in the salon by a bald headed old party who brought his own oysters to luncheon.

Monday morning. Then the bell rang for dinner & I went down & afterwards sat in the salon & talked with the lender of the Roman. What a night I spent, Bogey! My left leg rushed up to reinforce my other ills and it has won the battle. In fact Im a complete prisoner to it today & shall have to give this letter to foreign hands to post for I cant walk at all. However its just my old rheumatism — you know what its like. Dressing took me nearly 2 hours & I nearly gave it up wore only one stocking, one leg of my 'pantalons' etc today but the old trick of looking at myself in the glass & saying 'Courage Katherine' won after all — & here I am complete even to Flowering Gorse.[3]

I got 2 papers from Kot today. They will be a great feast & as always happens I am now so tied and bound so *caged* that I know I'll *sing*. Im just on the point of writing something awfully good, if you know that feeling. So there is compensation.

The sun shines today but the wind is still high & 'foam flies white over rocks of black', opposite.

I feel cut off from all human kind — but I am not sad today, sweetheart. I am *hoping* for a letter from you by the courier this afternoon — Give Kot my love. Just a minute I am in your arms & now goodbye my treasure

Tig.

I have opened my letter again to say there is a review of *Mother Goose* under the title Nursery Rhymes in the Lit. Sup. for December 9th which is one of the most delightful reviews I ever read. If de la Mare wrote it[4] & you see him please say how enchanting I thought it was.

MS ATL. *LKM* I. 41-3; *BTW*, 374-5; *LJMM*, 50-3.

[1] Probably Charlotte Hannah Lassetter, née Iredale, wife of the Sydney businessman Frederick Lassetter (see p. 8, n.3); she was not in fact KM's great-aunt, but the sister-in-law of her great-uncle, Henry Herron Beauchamp.

[2] Murry briefly rented a room above a shop which sold pottery, at 41 Devonshire Street, Theobald's Road. It was close to Harold Monro's Poetry Bookshop at no. 35.

[3] KM's favourite perfume was 'Genêt fleuri'.

[4] He did. Cf. *TLS*, 9 Dec 1915.

To J. M. Murry, [13 December 1915]

[Hôtel Beau Rivage, Bandol]
A week today you went away.

My dear Heart,

After giving your letter to my 'bonne' yesterday I gave up the fight & retired in good order to bed, where I am still. The day seemed very long yesterday but I must say my 'bonne' was very good to me. She gave me an extra pillow, kept me supplied with boiling bottles, brought me Vichy, and my meals on a little round table, actually produced a bottle of alcool camphré & frictioned me & gave me some lime flower tea before I went to sleep. Not counting the number of times she put her fat face round the door & said, nodding & *smiling* as only a Frenchwoman can, with an air of delighted gaiety (!) 'Vous souffrez toujours.' You see little Wig giving her smile for smile & nod for nod & saying 'Ah, oui, un peu.' Shes the only creature I've seen. I am rather surprised that neither of the kind ladies who were so ready to welcome us to their haven should not at least have inquired. But no. And I must confess that notice that the repasts served in the room se paient en supplément rather rings in my ears. But Kay's money has come and as I am spending nothing else it will be *perfectly alright*. It is such a beautiful day today — Oh, so lovely. There seems to be a ring of light round everything — It is still and sunny — so still you could hear a spider spin. I dreamed last night that I sat by a fire with Grandmother & my brother & when I woke up I still held my brother's hand. That is true. For my hands were not together — They were holding another hand — I felt the weight & the warmth of it — for quite a long time.

I am hoping for a letter by this afternoon's post. Goodbye my lovely one. Do not forget me & WRITE often to your

Tig
I
am
quite
happy.

MS ATL. *LKM* I. 43-4; *LJMM*, 52.

To J. M. Murry, [14–15 December 1915]

[Hôtel Beau Rivage, Bandol]
Tuesday.

Dearest of all

Don't you worry about me. My femme de chambre, when she goes off duty leaves me in her 'friends' charge & her 'friend' is a little spry creature with a pale blue nose who is very gentille indeed to me. 'Il ne faut pas vous gêner' — she keeps saying to me — 'Je veux faire tout ce que je peux pour vous.' In fact the servants here seem to think Im a *dear* little thing! *And* after midday that Englishman, terribly shy, knocked at my door. It appears he has a most marvellous cure for just my kind of rheumatism. Would I try it? All this was explained in the most preposterous rigmarole, in an attempt to appear off hand and at his poor unfortunate ease. I never saw a man so shy! Finally he says that if the pharmacien can't make it up here he will take the first train to Toulon this afternoon & get it for me. It is a rubbing mixture which he got off a german doctor one year when he was at Switzerland for winter sports & had an attack of sciatic rheumatism. It sounds to me — very hopeful — but I'd catch any straw! So I thanked him and bowing and humming and hawing he went off. I cant think what frightened him so. I shall have to put on a hat and a pair of gloves when he brings me back the unguent. Oh, that postman is a tortoise, a detestable tortoise — half a tortoise — for I am hot and he is slow. (Bogey I am an awful little cod. My bed is going to my brain. Now I'll wait for your letter before I go on.) *Later.* I did wait with a vengeance. At half past 3 I rang the bell. 'Le courier — a-t il déja passé?' '*Ah oui*, Madame — une *bonne* demi heure!' 'Merci bien.' But when she had gone I confess I turned to the wall & cried bitterly. . I think mostly from rage. Then I began to think how my Father always always had time to write every single day to my Mother etc etc etc. Then in despair I climbed out of bed, found a piece of ribbon and sat up & made myself a hat. Once before, I remember when I was ill at Rottingdean[1] and alone & waiting for a letter that didn't come I made myself a hat out of pins and fury & it was the hat of my life. So is this. But I am desperately disappointed, I must confess. And I think it is awfully awfully cruel. Once I get better I'll forgive you if you don't write but Oh — to lie in this silent room & know the postman has *been.* You wouldn't like it, Bogey. Now I've had diner, an omelette, some cauliflower & stewed apple. I am getting thin. There are 2 hollows in my cheeks but no little love kisses them. My Englishman has arrived with his pot of ointment & refuses to take even a pin or a bead in payment. How kind he is. Its easy to see *he* hasn't lived with me 3 years.

I am very angry, but not really with you — you couldn't help your letter missing the post I suppose — or perhaps you were handing cups & saucers for that quiet lady with the cast eye.[2]

I should like to be at a large circus tonight, in a box — very luxurious, you know, very warm, very gay with a smell of sawdust & elephants. A superb clown called Pistachio — white poneys, little blue monkeys drinking tea out of Chinese cups — I should like to be dressed beautifully, beautifully down [to] the last fragment of my chemise, & I should like Colette Willy to be dressed just exactly like me[3] & to be in the same box. And during the entr'actes while the orchestra blared Pot Pourri from The Toreador we would eat tiny little jujubes out of a much too big bag & tell each other all about our childhood. A demain, then. *Are* you a darling? Oh, I forgive you. I love you. I hug your blessed little head against my breast & kiss you — I love you you bad wicked precious adorable and enchanting boge. I am

Wig Tig
Wednesday

Dear Jack I have opened my letter to say that now another day has come & again I have no news. I am sending the maid with a wire this morning, for I cannot but believe there is something terribly wrong. I do not deny that today I am *dreadfully anxious.*

Oh, Jack, I appeal even to your imagination as a novelist — do not leave me like this without news. It is so cruel — cruel — I weep bitterly as I write but if you do not answer my wire I shall weep no more but face the fact that — no I can't write it. Ever since Sunday my hope has been for letters & Ive not had one — Your silence makes me ashamed to so let you see my heart — and its need of you. I am still in bed.

[3]

[*Very heavily scored line*]

MS ATL. *LKM* I. 44-5; *BTW*, 375-6; *LJMM*, 52-4.

[1] From April to ?July 1910; see p. 97.
[2] Murry wrote on 9 Dec 1915 (ATL) that when he announced his name to the landlady of the Devonshire Street room, who had a cast in her eye and a quiet voice, she exclaimed, 'Not Middleton Murry, the writer!'
[3] KM must have heard the story — perhaps from X. Marcel Boulestin who records it (60) in his *Myself, My Two Countries* — that at one time Colette appeared at first nights dressed identically with the music-hall star, Polaire.

To J. M. Murry, [15 December 1915]

[Hôtel Beau Rivage, Bandol]
Wednesday night.

Dear Jack
The maid came back with the wire. She couldn't send it. I had to appear in person with my papers — so it lies here — However this afternoon I got your Sunday letter so I know my fears were quite groundless. The room does not sound very comfortable — Thank you for sending me Belle's and Mother's letter. Belle's letter was awfully

sweet & friendly & my Mother's too, I understood very deeply. I am sorry you should have waited for my letters before writing to me — that is what made the situation.

To tell you the truth I feel exhausted now as though the sea which has been tossing me so rudely has thrown me on a flat rock. Of course I do not want you to write if you do not 'feel' like it, but you are a strange being, Jack & you have hurt me terribly. You were so SURE I would be lonely in this quiet room — but once away I suppose you 'forgot' — However I DONT MIND NOW. Its all over. It is getting dark again — after a long, bright day. The moon shines in my room — Goodnight, dearest

Tig.

MS ATL. *BTW*, 375; *LJMM*, 54-5.

To J. M. Murry, [16 December 1915]

[Hôtel Beau Rivage, Bandol]
Thursday Night.

Dearest Boge

I am better but still in bed for there is a bitter east wind blowing today and I feel it is not safe for me to start my normal life in it. I think my Englishman's stuff is going to do me a great deal of good & he has made me so perfectly hopeful — and has been in so many ways such a *comfort* to me. Should this stuff not quite cure me he has given me the address of a place in Normandy where one goes for a cure once a year — the cure only takes 3 weeks; it is a small inexpensive place and he says its simply miraculous. Well, I am sure I can get my Father to give me a little extra a year for this purpose — 'Youll be skipping like a 2 year old after a week there' says my nice, funny man. I am being rubbed twice a day and dieting carefully and only drinking Vichy. This man isn't really a doctor. He's the Head of Guys Dental Hospital[1] — but he is a queer, delightful, goodnatured person and he has certainly been a comfort to me.

I feel very sober today — I am afraid you will think my last letters very silly — They won't happen again — I understand you far better now — somehow — and Ill not ask for the moon either.

A Knock at my door. A letter in pencil from you & funnily enough almost the second sentence is about crying for the moon. Thank you darling for your letter; its an awfully sweet one. I do hope you get your studio at Haverstock Hill — it sounds really delightful — et pas trop cher — Your present room must be horrid. I am sorry too — you do not know how sorry — that we have not talked more about the things we have read and seen & felt. Still, it was fate and can't be altered —

Kiss those fingers for me, dear one. Kiss the chewed up one & the grimy one & particularly the drunken old villain of a first finger.

Tell you all that I am doing? Why, Bogey, I'm lying down or sitting up in bed. All Im feeling? Ah, I cant — Ive lost The Key just for the minute — you know how things do get lost in bed.

Since I have been alone here the loss of my little brother has become quite real to me. I have entered into my loss if you know what I mean — — Always before that I shrank from the final moment — but now it is past.

As I write it is raining fast with a loud noise on the windows — I have the bed covered with copies of the Times, marked at certain places with large blue crosses & a copy of Le Temps with arrows in the margin & "this will interest you" written underneath. All from the same kind and only donor.

Again, my dear one — your last letter is very precious — such a Jag like letter — I see every bit of you in the way you write your name. Goodnight, sweetheart and bless you —

Always
Wig.

MS ATL. *LKM* I. 45-7; *LJMM*, 55-6.

¹ See p. 203, n.3.

To J. M. Murry, [17–18 December 1915]

[Hôtel Beau Rivage, Bandol]
Vendredi.

My dear love,

I am afraid that the courier is past & my letters are drowned for it is as wild a day as ever I have seen — a sky like lead, a boiling sea, the coast hidden by thick mist, a loud noise of wind and such rain dashing on the windows. It is very cold, too, and (3.30) dark already. My maid however lit me a splendid fire this morning & after lunch when the room was warm I got up & am sitting by it now in the arm-chair. I don't feel *very grand* & though the fire isn't like that wretched affair at Cassis and burns merrily and warm, it seems to light the shadows & to prick an ear to the quiet. How quiet it is — except for the storm outside! Much quieter than Day's Bay!

No, the courier has just come & there *is* a letter after all with no address — "Somewhere in Hampstead."¹ I am glad you have moved there if you are more comfortable, darling. I am sure you were wretched doing your own chores in the other place. And I do hope you will soon be able to get your studio and be free of your wretched worries in that respect. It always seems such a waste of time looking for a bed — especially for people like you and me who are so particular — I hope you have a big fire and a GOOD breakfast, darling Bogey and that you will now refresh yourself with one of your Turkish Bath Tickets — (which are in your "gentleman's companion".)

I am sorry I made you sad about that little villa. I heard of another last night from my englishman — four rooms — good stoves — electric light, heating, a verandah, a garden all furnished, and so sheltered that you can dine out every day — 88 francs a month. The man who has just taken it says he buys fish at the market for practically nothing and rosebuds at 1d a dozen — so I should live off fish and rosebuds — But no, Ill not speak of these things — for its useless & foolish — Ill remember that England & the Printing Press won the day & left me on the field[2] — Dont think I don't understand — I do understand, absolutely, my love. Ah, Bogey, as I write to you my heart is full of love for you — and I long to press your head to my breast. Do not forget me — we have had the loveliest times together — you know. Shut your eyes and so many sweet things press on your eyelids —

I am
Tig.
Saturday.

I must write a little more for 'le temps' is so exciting. I had a very vivid dream last night that I and my brother were in Berlin without passports — We were having lunch in the waiting room of a railway station at a long table — with several german soldiers just back from the front with their equipment etc. I see now the proud wives carrying the men's coats for them etc. Suddenly in a dreadful pause I began to speak English. I said one woman reminded me of a Miss Lindsay, bootmaker's assistant in Lambton Quay.[3] In a flash I knew we were done for. Brother said "make for the telephone box" but as we got in a soldier smashed his helmet through the glass door. Crash! I woke to a violent peal of thunder. It was raining, hailing, the shutters flashed pale yellow with the lightning. I heard the bells ringing in the hotel — the servants in felt slippers running along the corridors. Bang! went the thunder — rolling & tossing among the hills. The air was so electric that ones hands and feet sang. Finally I got up, put on my mackintosh & opened the shutters. I felt sure that I'd be struck especially as my room, being at the corner got the full force of the storm. It was a wonderful sight. I shall never forget the dignity of the sea. It drew back from the land a long way. There were no waves — only a fold or two where it touched the shore — and it looked as cold as stone. Above the coast ·the sky was light

silver & above that a bright fantanstic green. As I opened the window
I smelled the sharp smell of the wet blue gum trees — Oh, it was
exciting — it was lovely & all the while the hail springing against the
window pane & the loud thunder & the fluttering light. I rang for
my breakfast & that became a kind of thrilling feast too. I put the
milk jug under the edredon when I had poured out my first cup of
coffee & it stayed there warm as a pigeon & I had a second boiling
cup. That seemed a miracle of ingenuity and forethought! Then the
spry maid tripped in & lit the fire. I heard the little twigs cracking:
she sat back on her heels & told me which rooms the water had
flooded — when such a thing had happened before etc. I felt that I
was going to jump out of bed, wash & dress as quickly as possible
pack a small bundle and catch the ark at about half past ten. But it
is half past ten now & the wind has dropped, 2 roosters are crowing
somewhere & the sky is silver.

This letter will arrive dreadfully near Xmas & I have no present for
you and I shall not be able to send you one — only my love, dearest
and my loyalty. I shall make them both into a little something that
you can hang round your neck as a charm — like the Russians do.
(Wouldn't you hate [it] too.) No, I shant. But forgive me for not
having a gift for you.

I am very much better — in fact to all intents & purposes *cured* I
believe by that unguent. Here is a geranium — I quite forgot they
were there. Here is your Xmas box, Bogey.

Wig.

MS ATL. *LKM* I. 47-9; *LJMM*, 56-8.

¹ Murry had moved to 23 Worsley Road, Hampstead.
² One of Murry's reasons for going back to England was to buy a printing press. He
replied on 22 Dec 1915: 'Why did I leave you? I keep on asking myself the question, and
I find no answer. I can remember nothing of what urged me back. It must have been strong
and overwhelming — but it is all gone. There is no printing press — that vanished like
smoke.' (ATL)
³ At Alfred Lindsay Ltd., bootmaker, 127 Lambton Quay, Wellington.

To J. M. Murry, [19 December 1915]

[Hôtel Beau Rivage, Bandol]
Sunday morning.

Dear Jag.

From sheer laziness Im sitting up in bed. The 'l eau chaude' is
warming its enamel bosom before a fresh lighted fire, & I ought to
be up — but its so pleasant here & the smell of burning wood is so
delicious & the sky & the sea outside are all pearly. After I had

written to you yesterday down came the rain again — & this time the courier really was drowned — so I got a letter of yours about the landlady etc. just this moment. You sound to me peculiarly snug in a way — a clean bed, a fire & a landlady who has a sense of the horrific.[1] Très Anglaise! But you mustn't send me money yet, not until you have more, darling. I'll keep this as an iron ration & buy myself a little tiny noël — but guard your money. I hate to think you may want it et tout va bien chez moi — tu sais. My rheumatism this morning — *n'existe pas*. Ive not been so free for a year. I can positively jump. I'm to go on using the unguent and my Englishman is going to give me the prescription today for he leaves here on Monday. He is also going to conduct me to the post & see Im not cheated with my mandat from Kay, so that is all to the good. I dined downstairs last night. A good many people have arrived — and the hotel is rather changed. More flowers, more fire still & an 'atmosphere'. I met the 'Madame' on the stairs. Elle me demandait si je souffre toujours. I said no — said she, Heureusement le climat est très sec! What a *fool* with rain teeming on everything. I paid a bill here too which was a relief off my mind —

Dear *do* send me summat to read when you can. I am still confined to Shakespeare & the Times. I don't know what to ask for. I'd like a 1/- Dickens that I haven't read — or one I don't remember — but which is it? Oh, I'd like to read Oliver Twist again for one — And Ill send you something for the Signature but don't flatter me[2] — Im only the jam in the golden pill — and I know my place, Betsy. You suddenly mentioned Belgians in connection with your studio, but what Belgians? I hope they don't wrest it from you.[3] It sounded such a good place & Haverstock Hill is près de Hampstead isn't it? I must get up — this paper is being supported on the edredon & its dreadfully heaving.

I have a présentiment that I shall never see Albion's shores again (but then I always feel like that once I am away.) Still, Bogey, in case I should be taken sudden preserve these words & show them to the landlady.

It is such a Sunday morning — so quiet and so tending towards la messe. The lovely air must be the result of the storm, I suppose, for breathing is a delight — Its what you might call very *choice*, this morning, too. I should like to embrace my Father this morning. He would smell of fine cloth with a suspicion of cigar added, eau de cologne, just an atom of camphorated chalk, something of fresh linen & his own particular smell — his 'blood smell' as praps Lorenzo [D.H. Lawrence] would say —

Addio — dear love. Je suis à toi

Tig.

MS ATL. *LKM* I. 49-50.

¹ Murry's landlady had told him about her daughter's dying from an abortion; cf. *BTW*, 377.

² Murry had written on 15 Dec 1915, 'please send me something immediately for the *Signature*. You are the real success of it . . . we shall eventually pull thro' with it, trading on your popularity.' (ATL).

³ In the same letter Murry wrote: 'About that studio, it's all up in the air still — and I'm rather afraid the Belgians will get it, because the landlord will have some stupid idea of doing a charity by letting them teach little Belgian brats in it, instead of giving it to us.'

To J. M. Murry, [19–20 December 1915]

[Hôtel Beau-Rivage, Bandol]
Sunday before Xmas.

My dearest love,

I have just got the letter that you wrote me on Thursday night — with the money in it. Papers have come, too, which I have not opened yet and other letters are waiting — but I want to speak to you tres serieusement — Your letter made you 'real' to me in the deepest sense of the word, I believe, almost for the first time. You say just those things which I have felt. I am *of* you as you write just as you are *of* me.

Now I will say toujours because now at last I know you. We are in a world apart & we shall always be in a world apart — in our own Kingdom which *is* finer and rarer.¹ Shut the gates of it for a minute — & let us stand there. Let us kiss each other, we three.² Yes, Bogey, I shall love you *for always*.

Tig.

Later. Ive just read the Times Lit Sup the New Statesman, the Daily News, a letter from Beatrice Campbell, Kay and Marie. For the papers many thanks darling; they were a great feast. The New Statesman is a dead horse — but still — horse it is & there you are — Beatrice (très entre nous) wrote me a nice letter. Shes a queer mixture for she is really loving & affectionate & yet she is malicious. She was about you and Lawrence *re* me, you understand. How you were so happy on your own and a lot of rubbish & how Lawrence had spoken against me at Clive Bells. It is unpleasant hearing, that kind of thing, and smells faintly of their drawing room which is a most distasteful memory to me.³ By the way, I wrote to Lawrence the other day — a wild kind of letter, if I think of it and not fair to 'us'. You understand? It was just after I had been in bed and without letters & I had a fit of positive despair when life seemed to me to be absolutely over — & I wrote rather in that strain. I only tell you because when I have read your despairing letters to your friends I have always felt that you betrayed us and our love a little and I feel if you should see mine (don't! for its nothing & the mention is making it a

mountain) you might feel a little the same. I am sorry I wrote it[4] —
To tell you the truth I am come to the conclusion that our happiness rests with us and with nobody else at all and that we ought to
build for ourselves and by ourselves. We are very rich together for
we are real true lovers — and we are young and born in each other.
Therefore I think we ought to develop together — keep very close
together (spiritually, mon chér!) and make ourselves, on our island,
a palace and gardens and arbours and boats for you and flowery
bushes for me — and we ought not to court other people at all yet
awhile. Later it will be different. Do you know what I mean and do
you agree with me? Writing to you I love you simply boundlessly.
My love for you is always being new born; the heavenly dews
descend upon it & I'll not believe it is the same flower as yesterday.
You see — how I believe in you! I have a store of belief in you that
couldn't be exhausted! How I admire you! How I love you — we are
two little boys walking with our arms (which won't quite reach)
round each others shoulders & telling each other secrets & stopping
to look at things. . We must not fail our love.

At the end of your letter you ask me how long I am going to
stay — I do not know at all, my precious. You'd better tell me what
you think. Now Ill add a word tomorrow.

Lundi le matin.
A lovely 'gold dust' day — From early morning the fishermen have
been passing & the little boats with red sails put out at dawn. I am
dressed to go to the post office with my 2 mandats —

When I woke this morning & opened the shutters & saw the
dimpling sea I knew I was beginning to love this place — this South
of France — Yesterday I went for a walk. The palm trees after the
rain were magnificent — so firm and so green and standing up like
stiff bouquets before the Lord. The shop people, too, are very kind.
You are a regular customer — after a day or two — & my englishman
says they are very honest.

Last night in the salon I had a long talk with a woman who is here
for her health. A woman about 50. She has been nursing since the
beginning of the war somewhere near Arles. She is of the Midi and
has a very pronounced accent — whch is *extremely* fascinating —
and she knows and adores 'mon pays' — She told me all about the
coast, about all sorts of little places "de toute beauté" — and as she
talked I began to see this place — not romantically but truly. I like
it and more than like it. This woman was reading the Letters of
Taine. .[5] She told me such good stories of the black soldiers — I
must not forget them. I hope I shall speak a great deal with her
because she is very good for my french too. She has a good vocabulary and a way of *spacing* her words giving them a very nice, just

quantity. Oh, Bogey, it is the most heavenly day. Every little tree feels it and waves faintly from delight. The femme de chambre called to the gardener, just now as she beat the next door mattress out of the window — 'Fait bon?' & he said 'Ah, delicieux!' Which seemed to me very funny for a gardener, especially this little chap — Now I must button my boots with a tiger's tail[5] and go out —
Goodbye dearest love

Tig.

MS ATL. *LKM* I. 50-1; cited *BTW*, 378, 389; *LJMM*, 60-2.

[1] Murry wrote on 17 Dec 1915, 'For that is our business in life, my dearest, to . . . walk, hidden from the world, beneath the big leaves' (ATL).
[2] Murry later wrote (*BTW*, 389) of this inclusion of her brother: '"We three. . ." I wonder whether I grasped the significance of it at that moment. I doubt it.' KM, whose notebooks of these months record her obsession with her brother, had written soon after arriving in Bandol: 'I do not wish to go anywhere and the only possible value that anything can have for me is that it should put me in mind of something that happened or was when we were alive' (*Journal* 1954, 89).
[3] Although KM remained friendly with Beatrice Campbell, she and Murry had altered their opinion of Gordon Campbell, who was now Assistant Controller at the Ministry of Munitions. Murry wrote on 12 Dec 1915, 'Gordon is now completely done for, and terribly depressing. I think he is really a lost soul. Biddy is lovely as ever.' (ATL.) KM had met the art critic Clive Bell (1881-1964) through the Lawrences shortly before she left for the South of France. He had recently separated from Vanessa (Stephen) Bell (1879-1961), whom he married in 1907.
[4] Murry told KM on 20 Dec 1915 that when her letter to Lawrence arrived, 'Lawrence went for me, about you, terribly. Had I been alive I should have been hurt; but I'm not alive today. I'm just numbed. He said that it was all my fault, that I was a coward, that I never offered you a new life, that I would not break with my past, that your illness was all due to your misery and that I had made you miserable, by always whining & never making a decision; that I should never have left you there. . . . He let drop by accident that you had written that "there was nothing for you in life". (ATL.) KM's letter to Lawrence does not survive.
[5] Presumably *H*[ippolyte] *Taine: Sa Vie et sa correspondence*, ed. M. Taine and André Chevrillon, 4 vols. (1902-7).
[6] KM was fond of quoting the nursery-rhyme variant which begins:
　　Come button your boots with a Tiger's Tail
　　And let down your golden hair
　　And live for a week on Bubble and Squeak
　　At the foot of the winding stair. . .

To Mary Hutchinson, [20 December 1915]

[Bandol]

I do hope you have forgiven me, for I am so sorry that I did not see you before I left England. It is lovely here — very early spring and sunshine which melts in one's mouth.

Salutations sincères
Katherine Mansfield.

MS (postcard) Texas.

To J. M. Murry, [21 December 1915]

[Bandol]

AI RECU LETTRES TOUT VA TRES BIEN ECRIT

BOWDEN

Telegram ATL.

To J. M. Murry, [21 December 1915]

[Hôtel Beau Rivage, Bandol]
Tuesday

My darling,

This will just be a note today for I wrote you at such length yesterday. Last night at about 6.45 your telegram came. It was very worrying because now I am better & you are still getting letters to say that I am ill. That is the horrible part of distance. If ever I'm ill again I'll [not] breathe a word of it. Oh, my precious darling I am sorry you should have been so worried, & I hope my wires arrive early. The reason for the 2 wires was this. The Courier who brought me the telegram said it was défendu to send wires in English from France from here so I believed him & sent you the first cold acknowledgement, but when he had gone I thought it was absurd and I hated to think of you getting that chill reply so I ran to the post office — The postmaster said of course I could "dire ce que vous voulez" and thankfully I sent the other. It was bright moonlight when I went to send your wire. I felt I could have spend pounds upon a long long telegram but you will understand that I used our secret word with intent in the English telegram.[1] Is all well, now, my dear love and do you understand?

Last night I dreamed I was back in England looking everywhere for rooms behind the South Kensington Museum. It was pouring with rain & nearly dark — and the agent said how about a small house with a studio attached! We were *seriously considering* this when I woke up & praised the Lord. I am writing something for *The Signature* but it will not be finished before Friday. That means you will get it on Tuesday. Is that time? It is called *Et in Arcadia ego*[2] — I hope you will like it.

This is a scrappy and insufficient letter today — but you know it is sent with all my love. How distracting it is that I cannot say how much I love you — however I may long to — but you know. You have written me such wonderful letters. It is strange. I feel that I only really know you since you went back to England. I feel as though a miracle had happened to you and you are rich and bathed in light. While I sit here writing to you time is not. I am one with our love for ever — The fishing boats are putting out to sea. There is a breeze today and white wings in the sky — they mean happiness.

Again again I love you

Tig

MS ATL. Cited *BTW*, 386; *LJMM*, 62-3.

¹ KM's telegram in English has not survived.
² A short piece with this title is in the *Journal* 1954, 92-3.

To J. M. Murry, [22 December 1915]

[Hôtel Beau Rivage, Bandol]
Mercredi.

Bogey, my dearest love,

I wish you could see the winds playing on the dark blue sea today, and two big sailing vessels have come in & are rocking like our white boat rocked when you were here — The sea is what *I* call very high this morning and the clouds are like swans — Its a lovely morning; the air tastes like fruit. Yesterday I went for a long scrambling walk in the woods — on the other side of the railway. There are no roads there — just little tracks & old mule paths. Parts are quite wild and overgrown, then in all sorts of unexpected faery places you find a little clearing — the ground cultivated in tiny red terraces & sheltered by olive trees (full of tiny black fruit) There grow the jonquils, daffodils, new green peas and big abundant rose bushes — A tiny (this word is yours really: its haunting me today —) villa is close by with a painted front and a well or a petite source at the bottom of the garden. They are dream places — Every now and then I would hear a rustle in the bushes and an old old woman her head tied up in a black kerchief would come creeping through the thick tangle with a bunch of that pink heath across her shoulders. "B'jour ma petite dame" She would munch and nod — and with a skinny finger point me my way — Once I found myself right at the very top of a hill and below there lay an immense valley — surrounded by mountains — very high ones & it was so clear you could see every pointed pine, every little zig zag track — the black stems of the olives showing sooty and soft among the silvery green — One could see for miles and miles — There was, far in the distance a tiny town planted on a little knoll — just like a far away city in a Dürer etching — and now and again you would see two cypresses & then if you looked carefully you found a little house — for two cypresses planted side by side portent bonheur — On the other side of me there was the sea & Bandol & the next bay Sanary — Oh, Bogey, how I longed for my playfellow. Why weren't you with me — Why didn't you lean over the fence and ask the old old man what that plant was & hear him say it was the immortelle & it flowers for eight years and then dies and its yellow flowers come out in June — The sun went down as I found the Saint Cyr road back to Bandol. The people were coming home — & the children were running from school — As I came into Bandol I heard a loud chanting & down the Avenue des Palmiers there came four little boys in white carrying a cross & incense braziers — an old priest with white hair chanting — four men follow-ing each carrying a corner of a black & silver cloth — then a coffin carried on a table by six men & the whole village following — the last man of all being an old chap with a wooden leg — It was extremely fantastic and beautiful in the bright strange light.

No post came yesterday. I expect it was delayed. I am longing for a letter today, my precious — Do you feel in this letter my love for you today — It is as warm as a bird's nest — Bogey — but don't mind when I say that in all these walks & in all my growing love for this country and people I cannot but wish infinitely that you were here to share it and complete my happiness —

My own — my darling love. Take me in your arms and kiss me — and I will kiss you too and hold you Bogey & tell you all I can't write. I am your woman

Tig.

[*Across top of first page*]
As I write a *third* ship is coming in & you are walking on the deck in your corduroy trousers & spanish boots — an Awful Knife in your sash. Can you see me if I wave?

MS ATL. *LKM* I. 51-2; *LJMM*, 63-4.

To J. M. Murry, [23 December 1915]

GD. HOTEL BEAU RIVAGE | BANDOL (VAR)
BANDOL LE 23rd I think

Dearest

I had 2 short notes from you this morning one written on Saturday and one on Sunday — They are arrived so late that I can only think the post is out of order with the Xmas mails — & we'll have to expect delays for a day or two. I (*unlike* you, false wretch) have never missed one day in writing to you. I expect by this time the letters are come. The Daily Sketch arrived yesterday. Its a fat rag and thank you for it, Jag dear, but don't be offended if I say I don't like it — will you? I am longing for my Colette books & I am also *absolutely certain* that letters from Lesley Moore have fallen into Farbman's hands. Is Kot my enemy now? I feel he is. You know I have not heard from Lesley for a long time and I know she writes to me every week. My heart burns with rage when I think that her poor letters come & I do not see them — Chastise Kot for me — will you, Bogey?

I am glad you are going to Lady Ottoline's,[1] darling for Xmas. You are bound to have what Marie calls a "very merry time." I lay in bed this morning wondering how many wenches you'd take under the mistletoe & swear you'd been amorous of these three years — Tell me all about it, darling of my heart & don't forget among your faeries to think of me on New Year's Eve —

The sailors in the sailing ships have been washing — they are all pegged out along the masts and spars — Its a very still primrose & cowslip day. I am going to drive in a kerridge to that little Durer town I told you of — The Englishman did not go away on Monday. He stayed till the end of the week to show me the different walks he has discovered here & it is he who is taking me there this after- noon. How we get there heaven only knows but he says there *is* a road — This man has certainly been awfully kind to me. You he cannot understand at all & for all I say I am afraid you will remain a villain. I can't persuade him that I am more than six years old and quite able to take my own ticket & manage my own affairs. "But why should you"? says he. "What did he marry you for if it wasn't because he wanted to look after you?" He is 62 and old fashioned at that but I feel in a very false position sometimes and I can't escape from it. However its no matter.

I am glad Lawrence is nice to you & I think your lunch sounded quite *too horrid*.[2] Please tell me how money is with you, Bogey — I don't like your sausage & mashed dinners — & your free meals. Thank goodness the Lady Ottoline will feed you well, & youll have good baths and beds —

Ten new people are coming here today — There is a kind of flurry in the corridors —

You know I really am a little tempted to take a minute villa later on here. Would it be more expensive than living here, do you think? Its not that I don't like this hotel — I *do*, and (this is like my brother) I am awfully popular with all the people here — you would laugh. I know all their separate histories & married lives etc — I sit and listen — they talk. I feel sometimes very much like Ferguson. But a little villa with a handkerchief of garden is a very attractive idea —

Talk to me about it. I am so sorry, love that the Belgians have got your studio. Have you any other place in your life?

Your two letters today for some reason have made me rather stiff — rather dumb. I feel it as I write — I don't know why. I feel I am talking over a fence — & my voice is tiny like a grasshoppers — Write to me again at length — and know that this little stiffness or dumbness est rien and that really and truly there isn't a fence & we are sitting together hand in hand under a rhubarb leaf & I am showing you what I have got in my pocket and you are showing me what you have got in yours —
My dear love!

Tig.

MS ATL. *LKM* I. 52-3; *LJMM*, 65-7.

¹ Lawrence had arranged for Murry to spend Christmas at Lady Ottoline Morrell's at Garsington.
² In a letter of 18 Dec 1915 (ATL) Murry described how Frieda Lawrence had asked him to lunch with her. He 'waited for twenty minutes in the cold before she deigned to appear', and then found there were several other people present — 'a vile experience'.

To J. M. Murry, [24 December 1915]

[Hôtel Beau Rivage, Bandol]
The Morning of Christmas Eve.

My Very Dearest,

Yesterday I had *four* letters from you and a copy of the Daily News. I have never had such richesse upon a single day — but my love, my darling, in all the letters you were worried about me and I simply curse myself for having told you about my rheumatism at all — Fool that I was — I will never never do such a thing again — I am only praying that my telegram was not very delayed with the Xmas posts and that you go away for your festivities with a light heart — Oh, Bogey I do reproach myself, but it is over now, isn't it and we are in harbour aren't you & you will be able to work in peace when you get back to London. I wish I had known how long you were staying for I wanted to send you a small panier de fleurs for the New Year. They are in such profusion here and they can be safely sent to London.

Thank you for Lesleys two letters and for dear Maries. She sent me, as you know a pair of mittens to write in, but apologised that they had no '*thum*' as she had no one to teach her to make one — If they are large enough for you do wear them, my precious, and keep your knobbly hands warm — Oh, I wish I could *cherish* you as

I long to. I wish I could care for you & hold you in my arms and say "Yes Boge, I know —"

Although you are as near me as my own blood, in one way, in another, here is the physical fact that you are not here — that when I go for my walks and scramble on the rocks there is no Bogey somewhere with a little worn Homer in his hand — that when I fly round a particularly lovely corner I do not see — coming to meet me — No, that idea that you should come and meet me, happily, not as we have met at Tube Stations & street corners — but you careless, whistling frightfully out of tune is too sweet and too painful to imagine even in play. I can never be completely happy without you and the nearer I feel to life and to being myself the greater is my longing to have you with me — that is quite absolute and final.

Yesterday after I had posted your letter I went to the Market. You know where it is — in front of that square, curious little church. Yesterday the market was full of branches of roses — branches of mandarines and flowers of all kinds. There was also a little old man selling blue spectacles and rings "contre la rheumatisme" and a funny, fat old woman waddling about and pointing to everything she wanted with a fat fowl that she held by the legs. The fowl was furious.

Then I went up to that untidy funny villa with the oranges growing against the walls close to the cemetery — You know the one I mean? It has a long 'sticky' garden in front and a large blue board advertising apartements. White roosters peck among the gravel and all the paths are spanned over with brown sprigs of vine — The villa is stone and carved with doves, cauliflowers, lions, monkey trees and setting suns. Very gay —

In the garden, mounted on a very nervous chair a huge old man in a blue apron and horn specs was snipping twigs — & below him a tiny little boy in pink and white socks was receiving them in his pinny. I asked if Madamoiselle Marthe lived there — Certainly said the man while the chair wobbled fearfully & then he stood up raised his snippers and *roared* "Marthe Marthe." Open flew a window, out popped a little round head. "On demande" said the old man. Then a glass door opened and a little creature in a white cotton jacket with red wool shoes on stood smiling by me. I asked her if she would lift the shoulders of my brown jacket for me — And she said she would — but after the days of fête — n'est ce pas? And then, her head a little on one side, with a charming timid smile and one hand with a silver ring on it keeping the sun from her eyes she came to open the gate for me, because she said it was a very difficult gate — I went away longing to write a little play with this setting — I could even hear the music to it. I especially saw the garden by moonlight & the shadows of the oranges and Marthe with a shawl over her head — and her telling *him* it was a difficult gate.

Two of the big sailing ships have come right into the port this morning and are anchored close to the quai. I think they are unloading something. I must go and ask the paper woman all about it. She is a fund of cheerful gossip and she's a nice soul. When the air is 'frais' she produces a tiny charcoal bucket with a pierced lid — and says — "warm your hands one good little moment" —

My dear! Ten *children* with their parents and 2 nurses arrived here last night. They are all 'une belle famille' as my maid says — I have not seen them yet — but my brain reels at the idea of their weekly bills —

Bogey, Bogey Bogey.

I am not going to write any more now for I am so longing to see you today & to talk to you that it's useless.

Dear love I am

Tig

Do you want *any money*. Tell me your exact finances will you? I am quite in the dark about so many things that concern you.

MS ATL. *LKM* I. 55-6; *LJMM*, 67-9.

To J. M. Murry, [24 December 1915]

[Hôtel Beau Rivage, Bandol]

Bogey darling, I received this yesterday and I don't know what to do with it. How can I get the £2.0.0? Must I sign something or — enfin what must I do?[1] If I have to sign it & return it to you mark the place for my signature with a pencil — will you & instruct me how to proceed. Its an excellent advent for it will pay for all my unavoidable recent extras. It could not be more welcome — Dont send me *another farthing* for I'll send it back. I am perfectly well, you know, not a touch of rheumatism — and I am taking care of myself like Billy-O.

Observe the spelling of Marie's name — Mrs Perk*ins* — but if we were together we'd have a TERRIFIC Time with the £2.0.0. Wouldn't we? — I have just had lunch — vin blanc & grilled sardines carottes à la crême and saucisses pommes parmentier — & oranges — One must *never* drink vin rouge in the Midi — on m'a dit. Its true the vin blanc is wonderful. I wish you had tasted it. Then I make these people give me toast at all my meals instead of the Van Gogh[2] & that makes "le repas deux fois plus discrèt" — Im just off for a long promenade — If you were here we could walk to Sanary — watch the fishermen pull in their nets, have coffee at the Café on the quay and come back by train — carrying a big bunch of yellow roses. Sanary is simply a bower of roses pour *rien* — Monsieur.

Whether it is because I feel so well & my bête noir of rheumatism is gone or whether it is the vin blanc *or* the climate or all three, I don't know, but I feel so terribly happy this afternoon I have such a desir vif d'embrasser quelqu'un — *bien bien* —

Mon plus que chéri — voici ma secondre lettre aujourdhui — il faut que ça finit, et tout de suite —

Can you send me Maries £2.0.0 by a Mandat Internationale. I mean isn't there a way to send money so that the postman comes and gives it to you while you curl in bed, pays you out of a bag. That used to happen to me. How is it done?
A bientôt, mon amour

Tig

MS ATL. *LJMM*, 64–5.

¹ KM's sister had sent her a 'sola', a kind of money order which had to be endorsed with the recipient's signature before it could be cashed.
² Murry's note (*LJMM*, 65), explains: 'An ordinary French long *pain*, so christened because of a Van Gogh still-life containing one.'

To J. M. Murry, [25 December 1915]

[Hôtel Beau Rivage, Bandol]
It is Xmas Morning.

My Little King,

The rain is pouring down & the sea is roaring out the Psalms — Even in the harbour the boats are rocking — but I am so happy and there are so many candles and angels burning on the tree that you have planted in my heart that I can hardly write to you. I want to come flying into your arms and I want us to stay close — close kissing each other because we are in love. There is a large pine cone on the fire. I put it on just before I began this letter — to be a kind of celebration. And do you remember that black headed pin you stuck in my curtain to make it 'hang'. Its still there — it has got to look very like you. I am going to write a fearfully long letter this morning for if I do not I shant be able to keep my heart from going off like a Xmas cracker.

Dear love — my own beloved, precious marvellous and adorable little Boge. If I live to be the age of those first and original Pa men in the Bible I shall never be able to love you enough. I quite understand God making eternity — Catch hold of me Bogey — stop me.

Oh, dearest hold me close. My body trembles for love of you today — I can feel you in every minutest part of me.

Before I write any more I must tell you something. I hope you don't kiss anybody at Lady Ottolines. After all I have said — it does sound absurd! But I minded you kissing even Anne [Drey] 'seriously'. I minded you *really* kissing. For this reason. If I wished to — I could not. There is no question of will or reason, but I have to be physically faithful to you because my body wouldn't admit anyone else — even to kiss *really* you know. That was why I wrote so stiffly about your going there for Xmas. Is this jealousy? I suppose it is. But you're mine — you're mine and when we have not been lovers for so long I feel I could not bear anyone else to touch even the threshold of your lips. But tell me *all* that happens at Lady Ottolines and if you have kissed somebody — (I'm laughing a little, precious, as I write that because it is a little absurd.) Tell me and I'll bear it and understand and not take it to heart. Only, *tell me* always. Now you'll say 'good God, my goblin is changing into a dragon.' I'm not.

Two letters came from you today. One you had been to see Lawrence (but I explained that away — didn't I?) and in the other, thank God, you had got my telegram at [last].[1] Ah, dear heart, really our stormy passage is over. Then just as I had brushed my hair 100 times I had your telegram. You couldn't have sent me a lovelier present — I keep on reading it and it looks so awfully funny and sweet because its so written wrong — by the man here and scratched over. Tenderest *lion* (I read that *love*) wonderful LItters received perfectly haRpy and your name is MErcy!! It is even nicer like this. I feel as though fate did it on purpose to show that she really does love us and we really are her funny little children. . .

Although it is damp and raining I have not even a touch of rheumatism. That cure is wonderful.

When I went out to put your letter in the Palais D'Azur yesterday I found out why the boats had come in — for there was a procession of dark young sailors, barelegged, their bright blue trousers rolled to the thigh in big full blouses & with their [hair] cropped "en pudding" carrying on their shoulders little red kegs & filling them at the fountain. A great dispute went on because it was midday & the women had come to draw water too — & the sailors would not take the kegs away and only laughed — They had a tiny boat rocking at the steps of the quai — On deck, three sailors hung over a rail plucking three ducks. The feathers floated on the water. The boat is called the *Felicina* and she comes from Verragia. The other boat hasn't got a name. Today they are dressed & flying five or six snippets of flags.

Yesterday afternoon I went off by myself into the woods & spent all the afternoon exploring little tracks and 'chemins de chamois'. I picked such lovely daisies too, with pink tips — It got very faery after the sun went down, and when I go to the road to come home, still deep in the woods there came a tinkle and round the corner came an old man with a herd of brindled goats. As I came into the town all the babies were flocking in the streets looking at the Xmas toys. Heaven knows they are a sorry little show, but you should have heard the screams of joy. "Ah, ah, le beau chemin de fer. Dis! Dis! Qu'il est mignon le p'tit chien! Ah, la grande — la belle!' I began to look too & I nearly bought an elephant or a dog with one ear standing up, or a *lovely* tea set with roses painted on it & a sugar basin with a tiny strawberry for the handle on the lid. Then the captain of the Felicina landed & came marching up the street — very grand — all gold braid — little clipped beard — stiff linen. He was followed by 2 sailors and he disappeared behind the bead curtain of the butcher's shop. Then another ship came sailing in. Which makes *five*. Can you feel how thrilling they are in this tiny place? And how one longs to go on board and walk up and down little ladders?

There is a crèche in the church. It has been all made by the children. It is simply beautiful. A landscape with painted cardboard houses — even shutters to the windows. A windmill — little bridges of twigs — fountains made of falling silver paper cut in strips, the roads all of fresh sand the hills and the valleys all of moss that they gathered in the woods. Trees are planted in the moss & hung with silver stars (far too big for them). There are sheep under the trees — shepherds, holy men — the three kings — one with a black face and awful whites to his eyes. Fat little angels perch in all sorts of places and in a neat cardboard grotto is Mary, St. Joseph (a very old Dotty) and a naked 'p'tit *Ch*esau' as they say, who can open & shut his eyes. The priest was showing this Marvel to a baby when I was there but she could say nothing except in a very hushed voice "il est tout nu." The dove is also perched on a tree — a drunken fowl bigger than the ox & the ass — & out of one house there is the head of the inn-keeper in a night cap with a tassel on it telling Mary he hasn't got a room. . .

My love. I have only time to run to the post with this. I love you — *love* you. I am always your own

Tig.

Plus tard. Colette has come — thank you love.

I have opened my letter (I am always doing that — its like popping just ones head in again) to say that when I ran to the post it was shut for all today & I am afraid this letter will not go until tomorrow, love. But I am glad I opened it for I want to ask you something.

Do you want me to come back? Do you think you will work better at your Dosty Book alone?[2] Shall I stay here until it is finished or until the Spring, or when? I am willing to come back today if you want me — you know that, my heart. But speak to me frankly about this, will you? And when you DO want me back write me a note saying that Hara is ill and you would be very relieved if I would come to England immediately etc. just so that I will have a definite something to show the consuls and the passportiers. (We are still quite babies enough to play with dolls and I'd much rather pretend about Hara than about a real person. I would so see her, with her little hands in her kimono sleeves, very pale & wanting her hair brushed.)

I have just had a Xmas dinner — very dreadful and indecent to be partaken of alone. The "belle famille" had an *enormous* feed. I left the little tiny ones leaning back in their chairs with their legs stretched out utterly helpless — & slightly the worse for wine. For even the baby who is not yet three drank until her glass rested on her nose, where she left it and blew into it & stared at me through the top. Now I am going for a walk with the Englishman who leaves definitely the day after tomorrow.

Later. It was a long walk through the woods & then we left the paths and he taught me *how* to climb as taught by the guides in Norway. It was boring beyond words but absolutely successful — We scaled dreadful precipices & got wonderful views. Then I had to learn *how* to descend — and how to balance if the stones roll when you put your foot on them. What a pa man! All this of course he takes deadly seriously — and I find myself doing so too and I don't get one bit tired. I wish you could see my room. Even the blue glass vases we put away have had to come out for the big bouquets of yellow and pink roses. Tonight I have promised to dine with this pa man. I don't doubt I shall get a lecture on touring in Spain. I already know more about how to travel in Italy than any living being, I should think —

I am going to try to send you a nutshell in this letter for a little hat. Its dark now and the waves are beating right up the road among the palms.

Do you feel my love?

Always & toujours
Tig

MS ATL. *LKM* I. 56-8; *BTW*, 387-8; *LJMM*, 69-73.

[1] i.e., that of 21 Dec 1915; see p. 222.
[2] Martin Secker had commissioned a study of Dostoevsky from Murry, to cancel the £30 debt still owing from the collapse of *Rhythm*.

To J. M. Murry, 26 [December 1915]

[Hôtel Beau Rivage, Bandol]
26th

My own!

Just a little note so as not to let the day pass. It is a lovely day & even yesterday became fair after all. If you could but see my roses! I heard today from Kay — whose card I send you (!) and from Father and Mother. Their letters I have just answered, Bogey. They made me very sad — Indeed I understand that as 'the silence' descends on them their loss becomes even greater. Now, for instance that letters about him are infrequent and few — and the English mail arrives, as Father says, and seems each week to make the dreadful gap more real. Dearest, in my letter I wrote a great deal *about* you and Chummie. I wanted to make them feel that you had been real to each other and played together. I wish you would write a note to them. Please *do* if you can, but send it to *me* to post for I have not told them that you have gone back to England. I thought it wiser not to; it was so difficult to explain from this distance and not necessary —

I heard from Lawrence today. Shall I send you his letter? It left me cold. He wants us to join him, but you know we are not made to do that kind of thing ever.[1] We are two, rich & happy apart — If you do not want me back yet, Bogey (you understand) I would like to stay here a little longer — I send you all my love

Tig.

MS ATL. *LJMM*, 73.

[1] Lawrence wrote to KM from Hampstead on 20 Dec 1915, telling her of the new life they must live, and informing her that after Christmas he and Frieda were removing to Cornwall: 'When you come back, I want you and Murry to live with us, or near us, in unanimity: not these separations. Let us all live together and create a new world. If it is too difficult in England, because here all is destruction and dying and corruption, let us go away to Florida: soon.' (*LDHL* II. 482.)

To J. M. Murry, [27 December 1915]

[Hôtel Beau Rivage, Bandol]

Dearest

Just a line which may not reach you. It is 7.30 *A.M.* & I am just off to send the telegrams. I have been awake all night — hugging my joy — If you come, Bogey,[1] in all probability I shall fly into two bits as the train comes in — I hate the journey over again for you that is why I am putting 'dont feel bound to', but once you arrive you will be *happy, happy*. I keep making out little lists & having conversations with imaginary charbonniers! Bogey, my heart, my treasure — I have been sent £10.10. for a Xmas present which will come in handy. No more now. I will write again at length when your wire comes if it says 'no' but until then I cant write. We can easily live here on £3 a week. A woman to 'do' for us only costs 15-20 francs a month. We shall become very brown indeed with little bits of orange peel in our hair. I am praying — to really the old God — I feel He can do it and will —

A Happy New Year to my little big husband — Your infinitesimal wife

Wig.

The white bear[2] is waving at you.

MS ATL. *LJMM*, 73-4.

[1] Murry had written on 23 Dec 1915, 'I want either to go right away — perhaps to some up-country station in your back-blocks — or I want to stay in England. Only before either of those things, I want to be with you. Therefore, if you decide to stay, I must come, even if I starve for it.' In the same letter, he said both to 'forget . . . I said "Find a villa." It was mainly cowardice', and 'If you want me, I will come *immediately*'. (ATL.)

[2] Another of KM's dolls.

To J. M. Murry, [27 December 1915]

[Bandol]

PERFECT IDEA BELLE HAS SENT TEN GUINEAS ALWAYS

KATHERINE

Telegram ATL.

To J. M. Murry, [27 December 1915]

[Bandol]

ILL COME IMMEDIATELY URGENT WIRE ARRIVAL

KATHERINE[1]

Telegram ATL. Cited *BTW*, 391.

[1] The wire professing illness was to help Murry obtain permission to travel during wartime. Lady Ottoline noted in her journal in January 1916 (Morrell, 84-5) that a telegram asking him to come arrived while Murry was at Garsington. 'I let him talk on and on about her, telling me of their wonderful times together, . . . and the way they "wisped away together", as he called it — by which, I suppose, he meant flights of thought and talk.' She advised him to go at once, and gave him £5 for his journey.

To J. M. Murry, [27 December 1915]

[Hôtel Beau Rivage, Bandol]
Monday morning.

Even if you never came I cannot but love you more for the evening and the night and the early morning I have spent thinking that you *are* coming. It was Sunday so I could not send you a telegram until today. I somehow — Oh, how did I? got through last evening but sitting in the salon among unreal fantastic people & sewing and talking. For I knew I would not sleep. What drowsy bliss slept in my breast. Oh Jack, I hardly dared to breathe. A woman here told me how to buy our stores & what to pay & how to make soup with 2 sous worth of bones — and what day the woman with the good apples was at the market and how to manage une femme de ménage. I heard — I dared not look at her — I felt my smiles chasing in my eyes — I saw the villa, perhaps a cactus near the gate, you writing at a little table, me arranging some flowers & then sitting down to write, too. Both of us gathering pine cones and drift wood and bruyère for our fire — I thought of what I would have ready for you, soup & perhaps fish, coffee, toast because charbon de bois which is *much* cheaper than coal makes lovely toast, I hear, a pot of confitures, a vase of roses. And then I thought de notre bon lit et de nous deux tout seule, seule cachée dans la nuit — the fire perhaps just tinkling — the sea sounding outside et vous et moi, mon cheri. . . . with happiness fast asleep on the roof with its head under its wing, like a dove. And then I saw us waking in the morning & putting on the big kettle & letting in the femme de menage. She hangs her shawl behind the kitchen door. "Vous savez il fait beau —"

Finally I could bear it no longer. I came up to my room & took a hot bath & then curled up in bed & smoked & tried to read a new Dickens. No use. The sea was very loud. I looked at the watch and saw it said 25 to 12 & then I went to sleep. When I looked again it was nearly four. So I turned on the light & read & waited waited for day. How the light changed I never shall forget. I put on my big purple hat & opened the shutters & sat on the window sill. It was all primrosey with black mountains — A sailing ship put out to sea. I saw all the little men on board — and how the sail was put up & how when it caught the breath of wind the ship went fast. Two more of our big ships, with a rattle of chains, hoisted anchor & put out to sea. I saw the bending straining bodies of the men. And then came the fishers bringing in their pots. Then the first bird — At seven I heard my little maid lighting the stove so I ran out and asked for my déjeuner, washed in cold water, kissed my roses — put on my goblin hat and flew into the garden. The market was there — with 2 funny

Spaniards beating drums. Such flowers! Such violets! But I kept my pennies for you & me. I thought I should have to have a small fête so when I went to the post office I put *new relief nibs* in all the awful old crusty pens — The sea, and sky this morning are LITERALLY a DARK NAVY (See Aunt Li). I sent your telegrams ran home to find the maid beating the carpets and the white dog overslept & pretending he had been awake for hours on the terrace. Now I am going with a gent in corduroys to look at a furnished villa of his.

This letter may never reach you for I shall not send it until your answer comes. Oh, my love, I cannot walk fast enough. My heart is eaten by love like the Spartan boy's inside.[1] Love eats & eats at my heart and I feel everybody must know. I keep thinking "we shall go to Sanary — to that little village in the mountains — I will show him all the walks", and then I think and think of the long journey & perhaps you will not come — If you do then it is the miracle.

There are faeries, faeries everywhere. I would not be surprised if I were to find them putting fir boughs in the hall, and wreaths upon the door handles and swags and garlands over the windows.

Love presses on my forehead like a crown — my head is heavy — heavy — I must not think of you . . . But I keep talking to myself in my Tig voice as though you could hear . . . The other coming to France I can hardly remember. It was all so curious, so uncertain, and so joyless. Was it? Or is it my fancy — I feel we are coming together for the first time. In your letter you say "we shall go from sunshine to sunshine." Yes, that is just what I feel. Today too, my brother smiles.

Two more ships have put out to sea. One had 11 sails and one had 12 twelve. And now a little destroyer has come rushing in. My only thought is — are you on the destroyer? A little low gray boat snipping through the water like a pair of scissors.

[No signature]

MS ATL. *LKM* I. 59-60; *BTW*, 388; *LJMM*, 74-6.

[1] Cf. the story in Plutarch's *Lives,* Lycurgus, XVIII. 1: a boy who was carrying a stolen fox under his cloak, allowed the animal to tear out his stomach rather than have the theft detected.

To J. M. Murry, [28 December 1915]

[Bandol]

LETTERS RECEIVED IMPLORE DON'T COME DON'T WANT UNDERSTAND PERFECTLY

KATHERINE.[1]

Telegram ATL.

¹ While KM assumed Murry was anxious to come, his letters continued to be ambiguous, for he would have preferred her to return to England. But on the night of 28 Dec 1915 he wrote: 'I came back from Garsington today. Then this morning I had both your telegrams saying that I should come. When I arrived here another came — imploring me not to. That one finished me. It seemed suddenly so childish — not childish, but criminal — to stay away from you a day longer. Whatever happens I must be with you; we will live together in our villa, until the summer comes.' (ATL.)

To J. M. Murry, [28 December 1915]

[Hôtel Beau Rivage, Bandol]
Tuesday

Boge, I ran about yesterday and surveyed the land, but it was only prospecting, and nothing definite. Then when I came in I found your happy letters & realised that the Xmas telegram had meant to explain that the villa, too, was not necessary any more. Then I had a most terrible feeling that you did not want to leave England and that it were better for you *not* to come again — You see I love you so and I shan't be bitterly disappointed if you don't come — I want you to do what you please, my love and I shall really understand and love you more because then I know you are free in our love as I am. So I rushed off in the dark & sent the third wire. Cost of wires that day 9 francs. Happily Leslie sent me 10/- for Xmas so I spent that and did not feel so guilty. I am sending it to you a little later with the *Sola* too — My own, my little Boge, I shall be glad when this is all settled. Its frightfully unsettling. This morning I am in terror lest you should come —

If you don't I shall go on living here for a while & then I will return later — I had such lovely letters from you but I am a little bit distracted, my precious & wish the crisis was over. Also I have appointments with various people all day in case you should come — — —

But my love will always endure & it will never be faint or be less — You must believe that — for it is true for ever — neither shall I be unhappy nor think the miracle is anything but postponed.

Wig.

FEEL how I love you.
The white bear sends O Hara San his respects.

MS ATL. *LJMM*, 76.

To S. S. Koteliansky, [late December 1915]

[Hôtel Beau Rivage, Bandol]
Nearly the end of the year.

My extremely wicked and neglectful and utterly faithless friend! At last you have sent me a letter and although it only arrived a few moments ago and you certainly do not deserve an answer I *will* just write two words to prove once and for all my complete superiority of nature over you. You need not bother to write me letters if it is a trouble to you; its enough if, *occasionally* you send me a little card and tell me that you have not forgotten. For I shall not forget you. I often think of you. I wish you would come into my room now & smoke a cigarette with me. It is very quiet here and outside the window the sea is trembling under the moon. My room smells faintly of wood from the fire — you would like it.

I am very happy here. The place is so beautiful and the sun shines — or it doesn't — There is the sea and a wild beautiful coast — and behind the village there are woods and mountains. Already I have so many 'secret' places — The people are awfully nice too. They are honest one can be onself with them. You know, you can lean over the fence and talk to the old man who is cutting flowers or you can sit on a rock and talk to the old old woman who is cutting heather — and you are "at home". There are many fishermen, too; fishermen are always very true. Oh, my God! I am very happy. When I shut my eyes I cannot help smiling — You know what joy it is to give your heart — freely — freely. Everything that happens is an adventure. When the wind blows I go to the windiest possible place and I feel the cold come flying under my arms — When the sea is high I go down among the rocks where the spray reaches and I have games with the sea like I used to years ago. And to see the sun rise and set seems enough miracle.

When I first came here I was really very ill and unhappy but that is over now — and London, you know seems remote — remote — as though it did not exist. Those last hateful and wasted months are blotted out. Next time we see each [other] really we will be happy. Don't always remember the 'wicked' me. But one day, darling, we shall see each other again and be frightfully happy — Let us promise each other. I want to tell you all about the people here (but that would fill books) and all about the place (and that would not interest you). So pretend I have told you. At any rate it is too dark to see anything or anybody now. My brother is here often, laughing, and calling "do you remember, Katy?"

It is a beautiful night — so beautiful that you are half afraid to take it into your breast when you breathe —

This is not a letter at all, darling — only a message — Take care of yourself. I do not know why but just this moment I see awfully clearly the elephant on your big inkstand. And I want a reply *immediately* but you won't send me one — You will be wise and severe with me as you always are —
Goodnight.

Katiushka.

MS BL. *LKM* I. 53-5.

To J. M. Murry, [29 December 1915]

[Hôtel Beau Rivage, Bandol]
Wednesday early

Dearest only only one

Of course I really *don't* expect you & yet. . .I am waiting for the answer to the telegram and I cant stop my heart leaping whenever steps sound in the corridor. If you *should* come I have found a tiny villa for us — which seems to me almost perfect in its way. It stands alone in a small garden with terraces. It faces the 'midi' & gets the sun all day long. It has a stone verandah & a little round table where we can sit & eat or work. A charming tiny kitchen with pots & pans & big coffee pot, you know. Electric light, water downstairs & upstairs too in the cabinet de toilette. A most refined 'water closet' *with* water in the house. . . . The salle a manger is small & square with the light low over the table — It leads on to the verandah & overlooks the sea. So does the chambre à coucher. It is very private & stands high on the top of a hill. It is called the *Villa Pauline.* The woman (wife of the mobilier) who showed it me would also find me a servant for 3 hours every day. Yesterday I *ran ran* all day long to find something & saw such funny places. Every little street I came to there seemed to be an old woman in woolen slippers with keys in her hands waiting to show me "votre affaire". Oh, such funny experiences! But I have been very careful to go to each other whom I left in a state of uncertainty & to say I regret that I cannot take their particular treasure so that I shall not have to spend the rest of my days in dodging streets, houses & people as I usually do on these occasions. And they are neither heartbroken nor do they call me a 'sausage' — to my *great* surprise.

It is a sunny windy morning with a high sea and dancing light on all the trees. The vent de l'est is blowing as a matter of fact but it has no terrors for me now that I have my legs again. Do not, my reckless dearest wire me now I have found the villa that you *will* come for I have to give my answer tomorrow at latest & I don't think there is another — at any rate I think we had better have done with the idea — and I will stay on here for the time being.

Mdlle Marthe has just been although I am still in my pignore. She is not a girl; she is a *sparrow*. It is so awfully nice to have your jacket mended by a charming little sparrow instead of a monster with icy hands & pins in her mouth and all over her non-existent bosom. But Marthe hops about, smiling, with her head a little on one side. She is a sweet little being; I wish to goodness I could somehow adopt her for us.

My roses — my roses are too lovely — They melt in the air (I *thought* that in French where it sounds sense but in English its nonsense.) I have 23. I just counted them for you & if you turn these blue glass vases back to front so that you don't see the handpainted horrors on them they are very lovely — the dark red stems and a leaf or two showing through the water.

I didnt have a letter from you today or yesterday — I expect they take longer from marbil halls than they do in London. If only I knew how long you were to be there — Perhaps you won't get my telegrams. Bogey *make* me wash & dress. Ive lighted another cigarette & in spite of my absolutely cold, calculating mind, my heart keeps on *perpetually* like this. 1 large vase of white & yellow jonquils in the middle of the table. Roses in the bedroom. Some little red anemones on the mantlepiece. "This is the place, Bogey." A ring at the door. The man with your boxes from the station — — Now we are sitting down, hardly daring to look at each other, but smiling — Now you have unpacked & put on your corduroys & your boots. I am downstairs & you are upstairs. I hear you walking. I call out "Bogey do you want coffee or tea?" We arrange to work every morning — have lunch — go out until it is dark, come home have tea and talk and read & get our own supper — & then work. On our walks we will take that satchel you bought — for pine cones & wood and oranges. Oh God, this place is as far as New Zealand to me — as apart, as secret as much a place where you and I are alone and untroubled — But so I dream — & do not take my dreams too much to heart, my very dear, for you know that when I know you are not coming I shall be alright & come up again smiling & pin our colours to the mast of another little boat & put out upon another sea.

I love you. Now I am going to get up — I've got some *awful* tooth paste. It is called Isis and it has funny woodeny birds on the tube. It has all come out the wrong end, too, and its *much too pink*.

I don't want any more books, my heart. Thank you please for all your dearness and sweetness to me —

The black pin and the white bear send their love.

But I send you everything I have got — yes, yes, even this throbbing, sweet anxiety that beats in my forehead and makes my hands so cold & my heart intent and ready.

Always your own
Tig.

MS ATL. *LKM* I. 60-2; *LJMM*, 76-8.

To J. M. Murry, [29 December 1915]

[Hôtel Beau Rivage, Bandol]
Wednesday night.

I am like that disciple who said: "Lord I believe. Help thou my unbelief."[1] As I was dressing & your letter was already sealed the heavy steps really came along the corridor — the knock at the door — the old man with the blue folded paper that I scarcely dared to take and having taken — could not open — Oh, I sat by the side of my bed — & opened it, little by little. I read all those directions for the sending of urgent telegrams & telegrams in the night — At last I said: He is not coming & opened it and read your message. Since then I have never ceased for one moment to tremble — I shall never never be calm until I am on your heart. I felt "now he is coming that villa is taken" and I ran, ran along the quai. One day I shall tell you all this at length, but it was not taken until I saw the woman & took it. I went through it again. It is quite perfect in its way — It is always what I felt there was somewhere in the world for us — in Spain or Italy — And the people to whom it belongs who live next door are such good decent, honest people, eager to have us, eager to make us comfortable & happy. "Je suis toujours là. Vous avez seulement de frapper si vous aurez besoin de quelque chose." The sun shone in every room & on the little stone verandah danced the shadow of a tree. Is this true? Is it coming true?

I have to sign the agreement & pay a month in advance tomorrow. Then to order the coal & wood & see my femme de ménage who has already been found "pour 3 heures le matin et pour faire mes petites courses, n'est ce pas?"

All the rest of the day I do not know how I have spent it. Such a lovely wild day brimming over with colour & light. I have found the shortest way to our home by a road you do not know, through fields of jonquils & past the olive trees that blow so silver & black today. There are high walls on the road & nobody goes — I thought — we shall stand here & kiss each other. Then I thought, but if we do I think I shall faint for joy — Yes, I have found a lovely way — And

I have made out a list of our modest provisions — that I shall buy on Friday. In fact I have made out more than one list — For I cant even write nor read. This evening in the salon someone said that already there was conscription in England — Oh, God is it too late — Are you coming?

I have loved you before for 3 years with my heart and my mind but it seems to me that I have never loved you *avec mon âme* as I do now. I love you with all our future life — our life together which seems only now to have taken root and to be alive and growing up in the sun — I do not love you — but Love possesses me utterly love for you and for our life and for all our richness and joy. I have never felt anything like it before. In fact I did not comprehend the possibility of such a thing. I seem to have only played on the fringe of love and lived a kind of reflected life that was not really my own but that came from my past — Now all that is cast away — Oh, my soul — if you come now we shall realise something that it seems to me never has been — such warmth and such richness and such virtue there is in you and in me — Is it too late? You are *really* coming?

This morning I went to the little church and prayed. It is very nice there — I prayed for us three — for you and me and Chummie. It was so gay and yet solemn there —

Bogey, come quickly quickly. My heart will break.

[*No signature*]

MS ATL. *LKM* I. 62-3; *BTW*, 387; *LJMM*, 78-80.

¹ Cf. Mark 9: 24.

To J. M. Murry, [30–31 December 1915]

[Hôtel Beau Rivage, Bandol]
Thursday

I must be brave so that you will not be afraid & make the officials suspicious. I shall just go on believing & believing in God and preparing a place for you — Your letter written on Xmas Day has come — with that about the horrid woman in the shop — "There is no doubt that I hate life"¹ — My dearest, my darling I will stretch a lovely rainbow wing over you & not let them make you hate life. You must not really hate life. I promise you if you come here I will not let you hate it. I will always talk to all the uglies and you can talk to the nice ones — For there is no doubt that I love life — and now that I have cast away for ever that dark shell that I used to creep into in London I will face anybody and I am not afraid. The only thing that frightens me is that you cannot come. Money doesn't frighten me a *bit*. We'll be 2 little silk worms & live on mulberry leaves. If you come here we shall both write poetry — a mutual book which we will publish together — Also we shall both write a kind of 'paysages' and we shall both write — — well, I shouldn't be surprised if we both wrote *anything*.

The little house is there, waiting for us. Its eyes are shut until I open them. The sun touches the verandah and warms the place where your hand will rest. Tout bas tout bas mon coeur chante: "Cinquante kilos de charbons de pierre — 50 kilos de charbon de coke et des poids pour allumer pour cinq sous — c'est presque un sac." I have such a lot to do today. I must go out soon. Again I am not dressed, but idling here with your adorable letter beside me — Bogey I hardly slept at all — I shant sleep again until I have your head on my shoulder and your burnt gorse hair sous mon nez. Goodbye for now. You are on your way? Will you send me a wire from Dieppe with just "all serene"? Are you in Paris tonight?

Midi. This morning I went to the woman who introduced [me] to the Villa. She is a Spaniard, from Barcelona, and we are *really sincerely* friends. She is a dear creature — and at first I know she didn't like me but now really we have jokes together and she laughs, showing her pretty teeth. She tried to find me a femme de ménage but could not so her daughter 'Marie' a darkeyed Spanish beauty, a really fascinating creature with a fringe, big eyes & bright colour is coming instead. But do we mind 'cuisine espagnole'. 'Pas de tout!' Then I went to the church for a minute — I feel I must keep in close touch with God. They were dressing the altar with white yellow jonquils — a sweet savour must have mounted — I prayed that my prayer was heard at the same moment & that God was pleased. Then I went to the station to ask what trains arrived & then to our villa by the path that you are coming. The door was open. The owner was inside hanging up saucepans. So we went through the inventory together & she said she would give me teacups and a teapot — because we were english. Also she offered to take me to any shops where I wanted to buy anything. I then went over the villa again. There is the loveliest green water pot like you admired. We must find something to fill it with. Then I went back to her house & together with her husband made out a lease, signed, paid, and put the key in my pocket. A friend came in & we sat talking a little. They told me not to buy flowers for your arrival. They had enough in their garden — & she said she would come in when Marie arrives on Saturday & show her how to make the fire. I walked home with the key in my hands. I kept thinking — where is he now? Are you near Folkestone — — I simply don't know how I shall wait until you come. Every time I see the telegraph man I run out of his way in case he has a telegram for me 'impossible to come'. What should I do? I feel we simply *must* be here together — I feel its absolutely necessary — It has been a dark morning, but as I write a pale sun is over everything. The clouds are white as marble. Tomorrow I shall buy stores and settle everything. On Saturday morning I shall go there and stay there — But I simply don't know how to exist until I know if you will be here Saturday or Sunday.

— — Now it is late night. I have been playing games in the salon with 3 men and a woman from Avignon — Playing games that one only plays at school. Oh I wish we had played all night long for I shall never sleep. You are arriving in Paris if you are on your way — That is all I can think. All the evening I have hid my joy & my heart has said "now he is dans le même pays" — but I am still so frightened that my breast hurts me to breathe. I shall know for certain tomorrow because if you have not come there will be a telegram — And I know you will telegraph me from Paris, my love, tomorrow — So courage — courage. In quelques heures I shall know. But I am in a fever.

Friday. Noon. No telegram yet. I asked this morning at the post. They said that a telegram from Paris took perhaps one or two hours only. And yet if you have not left I cannot but think you would have already let me know — Now I am just waiting.[2] I have ordered the little stores and the wine and the wood. All the windows are open — all the doors — the linen is airing. I went to the flower market and stood among the buyers and bought wholesale you know, at the auction in a state of a lively terrified joy 3 dozen rose buds and 6 bunches of violets.

MS ATL. *LKM* I. 63-5; *LJMM*, 80-2.

[1] Murry was distressed after arguing with a woman about renting rooms.
[2] Murry arrived on Saturday, 1 Jan 1916.

To Ottoline Morrell,[1] *[21 January 1916]*

[Villa Pauline,[2] Bandol]
Friday Night.
I have been wanting to write to you for nearly three weeks — I *have* been writing to you ever since the day when Murry came and said: "there's a perfectly wonderful woman in England" and told me about you. Since then I have wanted to send you things, too — some anemones, purple and crimson lake and a rich, lovely white, some

blue irises that I found growing in the grass, too frail to gather, certain places in the woods where I imagine you would like to be — and certain hours like this hour of bright moonlight, when the flowering almond tree hangs over our white stone verandah a blue shadow with long tassels. So please take, if you care for them, all these things from me as well as the letters I have not sent but have written and written to you. All that Murry tells of you is quite wonderful and perfect — But its strange — I feel that I *knew* it (although I denied the knowledge over and over) from the first time that I heard of you — and I felt it, even through the atmosphere of that evening at your house[3] — When you were ever so far away —

I long to meet you. Will you write to us again? But until we do see you — will you remember that you are real and lovely to us both and that we are ever grateful to you because you are.
Goodnight

Katherine.

MS Texas. Morrell, 88-9.

[1] Ottoline Violet Anne Cavendish-Bentinck (1873–1938), half-sister of the 6th Duke of Portland, married in 1902 Philip Edward Morrell, a Liberal MP 1906–18. An influential hostess and patroness of the arts, she moved in June 1915 to Garsington Manor, near Oxford, which at once became a centre for artists, writers, and intellectuals.

[2] The villa KM had taken at the end of December 1915 remained their home for three and a half months.

[3] KM had met Lady Ottoline briefly in February 1915, when she and Murry were taken by Lawrence to the Morrells' home at 44 Bedford Square, Bloomsbury.

To Vera Beauchamp Bell, 26 February 1916

Villa Pauline | Bandol (Var)
February 26th 1916.

Dearest Sister V.

Our letters have crossed. I wrote & posted to you just the other day & this afternoon a long lovely letter has come from you — I am more than glad to have it and to hear of you at last, darling. How strange that you should have mentioned the snapshots when I had asked if you had any — I do hope that they arrive — Thank you for this letter: it was such a very great delight to hear from you again — for I think of you often — I envy you indeed with the lovely prospect of a visit from Mother and Jeanne. Unfortunately I am rather in the dark about their plans for Father has only mentioned the idea of their voyage to me once & that was in his last letter and he has never breathed a word that I should come — Yet, if he had offered the trip to Chaddie that means he *could* afford it — doesn't it? Oh,

my dear, of course it would be a wonderful wonderful pleasure and
I can think of nothing that I would more greatly love to do than to
be with you all and tell you all I know of our dear Chummie. But,
Vera, Father is so good and generous to me[1] that I could not *possibly*
mention it to him. You understand — don't you? *We* have not the
money and I should never ask Father for it. If he had wanted me to
come or if he had thought of me coming he would have suggested it
to me. I feel it simply isn't my place to do so. Perhaps, later on, he
may and if he did of course I should come by the first possible boat.
I told Jack about the idea and of course he understood it just as I did
and as our house is sublet and we are only spending the summer
visiting friends it would be very easy — But these are at best, my
dear, dreams. Only *in case* anything definite was proposed I felt I
ought to write to you at once and let you know exactly how the land
lay — Our present intention is to return to England at the end of
April — We shall be here until then, but all my letters etc. go to our
good Mr Kay at the Bank and he sends them on to me — Jack says:
"Give Vera my love" but you refer to him so formally that Im half
afraid to.

I would love to tell you a great deal about our brother — One day
I shall, dear — There was no one like him and his loss simply can't be
ever less for me. Oh, Vera, I loved him — more than I can say — and
we understood each other so wonderfully — When we talked together
we were like 'one being'.

Do tell me what your boys look like when you write to me again
— and how big they are and what they wear — so that I may have a
picture of them. I knew that John would be a 'thorough boy' — I
don't know why — I always felt it — Is he like our family? Put your
arms round the darlings and give them a special *bon baiser* from their
Aunt Katherine.

I expect that Mack will be in Europe by the time that you get this
letter — Will you give me an address where I might write to him —
How I feel for you without him, my dear — but you must be very
proud, too.[2] Jack was desperately upset that he could not get into
anything — and I was too, for him — He and Chummie were such
friends. They were great pa men together — They even had their
baths together and went in for what Chummie called "a very special
kind of walrusing" — We talk of him continually, and when I am
alone I feel he is quite close to me — indeed I am *sure* he is — but all
the same it is not comfort enough — For he loved life so and he took
such a great joy in being alive — That is what makes his death so
hard to bear.

Chaddie wrote to us a day or two ago from Sangor — some mysterious, lovely place — She sent us a postcard of it.[3] Yes, she has a

perfect nature. It is four years since I have seen her but her letters bring her right into one's presence immediately —

I am longing for my next home letters. Perhaps I shall hear more of their plans. Vera, you will tell me *all* about Mother when she is with you — & do tell me about my little almost unknown sister Jeanne — too — Is Father coming? Oh, that you were nearer!

Goodbye, dear, for just now. I must cook the dinner and blow up the charcoal fire first.

Always your sister
Katherine.

MS ATL.

[1] KM's father was shortly to increase her allowance from £120 to £156 a year.

[2] James Mackintosh Bell, a major with the 73rd Royal Highlanders of Canada, served first in France, then later in Russia.

[3] Probably of the Sangar River in Derajat province, West Pakistan. It seems that Harold Beauchamp was paying for Chaddie to come to England, before going to Canada. In fact her husband, Lieut.-Col. Perkins (see p. 121, n.1), died in India the day after this letter was written.

To Ottoline Morrell, 26 February 1916

Villa Pauline | Bandol (Var)
February 26th 1916

Dear Lady Ottoline

The days go by so quickly and I have wanted to write to you on nearly every separate day — and just *not* written — to say how glad we were to have a lovely letter from you and to tell you how much we both long to come and see you when we are back in England. Thank you for letting us see Frieda's letter, too. I am thankful that the Armenian is gone but I wish he had taken Haseltine with him.[1] I suspect Haseltine. I did from what Jack told me of him before I knew that he had 'confided' in Frieda. What a pity it is that dear Lorenzo sees rainbows round so many dull people and pots of gold in so many mean hearts.[2] But he will never change —

We have decided to spend the summer with them in a farm-house somewhere near the sea — Lawrence seems to be much better — I am glad. One hates to think of him being ill.[3] We are leaving here at the end of April — Jack is very busy at present with his book on Dostoievsky. And I have a book on my hands too: we feel they won't be old enough to travel until then. I am awfully anxious for Jack's book to be published. It is really brilliant — The weather has changed. All the almond flowers are gone — A cold wind blows, the sea makes a loud roaring and at night it rains. Our walks and climbs are over — We sit by the fire and work nearly all day — Only in the late afternoon we put on our hats and run into the wind and go down to the sea and wish that the waves would be still bigger — they're never high enough — In the evenings we read and talk and "make plans". . . . . We are awfully happy — and I know that we always shall be wherever we are together.

Katherine.

[*In Murry's hand*] .
We are going to stay with the Lawrences for ever and ever as perhaps you know; I daresay eternity will last the whole of the summer.

MS Texas. Cited Alpers 1980, 195.

[1] Michael Arlen (1895-1956), born Dikran Kouyoumdjian in Bulgaria, of Armenian parents, but raised in England from an early age, enjoyed a remarkable vogue in the 1920s for his pertly sophisticated fiction. At the end of 1915 he and Philip Heseltine (1894-1930), composer and editor of early music under the name of 'Peter Warlock', became briefly enthusiastic over Lawrence's plan for a congenial group of people to settle together in Florida.

[2] 'Rainbows' is a reference not only to Lawrence's novel *The Rainbow*, suppressed by legal action the previous November, but to a scheme for a private publishing venture, 'The Rainbow Books and Music', for which Lawrence had sent KM and Murry a circular on 17 Feb 1916. The venture was to publish Lawrence's works; the circular, declaring that 'It is monstrous that the herd should lord it over the uttered word', was signed by Philip Heseltine. Since the establishment of such a private press had been Murry's idea, he and KM must have written back in some heat, for Lawrence replied on 24 Feb 1916: 'Now don't get in a state, you two, about nothing. The Publishing scheme has not yet become at all real or important, to me.' (*LDHL* II. 542, 548.)

[3] The Lawrences, having moved to Cornwall at the end of 1915, were urging KM and Murry to join them there. Lawrence had been bedridden for much of January with inflammation of the chest.

To [Frederick Goodyear],[1] [4 March 1916]

Villa Pauline | Bandol | (Var)
Mr F.G.   Sunday.
Never did cowcumber lie more heavy on a female's buzzum than your curdling effugion[2] which I have read twice and wont again if horses drag me. But I keep wondering, and cant for the life of me think, whatever there was in mine to so importantly disturb you. (Henry James is dead.[3] Did you know?) I did not, swayed by a resistless passion say that I loved you. Nevertheless I'm prepared to say it again looking at this pound of onions that hangs in a string kit from a saucepan nail. But, Betsy love, what has that got to do with the Kilner Idea?[4] I recognise the Kilner Idea, I acknowledge it and

even understand it, but whats it got to do with me? Nothing. I don't want to rob you of it. . .And why should you write to me as though I'd got into the family way with H.G.W[ells] and driven round to you in a hansom cab to ask you to make a respectable woman of me? Yes, youre bad tempered, suspicious and surly. And if you think I flung my bonnet over you as a possible mill, my lad, you're mistook. So shut up about your Fire Whorls *and* a Hedgehog[5] and send me no more inventories of those marbil halls wherein of aforetime they did delight to wander.

In fact, now I come to ponder on your last letter I don't believe you want to write to me at all and Im hanged if Ill shoot arrows in the air. But perhaps that is temper on my part; it is certainly pure stomach. Im so hungry, simply empty, and seeing in my minds eye just now a surloin of beef, well browned with plenty of gravy *and* horseradish sauce and baked potatoes I nearly sobbed. There's nothing here to eat except omelettes and oranges and onions. Its a cold, sunny windy day — the kind of day when you want a tremendous feed for lunch & an armchair in front of the fire to boaconstrict in afterwards. I feel sentimental about England now — English food, *decent* English *waste!* How much better than these thrifty french whose flower gardens are nothing but potential salad bowls. There's not a leaf in France that you cant 'faire une infusion avec', not a blade that isn't bon pour la cuisine. By God, Id like to buy a pound of the best butter, put it on the window sill and watch it melt to spite em. They are a stingy uncomfortable crew for all their lively scrapings. . . For instance, in their houses — what appalling furniture — and never one comfortable chair. If you want to talk the only possible thing to do is go to bed. Its a case of either standing on your feet or lying in comfort under a puffed up eiderdown. I quite understand the reason for what is called french moral laxity — you're simply forced into bed — no matter with whom — there's no other place for you . . . Supposing a *young* man comes to see about the electric light & will go on talking and pointing to the ceiling, or a friend drops in to tea and asks you if you believe in Absolute Evil. How can you give your mind to these things when youre sitting on four knobs and a square inch of cane. How much better to lie snug and *give yourself up to it.*

Later.

Now I've eaten one of the omelettes and one of the oranges. The sun has gone in; its beginning to thunder. There's a little bird on a tree outside this window not so much singing as sharpening a note —

He's getting a very fine point on it; I expect you would know his name . . . Write to me again when everything is not *too* bunkum.[6]

Goodbye for now | With my 'strictly relative' love

'K.M.'

MS (draft) ATL, Notebook 34. *Journal* 1927, 59-61.

[1] Frederick Goodyear (1887-1917), fellow student with Murry at Oxford and the author of 'The New Thelema', the introductory essay in the first issue of *Rhythm*, Summer 1911, became one of KM's close friends. His letters were among the few, apart from Murry's, that she kept until her death. Now serving in France as a corporal with the Meteorological Office of the Royal Engineers, Goodyear later transferred to the Essex Regiment in order to see action at the Front, received a commission, and in the middle of May 1917 was wounded during an attack on Fampoux, near Arras. He died on 23 May 1917.

[2] Apparently close to some kind of breakdown, Goodyear had written to KM from France on 14 Feb 1916, 'I greatly miss your talent for double entendre, which made conversation with you one of the consolations of life', and declared: 'You're a genuine old darling, for all your mendacity.' On 28 Feb 1916 he told her, 'All the time I have known you you have been fixt up with Murry, & that's been final so far as I am concerned, though it has made things very awkward between us.' (Both ATL.)

[3] The novelist Henry James (1843-1916) died in London on 28 Feb 1916.

[4] The 'Kilner Idea' — perhaps a hope for greater intimacy, or simply some personal plan — is unexplained. There is a comic poem dedicated to 'G.W. Kilner, 1912', in *Frederick Goodyear, Letters and Remains, 1887-1917* (1920).

[5] On 28 Feb 1916 Goodyear wrote, among other details of his sexual life, of '5 whores, 1 engagement, several interminable sentimental friendships. Like the hedgehog, I've never been buggered at all.' (ATL.)

[6] Goodyear concluded his 28 Feb 1916 letter, 'If love is only love when it is resistless, I don't love you. But if it is a relative emotion, I do. Personally, I think everything everywhere is bunkum.'

To [Frieda Lawrence], 4 March [1916]

March 4th

Dear Frieda

The new house sounds very nice and I am glad to think we shall be there — all of us together — this spring.[1] Thank you for your letter, dear, but you really haven't been right in judging us first the kind of traitors that you did.[2] Jack *never* would hear a word against Lawrence

MS (draft) ATL, Notebook 34. *Journal* 1954, 114.

[1] KM's draft seems to predate a letter from Lawrence of 8 Mar 1916 about the two cottages he had found near Zennor; he and Frieda had taken one, and 'Really, you must have the other place. I keep looking at it. I call it already Katharine's house, Katharine's tower.' On the same day Frieda wrote to KM, 'I am so anxious now to *live* without any more soulharrassing, we are *friends* and we wont bother anymore about the *deep* things, they are all right, just let us live like the lilies in the field.' (*LDHL* II. 569, 571.)

[2] In her letter of 8 Mar 1916, perhaps in response to this from KM, Frieda added: 'Did the old Ott. say *horrid* things about me to Jack? I hope he did not swallow them all'. Lawrence had already told Koteliansky on 25 Feb 1916, 'The Murrys accused me of being treacherous and not taking them in to the publishing scheme. I tell them of course they are included, and they are far more treacherous to me, intrinsically, than ever I shall be to them.' (*LDHL* II. 571, 554.)

To Harold Beauchamp, 6 March 1916

Villa Pauline | Bandol | (Var) | France.
March 6th 1916.

My dearest Father,

This morning I received a letter from you telling me that you had instructed the manager of the Bank to pay me £13 a month instead of £10, as formerly. I scarcely know how to thank you for yet another proof of your unexampled generosity to me, darling. It puts my finances on such a secure and easy footing at a time when so many are in want and it gives me a very real feeling of security and added comfort. Thank you a thousand times, my darling Father: I am deeply grateful.

Two days ago I received from you a copy of the Free Lance. Like a book which Mother sent me it had been much detained by the censors and it arrived in a perfect wrapping of various labels signifying that it had been "opened and examined". I was very much interested to read the contributions by 'little Ethel'. She must be quite a leading light of Picton City.[1] I remember her as a little pale girl, very thin, with flaxen hair in the charge of Cousin Ethel who always seemed to wear a mackintosh and a sailor hat tied on with a white silk motor veil!

I am extremely glad to think that you and Mother and Jeanne are going to Canada to spend some time with dear old Vera. She wrote to me the other day, full of delight at the prospect. I hope you have a successful peaceful voyage, darling and I do pray that later in the year we may meet in England. I wish I could tell you, Father, how I long to see you. Our dear one, when he was with me even, seemed to bring me so near to you, and talking of you with him I realised afresh each time how much I love and admire and how very much you mean to me. Forgive my childish faults, my generous darling Daddy, and keep me in your heart. I feel that we shall have so much to talk over when we do meet. If only this war would end and make the Atlantic safer. It is a terrible, tedious calamity and the end seems still far away. As I write the papers are full of the news of the awful battle of Verdun and they seem to agree that the german offensive is only beginning![2]

I had a wonderful letter from Mother this morning to which I have sent a reply to Almonte.[3] Her courage and faith is very beautiful. I am afraid you will miss her and Jeanne very much in those eight weeks when you are alone. I wish I could 'housekeep' for you and give you your slippers in the evening!

At present we intend to return to England in the second week in April and as our small house will still be let we are staying with friends for the time. I shall be very glad to be 'home' in England, although I am thankful for this experience here and it has by no means be[en] wasted. I shall make it my duty to call upon Mr Kay at the Bank as soon as I arrive. He wrote me today, telling me the good news. "Extremely generous of your Father". He is awfully kind in sending on all my letters promptly and always with a cheering little note and a very large, powerful signature.

Father dear, I do so reproach myself for writing you a sad letter from Marseilles and thereby adding even a little to your sorrow. But by now, I trust that you have had other letters from me and that I have made it plain that I am happier. Not that the loss of our darling one is any less real to me. It never can be, and I feel that it has changed the course of my life *for ever* but I do feel very strongly, that I fail in my duty to his memory if I do not bear his loss bravely, and I could not bear to fail him. I often think of you and of him together and I remember the way he used to look at you — a kind of special loving look that he had for you — it is unforgettable. It is truly marvellous how many people were influenced by him and how many people mourn him. I should much like to have seen the copies of the letters that Mother sent to Belle and I hope to do so on my return to England.[4]

Chaddie and I write frequently: she is a sweet nature. We are just as natural together as when we were girls and shared the same room together. Do you remember, at Johnsonville,[5] I think it was, coming into our room in the middle of an earthquake and carrying us out into the garden? I can see Chaddie now, who was very "weedy" at the time and only had a wisp of hair tied up with a piece of pink wool for the night. It must be a long time ago but I remember Johnsonville very well, even to the smell of it. Like Chummie, I always remember by smells.

Well, dearest and best of Fathers, I must end this letter. Again, from my heart I thank you. I think of you every day and I long for the time when we shall meet again. God bless you darling.

Always your own child
Kass.

MS WDPT. Beauchamp, 203-6.

[1] The *New Zealand Free Lance*, a paper of social and sporting news, was published weekly in Wellington. KM's cousin Ethel Beauchamp, grand-daughter of Harold's brother Craddock, had two short stories in the *Free Lance Christmas Annual* for 1915. Picton at that time had a population of only a few hundred.

[2] The battle of Verdun had begun on 21 Feb 1916.

[3] Vera Bell lived in Almonte, Ontario.

[4] KM's letter to her father from Marseilles does not survive. Her mother wrote to a Wellington friend on 16 Mar 1916: 'You will be glad our darling Leslie was the means of bringing poor old Kass *right* into the fold again, as she writes to us all most loving letters. . .' (ATL.)

[5] A settlement a few miles north-east of Wellington.

To J. M. Murry, [21 March 1916]

Hotel Oasis [Marseilles][1]
The Same Afternoon.

Dearest of all —

I got through to the 2nd & had a very comfortable journey. I nearly fell out of the train at the last moment looking for & then at you — But no, you walked away. It was rather awful — wasn't it? The country on the way here is so lovely — Where there used to be pink heath there is gorse now & white & red trees everywhere. Cooks weren't much consolation — but they referred me to the P and O people Rue Colbert (opposite the Post office) And I found out from them that the Sardinia is *definitely* expected at 8.30 AM. on Thursday morning.[2] Also I explained my situation and obtained from them a card permitting me to go on board. So I must stay. Its a good thing I came. She "moors" says my card further at MOLE C — Bassin National. I shall find it. Cooks will tell me the way — The P and O. people were *not* inclined to over amiability. Then (very hungry as usual when en voyage) I went and bought my bag for 13 francs. It was expensive, but it is just what you would have bought (Oh, how she flatters him!) Darling, its a lovely bag, though, *mouse blue* well finished & strong & with or without a handle — & the shape you said & deep enough to hold my passport. But my things somehow don't belong don't quite belong to me now until you have seen them & they've spiritually passed through the customs Until you've more or less put a little white chalk squiggle on this bag it isn't quite mine — though I am very pleased with it.

Then I came here & was remembered — but it was 'et comment va Monsieur?' From Monsieur, Madame & especially that nice rather slatternly maid, who was very friendly & shook hands — I have the same room (Im in it now) the same flowers on the wall paper (that came out & bowed when I had fever). Only the couch has been 'recovered' in large yellow and black 3 eyed beetles. The same little chap has gone for my bag, because it is pouring with rain and has been ever since I set foot — A nuisance — for I don't feel I *can* buy a 3.75 umbrella. However the rain is warm, and smells of spring. I don't really mind it, but my boots do — & they wouldn't be protected with an umbrella anyway. . . I had 2 mingy eggs cooked in margarine a pot of tea & one lumpish little roll for lunch 1.70. Two eggs are *1 franc*: tea *60* — bread 10. It was at the place we always went to. I protested but was told a long story. Everything has augmented. I was very angry — especially as I couldn't eat the eggs for all my hunger. Our cooking spoils one for anything else. I bought 2 penny packets of note paper a pen a bottle of ink, a Daily Mail & Radical & Tabac.

So here I am waiting for the bagage as usual. Madame Ferrand[3] was at Cassis station in the corridor of the train we met and she did *not* acknowledge my bow. Why are people so *horrid*? Im glad youve not come. What could you do here? And there's not the ghost of a *home comfort*. But it isn't horrid & Im quite alright & shall be very careful of the money. I hope to be home on Thursday night, but I will *wire* you again after I have seen Chaddie. Make no preparations — but look after your darling darling self — Oh, Bogey, how *can* you be such a darling? I shall sit here & write all the afternoon. I feel so 'settled' — it is because of our love. I feel so rich and my heart is quiet — you know that feeling?

Always your own
Tig.

MS ATL. *LKM* I. 65-6; cited *BTW*, 397; *LJMM*, 82-3.

[1] The hotel at which KM and Murry had stayed in November 1915.

[2] KM was in Marseilles to meet her sister Chaddie, now a widow, who had sailed from Bombay on the *Sardinia* on 5 Mar 1916.

[3] Mme Ferrand is unidentified.

To J. M. Murry, [22 March 1916]

[Hôtel Oasis, Marseilles]

My precious,

Even though I hope to be home soon after this letter I will send you a 'Bon jour' — Im smoking my after breakfast cigarette. This morning I am going to find my way to the Bassin Nationale in preparation for tomorrow. Cooks could not explain exactly; they advised me however to take a cab (!) it is about half an hour's drive — Très, très bien. But the man here says I can go by tram from the Vieux Port all the way. This Ill find out by trying to do it this morning. Bogey — I had a funny night. All my fever came back — I shivered and my blood buzzed as though bees swarmed in my heart — & the lilies came out and bowed. Also it was rather late before I went to bed *after* locking the door — fastening the bolt etc — and to my horror just as I began to fall asleep I heard SOMEONE turning the handle — Then the door was gently rattled — Then came a KNOCK. This is all true. I called out 'qui est là' — No reply. So I leapt out of bed — threw my kimono on, and arming myself with a pair of scissors I opened the door — There stood a horrid creature in his night shirt who began mumbling something about the wrong door — but he *leered*. Oh I *slammed* the door in his face & walked up & down my room — furious — I was not at all frightened.

Today it is very warm (so far) and sunny — The trams roll up and down, & clatters & squeaks fly up. Now I have had a scrupulous cat like bath & washed my ears beyond words. I feel we are about 15 today — just children. You and I don't live like grown up people, you know. Look at the way we soap each others backs & hop about in the tops of our pyjamas and scrabble into bed winking our toes — & I keep seeing in my minds eye, your back view as you go down to the cave for wood — & then your front view as you come up with your arms full. Life isn't half long enough to love all the different things about you in. I shall die in the middle of a little laugh at some new funny thing that I adore you for. Now I must go out & stop writing love letters — Perhaps I didn't quite know until I came away what these months have brought or how they have changed everything.

(Dont think I forget the army. I don't, but I simply feel it *is* a false alarm — It must be. But I know how you feel about it & my love, don't think me unsympathetic. For I'm not. It's only I can do nothing from here — & ∴ we've got to wait.[1] But it wont catch you, Bogey.)

Always your girl

Tig.

MS ATL. *LKM* I. 66–7; cited *BTW*, 397; *LJMM*, 84–5.

[1] After the German attacks on Verdun towards the end of February 1916, there were new fears of conscription. The Conscription Bill requiring military service of all men of military age was passed the following month.

VI

ENGLAND: 1916–1917

KM and Murry returned to England early in April 1916, when it seemed that under the new more comprehensive classification Murry would soon be called up for military service. They had agreed to take the cottage in Cornwall next door to the Lawrences at Higher Tregerthen, but at first, while they worked at renovating the house, they slept at the Tinner's Arms in Zennor.

There was considerable strain between the two couples from the start. KM disliked Frieda's influence on Lawrence, and Lawrence's theorizing about sex. Murry for his part was unable to respond to his friend's demands for *Blutbrüderschaft*, and the two men quarrelled so violently that in mid-June KM and Murry left the house at Higher Tregerthen and took a cottage further south at Mylor. They were again unhappy together, and for a time considered separating. The unsuccessful Cornwall months concluded when Murry secured a War Office post in London, and KM began her closer association with the milieu of Garsington.

KM wrote nothing in Cornwall, nor for several months afterwards, apart from letters and occasional jottings in her notebooks.

∽

To Ottoline Morrell, [7 April 1916]

Higher Tregerthen[1] | Zennor | St. Ives | Cornwall.
Friday.

I cannot say how sorry I am that we have not yet been able to come to you. For I do want to meet you. Dear Lady Ottoline, I hope you understand why we did not come immediately. Jack has really been ill and he is still very thin and pale: I was thankful when he left London for we had so much to do and it was all so trying. But we may come later — mayn't we?

We are making a house — but everything seems to be made of boulders — We shall have to eat off stones as well as have them for our pillows. Money is dreadful: we've none — We wondered this morning whether you could lend us a chair or a table or a piece of stuff or anything that could be made into something. They have got a needlework picture of yours and a lovely lovely bed cover but we've nothing and we really love you. Now we are begging — handing round Jacks big black 3 francs 50 hat. But of course if you haven't we do understand.

I want to write again. I am writing on my knee — between scrubbing a floor and cleaning paint.

It is all going to be nice and perhaps later you really will come?

With both our loves
Katherine —

MS Texas. Cited Alpers 1980, 203.

[1] Of the grey granite cottage at Higher Tregerthen, rent £16 a year, into which KM and Murry moved early in April 1916, Lawrence had written to them on 8 Mar 1916: 'It is only twelve strides from our house to yours: we can talk from the windows: and besides us, only the gorse, and the fields, the lambs skipping and hopping like anything, and sea-gulls fighting with the ravens, and sometimes a fox, and a ship on the sea' (*LDHL* II. 569).

To Beatrice Campbell,[1] [4 May 1916]

[Higher Tregerthen, Zennor]
Thursday.

My dear Bici

I have been wanting to write to you but felt that Ireland wouldn't permit — Now that Ive heard from you and seen Mary Clarke (whom I quite understand) I feel free to ask you for that prescription for poor Murrys remaining hair. For though he is about to be taken he must rub something into his roots while he is on sentry go — Send it when you find it. . .I can imagine what you and G[ordon] must have felt. This morning there is news that 3 leaders are shot & its horrible reading. It['s] difficult to get any coherent account of anything down here but Garvin in the Observer last Sunday very nearly brought one off.[2] There is no accounting for Ireland — The fact that while one street was under hot fire & people falling in all directions the milkmen with their rattling little vans went on delivering milk seemed as Lawrence would say "pretty nearly an absolute symbol". Tell me more about Mary Clarke and hers when you know.[3]

If I had a box I'd send you flowers but Ive nothing but a Vinolia Soap box & the violets would arrive in a lather. As soon as I have a box you shall have some. This country is very lovely just now with every kind of little growing thing — and the gorse among the grey rocks is as Mrs Percy H[4] would agree "very satisfactory". There are a great many adders here too — How does one cure oneself of their bite. You either bathe the afflicted part with a saucer of milk *or* you give the saucer of milk to the adder — There is a creek close by our house that rushes down a narrow valley and then falls down a steep cliff into the sea — The banks are covered with primroses & violets and & bluebells. I paddle in it & feel like a faint far off reflection of

the George Meredith Penny Whistle Overture[5] — but awfully faint —
Murry spends all his time hunting for his horn rimmed spectacles
for whenever he leaps over a stile or upon a mossy stone they fly
from him — incredible distances & undergo a strange and secret
change into caterpillars dragon flies or bracken uncurling.

Today I cant see a yard — Thick mist and rain and a tearing wind
with it. Everything is faintly damp. The floor of the tower is studded
with Cornish pitchers catching the drops. Except for my little maid
(whose *ankles* I can hear stumping about the kitchen) Im alone — for
Murry & Lawrence have plunged off to St Ives with rucksacks on
their backs & Frieda is in her cottage looking at the childrens photographs, I suppose.[6] Its very quiet in the house except for the wind
and the rain & the fire that roars very hoarse and fierce. I feel as
though I and the Cornish Pasty[7] had drifted out to sea — and would
never be seen again. But I love such days — rare, lonely days. I love
above all things, my dear, to be alone. Then I lie down and smoke
and look at the fire and begin to think out an EXTRAORDINARILY
good story about Marseille — Ive reread my novel today, too and
now I cant believe I wrote it —[8] I hope that G. reads it one of these
days. . .

I want to talk about the Ls, but if I do don't tell Kot and Gertler
for then it will get back to Lawrence & I will be literally murdered —
He has changed very much — Hes quite 'lost' — He has become very
fond of sewing, especially hemming; and of making little copies of
pictures — When he is doing these things he is quiet and gentle and
kind, but once you start talking I cannot describe the frenzy that
comes over him. He simply *raves*, roars, beats the table, abuses everybody — But thats not such great matter. What makes these attacks
insupportable is the feeling one has at the back of ones mind that he
is completely out of control — swallowed up in an acute *insane*
irritation. After one of these attacks he's ill with fever, haggard and
broken. It is impossible to be anything to him but a kind of playful
acquaintance. Frieda is more or less used to this. She has a passion
for washing clothes — & stands with big bowls of blue and white
water round her wringing out check tablecloths — & looking very
much at home indeed — She says this place suits her. I am sure it does.

They are both too rough for me to enjoy playing with. I hate
games where people lose their tempers in this way — Its so witless.
In fact they are not my kind at all. I cannot discuss blood affinity
to beasts for instance if I have to keep ducking to avoid the flat
irons and the saucepans. And I shall *never* see sex in trees, sex in
the running brooks, sex in stones & sex in everything. The number
of things that are really phallic from fountain pen fillers onwards!
But I shall have my revenge one of these days — I suggested to

Lawrence that he should call his cottage The Phallus & Frieda thought it was a very good idea. . .

Its lunchtime already & here is the Pasty looming through the mist with a glimmering egg on a tray. Have you read so far? Give G. my dear love and keep it for yourself

[*No signature*]

PC ATL. *LKM* I. 68-9; Alpers 1953, 225; Glenavy, 93-4.

¹ Beatrice Campbell, née Elvery (1885-1970), later Lady Glenavy, was born in Dublin, and attended the Dublin Metropolitan School of Art and then the Slade School in London. She married Gordon Campbell in 1912, the year that she and KM began their close friendship.

² On 21 Apr 1916 the Irish Republic was proclaimed, and the centre of Dublin occupied by the Republicans. The rebellion collapsed on 29 April, and in the following weeks 15 of the leaders were executed, among them, on 3 May, James Clarke, Padraic Pearse, and Thomas Macdonagh, three signatories to the Proclamation of Independence. A long unsigned article on the Rebellion, 'Ireland's Ordeal', published in the *Observer* on 30 Apr 1916, was by James Garvin, the paper's editor.

³ The daughter of the Revd George Clark, rector at Carrickmines, Co. Dublin, was a childhood friend of Beatrice Campbell, who recorded (Glenavy, 45) that for KM the name of Mary Clark became 'a sort of symbol for talks about our childhood'.

⁴ 'Mrs Percy Hutchinson', according to Murry's note on the MS; Percy Hutchinson (1875-1945) was a well-known actor manager, married at this time to Lilias Earle.

⁵ Cf. 'A Diversion Played on a Penny Whistle', ch. XIX of George Meredith's *The Ordeal of Richard Feverel* (1859), which begins with a celebratory evocation of the countryside.

⁶ Frieda's three children, in the custody of her former husband, Ernest Weekley, were the cause of bitter disputes between the Lawrences. KM had acted as a go-between for Frieda and her son Montague when they were legally prevented from seeing each other.

⁷ Hilda, the servant.

⁸ The Marseilles story was not written. KM's novella, *The Aloe*, was completed at Bandol.

To S.S. Koteliansky, [11 May 1916]

[Higher Tregerthen, Zennor]
Thursday.

I am quite alone for all the day so I shall write to you. I have not written before because everything has been so 'unsettled'; now it is much more definite. I wish I could come and see you instead of writing; next month I shall come to London probably for a little time and then we shall be able to meet and to talk.

You may laugh as much as you like at this letter, darling, all about the COMMUNITY. It *is* rather funny.

Frieda and I do not even speak to each other at present. Lawrence is about one million miles away, although he lives next door. He and I still speak but his very voice is faint like a voice coming over a telephone wire. It is all because I cannot stand the situation between those two, for one thing. It is degrading — it offends ones soul

beyond words. I don't know which disgusts one worse — when they
are very loving and playing with each other or when they are roaring
at each other and he is pulling out Frieda's hair and saying "I'll cut
your bloody throat, you bitch" and Frieda is running up and down
the road screaming for 'Jack' to save her!! This is only a half of what
literally happened last Friday night. You know, Catalina, Lawrence
isn't healthy any more; he has gone a little bit out of his mind. If he
is contradicted about *anything* he gets into a frenzy, quite beside
himself and it goes on until he is so exhausted that he cannot stand
and has to go to bed and stay there until he has recovered. And
whatever your disagreement is about he says it is because you have
gone wrong in your sex and belong to an obscene spirit. These rages
occur whenever I see him for more than a casual moment for if ever
I say anything that isn't quite 'safe' off he goes! It is like sitting on a
railway station with Lawrence's temper like a big black engine
puffing and snorting. I can think of nothing, I am blind to everything, waiting for the moment when with a final shriek — off it will
go! When he is in a rage with Frieda he says it is she who has done
this to him and that she is "a bug who has fed on my life". I think
that is true. I think he is suffering from quite genuine monomania
at present, through having endured so much from her. Let me tell
you what happened on Friday. I went across to them for tea. Frieda
said Shelleys Ode to a Skylark was false. Lawrence said: "You are
showing off; you don't know anything about it." Then she began.
"*Now* I have had enough. Out of my house — you little God Almighty
you. Ive had enough of you. Are you going to keep your mouth
shut or aren't you." Said Lawrence: "I'll give you a dab on the cheek
to quiet you, you dirty hussy". Etc. Etc. So I left the house. At
dinner time Frieda appeared. "I have finally done with him. It is all
over for ever." She then went out of the kitchen & began to walk
round and round the house in the dark. Suddenly Lawrence appeared
and made a kind of horrible blind rush at her and they began to
scream and scuffle. He beat her — he beat her to death — her head
and face and breast and pulled out her hair. All the while she screamed
for Murry to help her. Finally they dashed into the kitchen and
round and round the table. I shall never forget how L. looked. He
was so white — almost green and he just hit — thumped the big soft
woman. Then he fell into one chair and she into another. No one
said a word. A silence fell except for Frieda's sobs and sniffs. In a
way I felt almost glad that the tension between them was over for
ever — and that they had made an end of their 'intimacy'. L. sat
staring at the floor, biting his nails. Frieda sobbed. Suddenly, after
a long time — about a quarter of an hour — L. looked up and asked
Murry a question about French literature. Murry replied. Little by

little, the three drew up to the table. . Then F. poured herself out some coffee. Then she and L. glided into talk, began to discuss some "very rich but very good macaroni cheese." And next day, whipped himself, and far more thoroughly than he had ever beaten Frieda, he was running about taking her up her breakfast to her bed and trimming her a hat.

Am I wrong in not being able to accept these people just as they are — laughing when they laugh and going away from them when they fight? *Tell me.* For I cannot. It seems to me so *degraded* — so horrible to see I cant stand it. And I feel so furiously angry: I *hate* them for it. F. is such a liar, too. To my face she is all sweetness. She used to bring me in flowers, tell me how 'exquisite' I was — how my clothes suited me — that I had never been so 'really beautiful'. Ugh! how humiliating! Thank Heaven it is over. I must be the real enemy of such a person. And what is hardest of all to bear is Lawrence's 'hang doggedness'. He is so completely in her power and yet I am sure that in his heart he loathes his slavery. She is not even a good natured person really; she is evil hearted and her mind is simply riddled with what she calls "sexual symbols". Its an ugly position for Lawrence but I cant be sorry for him just now. The sight of his humiliating dependence makes me too furious.

Except for these two, nothing has happened here. A policeman came to arrest Murry the other day,[1] & though M. staved him off he will have to go, I think.

I am very much alone here. It is not a really nice place. It is so full of huge stones, but now that I am writing I do not care for the time. It is so very temporary. It may all be over next month; in fact it will be. I don't belong to anybody here. In fact I have no being, but I am making preparations for changing everything. Write to me when you can and scold me.

Goodbye for now. Dont forget me.

I am always
Kissienka.

MS BL. *LKM* I. 67-8; cited Lea, 52; Dickinson, 83-5.

[1] Rather, to ensure that Murry reported for military registration.

To Beatrice Campbell, [14 May 1916]

[Higher Tregerthen, Zennor]
Sunday Night.

Ma très chère:

I have been waiting for the time and the place to answer you in — & they both seem here. So first of all 'thank you' for the prescription (which you shall have back) and for your letter and the 2 papers. Nor must I forget Marjory's account *NOR* Gordon's comment upon her reason for not being a S.F.[1] We have just been talking about you and G. I hope your four ears kept up a pleasant burning for we are awfully fond of you always. G. is quite sincerely and for ever Murrys only love but G. knows that . . .

It is still awfully difficult to credit what has happened and what is happening in Ireland. One cant get round it — This shooting, Beatrice, this incredible shooting of people! I keep wondering if Ireland really minds — I mean really won't be pacified and cajoled and content with a few fresh martyrs and heroes. I can understand how it must fill your thoughts — for if Ireland were New Zealand and such a thing had happened there. . . it would mean the same for me — It would really (as *un*fortunately George-Out-of-Wells would say)[2] Matter Tremendously . . .

Dear woman, I am a little afraid of jarring you by writing about the whole affair — for I know so little (except what you've told me) and I've heard no discussion or talk.

Gracie Gifford's story was spoilt by her having broken down before the jeweller in Grafton Street when she bought the ring and confided in him. Otherwise it was almost an Irish On The Eve of Turgeniev . . Poor Plunket's picture too — a cross between Jack Squire and Willie Yeats.[3] There is a strange passionate cynicism about Orpen's drawing of women's hands. Even the Daily Mirror couldn't suppress it.[4]

It is Sunday evening. Sometimes I feel I'd like to write a whole book of short stories and call each one Sunday. Women are far more 'sensitive' to Sundays than to the moon or their monthly period — Does Sunday mean to you something vivid and strange and remembered with longing — — The description sounds rather like the habits contracted by Jean Jacques Rousseau when his blood was inflamed by his youth[5] — or like G[ordon] C[ampbell] lying on his bed reading the Police Court News — but I don't mean that — Sunday is what these talking people call a rare state of consciousness — and what *I* would call — the feeling that sweeps me away when I *hear* an *unseen* piano. Yes, that's just it — and now I come to think of it — isn't it extraordinary how many pianos seem to come into being only on Sunday. Lord! someone heaven knows where — starts playing something like Mendelssohn's Melodie in F — or miles away — some other one plays a funny little gavotte by Beethoven that you — simply can't bear — I feel about an unknown piano, my dear what certain men feel about unknown women — — No question of love — but simply "an uncontrollable desire to stalk them" (as the Crown Prince on Big Game Shooting says). Not that there is even the ghost of a pianner here. Nothing but the clock and the fire and sometimes a gust of wind breaking over the house. This house is very like a house left high and dry. It has the same 'hollow' feeling — the same big beams and narrow doors & passages that only a fish could swim through without touching. And the little round windows at the back are just like port holes — Which reminds me — there has been a calf lying under the dining room window all day. Has anyone taken it in? It has been another misty Highland-Cattle-Crossing-the-Stream-by-Leader day & the little calf has lain shivering and wondering what to do with its far too big head all the day long. What time its Mother has guzzled and chewed away and looked into the distance and wondered if she were too fat to wear a tussore coat like any Christian woman. Oh, Lord, why didst Thou not provide a tucking away place for the heads of Thy Beasts as Thou Didst for Thy Birds — If the calf were only something smaller I could send my soul out wrapped in a nonexistent shawl and carrying a nonexistent basked lined with non-existent flannel and bring it in to the dead out kitchen fire to get warm and dry . . .

I must stop this letter. Write to me again very soon, Bici love.

[*No signature*]

PC ATL. *LKM* I. 69-71; Glenavy, 96-7.

[1] Marjorie Elvery, Beatrice Campbell's younger sister, was then working at the Air Board in London. The term Sinn Feiner ('S.F.') was generally applied to those who supported political independence for Ireland, as well as specifically to members of Sinn Fein ('We Ourselves'), the organization founded by Arthur Griffith in 1905.

[2] KM thought the novels of W.L. George were derivative of H.G. Wells.

[3] Grace Gifford, the fiancée of Joseph Mary Plunkett, a member of the military council of the Irish Republican Brotherhood, and one of the signatories to the Proclamation, married him in his cell at Kilmainham Jail a few hours before his execution on 4 May 1916. Ivan Turgenev's novel *On the Eve* (1860) depicts a young woman whose Romanian husband wears himself out in the cause of his country's political freedom. The poet John Collings Squire (1884–1958) was literary editor of the *New Statesman* 1913-19.

[4] The *Daily Mirror* for 9 May 1916 carried on its front page an oil portrait of Grace Gifford, who had studied at the Slade School of Art, by the Irish painter William Orpen (1878-1931), who was extremely popular for his portraits and historical 'set-pieces'.

[5] Cf. especially Book One of the *Confessions*, where Rousseau writes of being inflamed by sexuality from an early age.

To Ottoline Morrell, [17 May 1916]

Higher Tregerthen | Zennor | St. Ives
A Tuesday Night. No, its Wednesday.

Dear Lady Ottoline,

I felt from your letter that you really did understand quite wonderfully what was happening here.[1] Murry has a way, too, of making things plain — a kind of sobriety of vision that I haven't. That is really one reason why I have not written of it all before: I felt about it all so 'violently' but now I do want to talk with you — for a little.

It really is quite over for now — our relationship with L. The 'dear man' in him whom we all loved is hidden away, absorbed, completely lost, like a little gold ring in that immense german christmas pudding which is Frieda. And with all the appetite in the world one cannot eat ones way through Frieda to find him. One simply looks and waits for someone to come with a knife and cut her up into the smallest pieces that L. may see the light and shine again. But he does not want that to happen at all. And that is the really hopeless part. Every day they seem to suit each other better; they seem more *at home*. I don't know which is the more distasteful — L. sitting in his kitchen and trimming a hat for Frieda while she sits smoking a cigarette and telling him (quite uncontradicted) that her first husband "really was an artist" — (Frieda, you know dandling her little Nottingham Nietsche[2] on her knee and tossing him over to L. who really considers him gravely) or open proclaimed warfare when they throw each other in and out of the window and declare "This is the end." But is never *is* the end and it never will be. I only realised this finally about a fortnight ago. Frieda asked me over to their cottage to drink tea with them. When I arrived for some unfortunate reason I happened to mention Percy Shelley. Whereupon she said: "I think that his Skylark thing is awful Footle." "You only say that to show off," said L. "Its the only thing of Shelley's that you know". And straightway I felt like Alice between the Cook and the Duchess. Saucepans and frying pans hurtled through the air.[3] They ordered each other out of the house — and the atmosphere of HATE between them was so dreadful that I could not stand it; I had to run home. L. came to dinner with us the same evening, but Frieda would not come. He sat down and said: "I'll cut her throat if she comes near this table." After dinner she walked up and down outside the house in the dusk and suddenly, *dreadfully* — L. rushed at her and began to beat her. They ran up and down out on to the road, scuffling. Frieda screamed for Murry and for me — but Lawrence never said a word. He kept his eyes on her and *beat* her. Finally she ran into our kitchen shouting "Protect me! Save me!" I shall never forget L. how he stood back on his heels and swung his arm forward. He was quite green with fury. Then when he was tired he sat down — collapsed and she, sobbing and crying, sat down, too. None of us said a word. I felt so horrified — I felt that in the silence we might all die — die simply from horror. L. could scarcely breathe. After a long time I felt: "Well, it has happened. Now it is over for ever." And though I was dreadfully sorry for L. I didn't feel an atom of sympathy for Frieda. It was awfully strange. Murry told me afterwards he felt just the same. He just didn't feel that a woman was being beaten . . . Then Frieda stopped crying and drank some coffee. Still they stayed in our kitchen and by and by Lawrence turned to Murry and began to talk . . . In about half an hour they had almost *recovered* — they were remembering, *mutually* remembering a certain very rich, very good, but very extravagant macaroni cheese they had once eaten . . And next day Frieda stayed in bed and L. carried her meals up to her and waited upon her and in the afternoon I heard her (I can't think it wasn't intentional) singing and L. joined in. Its not really a laughing matter — in fact I think its horribly tragic, for they have degraded each other and brutalised each other beyond Words, but — all the same — I never did imagine anyone so thrive upon a beating as Frieda seemed to thrive. I shall never be persuaded that she did not take some Awful Relish in it — For she began to make herself dresses and to put flowers in her hair and to sustain a kind of girlish prattle with L. which left Murry and me speechless with amazement *and* disgust — disgust especially! But I cannot help it — I hate them for it — I hate them for such falsity. Lawrence has definitely chosen to sin against himself and Frieda is triumphant. It is horrible. You understand — don't you — that I could not write like this to anyone but you . . .

We are going to leave here as soon as we can. We are at present, looking for a little cottage where we can put our pieces of furniture, for we must have a tiny home and a garden and we must be alone again. Murry and I are so happy together — its like a miracle. When we have found our cottage we both shall love to come to you for a little while. Dear Lady Ottoline, I long to know you. I love you in your letters. We read your last letter sitting with our feet in a little stream all among primroses and wild flowers — and dreadfully like the Overture to the Penny Whistle chapter in Richard Feverel. But your letter saved us from piping . . . and, at any rate, Im never Lucy and Murry is never Dick[4] — But oh! we do look forward to seeing and speaking with you.

He sends his love — and I mine.

Katherine.

MS Texas. *LKM* I. 71; Meyers, 91; Alpers 1980, 204-5.

[1] Lady Ottoline was implicated in the Lawrences' disputes, having recently been sharply attacked by both Frieda and Lawrence.

[2] Ernest Weekley was Professor of French at University College, Nottingham.

[3] Cf. Lewis Carroll's *Alice's Adventures in Wonderland* (1865), in which the platitudinous Duchess suffers the abuse and the hurled pans of her cook.

[4] Cf. p. 262, n. 5. Ch. XIX of Meredith's novel also portrays the rapturous love between Richard Feverel and Lucy Desborough.

To S.S. Koteliansky, [24 June 1916]

[Sunnyside Cottage, Mylor,[1] near Penrhyn, Cornwall]
Saturday.

I have been wanting to write to you for days. But I am too sad, my dear one. I hope to be in London within a fortnight and then we can meet. Life is so hateful just now that I am quite numb.[2] Do not let us forget each other . . You are so often in my thoughts — especially just lately.

[*No signature*]

MS BL. Dickinson, 85.

[1] KM and Murry had moved in mid-June 1916 to this cottage, rent £18 a year, on the milder south coast of Cornwall; Mylor, 30 miles away from the Lawrences at Zennor, was on an inlet of the Truro River.
[2] Their difficulties at Higher Tregerthen, and KM's feeling that Murry had been drawn from her by his involvement with Lawrence (see *BTW*, 408-9), had left her in an unsettled state of mind.

To S.S. Koteliansky, [27 June 1916]

[Sunnyside Cottage, Mylor]

Dearest friend

Your note came this morning. I have arranged to come to London on the 8th (a Saturday). I will send you the time of the train and you will come and meet me — will you? I have asked Beatrice C. to put me up for a few nights.

I have felt that you were very depressed. But don't be sad. Let us be happy when we see each other — if only for a minute of time. I will tell you my plans then & you will tell me all yours. Until then I am always

Kissienka.

MS BL. Dickinson, 85.

To Ottoline Morrell, 27 June [1916]

Sunnyside Cottage | Mylor | Nr Penryn
June 27th

Dear Lady Ottoline —

I was so glad of your letter. We have moved at last; that is why I have not written to you before for I have wanted to.

May I come and stay with you on the 13th of July for a few days? I have to go to London on the 8th and I should so love to come to you. Only I don't know whether you will have me — for I'll be alone — Murry can't be with me. I feel as though I have so much to tell you and to talk over. Even though we have barely met — its strange —

With my love to you always
Katherine.

MS Smith.

To S.S. Koteliansky, [3 July 1916]

[Sunnyside Cottage, Mylor]

My train arrives at Paddington at 4.45 on Saturday — I am going to stay with the Campbells for a little — then I want to find some rooms & perhaps to go to Denmark[1] for September . . . but I am not quite sure — Life feels wonderful and different for at last I am free again — Till Saturday —

[No signature]

MS BL. Dickinson, 85-6.

[1] A plan probably suggested by Frederick Goodyear, who was familiar with the country. He visited KM and Murry at Mylor early in July 1916, on leave from his unit in France.

To Ottoline Morrell, [4 July 1916]

Sunnyside Cottage | Mylor | Nr Penryn.
Tuesday.

Dear Lady Ottoline.

It is lovely to think that I really can come on the 13th. I am going up to London on Saturday (the 8th) and my address will be: —

24 Norfolk Road
St. John's Wood N.W.[1]

I will send you a little note from there. This morning I had a long letter from Lawrence[2] — but we will talk about him when I see you —

With my love | A bientôt
Katherine.

MS Texas.

[1] The home of Gordon and Beatrice Campbell.
[2] Lawrence's letter has not survived.

To Ottoline Morrell, [10 July 1916]

24 Norfolk Road | St. John's Wood.
Monday.

Thank you so much for your card — I shall come by the 2.30 train which arrives at Wheatley at 4.30 — on Thursday afternoon. Carrington[1] said she might travel down with me — which would be delightful —

I really long to come. I do hope that you will like me —

London is meaningless —

Katherine.

MS Texas.

[1] The young painter Dora de Houghton Carrington (1893-1932), with whom Mark Gertler was in love, but who was devoted to Lytton Strachey.

To J.M. Murry, [12 July 1916]

[24 Norfolk Road, St. John's Wood]
Wednesday —

My dear Bogey —

This morning I received a book and a note & a shilling on page 50. But the letter to which you refer has never come. Perhaps it is just delayed, but I don't see why — So your note was a little difficult to understand. I suppose the letter explained the book. I'll read it (the book) on my journey to Garsington.

You could not have given me much less news of you — Not a personal word — nor half a phrase —

So I suppose you don't want any from me & Ill not give it —

You are a funny boy — and you *do* rather offend me —

Tig —

Ever so many thanks for the 1/-. You should not have sent it —

MS ATL. *LJMM*, 86.

To Beatrice Campbell, [15 July 1916]

[5 Garsington Manor, Garsington]
Saturday —

Dearest Bici,

I am going to Cornwall on Monday to
Sunnyside Cottage
Mylor near Penryn.
and I will write to you from there. Do write to me, too, darling, and

tell me the news. I arrived at Paddington to find the station crowded with Sinn Feiners who had just arrived from Wormwood Scrubs[1] and were being taken, on the points of innumerable bayonets to some other prison.

Heavens! What a sight it was but they all looked very happy and they all wore bunches of green ribbon or green badges — I very nearly joined them and I rather wish I had.

In great haste, darling — Thank you again for my bed —

Always,
Mansfield.

PC ATL. *LKM* I. 71; Glenavy, 97.

[1] Irish political prisoners from the London prison.

To Ottoline Morrell, [27 July 1916]

Sunnyside Cottage | Mylor | Near Penryn
Thursday —

I loved hearing from you this morning, and I had intended to write to you today and tell you that Lawrence has gone home again. We walked with him as far as the ferry and away he sailed in a little open boat pulled by an old old man. Lawrence wore a broad white linen hat and he carried a ruck sack on his back. He looked rather as though the people of Falmouth had cried to him as the Macedonians did to Paul and he was on his way over to help them.[1]

He is really very happy just now but Murry is dreadfully depressed. The thought of this military service is haunting him and he cannot forget it or put it from him for a moment. Also Lawrence's description of his night at Bodmin didn't shed a milder light upon its horrors.[2] Has Lawrence told you fully about his time there? Even to the pillow he slept on which was like "an old withered vegetable marrow tied up in a bag"? I am thankful that he has escaped but I wish that I could help Murry in some way — He feels almost too hopeless to try and help himself . .

That journey with Fatty![3] I built myself a bower of newspapers and sat in it until the train reached Paddington but Fatty talked over and round it and kept pointing to little financial paragraphs . . . leaping upon them, you know, with a shout of excitement — with the ardour of a young man discovering mountains and torrents. Fancy *thrilling* to the fact that Pig Iron is nominal and Zinc Sheets are unchanged . . .

Thank you a thousand times for my three days with you; they were quite wonderful.

With love from us both | I am always
Katherine.

MS Texas. *LKM* I. 72.

¹ Lawrence had visited KM and Murry the previous weekend, after she had written inviting him to stay (see LDHL, II. 637). For the Macedonians, cf. Acts 16: 9: 'And a vision appeared to Paul in the night: there stood a man of Macedonia, beseeching him, and saying, Come over into Macedonia, and help us.'

² Lawrence had spent the night of 28 June 1916 at Bodmin barracks, waiting his medical examination.

³ The journey back from Wheatley to Paddington, after KM's visit to Garsington on 13-17 July. Her fellow traveller is unidentified.

To Mary Hutchinson, [? 5 August 1916]

Sunnyside Cottage | Mylor | Near Penryn

Dear Mrs Hutchinson

Thank you for your delightful letter. I'd love to spend a week with you, for every time we have met I have wished I could see more of Mary Hutchinson & the possibility has seemed so remote — But just let me tell you how I am situated — Murry is, at this moment, hovering too dreadfully between the Ministry of Munitions, the latrines of India, the flies of Aden & a certain Bureau Internationale in the Haymarket. One of these must absorb him in September¹ and until I know *which* it is and *when* it is to be I don't feel that I can even unreasonably leave him.

. . But that gay week end & the prospect of meeting Lytton Strachey again is awfully intriguing & hard to give up —² You do understand — dont you? that I hate to have to say 'no'. And will you let me know when you are in London again & if I may come & see you the next time that I am in town.

With infinite regret | Yours very sincerely
Katherine Mansfield.

MS Texas.

¹ Murry's recent medical examination at Bodmin had classified him as B2. His eyesight barred him from active service, but he was liable to be called up for service in a labour battalion unless he found work of national importance by 1 Oct 1916.

² After seeing her at Garsington in mid-July, Lytton Strachey, whom KM had met the previous November at Dorothy Brett's studio, wrote on 23 July 1916 to Mary Hutchinson: 'I wish I could tell you all about the Garsington whirlpool . . . .' , and mentioned 'Katherine Mansfield — an odd satirical woman behind a regular mask of a face — but probably you know her. She was very difficult to get at; one felt it would take years of patient burrowing, but that it might be worth while.' (Texas.) It was at Strachey's prompting that Mary Hutchinson now invited KM to visit her in the country near Chichester. When she received this letter from KM, she posted it on to Strachey on 7 Aug 1916.

To J.M. Murry, [18 August 1916]

[Sunnyside Cottage, Mylor]
Very late Friday night

My own,

I shall not be able to post this letter until I have heard from you where you are going to sleep after tonight.[1] Never-the-less I must write and tell you . . . .

That it only dawned upon me this evening that perhaps you will not be here again for a long time . . That you wont see these dahlias of this year again reflected in your mirror & that the lemon verbena in a jar on my table will be all withered and dry.

As I thought that, sitting, smoking in the dusky room Peter Wilkins[2] came in with a fallen-all-too-fallen leaf in his mouth, and I remembered that the michaelmas daisies were out and lo! it was autumn.

Is it just my fancy — the beauty of this house tonight? This round lamp on the round table, the rich flowers, the tick of the clock dropping into the quiet — and the dark outside and the apples swelling and a swimming sense of deep water. May[3] brought me this evening some of this years apples. "Good to eat". They are small & coloured like pale strawberries. I wish that you were with me, my love. It is not because you are absent that I feel so free of distraction, so poised and so still — I feel that I am 'free' even of sun and wind — like a tree whose every leaf has 'turned'.

I love you tonight beyond measure. Have I ever told you how I love your shoulders? When I hold you by your shoulders — put my arm round you & feel your fine delicious skin — warm & yet cool, like milk — and your slender bones — the bones of your shoulders . . . Goodnight, my heart.

I am your own girl.

[No signature]

MS ATL. *LKM* I. 72-3; *LJMM*, 87.

[1] Murry had gone to London to look for a war job. It may have been on this occasion that he was interviewed, thanks to his friend Edward Marsh, for a job at the Home Office (see Alpers 1980, 213).
[2] A black kitten.
[3] A servant.

To J.M. Murry, [19 August 1916]

[Sunnyside Cottage, Mylor]
Saturday Night.

Darling,

Your girl has been so 'down' today, so appallingly 'low'. I knew I could not expect a letter — and cannot until Monday. Monday is 11,500 miles away — — How I loathe being here alone — It gives me nothing, really. This place is only tolerable because of you, & even then it never inspires . . . Mrs. Hoblyn called & asked me to come to a Sale of Work on behalf of the Seamen's Mission. Her thread glove *squeezed* my hand, her father was vicar here 40 years — — She is a Whidow . . . A girl called & asked if I felt inclined to subscribe to the Red Cross. Little Keverns and parties from Kevern . . . "Please Mrs Murry can I go through?" And then a Mr Watson with a boat for sale £9.0.0 with centre keel etc etc. And that grocer & the oil boy — & Mary [*or* May] has broken the primus — & Mr Mustard says we use more than our fair share of water from the pump — That from *him*.

Then came your telegram which meant evidently that we'll be in a state of suspense until Thursday at earliest & dear only knows when I shall be in London. Do you want me? Would you love to have me? I want to reach out my hand & take yours & say Oh Bogey — I *should* have come. What is £2.10.0[1] to us? Soon the army may have you & then not all the £2.10.0 in the world can give us each other. What *can* Goodyear know![2] If only you had *made* me come — wanted me so that you wouldn't let me stay here!

Oh, I could cry — I could cry tonight — I'll write no more —

My dearest heart I am

Tig.

PLEASE SEND ME MONEY.[3]

MS ATL. *LKM* I, 73; *LJMM*, 87-8.

---

[1] The train fare to London.
[2] It is likely that KM's strong affection for Goodyear, and his own fatalism about going back to the Front after his visit of the previous month, had contributed to her recent unhappiness.
[3] Wrongly transcribed by Murry (*LJMM*, 88) as 'PLEASE SEND ME NO MONEY'.

To Ottoline Morrell, [? 20 August 1916]

Sunnyside   Mylor | Near Penryn

Dearest Lady Ottoline,

I will send back The Voyage Out[1] tomorrow; I hope that I have not kept it too long — I am afraid I have —

Murry is away in London. He left last Tuesday morning & since then I have had no news from him. I am very anxious. He went because of a letter from The Military Intelligence Department who asked him to call with reference to interpreterships — I hope very much that he is successful.[2]

Being here alone in rather an ugly little house with no news of what has happened is damnable. I sit up at night with all the doors and windows locked and wait for daylight with a hammer on the table by my side to beare me companie. What the hammer would do in an hour of need I really don't know, but I feel that to come upon a woman armed with a hammer *might* be damping to the spirits of the most Hardened Fiend . . . The frightening thing about this little house is its smugness — an eternal, a kind of Jesus-Christ-yesterday-today-and-forever quality of smugness which is most sinister. It is a perfect setting for a De Quincey murder.[3]

I do not know in the least when Murry will be home but if I am not done to death before I'll gladly write something for the Garsington Chronicle.[4]

With very much love
Katherine

MS Newberry. *LKM* I. 74.

[1] Virginia Woolf's first novel, published in March 1915.

[2] Murry describes his unsuccessful interview for this post at M17 in *BTW* (425).

[3] The two papers comprising Thomas De Quincey's *On Murder Considered as a Fine Art,* with their detailed case histories, appeared in 1827 and 1839, and the Postscript in 1854.

[4] The plan of having a news-sheet with details and gossip from life at Garsington had been proposed by Dora Carrington, who wrote on 30 July 1916 to Lytton Strachey: 'Will you write outrageous verse for the "Garsington Chronicle"? Ottoline has already written a personal review of her visitors. But so dull. Because she said nothing of them she has not told us all before.' (Carrington, 32.)

To J. M. Murry, [20 August 1916]

[Sunnyside Cottage, Mylor]
Sunday Night.

Dearest,

This evening I watered the flowers & went into the orchard and into that 'walled garden' where you cut down the nettles — on your birthday — wasn't it? I am simply prostrate with misery; I can do nothing — Are we *never* to be happy — never never? We haven't had any 'life' together at all yet — in fact its only on the rarest occasion that we have any confidential intercourse —

The day is dying — very grandly — I can hear the water lapping & I can hear some sheep on the hill. Its ages since I really talked to you — for when Goodyear was here — no — you *wouldn't* respond. But its all of little account. What misery I have known! If it goes on like this I'll make an end to it in October[1] — I can bear no more.

Tig.

MS ATL. *LJMM*, 88.

[1] Once Murry was working in London, KM seems to have felt she could not stay on in Cornwall alone, although the cottage at Mylor had been taken for a year.

To J.M. Murry, [22 August 1916]

[Sunnyside Cottage, Mylor]
Tuesday.

Dearest Jack

I am going up to Mylor to post this; Ill send you a wire from there too — to cancel if I can, my horrid letter of yesterday — But I could not help it. Now I shall write fully in answer to yours of this morning. IF they do accept you provisionally, would that be sure enough for you to decide finally to leave Cornwall for the present? If they don't accept you are you coming back here? Heavens! I am really very much in the dark! And won't you have to find some place to live in in London as soon as possible? The whole affair seems to me so dreadfully in the vague.

But I'll get down to earth. If they accept you provisionally I shall wind up here — pack your clothes & my clothes — & travel up to London on Friday morning. As to what books and papers you want — as you have said nothing — you must leave it to me — I'll do my best — I shall stay the night in London and come down to Garsington by a train which (I think) leaves Paddington at 2.30.[1] If this is all O.K. wire me to Charing X where Ill go for a telegram *or* letter post restante — in the name of Bowden — in case I have to produce my identification disc. Ill call for letter or wire on Friday evening and Saturday not later than twelve o'clock — Then *if* all this happens we may have a moment to talk things out & arrange our plans. I cant stay much after Monday at Garsington. Salute Lady Ottoline for me —

Always, dearest —

Tig.

Cheque for £1.15. enclosed.

MS ATL. *LJMM*, 89.

[1] Murry was invited to Garsington, where KM was to join him, for the weekend of 26–7 Aug 1916.

To J.M. Murry, [22 August 1916]

[Mylor Bridge]

REPLIED PROVISIONAL LETTER TODAY GOOD LUCK FOR TOMORROW[1] FONDEST LOVE

KATHERINE

Telegram ATL.

[1] For his interview at MI7.

To Mary Hutchinson, [late August 1916]

Sunnyside Cottage | Mylor | Near Penryn

Yes, I will send you a telegram. I long to come for a little before the end of September. But do I get out of the train at Chichester, & what happens then? I haven't an idea where West Wittering is. Can one row there in a little boat from anywhere, or does one walk.[1] Will you just tell me what happens, & then when I send the telegram if you will just wire back 'yes' or 'no' I can come without waiting for a letter.

It is a very grey day shot with red geraniums. I feel inclined to wear a little black toque with a lace veil to my nose & drive to West Wittering in a little closed cab with a bunch of parma violets in my hand for you.

Katherine M.

MS Texas.

[1] Eleanor, the St. John Hutchinsons' house at West Wittering, Sussex, was some 50 yards from the shore of Chichester harbour.

To Lytton Strachey,[1] [? August–September 1916]

Dear Lytton —

I think it ought to be allowed to die — No amount of Valerian Drops will keep alive a creature so unwilling —[2]

+

Katherine.

MS Strachey.

[1] Giles Lytton Strachey (1880–1932), critic and biographer, was a prominent member of the Bloomsbury group.

[2] Perhaps a reference to the proposed 'Garsington Chronicle', about which Strachey had not been enthusiastic. Carrington wrote to him, 5 Aug 1916, 'Of course I can hardly agree with you about the Garsington chronicle as I invented the idea! . . . But as it will be plentifully filled . . . your valuable services will be easily dispensed with!' (Carrington, 35.)

To Ottoline Morrell, [early September 1916]

[4 Logan Place, Earls Court][1]

Monday —

Dearest Lady Ottoline —

It was a good thing I came. For Murry has had an appalling attack of influenza. I suppose he caught it at that wretched cheap hotel[2] — I imagine it must have been included with the radiator & the hot bath and London's largest rifle range — Poor child! I kept him in bed all yesterday & fed him on milk and Oxo and this morning he has crept to the War Office[3] — wispy and wan — like a moth after a shower of rain — But he is certainly better.

It is Autumn in London and the streets smell of leaves — and the barrel organs sound as they never do at any other time of the year — —

If you are in London this week — shall we see you? The memory of Garsington is so entrancing —

Thank you for all, dearest — It was so lovely —

I am always

Katherine

MS Newberry.

[1] KM was staying temporarily in Dorothy Brett's Kensington studio.

[2] Murry was staying at the National Hotel, Bedford Place, Bloomsbury.

[3] After the failure of his initial attempts to get a war job, Murry had, through the intervention of Lady Ottoline's friend J.T. Sheppard (1881–1968), then Lecturer in Classics at King's College, Cambridge, secured a post as translator for the War Office. He began work at Watergate House on 4 Sept 1916.

To Ottoline Morrell, [12 September 1916]

[4 Logan Place, Earls Court]
Tuesday.

Dearest Ottoline

What am I to make of this? Of course *if* the coloured gentleman
with the young party with pink hair *was* Suhrawadi — then indeed I
do know the 'reverse of the story'. I am a little hazy about Suhrawadi
— — was he one of Lawrence's Bing Boys last winter?[1] At any rate,
Huxley's languid letter doesn't tempt me dreadfully to tell him — to
satisfy even his 'very idlest curiosity' and 'merest inquisitiveness'. I
am afraid I am not young enough to dance to such small piping.
Heavens! his letter makes me feel so old — and inclined to dress up,
alone in the studio here — Tie up my head in a turban, make myself
fat, don a fur coat with lace frills slightly spotted with tea, and act
Lady Mary Wortley Montagu receiving a morning leg from — Swift,
perhaps[2] (played by the charwoman, Mrs Squeaks.)

But again, this little note *may* only be the prettiest way of asking
me which I prefer — pistols or . . . indian clubs.

Frieda sent Murry a tremendous 'biff' yesterday. "Now I am going
to have my say" — It was just the same "Ach du hässliche Augus-
tine"[3] as usual — Sooner or later all Frieda's friends are bound to
pop their heads out of the window and see her grinding it before
their door — smoking a cigarette with one hand on her hip and a
coloured picture of Lorenzo and Nietzsche dancing 'symbolically'
on the front of the barrel organ. Murry, yesterday, very wisely
slammed the window down and refused to listen, but I hung on
every note — —

Murry is much better, but he does not yet seem to be out of the
wood — Yesterday the Colonel said that he could only stay in the
office on the condition that he received a special permit from the
Home Office — or the War Office — I forget which. He is writing to
ask Philip [Morrell] about it —

Thank you for sending the little bundle of remnants — Your note
was quite hidden but so lovely to discover — — Please give our love
to Philip and salutations to Clive Bell —
I think of you constantly

Yours ever
Katherine.

MS Texas. Cited Meyers, 91; cited Alpers 1980, 217.

[1] This refers to the occasion — first unravelled with clarity in Alpers 1980 (214-6) — when KM, Gertler, and Koteliansky visited the Café Royal on the evening of Wednesday, 30 Aug 1916. Gertler, writing to Lady Ottoline the next day, told her how they had to share their table with two 'University Blacks' and a woman with crimson hair. KM and her friends were irritated when the group began to talk 'Intellectually'. But, continued Gertler,
imagine our Hatred and Horror when the red headed peice of dried Dung produced a Volume of Lawrence's poems [*Amores,* which was just published] and commenced to discuss Lawrence with the other, in this perfect English and carefully picked, long words! We had been ragging them all the time, but now we knew something drastic must be done. We sat and thought. Suddenly Katharine leant towards them and with a sweet smile said "*Will* you let me have that Book a moment?" "Certainly" they all beamed back — even more sweetly. Imagine their horror and utter amazement when Katharine without a word more, Rose from the table, Book and all, we following most calmly — most calmly we walked out of the Café!!! (Alpers 1980, 216.)
One of the men was Huseyn Shaheed Suhrawardy, a Bengali Muslim, a law student at Oxford, and a friend of the novelist Aldous Huxley (1894-1963), who had taken him to Garsington. He met Huxley the next day, told him of the episode without knowing who the woman was who had taken the book, and Huxley passed the story on in a letter of the same day, 31 Aug 1916, to Lady Ottoline (Texas). When Huxley heard from Lady Ottoline of Gertler's report, he wrote again; this second letter she sent on to KM, and so drew this reply.
Koteliansky sent his own account of the episode to Lawrence, who, for his part, turned KM's action into 'Gudrun in the Pompadour', ch. XXVIII of *Women in Love.* The 'Bing Boys' (from *The Bing Boys Are Here,* a popular musical by Nat D. Ayer and Clifford Gray, first performed in April 1916) were the group of Lawrence's friends who had taken seriously his plan of the previous year to establish a community in Florida.
[2] Pope would have been a more likely morning caller than Swift, on the eighteenth-century traveller and letter-writer, Lady Mary Wortley Montagu.
[3] A play on the refrain of the Viennese song 'O du lieber Augustin'.

To Mary Hutchinson, [18 September 1916]

4 Logan Place, | Kensington.
Monday.

Dear Mrs Mary Hutchinson,

May I come & stay with you from this next Friday until Monday at West Wittering? I should like to so much. If this isn't 'convenient' to you please don't hesitate to say 'no' but if it is I will look out a train & send you a telegram saying when I arrive at Bosham. That is right, isn't it?

I cannot write a word for Monday morning is in full swing here, with laundry carts bowling by. Such a heavenly morning, too, far, far too lovely to be carted away in seven baskets.

I hope I shall see you on Friday.

Katherine Mansfield.

MS Texas.

When the Hon. Dorothy Brett became the tenant of Maynard Keynes's house in Gower Street, in September 1916, she took KM and Murry as lodgers, and for the next four months KM was closer to the Garsington 'set' than at any other time. She was drawn into Bloomsbury through her growing acquaintance with Lytton Strachey, and her brief but intense friendship with Bertrand Russell. 'I want to get to know [her] really well,' Russell told Lady Ottoline in early December 1916. 'She interests me mentally very much indeed — I think she has a very good mind, & I like her boundless curiosity.' (Ronald W. Clarke, *The Life of Bertrand Russell* [1973], 314.) In a 1949 note Russell wrote: 'The following batch of letters from Katherine Mansfield has surprised me as I have come upon them. They read as if we were having an affair, or about to have one, but it was not so. She withdrew, possibly on account of Colette [Lady Constance Malleson], though I never knew. My feelings to her were ambivalent: I admired her passionately, but was repelled by her dark hatreds.' (McMaster.) At the end of 1916 Russell was beginning an affair with Lady Malleson, whose stage name was Colette O'Neill.

By January 1917 KM was longing for the privacy which was not available in Gower Street, and felt yet again that a change of address would encourage her to write.

∾

To Mary Hutchinson, [early October 1916]

3 Gower Street — [Bloomsbury] [1]

Dear Mary Hutchinson

I hope that you will come to see me when you are 'settled' in your new house[2] — and for my part I hope that we shall continue the same conversation ever so often —

What will you think of Colette,[3] I wonder — — — and will you find her 'sympathetic'. For me she is more real than any woman Ive ever known. London is sad and dull — The only thing to do is to hug the fire and smoke & read & write —

We are almost established here. Carrington's friends climb up to her heaven kissing attics — I hear them like the younger generation passing my door — simply incredibly young —

Please give my salutations to Clive Belle — I am so glad to hear he is better —[4]

My love to you
Katherine Mansfield

MS Texas.

¹ The house of John Maynard Keynes (1883–1946), Fellow and Bursar of King's College, Cambridge, who was serving in the Treasury during the war. Dorothy Brett became Keynes's tenant at the end of September 1916, with KM and Murry as her lodgers on the ground floor, she herself living above them, and Dora Carrington on the top floor. As the new residents moved in two by two, the house became known as 'the Ark'.

² River House, Upper Mall, Hammersmith, which the next year was to be decorated by Vanessa Bell and Duncan Grant.

³ The French writer, whom KM very much admired.

⁴ Mary Hutchinson was openly the mistress from 1915 of Clive Bell, whose wife Vanessa was now living with Duncan Grant. Clive Bell had influenza in the early part of October 1916.

To Ottoline Morrell, [27 October 1916]

The Ark [3 Gower Street, Bloomsbury]
Friday.

Dearest Ottoline

I want to explain to you why I have kept silent for so long — and why I have written to you and simply not posted the letters. It is *only* because I have been so frightfully wretched and distracted — and for weeks and weeks I have not been myself at all — hardly for an instant — but just living on a kind of quaking crust with blackness underneath which has paralysed — paralysed me — I have known this state of mind before but never as 'violent a melancholy' as this and the diabolical thing about it is that I cant break through and tell the one whom I want to tell "it is like this and this with me." All the while I realise how incomprehensible it must seem and I know with a kind of anguish that its out of my power to lift a finger.¹

Forgive this dull explanation. But I have to tell you that I *am* like this, and all the while I love you and think of you and long to see you. Dearest friend, can you forgive me? I have been erratic and unstable to the outward eye, but I long to have you for my close friend.

If I have not been too infernally wicked — tell me and I will write you all I long to 'talk over' with you.

For I love you and I am always

Yours
Katherine.²

MS Texas.

¹ KM's burgeoning friendship with Bertrand Russell may explain why she had become reticent with Lady Ottoline, his mistress for some years. An intricate network of letters stretched between Gower Street and Garsington over these months, including Murry's extravagant protestations of affection for Lady Ottoline, and Brett's reports on Carrington, KM, and visitors to both. But there was a more mundane reason for KM's coolness. On the

same day as this letter, 27 Oct 1916, Brett wrote to Lady Ottoline that KM, on her last visit to Garsington, had been rather put out that when she wore a new Burberry coat, Lady Ottoline failed to remark on it. KM then gave it to the housemaid, who thought it just the thing for bicycling.

² Lady Ottoline sent KM's letter on to Brett, who replied on 2 Nov 1916, quite unaware of the ironies: '*I* think she is in *Love*, some man has risen like the dawn on her horizon like they all will all her life — the Call of the Wild is in her and she can no more resist the call when it comes than any other wild animal. Poor Katherine she is torn in two I believe — Pity for the shy gentle clinging man she lives with and the passionate desire for freedom.' (Alpers 1980, 221.)

To Lytton Strachey, [? October–November 1916]

3 Gower Street
Tuesday:

I shall love to come to tea on Friday at about 4.30, thank you.

K.M.

MS Strachey.

To Bertrand Russell,¹ [13 November 1916]

3 Gower Street.

Monday,

I shall be delighted to dine with you on Thursday the 23rd. The talk on Saturday evening was infinitely exciting. I wrestled hard with Murry after, but he remained a dark riddle.²

I wonder how true your party rang!

Yours very sincerely
K.M.

MS McMaster. *Adam* 370-375, 37.

¹ The Hon. Bertrand Russell (1872-1970), philosopher, radical activist, educationalist, author. He had been a Fellow at Trinity College, Cambridge, since 1895.

² Russell had met KM the year before, in July 1915, when he wrote to Lady Ottoline Morrell that Lawrence had taken him 'to see a Russian Jew, Kotiliansky, and [Middleton] Murry and Mrs. Murry [KM] — they were all sitting together in a bare office high up next door to the Holborn Restaurant, with the windows shut, smoking Russian cigarettes without a moment's intermission, idle and cynical. I thought Murry *beastly* and the whole atmosphere of the three dead and putrefying.' (*The Autobiography of Bertrand Russell, 1914-1944*, II [1968]. 53.)

To Bertrand Russell, [24 November 1916]

[3 Gower Street, Bloomsbury]
Friday afternoon.

Yes, it was a wonderful evening. The thrill of it stayed with me all night. Even after I had fallen asleep I dreamed that we were sitting at the same table, talking and smoking, but all the mirrors of the café were windows & through them I could see big waves of green water gleaming and lifting without sound or break as though we were far out at sea.

I shall read your book tonight.

I have written to my little maid in Cornwall to send me the MSS. You know how glad I am —

Yours
Katherine.

MS McMaster. *Adam* 370-375, 37.

To Bertrand Russell, [1 December 1916]

[3 Gower Street, Bloomsbury]
Friday.

I tried to write to you yesterday but there were so many interruptions . . Life seemed to rush in and out of my door like the teller of the tale in a Dostoievsky novel. But I thought of you. I reread your letter, sitting on a bench at the top of the steps outside the British Museum. Heavens! the morning was so lovely — a blue sky, and blue and white pigeons tumbling in the bright air, and little grass springing on those sunken lawns. Your friendship was delightful, so delightful to me then that I sat there for a long time with the sun on my hands, almost too happy to move, and I began to call the pigeons to me with all kinds of little endearing names . . . Which left them quite cold . . To feel that we are going to be truthful with each other, quite without reservation — that promises so great an adventure that it is difficult to remain calm.

Do please talk to me about your work if you can. I am returning you the letter. Thank you for sending it on to me. I understand perfectly what it made you feel; but at the same time I think it is extremely gratifying and important that you should receive such letters. Curious — isn't it — how one can trace your direct influence upon the young man's thought — while he writes.

Ottoline has written to me again, begging me to go down. I may go on Monday and stay until Wednesday morning.[1] I should love to have come to tea with you Wednesday but I have an engagement which I must keep. I shall not be 'free' before six. Supposing I were to come to your flat then?[2]

There is so much to be said, but do not let us hurry it.

Only one trembles at the shortness of Life. and all that there is to be done —

Katherine.

MS McMaster. *Adam* 370-375, 39-40.

[1] KM signed the visitors' book at Garsington on 3 Dec 1916.
[2] Although Russell kept a flat at 34 Russell Chambers, Bury Street, he had recently taken up residence in the house of his brother, Earl Russell, at 37 Gower Square. KM wrote to him at both addresses.

To Bertrand Russell, [7 December 1916]

[3 Gower Street, Bloomsbury]
Thursday Evening.

I have just re-read your letter and now my head aches with a kind of sweet excitement. Do you know what I mean? It is what a little girl feels when she has been put to bed at the end of a long sunny day and still sees upon her closed eyelids the image of dancing boughs and flowery bushes. To work — to work! It is such infinite delight to know that we still have the best things to do and that we shall be comrades in the doing of them. But on Tuesday night I am going to ask you a great many questions. I want to know more about your life — ever so many things . . There is time enough, perhaps, but I feel devilishly impatient at this moment.

You have already, in this little time, given me so much — more than I have given you, and that does not satisfy me. But at present, my work simply springs from the wonderful fact that you *do* stand for Life —

Adieu until Tuesday — I shall not read your letter again — It 'troubles' me too greatly — but thank you — Thank you for it.

Katherine.

MS McMaster. *Adam* 370-375, 38.

To Bertrand Russell, [? 8 December 1916]

[3 Gower Street, Bloomsbury]
Friday late afternoon.

I have been busy all day, and at times your letter of last night has . . haunted me. "Write and tell me what you think of it all." But I cannot just now. I should have to be far away from this house to write freely; it depresses me horribly today and I am only writing you this note just to let you know that your letter came, that I read it: That is all the sign I can give.[1]

Ah, but it is not for nothing that we know each other. We shall do great things — great things.

Katherine.

MS McMaster. *Adam* 370-375, 38.

[1] Brett was writing almost daily to Lady Ottoline, reporting on KM's visitors. Several weeks earlier she had reported "no one gets further than Katherine!! Bertie, Lytton, etc. all disappear like magic". (Alpers 1980, 221.)

To Bertrand Russell, [17 December 1916]

[3 Gower Street, Bloomsbury]
Sunday evening.

I meant to write to you immediately after you left me on Friday night to say how sorry I was to have been such cold comfort and so useless to lift even ever so little the cloud of your fatigue. For a long time I sat before the fire after you had gone feeling that your goodbye had been quite final — was it? And I did not explain myself as I wished to — I left unsaid so much that perhaps you were misled. Its true that my desire is to bring all that I see and feel into harmony with that rare 'vision' of life of which we spoke, and that if I do not achieve this I shall feel that my life has been a fault at last, and its my God terribly true that I dont see the means yet — I dont in the least know definitely *how* to live. But its equally true that life never bores me. It is such strange delight to observe people and to try to understand them, to walk over the mountains and into the valleys of the world, and fields and road and to move on rivers and seas, to arrive late at night in strange cities or to come into little harbours just at pink dawn when its cold with a high wind blowing somewhere *up* in the air, to push through the heavy door into little cafés and to watch the pattern people make among tables & bottles and glasses, to watch women when they are off their guard, and to get them to talk then, to smell flowers and leaves and fruit and grass — all this — and all this is nothing — for there is so much more. When I am overcome by one of the fits of despair all this is ashes — and so intolerably bitter that I feel it never can be sweet again — But it is — To air oneself among these things, to seek them, to explore them and then to go apart and detach oneself from them — and to write — after the ferment has quite subsided — — — —

After all youll cry me very vague & dismiss me perhaps as a woman with an ill regulated mind . . But —

Goodnight

Katherine.

MS McMaster. *Adam* 370-375, 38-9.

To Ottoline Morrell, [2 January 1917]

[3 Gower Street, Bloomsbury]
Tuesday Morning.

Ottoline dearest

I have just had a letter from you about Lawrence's Book.[1] I *do* hope that you will be able to persuade him *not* to publish it. Another book even anything like The Rainbow — (is it like The Rainbow —) would be a disaster for him.[2] I think that living alone engenders in him a real form of madness.

I would love to come & see you and talk about it and read it. But I am busy every day this week & in any interval I am searching desperately for a studio which I MUST find this month. May I come for a couple of days next week — dearest? From Monday until Wednesday for instance? I would come by an early afternoon train instead of that late one.

Our journey back to town[3] must be told, not written. I felt simply weak from trying not to laugh all the way to Paddington. For one thing we all seemed to change so incredibly on the journey — Lytton grew older & older & more & more feeble, sitting in a corner with his scarf over his mouth reading 'The Celebrity's Daughter' by Violet Hunt and just lifting up his feet occasionally to have them tucked in by Carrington who grew rounder & rounder & younger & younger and seemed to be turning into a little boy of about five, blowing over a picture book and asking her wa wa what the words meant, please. And Bertie became almost distracted, snapping open and shut the green attaché case & bringing out sheaf after sheaf of letters relating to persons forbidden to enter certain restricted areas[4] & scattering them over my lap. My purple coat & skirt got thicker & thicker & my veil blacker & blacker until I looked like a Norwegian lady of 45 on her way to a Peace Conference.

Is this heavenly weather descended upon Garsington, too? It is so lovely here that just to be alive is a kind of bliss almost too great to be borne. Oh, to love the sun so!

Yours ever
Katherine.

MS Newberry. Cited Alpers 1980, 231.

[1] At the end of December 1916 Lawrence sent Lady Ottoline the manuscript of *Women in Love*, with its character of Hermione Roddice very clearly based on herself.

[2] A review by James Douglas in the *Star* for 22 Oct 1915 had claimed that Lawrence's novel *The Rainbow* undermined England's war effort, and following other damning reviews the publishers, Methuen & Company, were obliged on 3 November to surrender all their copies to the police under the Obscene Prints Act. Ten days later a magistrate ordered the seized copies to be destroyed.

[3] KM and Murry had spent Christmas at Garsington.

[4] Because of his work on behalf of conscientious objectors, Russell was not permitted to travel to certain parts of England.

To J.M. Murry, [early January 1917]

[3 Gower Street, Bloomsbury]
Afternoon.

My dearest Boy,

I have just come in and smoked a cigarette staring out through these dirty windows on to the dirtier windows across the way. I am awfully tired and exhausted — not physically, but mentally. The business of entering an agents office, the sight of those huge unwieldy books being turned over and thumbed, the agent, leaning back in a revolving chair and toying with a pencil as he talks, the little boy clerk who is told to see if 'the key of No — is out or in' — all these things are so revolting to me now that its only by the greatest effort of will that I pass through that pinging door at all. I feel dont you know, like a professional flat-hunter; all my requirements are stated so pat — all my questions are so intelligent and inevitable. The first blow was that the tenants of the maisonette on the parade have decided to continue their lease. The second that there simply are not any flats in St. John's Wood under £100 a year — and that the maisonettes at from £75 to £85 are always *lower* maisonettes i.e. entrance floor and basement. Each agent had the same story to tell. All the houses at a high rent were vacant; people were clamouring for flats — were even prepared to pay a large premium for the privilege of moving into one — etc etc. I took some addresses for maisonettes at £75 in Abbey Road and Finchley Road, but they were hideous — Rather worse than those we saw in Alexandra Road, with the same preposterous proportions etc. Finally I went to Elgoods in Vere Street and inquired if they had any of their flats off the High Street, in Henry Street, to let. Yes, they had one at £95 and one at £48 a year — payable by the month. But "the great thing about our flats is that we make the strictest possible inquiries about our intending tenants. We have some very nice people indeed in occupation and you quite understand Madam . . . Of course if one wants The Other Kind of Thing" said this lunatic, warming his bottom before an immense coke fire, "one goes to Maida Vale. But in *our* flats every tenant is known to be strictly correct!" Très bien! St. Johns Wood, my dear soul, is absolutely 'off'.

Now Ill be extravagantly frank. I think, seriously, that we ought to stay on here until June and ask Barnicoat[1] to let our house furnished or unfurnished if he can — We ought to save money against the end of the war, and if we start moving again you know we shant have a penny between us. If you were in the Army we *could* not move. In a way you *are* in the Army — I mean you are engaged all day long, you have no personal life, you are very uncertain as regards the immediate future because this immediate future is not in your control. You could not really enjoy your flat until the war is over — and the journey down to Cornwall, the moving of the furniture, the buying of all those extra things that we should *have* to buy would cost us every penny of £25. And then it is impossible for us to rent a flat of the size we need for less than a 3 years tenancy — and that seems to me madness. What do you intend to do after the war? You must be your own master. That means that you will probably not earn more than £3 a week at most, and the high prices will continue so your £3 will be more like 30/-. It is no good worrying about money, and feeling the awful burden of not being able to do what you wish — because you must pay away what you earn. No, we know that is torture. Its only a sweet dream to imagine that we can afford £60-£65 a year for our rent — and live like a little married pair — and me to take a studio in addition. My darling, we cant and I have not got the courage to face the prospect again. No, our experiences in the past have absolutely robbed me of my courage in that respect. When I am really faced with the practical prospect I draw back and shiver. Do you remember as vividly as I do ALL those houses ALL those flats ALL those rooms we have taken and withdrawn from. My valiant little warrior have you forgotten the horrors? For the time they have broken me and I must live from week to

week and not feel bound. Let us try and think of some other solution. Isn't there one? Do help me. Whenever I try & talk this all over with you my positive horror of hurting you always prevents me from really speaking my mind — My one overwhelming feeling is that we must both be free to write this year — and that even our full life together must mark time for that — Id far rather sit in a furnished room in an hotel & work than have a lovely flat & feel that the strain of money was crippling us again. Time is passing, and we cannot afford to waste another year. Do not be impatient with me. I hate to write all this —
You know I love you

Tig.

MS ATL. *LJMM*, 89-91.

¹ The landlord of Sunnyside Cottage, Mylor, which they were still renting.

To Ottoline Morrell, [14 January 1917]

[3 Gower Street, Bloomsbury]
Sunday Night.

Ottoline dearest,

I have been passing through crisis after crisis last week and do not seem to have had my head out of hot water even for a moment long enough to utter a cry of sympathy or natural feeling. The morning of the day when I had so wanted to come down to Garsington my Rhodesian Mountain was injured in her munition works[1] (which sounds like a part of her anatomy: Im not sure that it isn't.) And I had to tend her and take her to hospitals and tuck her up — At the same time the studio flat which I had just taken was snatched from me by the most perfidious Pole and indeed a perfect little Dostoievsky novel raged for days on this subject dressed out with such a deal of impossible complications that even now I am not sure what happened and I have not an idea *why*. The only *fact* which remained was that Pan Polak had pinched my studio for his fair and I had to begin my desperate search all over again. Aided by an appalling cold. But I think I have found a refuge in a tiny flat in Grays Inn. So quiet and delightful, looking over gardens and very remote, ideal for writing. I want Brett to take a top flat there when she comes back from Borneo,[2] rather than move to Fitzroy Street, or Chelsea. I don't think that one can afford to live in dreadful surroundings — and climb flights of dirty stairs & shiver past pails containing dead tea leaves & bitten ends of bread and marmalade outside other people's doors — The trace of those places seems to cling round the hem of ones skirt for ever. It is better to live in some very quiet place, where there are trees and sunken lawns and porters with brass buttons between you and empty bottles. Besides oh, I want to work so — and this year I must finish at least two books. Would you care for a copy of my wretched old book [*In a German Pension*]? It is young and bad, but I would like to send you one. It might amuse you a little.

Dearest I hardly know what to write about Lawrence. Brett has told me a great deal about the book & I can imagine how bad it is. There is no doubt about it: left to himself Lawrence goes mad. When he is with people he expands to the warmth and the light in them — he is a darling and often very wonderful, but left to himself he is cold and dark and desolate. Of course Frieda is at the bottom of it. He has chosen Frieda and when he is with real people he knows how fatal that choice is. But his cursed obstinacy eggs him on in his loneliness with her to justify his choice, by any means — by even the lowest methods. I feel I understand him so well and the whole huge unreal fabric that he builds up as his 'house' against the world. And I am *sure* there is only one way to answer him. It is very cruel, but its the only weapon to prick his sensitive pride. It is to laugh at him — to make fun of him — to make him realise that he has made a fool of himself. *Anything* else will only make him feel like Christ whipping out the templemongers. I have always realised that he needs to be laughed at more than anything. It cures his madness. At the time it makes him furious but then quite suddenly he sees himself spinning round on one toe and he laughs, too. But he ought not to be allowed to go on. He *must* be stopped. I think it is really *fatal* that such books should be published.[3]

By the end of this week I hope to have the affair of this little flat settled & then I shall be a nicer woman — and dearest, such a much better friend. You cannot imagine how dead I feel in this false existence.

Would you be a reference for me? Just to say I am a desirable tenant? It is a quite formal affair and Id be infinitely grateful. I have a dream that you will come & stay with me when I am 'settled' & we shall talk and hear singing — & really have time together —

My tenderest love — but my fingers are so frozen that the pen only dances.

Always your devoted
Katherine.

MS Texas. Cited *Exhibition*, 32; cited Meyers, 90; Delany, 274; cited Alpers 1980, 231.

[1] Ida Baker, when she returned from Rhodesia in the autumn of 1916, had reported to an office where women with college backgrounds were being recruited for the war effort. After six weeks' intensive training in metal work, she became a tool setter in an aeroplane factory in Chiswick.

[2] Dorothy Brett's younger sister Sylvia had married in 1911 Sir Charles Vyner de Windt Brooke, GCMG, who became Rajah of Sarawak in May 1917. Brett did not, as she intended, go out to Borneo for the celebrations.

[3] Lady Ottoline's anger over *Women in Love* did not abate, and she never saw Lawrence again. Philip Morrell warned Lawrence's literary agent, J.B. Pinker, that if the novel were published as it stood, he would bring a libel action against the publishers. It did not appear until the end of 1920, in a limited American edition privately printed for subscribers. Martin Secker published a British edition in 1921.

To Bertrand Russell, [16 January 1917]

[3 Gower Street, Bloomsbury]
Tuesday Night.

Here is the manuscript and the letter — I was so glad to hear from you tonight. I cannot tell you how much I value your friendship . . This isn't a letter; it is just a little note written rather in prison.

Jack Hutchinson rather incredibly refused.[1] He did not even take the trouble to let me know until late this evening when Mary phoned & mentioned, incidentally, that he was not willing. Why do such men exist except for such purposes? I shall never take the trouble to recognise him again.

Tomorrow I am acting for the movies — an "exterior scene in walking dress".[2] Doesn't that sound awfully strange to you? God! I have been unhappy today — in despair and walking idly over a dreadful world having no hiding place and no cover. Only when it grew dark I lit the candles & read Villon.

And now Goodnight mon ami.

Katherine.

MS McMaster. *Adam* 370-375, 37-8.

[1] Russell's own note on the original of this letter recorded that KM 'needed a reference to say she was respectable. She applied to St. John Hutchinson, who refused on the grounds that she lived in sin with Middleton Murry. Hutchinson's wife lived in sin with Clive Bell, but not in *open* sin.'

[2] KM acted as an 'extra' in a number of unidentified films.

To Bertrand Russell, [21 January 1917]

[3 Gower Street, Bloomsbury]
Sunday:

So many thanks for your letter. I too am looking forward to Tuesday. But please do not expect me too soon — between six and seven — I cannot come before. I have heard from Ottoline; she comes to town tomorrow for one or two days. I expect she will want very much to see you. I shall be the soul of discretion. Marie has really gone — with Brett's sister for chaperone — It must be an infinite relief to Ottoline to have her off her lap.[1]

I hope to move at the end of next week, but my cough is so disastrous in this Khaki weather that I can hardly conceive of leaving Gower Street except feet foremost. Will the sun *ever* shine again? My last day with the "movies" — walking about a big bare studio in what the American producer calls 'slap up evening dress' has laid me low ever since. But I shall be quite well by Tuesday — There is such lovely mimosa in my room — I can see the plumy trees and the brown hand that gathered it — oh, to be there!

Such absurd things have happened to me since last I saw you (it feels a very long time ago). But I will tell you about them on Tuesday —

I am sorry you are so busy — and I feel that this work makes you so weary — will it go on for very long?

And thank you, too for letting me see the letters. I will bring them back with me on Tuesday.   Goodnight

Katherine.

MS McMaster. *Adam* 370-375, 40.

[1] After the German invasion of Belgium, Maria Nys (d. 1955) came as a refugee to live with Lady Ottoline, who found her presence at first a trial, then a serious problem after her attempted suicide in 1915. After a time at Newnham College, Cambridge, she stayed briefly with Brett in Gower Street while she worked at India House. In January 1917 she went to join her mother, now settled in Florence. She married Aldous Huxley in 1919.

To Bertrand Russell, 22 January [1917]

3 Gower St | W.C.
January 22nd

I did not at all want to send you that telegram.[1] But what could I do? Nothing else. My cough is so vile that Ill not inflict it on others and I *must* try & cure it before it lays me quite too finally low. So I am staying in doors & praying for the weather to change —

I want to move at the end of this week if possible: then I shall be quite free.

But if only it were not so cold & one did not cough so.

No, I am too depressed to write even. Please forgive

Katherine.

MS McMaster. *Adam* 370-375, 40-1.

[1] The telegram, apparently cancelling their appointment for the 23rd (see preceding letter), has not survived.

To Bertrand Russell, [24 January 1917]

[3 Gower Street, Bloomsbury]
Wednesday Night.

You wrote me such a lovely letter, mon cher ami — Yes, let us dine together on Friday evening. I shall be well enough if you will please come for me here. Then *we shall talk*. I feel there is so much to be said that Im quite quite silent until then; that it is an age since we have seen each other. And yet while I haven't seen you my 'friendship' for you has gone on and grown ever so much deeper and profounder.

Let us be very happy on Friday night.

I give you my two hands
Katherine.

MS ATL. Alpers 1980, 233-4.

To Ottoline Morrell, [late January 1917]

[3 Gower Street, Bloomsbury]

Ottoline my dearest —

I have been thinking of you all this week. I seemed to see *nothing* of you while you were in town — simply nothing except a party which was no real party at all — and the divine moment when we heard that trembling glittering italian music shake out into the air from the old barrel-organ — And then last weekend I had to go to the silly sinema — and this I [knew] would be fatal — among so many and so many and such glee. But I have so much to tell you and to talk over that I do hope we shall meet soon. I really believe we ought to join together against The Deaders[1] and — all of us who are alive — live so happily and so thrillingly that they are left like the men on the mountain — gazing up at us while we fly in the air.

It is such a perfect day — For the last two days and nights I have felt that winter was over for ever and that my breast could not contain my heart. Such air — full of little lilac flowers and new grass and the first butterflies — What can one do with this intolerable love of almost sensational life — of the outsides of houses half moonlight and half black shadow — of the sounds of music and the shapes of people standing in those round pools of light that the street lamps shed.

I wish we had spent one long evening together — here — but perhaps next time you are in London I shall have a studio —

This is only a note I am giving to Murry — I shall write you a long letter tomorrow night. It is a kind of endless miracle to know that you exist and that you are *you*.

Ever your
Katherine.

MS Texas.

[1] KM's term for the group of mainly Cambridge people associated with Bloomsbury.

To Lytton Strachey, [late January 1917]

[3 Gower Street, Bloomsbury]

Dear Lytton,

I am in a state of suspension until the end of next week. God forbid that we should take tea once again in what Miss Chapman[1] calls "this coldblooded moratorium". But on Monday I am gone and as soon as the paint is dry I shall write to you and beg you to come & drink a dish of tea.

Yours ever
Katherine.

MS Strachey.

[1] Maynard Keynes's housekeeper in Gower Street.

To Bertrand Russell, 30 January [1917]

[3 Gower Street, Bloomsbury]
January 30th

I must tell you the horrid truth at once — I shall not be delivered or anything like delivered by tomorrow night — Please do not be angry for it is not my fault.[1] Indeed I feel that were I not leaving here soon Id despair of ever producing anything of any sort again. It is the Very Devil. And now I am in a state of transition — half here — half in my new flat — If you can bear me tomorrow night, empty handed, do let us dine together. If you feel I am guilty, Ill quite perfectly understand. I had a long letter from Ottoline today. I will tell you about it when we meet again.

So you really do quite understand that if you have the faintest feeling writing — — —

Katherine

MS McMaster. *Adam* 370-375, 41.

[1] If KM was writing something for Russell, or at his request, it remains untraced.

To Bertrand Russell, [31 January 1917]

[3 Gower Street, Bloomsbury]
No, there is nothing to say ± I will tell you as soon as I am away from here, and perhaps we can then arrange a meeting — if you are not too offended with me. But for the present I am quite dead — and I could not bear to be with you while I am — — so.

Goodbye for now.

Katherine.

MS McMaster. *Adam* 370-375, 40.

VII

ENGLAND: 1917

At the beginning of February 1917, Murry recalled, 'After making a vain attempt to find a comfortable flat. . .Katherine and I agreed to live apart. The rumour went around that Mansfield and Murry had separated. It was nothing of the kind. We took rooms as near as we could get them to one another. . . .I went every day to Katherine's studio [141A Church Street, Chelsea] for my supper on leaving the War Office, and then went on to Redcliffe Road to work. It seemed the best arrangement while I was living my half-life in the War Office.' (*LJMM*, 91–2.)

It was more than a year since KM had completed anything except for *The Aloe*, and even that was not the finished story which in 1930 Murry skilfully put together from several manuscripts. Early in 1917 she attempted a play which was left in its first draft. Then in May KM returned to the pages of the *New Age*; by the end of the year she had contributed ten pieces, mostly rather brittle sketches. But her main work through the summer of 1917 was to refashion *The Aloe* into *Prelude*. This in turn brought her acquaintance with Virginia Woolf to something like friendship, for the Woolfs requested the story for their recently established Hogarth Press, and the two women began to see each other regularly.

Although her 'rheumatism' continued to trouble her, from the time KM left Gower Street to the flaring up of her lungs in December was the last period she enjoyed of what could be called reasonable health.

∞

To J.M. Murry, [early February 1917]

[3 Gower Street, Bloomsbury]

Darling

Here is my week's share + £2 for rent. But I think it ought to be £3 for rent. I can't remember — I'll pay the rest next week.

I am going to have a second key made for my Yale lock[1] and give it to you. Then, when I am out, the door isn't shut to you — I don't like that idea, somehow. Suppose you want to come in you must be free to come. So I shall get another made.

Don't my precious lamb wear yourself out with broomsticks!

Your
Tig

MS Newberry.

[1] i.e. on the new flat, to which KM was in process of moving.

To Ottoline Morrell, [6 February 1917]

[3 Gower Street, Bloomsbury]

Dearest Ottoline,

I could not find the house, but beat round the Square trying 38 & 28 all to no avail[1] — that was why I did not come back.

I sold last nights tickets by great good luck to a man as was wanting some & bought 4 more for tonight. But I am afraid I can't possibly go tonight for my furniture is arriving in fits & starts today & I shall be a black wreck by tonight. I am just starting off for the Great Beyond & the Edge of Things now — very thankfully. I will write to Brett from there. I am so sorry we only saw each other for such an interrupted moment; it was like a cinema! And I do hope you will some day find your way to 141A Church Street Chelsea, which is the address of my nunnery.

I wish you were well of your headaches. They are the Devil — & in England too

Ever so much love
Katherine

TC Texas.

[1] The occupant of a house whose number ended in '8', apparently in one of the Bloomsbury squares, is unidentified.

To J.M. Murry, [? early February 1917]

[141A Church Street, Chelsea][1]

Cheri

je suis sorti pour 10 minutes — Attends moi ici — ai laisse le clef dans le cabinet sous la siege.

T.[2]

MS Texas.

[1] The small studio which KM took from the beginning of February 1917; Murry had rooms a few blocks away.

[2] (Translation)
Dear
    I am going out for 10 minutes—Wait for me here—have left the key in the cupboard under the seat.

T.

To Ottoline Morrell, [? 13 February 1917]

141A Church street | Chelsea SW3
Tuesday.

My dearest —

A letter from you, unopened, has been lying on my writing table for days & days. At first I had not the *heart* to open it and then I hadn't the courage — only tonight I read it through.

Ah, my lovely friend, it was such an enchanting letter. It was so wise and so perfect that it took my breath away. It "went to my heart" like Music — and I seemed to see, in the dark pool of silence that lies between us, our wonderful friendship that we so very nearly achieved, shining, gleaming, heavenly, and longed for, like the moon in the trembling water of the pond — I stretched out my arms to it — I feel I *must* have it: it COULD not be gone —

Who, among women, loves you as I love you? Who appreciates you and understands you more nearly than I? I want you — I want you so immensely and so utterly for my friend — There is no one like you — and now I am terrified that I have lost you — — —

Shall I explain why I wrote like that and ran away? Yes I shall explain, but not now. I will tell you or I·will write at length. I tried, this evening, to explain to Brett — perhaps she did 'understand' —

But until I do — know that whatever you may feel for *me* I can never feel for you anything but love and deepest friendship. Do let us meet if it is possible & be really together & talk and talk — endlessly. I feel that if I were with you all would be plain between us — until I do I am yours for ever

Katherine

MS Texas.

To Bertrand Russell, 24 February 1917

141A Church Street | Chelsea | S.W.
24 : II : 17

Yesterday I received the Plough Share. It is very kind of you to have thought of me & I reread your letter to President Wilson with the liveliest interest.[1] It is splendid to find a paper that has printed it in full — more especially because of the hideous journalist habit of quoting 'extracts'. The other article 'The World After the War' I thought admirable until — may I be quite frank? — I came to the last sentence.[2] That so surprised me, having climbed so high with you and up such painful & dark stairs to find that there wasn't any landing at all — so that on your part, at least, the journey had been more or less cynical . . I am not yet recovered.

Dear knows you are perfectly free to think that — & to say it — I can hear you saying it. But I don't think it was the time or the place. Aber nein! Unless of course I was mistaken in your 'tone' throughout — quite taken in, in fact, like all the other little Plough Shares must have been. Is that what you intended? Were you getting your philosophic own back on us all — or — — — I really don't know even now. But very many thanks all the same. I hope you do not think me too rude —

I am a recluse at present & do nothing but write & read & read & write — seeing nobody & going nowhere. As soon as I have finished my Geneva story[3] you shall have it —

London feels to me quite remote & Garsington — over the brim of the world.
Addio.

Katherine.

Please excuse my penmanship: my right hand is out of action at present.

MS McMaster. *Adam* 370–375, 41.

[1] Russell's letter 'To the President of the United States', urging President Woodrow Wilson to bring the war to an end, was published in the Quaker journal *The Ploughshare*, February 1917. The letter, dated 4 Dec 1916, had appeared earlier in the United States.
[2] Russell's article 'National Defence', in the *Ploughshare*, January 1917, part of a series by prominent authors on 'The World after the War', concluded that unless there was a genuine desire for peace, 'civilized man will perish off the face of the earth. Whether that would be regrettable, I do not venture to determine.'
[3] A few pages of 'Geneva' survive in manuscript (ATL). Murry conflated this with other fragments as 'The Lost Battle', in *The Scrapbook of Katherine Mansfield*, ed. John Middleton Murry (1937), 61–5.

To Ottoline Morrell, [3 April 1917]

141A, CHURCH STREET, | CHELSEA, | S.W.
Tuesday. Midnight

Ottoline dearest,

When the postman handed me a letter from you this afternoon I felt as though it had come from a far country — — It is so long since I have heard from you and so much seems to have happened. It is so dear of you to ask me to Garsington for Easter. But I cannot come. I am working fearfully hard just now and simply dont dare to court any interruption. Here I stay in my home, and except for the most occasional alarum and excursion to my dentist I don't go out at all. Ive a play half written[1] and God knows how many long short stories and notes and sketches for portraits. And to tell you the truth I have hugged my shelter so long, not daring to issue forth & pick my way over the stones and rocky spikes to the edge of the sea where the impatient muse or fury in a quivering bonnet waits to drag me in and duck me, that I dont dare delay a moment longer. So until I can come to you with a lovely infant on each arm I'd better stay away (which last sounds like an extract from an unwritten play by Gilbert C[annan]).

How are you? Are you writing? Have you read anything 'good' lately? I wonder what you think of the new Conrad book now that it is complete.[2] I feel there is something wrong with it — that it doesn't get any further than he has got before — and no artist has any right to be able to afford to let it happen again. But perhaps I am quite wrong.

I am sitting writing to you with my feet in the fire. Its very quiet except for the clock that gallops away like a lonely rider with a long plume in his hat beating along a dark road — Sometimes I can hear the trains hoot or a strange mysterious tapping starts — and I am frightened. Only it is devilishly cold. I must go to bed. If I knew you were not offended with me I should love to write you — but pages.

Yours ever
Katherine.

MS Newberry. Cited Alpers 1980, 238.

[1] 'A Ship in the Harbour', published as 'Toots', *Turnbull Library Record*, May 1971, 4-20.
[2] Joseph Conrad's *The Shadow Line* ran as a serial in the *English Review* from September 1916 to March 1917.

To Ottoline Morrell, 24 April 1917

141a Church Street | Chelsea S.W.
April 24th 1917

My dearest Ottoline,

I would love to have a talk with you — a long talk to ourselves. I will come as soon as I can — just sending you a note beforehand to ask if you can have me. I was so glad to hear from you this morning. Heavens! What an exquisite early morning it was with little Poussin cherubs[1] climbing up & down the budding tree outside my window! I have so many trees to watch from here — two in my front garden and three graceful young bushes and a big fig tree at the back. It is so hard to be patient with them; one feels inclined to stamp and say:

come into leaf immediately! But no, they unfold in their beautiful reluctant way & I suppose one wouldn't have it otherwise — if one were a saint. But I am not & I wish the Lord were a little more like a Chinese conjuror.

I have been reading this past week the poems of Mistral and of his young friend Aubanel. I wonder if you know a book called La Miougrano — the Pomegranates by Aubanel — Dans les preaux il y a des violettes; voici, de nouveau des hirondelles; de nouveau voici le soleil plus roux, plus beau. Il y a des feuilles aux plantanes, l'ombre est fraiche dans les allees, et tout tresaille. La rive est verte; sur la rive je suis couché; cependant me viennent des grands arbres et des buissons, chants et parfums. Toutes les branches sont en fleurs; tout chante, tout rit, car la vie est si charmante![2] — — — These men write with such lovely ease. But oh they make one feel what madness it is to live out of the sun.

My play, which is called 'A Ship in the Harbour,' is at its Third Act. I hope it will be good; I know the idea is good. But there is an unthinkable amount of pruning to be done before one can liberate one's people in a play. I hadn't realised it before. It is very hard work. I wish I could see what you are writing. I am sending you some *snippets* of mine.[3]

I heard that Lawrence was in London or expected to arrive.[4] I wonder if you have heard from him. I found some of his letters the other day — and re-reading one I set to wishing that he hadn't 'Changed'. Lawrence was one of the few real people — one cannot help loving the memory of him.

One can just see darling Murry's toes sticking out from under the immense umbrella that he sits under and which is the war. I walk all round the umbrella very often and talk to the toes and a small voice answers me — but that is nearly all, one is tired of wondering when this infernal war will end, and tired of being buoyed up by false hopes one moment and crushed down again the next. But it cannot go on long, can it?

If ever you come to London you will come here? Really it is not quite in the wilds, and you know I should love to welcome you.

My love
Katherine

MSC Alpers.

[1] The canvases of the French classical painter Nicolas Poussin (1593–1665) often contain *putti*.

[2] The French poets Frédéric Mistral (1830–1914) and Theodore Aubanel (1829–86) were active in the nineteenth-century revival of Provençal literature. The lines KM quotes are from section XV of Aubanel's *La Mióugrano entraduberto* (1860), translated as *La Grenade entr'ouverte*.

[3] During the past year Lady Ottoline had begun writing pieces of short fiction and 'imaginative' prose; one of her sketches is included in Morrell (238-43). The *'snippets'* of KM's enclosed have not survived.

[4] Lawrence stayed in London between 19 and 27 April. He had written to Murry at Gower Street, unaware of his changed address, and no meeting took place.

To J.M. Murry, [19] May 1917

[47 Redcliffe Road, Fulham] [1]
Saturday Night. | May 18th[2] 1917.

My darling

Do not imagine, because you find these lines in your private book that I have been trespassing. You know I have not — and where else shall I leave a love letter? For I long to write you a love letter tonight. You are all about me — I seem to breathe you — hear you — feel you in me and of me — What am I doing here? You are away — I have seen you in the train, at the station, driving up, sitting in the lamplight, talking, greeting people — washing your hands — —[3] And I am here — in your tent — sitting at your table — There are some wallflower petals on the table & a dead match, a blue pencil and a Magdeburgische Zeitung.[4] I am just as much at home as they.

When dusk came — flowing up the silent garden — lapping against the blind windows — my first & last terror started up — I was making some coffee in the kitchen. It was so violent so dreadful I put down the coffee-pot — and simply ran away — *ran ran* out of the studio and up the street with my bag under one arm and a block of writing paper and a pen under the other. I felt that if I could get here & find Mrs [*illegible*] I should be 'safe' — I found her and I lighted your gas, wound up your clock — drew your curtains — & embraced your black overcoat before I sat down — frightened no longer. Do not be angry with me, Bogey — ça a été plus fort que moi . . . . That is why I am here.

When you came to tea this afternoon you took a brioche broke it in half & padded the inside doughy bit with two fingers. You always do that with a bun or a roll or a piece of bread — It is your way — your head a little on one side the while . .

— When you opened your suitcase I saw your old feltie & a french book and a comb all higgledy piggledy — 'Tig. Ive only got 3 handkerchiefs' — Why should that memory be so sweet to me? . .

Last night, there was a moment before you got into bed. You stood, quite naked, bending forward a little — talking. It was only for an instant. I saw you — I loved you so — loved your body with such tenderness — Ah my dear — And I am not thinking now of 'passion'. No, of that other thing that makes me feel that every inch of you is so precious to me. Your soft shoulders — your creamy warm skin, your ears, cold like shells are cold — your long legs & your feet that I love to clasp with my feet — the feeling of your belly — & your thin young back — Just below that bone that sticks out at the back of your neck you have a little mole. It is partly because we are young that I feel this tenderness — I love your youth — I could not bear that it should be touched even by a cold wind if I were the Lord.

We two, you know have everything before us, and we shall do very great things — I have perfect faith in us — and so perfect is my love for you that I am, as it were, still, silent to my very soul. I want nobody but you for my lover and my friend and to nobody but you shall I be *faithful.*

I am yours for ever
Tig.

MS ATL. *LJMM*, 92-3.

[1] Although Murry regularly spoke of his two ground-floor rooms as being in Fulham, and gave that as his address, Redcliffe Road is in the present Borough of Kensington, on the border of Chelsea.

[2] Saturday was in fact the 19th.

[3] Murry was on his way to Garsington for the weekend.

[4] The 'task of extracting from the newspapers of the Central Powers' for his War Office job 'a picture of their economic, political and moral conditions, roused all [Murry's] zeal,' observes Lea (54-5). Within six months of his appointment he was made editor of the confidential *Daily Review of the Foreign Press*, which circulated among heads of Government departments.

To Ottoline Morrell, [22 May 1917]

141A Church Street | Chelsea | S W.3.
Tuesday.

The lovely flowers and the piece of sweet scented geranium have brought all your garden into my studio. A thousand thanks for them. I was rather wondering when I was going to hear from you again. You *did* have a long letter from me a little while ago — didn't you? This month I must simply *slave.* I don't dare to go away again even for a night, just now. I click away on the typewriter all day & in the evening rush to the Queens Hall[1] & get back my nerves. But I do hope that Brett will come and see me — Murry told me so little about Garsington this time. What wretched little bones has Clive been stealing from grubby little plates & tossing to his friends now — I wonder.[2] Let them pick them clean if they will — and snigger and crack them up as they please. He is an appalling creature — but I cannot bear to look in his direction.

I re-read some poems by Walt Whitman this week. He is tremendously good at times — don't you think? And I am re-reading that wonderful, wonderful War and Peace. I could talk about *that* for ever.

I am so sorry about B.R.[3] Yes I saw him once; he was awfully kind about my work, and I enjoyed talking to him. He was "in the mood". We didn't talk about present people and present affairs but of all kinds of 'odd' things — like Flattery and Praise and what is it one really wishes to convey in writing — You know . . .

If you do come to London you will let me know — Yes I'd like a talk with you *here* and *now*. There is a great deal to say.

I am *always*
Katherine.

MS Newberry. Cited Alpers 1980, 235.

[1] An afternoon concert at the Queen's Hall on Saturday, 19 May 1917, featured the pianist Benno Moiseiwitsch and the New Queen's Hall Light Orchestra.

[2] Clive Bell, a conscientious objector, was employed by Philip Morrell as a farm labourer; he was a constant purveyor of gossip between Garsington and Bloomsbury.

[3] Bertrand Russell was suffering from severe depression at this time. He wrote to Lady Ottoline on 5 May 1917: 'I must be half asleep while the war lasts. And I don't want to go on talking about despair, but nothing else is quite sincere . . . I really can't ask anybody to enter into my inner life now — it is bad enough having to live it myself —' (Texas.)

To Ottoline Morrell, [after 3 June 1917]

141A, CHURCH STREET, | CHELSEA, S.W.

Dearest Ottoline,

I gave up trying to telephone you in despair this morning; and sent a telegram instead: I wish I could have come, but I have promised to go to Margaret Morris' Theatre[1] — and I cannot *not* go. Tomorrow I'm free until 7.15. I shall try again in the morning to see if I can get through to you by phone. It would be so lovely to see you: yes, my dear friend, I enjoyed myself immensely this weekend. I enjoyed talking to you. I *hate* to think that you have been feeling so unhappy, though.[2] Virginia [Woolf] came to tea this afternoon.[3] How hot it has been. The birds are making such a loud chatter & everybody from far and near is on the point of having dinner the air is all gongs and tinkles. [How] wonderfully beautiful Garsington [was] this time: There were even two white petals in my water jug the night I arrived. *Can* they have been Milly?[4] . . . !

I tried to make Chili[5] talk about Chili on the way up — but it seemed Most Mysterious. Full of tea shops like "Rumpelmeyers" and people in lovely french clothes walking up and down boulevards by the side of a dashing sea, eating water melons to the sound of large permanently playing brass bands!

My fond love
Katherine.

If only something wonderful would happen. . .

MS Newberry.

[1] Margaret Morris (1891-1980), who lived with KM's friend, the painter J.D. Fergusson, evolved her own technique of creative dance while a teenager. In 1914 she had started The Club, a small theatre with a club for dancers, musicians, and painters, in the Temperance Billiard Hall in Flood Street, Chelsea. One night a month it offered original dance; another was given to discussion; and the 21st of each month was a social occasion.

[2] Soon after Bertrand Russell concluded his long affair with Lady Ottoline, Philip Morrell had formed a liaison of his own, which his wife had doubtless discussed with KM when she and Murry were at Garsington the weekend of 3 June 1917.

[3] On 26 Apr 1917 Virginia Woolf (see p. 314, n.1) wrote to her sister, Vanessa Bell, 'I am going to see Katherine Mansfield, to get a story from her, perhaps' (*LVW* II. 150), for her and Leonard Woolf's recently established Hogarth Press. Mrs Woolf frequently visited the studio in Church Street over the summer of 1917.

[4] The parlourmaid at Garsington.

[5] Another guest that weekend was the Chilean painter Alvaro 'Chili' Guevara (1894-1951), born in Valparaiso. He came to England to study painting, first at Bradford, then in London, and was associated with the New Art Club; he held his first exhibition in 1916.

To Ottoline Morrell, [16 June 1917]

141A, CHURCH STREET | CHELSEA, S.W.
Saturday afternoon. In the garden.

My dearest Ottoline,

I would love to have lunch with you on Tuesday at 12.30 on the second floor of Lyons. But, darling, which Lyon do you mean — they are thick as violets everywhere. I imagine you mean the ragtime band one nearly opposite Bond Street Tube Station.[1] Do you? If you *do* don't bother to let me know, but if you mean another — just let me have a card — and I will attend it.

I have been thinking of you ever so often these last days & Murry has seen a lovely blue vision of you — at least twice. Oh, Ive felt so near you and so much your friend ever since my last time at Garsington — I wish you were here — no, that we were together now this very instant. I would tell you that I loved you and you would believe me — *Do* let us meet on Tuesday: there is so much to say that no earthly letter could hold. I want to talk to you about Sassoon (who seems to me at present, in the *Dostoievsky* sense, 'delirious').[2] I want to make you laugh about my dinner with Rasputin & Aldous &

his Khaki brother & French Polish Elliot[3] — And I want to ask you if I may come to Garsington at the end of next week perhaps & stay for some days. Is there a corner? And we shall sit in a field and walk in your heavenly garden —

I am writing to you in my backyard, now. The tree makes a wavy pattern on the table and a 'sad number' (as the early Vics. would say) of green beetles are walking on my neck — The fig leaves look tremendously tough, like metal. A pair of white stockings is hanging to dry on the back of the garden roller — Now and again I offer up an ave to Our Mother of Joy that they may be dry by this evening. But as far as I can make out she replies: "the legs which are of silk shall be dry but the tops and bottoms which are of cotton — yea, even of 'lisle', they will not be dry" . . . Hail Mary!

Alas! Poor Murry! I shall see him this evening & see how soon he can get his holiday. I have never seen anyone look more ill: he horrifies me. But he is so cheerful — — — a *straw* hat now — I will make him send your books. Yes, I must tell you about my meeting with Murry & Sassoon in Murry's room[4] — And walking along with them, very late at night, down the dark shiny road — Sassoon said: "How lovely she looked today." "Yes", said Murry, airily, blinking at the stars "it was that blue dress with *scallops*" . . .

If this weather goes on we shall all of us be angels. Only at the back of my mind there is that dark place — the *war* — but I cant *feel* it I cant get through to it just now. I feel as if I had got drunk to drown a sorrow — do you know what I mean —
Tuesday then — & until Tuesday —

my love
Katherine.

MS Texas. Cited *Exhibition,* 32; cited Alpers 1980, 244.

[1] The Lyons chain of tea-rooms had recently opened a Maison Lyons in Oxford Street.

[2] The poet Siegfried Sassoon (1886-1967), with whom Lady Ottoline was then infatuated, was an officer in the Royal Welch Fusiliers. Already decorated for bravery, Sassoon, believing that the war could no longer be justified, was at this time preoccupied with his decision not to return to the Front. Dostoevsky's anguished heroes are frequently 'delirious', in the grip of an *idée fixe.*

[3] 'Rasputin' was perhaps Floryan Sobieniowski, KM's tiresome Polish acquaintance; the real Grigori Yefimovitch Rasputin (1871-1916) had been murdered shortly before. Aldous Huxley's elder brother Julian (1884-1975), prolific writer on scientific and social subjects, had left his teaching position at the Rice Institute, Houston, Texas, and in the spring of 1917 was training at Aldershot as a cadet in the Army Service Corps. 'French Polish Elliot' can only have been the American poet and critic T.S. Eliot (1888-1965).

[4] On Lady Ottoline's prompting, Sassoon visited Murry on 11 June 1917. Murry helped him prepare his 'Declaration', released to the press at the end of July, stating why as an officer he could not continue to support the war.

To Ottoline Morrell, [? 24 June 1917]

[141A Church Street, Chelsea]
Sunday.

Dearest Ottoline

'They' tell me that you are coming to town this week. I do hope that you are, so that we shall have a laugh and a frisk together. Of course I longed to tell you of my meeting with Greaves — Mary Hutch gave a dinner party at her new house — Robby Ross, Roger Fry, Greaves, Eliot, Jack [St. John] Hutch[inson], she and I . . .[1] Oh God! Those parties. They are all very well in retrospect but while they are going on they are too infernally boring. Mary, of course went all out for Roger Fry and Robby Ross with an *eye* on Greaves and an *eyebrow* on Eliot. From Marys end of the table whiffs of George Moore and Max Beerbohm and Lord Curzon and Duhamel floated[2] — while Jack tied a white apron round himself and cut up, trimmed and smacked into shape the whole of America and the Americans. *So* nice for poor Eliot who grew paler and paler and more and more silent. In the middle sat Greaves chat chatting incessantly of what I told my sergeant and what my men said to me and how I brought them back at the point of my revolver etc. etc. I did not like that young man at *all*. In fact I longed to snub him and to tell him that one does not talk unless one has something to say. He seemed to me, too, to be so stupidly callous about the war and he was so frightfully boring about how the beer was diluted at La Bassée.[3] Roger Fry looked like an undiscovered unauthentic portrait by Jimmy Whistler and Robby Ross' teeth rang so false. And in and out among us all Mary moved like a spilt liqueur. I came away with Eliot and we walked past rows of little ugly houses hiding behind bitter smelling privet hedges; a great number of amorous black cats looped across the road and high up in the sky there was a battered old moon.[4] I liked him very much and did not feel he was an enemy.

Its so late: I must continue this tomorrow. Goodnight, my dearest friend. Always your

Katherine

MS Newberry. Alpers 1980, 243-4.

[1] Mary Hutchinson's guests on this occasion at River House, Hammersmith, included Robert Ross (1869–1918), critic, connoisseur, and close friend of Oscar Wilde; the painter and critic Roger Fry (1866–1934), a Cambridge science graduate who became a formative influence on Bloomsbury, (it was principally through his efforts that Post-Impressionism was accepted in England); and the poet and later novelist Robert Graves (b. 1895), then a captain in the Royal Welch Fusiliers. Graves was recuperating from a lung illness in Oxford, and through Siegfried Sassoon, frequently visited Garsington at this time.

[2] George Nathaniel Curzon, Marquess Curzon of Kedleston (1859-1925), had in December 1916 become a member of the War Cabinet. Earlier in the war, he strongly advocated compulsory service, and was now pressing for the creation of an Air Ministry. The *Vie de martyres* (1917), by Georges Duhamel (1884-1966), poet and novelist, was a realistic account of the author's own experiences as an army surgeon.

[3] Graves had taken part in the offensive against La Bassée in September 1915. In chapter 16 of *Goodbye to All That* (1929), he quotes from a letter home at that time, saying he had seen 'already their beer being watered from the canal with a hose-pipe. The *estaminet*-keepers water it further.'

[4] Lady Ottoline would have appreciated KM's parody of the imagery of 'Rhapsody on a Windy Night' and 'Conversation Galante', poems in T.S. Eliot's *Prufrock and Other Observations* (1917), published that month by the Hogarth Press. Clive Bell, in *Old Friends* (1956), records (122) how KM read 'Prufrock' aloud at Garsington, although the date he gives must be amended to that of her visit at the beginning of June.

To Virginia Woolf,[1] [? 24 June 1917]

141A, CHURCH STREET, | CHELSEA, S.W.

Virginia dear

I shall love to come and dine on Wednesday night with you alone:[2] I cant manage Friday. Ever since I read your letter I have been writing to you and a bit 'haunted' by you: I long to see you again. The memory of that last evening is so curious: your voice & Vanessa's voice in the dark, as it were — white rings of plates floating in the air — a smell of strawberries & coffee — Murry telling Woolf that you worked it with a handle & it had a cylinder[3] & then M. and W. disappearing — and a feeling that outside the window floated a deep dark stream full of a silent rushing of little eels with pointed ears going to Norway & coming back . .

My God I love to think of you, Virginia, as my friend. Dont cry me an ardent creature or say, with your head a little on one side, smiling as though you knew some enchanting secret: "Well, Katherine, we shall see" . . . But pray consider how rare is it to find some one with the same passion for writing that you have, who desires to be scrupulously truthful with you — and to give you the freedom of the city without any reserves at all.

Curse it! Here is the laundry boy snatching at my flying feet. Ill tell you about Garnett[4] on Wednesday.

(Come in, little boy and sit down. I won't be two shakes of a lambs tail) and we'll talk about Asheham,[5] please & lots & lots of other things.

Yours ever
K M

MS Sussex. *Adam* 370-375, 19.

¹ Virginia Woolf (1882-1941), novelist and critic, whom KM first met towards the end of 1916.

² This was the dinner—brought forward to Tuesday the 26th—after which Virginia Woolf reported to Vanessa Bell, on 27 June 1917: 'I had an odd talk with K. Mansfield last night. She seems to have gone every sort of hog since she was 17, which is interesting; I also think she has a much better idea of writing than most.' (*LVW* II. 159.)

³ i.e. the hand press which the Woolfs had set up at their home, Hogarth House, Richmond, in March 1917.

⁴ Murry was trying to find work for David Garnett (1892-1981), the son of Edward Garnett and his wife, the translator Constance Garnett.

⁵ The farmhouse the Woolfs rented a few miles from Firle, Sussex.

To Ottoline Morrell, [3 July 1917]

[141A Church Street, Chelsea]
Tuesday.

My dearest Ottoline

I have just received a card from Philip telling me that it really is measles. How utterly cursed! What can I say . . . sympathy is no good at all — and rage against the Lord more futile still. The weather is heavenly again too. I hate to think of you missing it: it must be divine down at Garsington. Last night, sitting under my fig tree, half of it was gold in the sunset and half silver in the rising moon. But all the figs have fallen off before their time: the sound of them falling in the grass reminds me of all the autumns that I have ever really *lived* through and heard the fruit falling in the long grass — which is not a cheerful thought for July.

I had to go down to the City today and found Baby Week in the fullest of full blasts.¹ Really, I believe I was the only woman with her quiver empty between Charing X and Victoria Station. I walked along crossing myself and saying the Spanish Nuns Hail Mary terrified lest this fruitfulness should be contagious. And the horrible thing was that I didn't see one couple who weren't more or less revolting — flushed untidy women with their hats on one side carrying little miniature Queen Victorias — ugh! What an appallingly bad job human beings have made of themselves. I kept wondering if they were all like this all over the world, or if it was only in England that we bred such monsters — but I am afraid not. I suppose that all the babies in Samoa have rubber comforters and all the mothers aspire to owning perambulators far too big to go through their front doors.

I wonder if you have heard from Virginia. I had a mysterious little postcard from Leonard on Saturday saying that Virginia was ill — but since that nothing. I think that she is still VERY delicate —

and I shouldn't imagine she was ever well enough to leave her own home and surroundings.[2] I dined with her one evening last week and she was charming — I do like her tremendously — but I felt then for the first time the strange, trembling, glinting quality of her mind — and quite for the first time she seemed to me to be one of those Dostoievsky women whose 'innocence' has been hurt — Immediately I decided that I understood her completely . . . I wonder if you agree at all.

Murry came to see me late last night, very gay after a dinner at the House with your brother.[3] I had spent a very dull solitary evening finishing a story about a woman who goes to see a friend of hers who has entered a convent — and when Murry came in, twinkling with champagne and smelling of the fleshpots I felt like Mrs Jellaby who spent her life, you remember, staring at the ink spots on the wall and writing tomes about some mission that need never have existed.[4] What does one do when one is not writing? Does one read and lie on the sommier and smoke — Yes, that is all there is to do — well — why can't one accept that and quench for ever this last spark which remains? But one cant. I fan and fan it & warm myself at it and never give up —

Aldous came to see me last Wednesday. He told me more news in half an hour than I have heard for months. At present he seems to be a great social success and 'incredible' things happen to him *at least* every evening. He spoke of the Isola Bella[5] as though it were the rendezvous of Love and High Adventure — and then his description of Mary Hutch's party to celebrate the rebirth of Gilly after his own private revolution — Gilly with his face to the dawn and Gwynnie Wilson upon his arm![6] . . . Very powerful indeed. I felt my mind flutter over Aldous as if he were the London Mail. There was a paragraph about simply everybody —

Dearest, this dull letter must fade away. Do make Brett let me know how you are. I wish I were not so helpless. If you should want a new nurse and would like to try me — I am really rather an admirable one —

Goodnight, my lovely friend

Katherine.

MS Texas. Cited *Exhibition,* 33; cited Meyers, 141.

[1] National Baby Week, marked by public functions and royal patronage, was held 'to decrease infant mortality from preventible causes'.

[2] Virginia Woolf was at this time recovering from a recent breakdown.

[3] Henry Cavendish Bentinck (1863-1931), though Conservative MP for South Nottingham, was strongly opposed to the war.

[4] Cf. Dickens's *Bleak House* (1853).

[5] A restaurant at 15 Frith Street, Soho.

[6] Gilbert Cannan, having recently suffered a nervous breakdown, had left his wife Mary and taken up with Gwendoline Wilson, later Lady Melchett.

To Ottoline Morrell, [13 July 1917]

[141A Church Street, Chelsea]
Friday

. . . I am thankful to know that you are better and that we shall soon be able to see each other again. What a dreadful time you have had, I had no idea that the measles were so formidable and overwhelming. I envy you going to the sea — even for a few days. Oh, I have such a longing for the sea as I write, at this moment. To stand on the shore long enough to feel the land behind one withdrawn into silence and the loud tumbling of the waves rise and break over one's whole being . . . .

But the English summer sea is not what I mean. I mean that wild untamed water that beats about my own forlorn island. Why on earth do I call it 'forlorn'. My bank Manager assures me that it's a perfect little gold mine and whenever I go down to the Bank of New Zealand I turn over a heap of illustrated papers full of pictures of electric trains and American buildings and fashionable ladies and gentlemen who might have walked out of the Piccadilly Grill . . . But all that sham and vulgarity is hard to believe in: I don't believe in it all. There is another side that you would believe in too. Ah, my dear, I know the most heavenly places that cannot be spoiled — and that I shall go back to as surely as if they were 'Dixie'.[1] And I shall think of you, and wish to God I expect that I were sitting opposite you at the Maison Lyons! Life is a queer, a damn queer business!

It's a golden day. The blinds are down. I have some big yellow lilies in the studio. The garden door is open and the fig tree throws a wavy pattern on the floor and walls among big soft spots of sunlight. Four o'clock in the afternoon. I've been sitting at this table since morning, writing and smoking. And somewhere quite near someone is playing very old-fashioned dance tunes on a cheap piano, things like the Lancers, you know. Some minute part of me not only dances to them but goes faithfully through, Ladies in the Centre, Visiting, Set to Corners, and I can even feel the sensation of clasping young warm hands in white silk gloves, and shrinking from Maggie Owen's hand in Ladies Chain because she wore no gloves at all —[2]

Talking about dancing reminds me of last Saturday night, when I really 'saw' [Augustus John][3] for the first time. It was at a show at Margaret Morris's theatre. He was there with two very worn and chipped looking ladies — the saddest looking remnants of ladies — in fact they reminded me of those cups without saucers that you sometimes see outside a china shop — all-on-this-tray-one-penny. But [John] was really impressive looking. I seemed to see his mind, his haggard mind, like a strange forbidding country, full of lean sharp peaks and pools lit with a gloomy glow, and trees bent with the wind and vagrant muffled creatures tramping their vagrant way. Everything exhausted and finished — great black rings where the fires had been, and not a single fire even left to smoulder. And then he reminded me of that man in Crime and Punishment who finds a little girl in his bed in that awful hotel the night before he shoots himself, in that appalling hotel.[4] But I expect this is all rubbish, and he's really a happy man and fond of his bottle and a goo-goo eye. But I don't think so.

MS lacking. *LKM* I. 76-7.

[1] The American popular song (1859) by David Emmett.
[2] The Lancers was a popular ballroom dance, a kind of quadrille. Margaret Owen was a girl in the same year as KM at Queen's College.
[3] The painter and bohemian Augustus John (1878-1961), was at this time suffering from deep depression.
[4] At the end of Part VI, section 6, of Dostoevsky's *Crime and Punishment*, Svidrigailov dreams he meets a depraved child.

To Virginia Woolf, [? 25 July 1917]

[141A Church Street, Chelsea]
Wednesday —
Dear Virginia —
That will be delightful — Friday at 4.30. It makes me *very* happy that you liked my little story;[1] thank you so much for telling me.
Yours ever
Katherine.

MS Sussex. *Adam* 370-375, 23.

[1] KM's *Prelude* was to be the second publication of the Hogarth Press.

To J.M. Murry, [late July 1917]

[141A Church Street, Chelsea]
Private
My dear Jack,
I got up at that moment to re-read your article on Leon Bloy.[1] The memory of it suddenly *rose* in my mind, like a scent. I don't like it. I don't see its use at all, even artistically. It's a 'Signature' style of writing[2] and its *appeal* is in some obscure way — to me —

mind me — I suppose only to me — indecent. I feel that you are going to uncover yourself and quiver. Sometimes when you write you seem to abase yourself like Dostoievsky did. Its *perfectly* natural to you I know, but oh my God, dont do it. Its just the same when you say — talking to Fergusson and me — if I am not killed — if *they don't kill* me. I always laugh at you then because I am ashamed that you should speak so.

What is it? Is it your desire to torture yourself or to pity yourself or something far subtler? I only know that its tremendously important because its your way of damnation.

I feel (forgive fanciful me) that when certain winds blow across your soul they bring the smell from that dark pit & the uneasy sound from those hollow caverns — & you long to lean over the dark driving danger & just not fall in — But letting us all see meanwhile how low you lean —

Even your style of writing changes then — little short sentences — a hand lifted above the waves — the toss of a curly head above the swirling tumble — Its a terrible thing to be alone — yes it is — it is — but dont lower your mask until you have another mask prepared beneath — As terrible as you like — but a *mask*.

K.M.

Forgive me for not telling you frankly when you read it to me — what I felt. I was wrong.

MS ATL. *LJMM*, 93-4.

[1] 'The Loneliness of Léon Bloy', *TLS*, 19 July 1917.

[2] To each of the three issues of the *Signature* Murry contributed a portion of an essay called 'There Was a Little Man'. Written when he was most under the influence of Lawrence, the essay condemns the war for the way in which 'It wells up like an ooze above the threshold of my consciousness', and confesses how 'there remains always a little cloud of self-contempt hovering within my mind'. (*Signature*, no. 1 (4 Oct 1915), 25, 29-30.)

To Ottoline Morrell, [after 22 July 1917]

[141A Church Street, Chelsea]

I purposely refrained from speaking of your work — One cant mention it with an 'oh, by the way', and I felt shy. I left it in the schoolroom in Murry's charge (who swore an oath not to read without express permission.)[1]

There are lovely things in all three — flying glimpses, flowers tossed one knows not whence — a perfume from hidden bushes — shadows moving, gleaming, mysterious —

In all three I think the opening is the best — the 'attack' — musically speaking — of Desire is wonderfully free and passionate. In all three I think the endings are rather too much 'to form' — rather consciously rounded off and finished . . . I hope you don't think me an upstart to criticise like this. God knows I am only a baby scholar myself, in the beginner's class — But one feels that you haven't quite the courage of your intentions — that you don't perhaps quite fulfil the promise of that first passionate gesture.

And one wishes you would be a million times more intimate — a million times more revealing — more absolutely, unmistakeably YOU. No, I don't feel that you have kissed her yet, or wakened the sleeping palace, or set the music leaping and playing. But there you *are* outside the wild hedges and I pray you may break through.

Katherine.

MS Texas.

[1] KM and Murry had stayed at Garsington the weekend of 21-3 July.

To Ottoline Morrell, [30 July 1917]

141A Church Street | Chelsea S.W.3.
Monday afternoon.

Ottoline dearest

Ever since I came back to my studio I have been thinking over the idea of the cottage[1] & trying to make it appear more practical and less impossible. But it wont. No. I am afraid I shall have to give it up before I take it — When I was down there with you it all seemed so easy and the question of 'money' no question at all. I utterly forgot how hard up I am — utterly ignored the fact that I really havent an extra sixpence to spend on an egg timer. And as I really must be in London a great deal it would mean railway fares — No, I will not plague you with details. I will only entreat you to forgive my thoughtlessness and thank you for your lovely generous gesture. So it is no use my coming down to see about it: I must learn to be wiser and to *realise my circumstances* more. I never do. I am afraid Murry will be dreadfully disappointed but — — you will let him come to you sometimes? He is dining with me tonight.

I saw Virginia last night but she was not alone — so I thought it wiser not to mention the story at all — if she did not. Clive had been there before me — I rather fancied that he had told all there was to tell.

That dreadful Mrs Galloway[2] keeps floating into my minds eye — She is a muddy little object.

How beautiful Garsington is. When I think of it my inward eye is a succession of flashes! I shall never forget it, *never, never*. But I cannot get into my stride today — you feel that — don't you? No, I'm mysteriously uneasy & walking painfully over awfully unfamiliar country — Why is that? God knows.

But do not turn against me for being so changeable — that I couldn't bear. It feels like years since I have seen Murry — Did he persist in writing endlessly about Péguy[3] or could you sometimes lure him away?. I couldn't, you know: every time I went near him I felt like an interruption.

How strange life is! Goodbye. One taps upon the counter & pays the waiter — pulls down one's veil & — goes —

I am ever
Katherine

MS Newberry.

[1] Lady Ottoline had offered KM the use of a bailiff's cottage at Garsington.

[2] After conscription was introduced, the Manor House at Garsington became something of a haven for conscientious objectors who were taken on as farm hands. The Galloways were a couple who lived for some time in one of the farm cottages.

[3] Murry published two articles on the French writer the next year, 'Charles Péguy' in the *Quarterly Review,* January 1918, and 'Péguy and Romain Rolland' in the *TLS*, 21 Nov 1918.

To Dorothy Brett,[1] [1 August 1917]

[141A Church Street, Chelsea]
Wednesday.

Dearest Brett,

I must tell you how excited I am that Murry is so enthusiastic about your picture — and I cant help delighting in the thought of you listening to all Clive's bubble blowing with this quite trump card up your monastic sleeve. Do tell me how it goes on & what you decide about the 'background'. Murry was especially impressed with the middle figure in the bonnet: with your easy, beautiful handling of it. There it *was*.

Thinking about you Ive got such a picture in my mind to entreat you to paint — that I long to describe it. But Ill wait till we meet. Cut my throat, Brett if its not a good 'un.

But if this weather goes on, my girl, Im afraid you'll have to make a canvas boat of your picture and I will have to turn my writing table upside down and float out of the window. But perhaps God in His goodness will allow us to bob near each other for a moment. I have been informed by my great aunt Charlotte (of Bangalore, Worple Avenue) that all those who are saved have expected a recurrence of the flood ever since the Kaiser was recognised to be Anti

Christ. And are Fully Prepared for it. Cant you see them, "done up in impervious cases, like preserved meats", like the Micawber family starting off for America — —²

I spent a mournful half morning yesterday being thumped and banged & held up by the heels by my doctor, who gave me no comfort at all, but half hinted, in fact, that given another hearty english winter or two — the chances were that I'd bend and bow under my rheumatism until I became a sort of permanent croquet hoop. So if, in a year or two (I don't think the rain will stop before then) you *should* come through my gate & find me in the garden as a sort of decorative arch with a scarlet runner growing over me you will know that the *worst* has happened.

Goodbye for now, mia bella. Salute my friends, frown on my enemies & remember me to Herr Mark [Gertler].

Yours ever
Katherine

MS Newberry. *LKM* I. 74-5.

¹ The Hon. Dorothy Brett (1883-1937), elder daughter of 2nd Viscount Esher, whom KM met in 1915. They became close friends through their visits to Garsington, before sharing 3 Gower Street. She had studied at the Slade 1910-16.
² Cf. ch. LVII of Dickens's *David Copperfield* (1850). The Micawbers, in fact, set off for Australia.

To J.M. Murry, 10 August 1917

[141A Church Street, Chelsea]
10. VIII. 1917.

My dear Jack

I am re-reading your poems¹ & taking a note or two. Here they are:

Torment is damned good. Better than Id even thought. The way the passionate pace of it quickens in verses 4 5 and 6 is amazing & then the way it 'ebbs' into quiet. Musically speaking its a little meisterwerk. Anyway its real love poetry and an achievement.

The effect of *The Tryst* is alright. The clichés are there once or twice but they are *fresh* rather than *current* (I mean rare by that).

The Quest comes off. Its what you might call legitimately romantic. And its got a kind of dark boyish plume in its hat thats very captivating. I like it immensely.

I *cannot* see anything in 'Backward'. Ive read it as fairly as I can. Its simply streaky with not even the best streaky Masefield, and so I tells you. Think well before you publish this. Ill blush for you if you do. Dear Jack, you may have a red carpet hassock with yellow flowers on it which makes you weep for tender remembrance but you wont put it in your lovely room. It *isn't* you. Enough! Its an awful thought the 'the coming man' may open your book at this!

The Critic in Judgment[2] is so good even as it stands that its hard to keep ones head about it. Its like a lifting of the mist, a glimpse of the Blue Mountains and you — blast you — a young poet walking airy in their bright shadow.

The *Tig* poem[3] will blow away if I lay even a feather on it. The last line is too easy.

You are 'in your stride' in *The Return*. There's a kind of dark mysterious sobbing in your love poetry — which shakes the heart. I feel that your lady, leaning from her tower, her hair all blowing out — says "is that he — or a dark shadow — or a young tree bending in the night wind". And really you are all these things.

To Jules Laforgue is frightfully good & brilliantly clear. Bitterness, fatigue, and a queer ageless quality — and all controlled. Its your control of that poem — the shaft of light you bring to bear upon Laforgue which is so good. You might be the wan moon at the window of the morgue where he lies.

Villa Pauline is charming but the last line is flat.

So is the last line of *I Know The Sea* — and the sentiment of the second half is fatigué.

Sanary is delightful.

The City of the Hills. Here you are again, singing your own song. Its a very lovely little poem — very 'rich' somehow in weight like dark grapes are rich in weight . . . if you know what I mean.

Nunc Dimittis for some reason which I cant quite explain leaves me cold.

Now, my dear friend for your poems of Remembrance. Ill not take them separately. To say that they are the only poems that have come out of this war isn't enough. They are *wonderful — wonderful — wonderful*. There they are — 'youve done it' as we say. If you knew how strangely each dead boy lies — lies in your poems as in a very perfect tomb — And at last, when they are all buried and hidden, you pause a little, and pluck a few forlorn notes and suddenly break into your song

"O unreturning travellers, O friends. . . ."[4] as the night falls.

Well, you see. Im quite overcome and weeping as I write. Je t'embrasse, mon ami

K.M.

MS ATL.

[1] Murry was putting together his collection, *Poems 1917-18,* published in 1919 by the Heron Press. Of the poems referred to in the letter, only 'The Return', and 'To My Dead Friends' from his 'Poems of Remembrance', appeared in the volume.

[2] See p. 160, n. 6.

[3] Possibly the poem in the 1919 collection called 'Ribni Speaks', in which Murry berates himself for leaving KM at Bandol. For the doll Ribni, see p. 348, n.1.

[4] 'O never-returning travellers, O friends' is the opening line of 'To My Dead Friends'.

To Ottoline Morrell, [11 August 1917]

[141A Church Street, Chelsea]
Saturday Night:

There are three unfinished letters to you in my writing case — one is even five pages long. I could not re-read them but I know why they were not sent. They seemed to me (and they *were*) as I wrote them hopelessly superficial and fatiguing — fatiguing like a conversation by telephone can. I heard my own little mocking, mechanical voice, *loathed* it, and chose silence. Quite suddenly, just after you had been so near, so thrilling and so enchanting — for no reason that I can explain away — it was as if the light changed, and you vanished from me. I wandered about in the wood among the wild smelling bushes and sometimes I thought I saw the dark plume of your hat, or your lips or your hands but when I went towards you — you *were* not — The strangest part was that my memory of the days we had just spent together was as perfect as ever — as bright as untroubled. I still saw the blue spears of lavender — the trays of fading, scented leaves, you in your room, and your bed with the big white pillow — and you coming down in the garden swinging the gay lantern — But between these lovely memories and me there opened a deep dark chasm — it *trembled* open as if by an earthquake — and now it is shut again and no trace of it remains.[1]

There — now I have told you 'all'.

For my part, my friendship for you couldn't end. There it *is* — I feel for all time, whatever may happen. I cannot tell you how gloriously sure I am of it and how I trust it. Not all the 'little people' in the world could destroy so fine a bridge. No, until you decide that you do not care to cross any longer, there it stands.

Thank you for your wonderful letters. I long to see you again *now*. Do you remember this time last year? It feels years away.

Murry came to see me this evening. He showed me a handkerchief you had given him. I took it in my hands and the scent of it shook my heart — Yes, just as if I had been a young person profoundly in love with you. Do make Murry show you his 'Poems of Remembrance'. I cant write about them calmly.

Ever since I came back except for two *hellish* days when the Rhodesian Mountain came out of her factory & filled every inch of my horizon, I have been 'at home' and working. It is the only life I care about — to write to go out occasionally and 'lose myself' looking and hearing and then to come back and write again. At any rate thats the life Ive chosen — But as soon as this bloody war is over I shall flee the country.

Today has been so strange, very sunny, with a loud wind blowing & the sky a bright dazzle. One simply wanted to run about and be blown about & if I dare quote Meredith to cry like Diana: 'I am like a leaf'.[2]

I am dying for something to read, but there is nothing. Every time my longing eye searches my shelves it sees Horace for English Readers, or Petit Larousse. . *Where* are the books?
Goodnight;

I am *ever*
Katherine.

MS Texas. *LKM* I. 77-8.

[1] Lady Ottoline records what must be the explanation for the 'three unfinished letters' and the 'deep dark chasm' of which KM writes. Murry, who had stayed on at Garsington after KM returned from the weekend of 21 July 1917, claimed when he came back to London that Lady Ottoline ' "had fallen deeply and passionately in love with him". . . . It was so absurd.' Brett informed Lady Ottoline that KM 'was very hurt with me and indeed she said she was bitter and angry against me.' (Morrell, 192.)

[2] In ch. IV of George Meredith's *Diana of the Crossways* (1885), the heroine writes a letter in which she admits to 'constantly wandering, like a leaf off the tree.'

To Virginia Woolf, [mid-August 1917]

[141A Church Street, Chelsea]

Virginia:
I should love to come to Asheham on the 17th. Do have me. My story [*Prelude*] I have sent to the typist who lets me have it back on Thursday. I couldn't cope with the bloody copying: I've been so 'ill'. Rheumatiz plus ghastly depression PLUS fury. I simply long to see you. I want to talk too about your Mark on the Wall.[1] Now shall I write about it or talk about it? Tell me, may I come & see you on Sunday at tea time or after supper time or whenever it suits you? Oh when may I come. I thought you had finally dispatched me to cruel callous Coventry, without a wave of your lily white hand. Do let us meet in the nearest future darling Virginia & don't quite forget
Katherine.

MS Berg. *LKM* I. 75.

[1] The first publication from the Hogarth Press, in July 1917, was *Two Stories*, one being Leonard Woolf's 'Three Jews', the other Virginia's 'The Mark on the Wall'.

To Ottoline Morrell, [15 August 1917]

[141A Church Street, Chelsea]
Wednesday.

Dearest Ottoline,

I am engaged on Saturday and on Sunday — tied by both legs — and though I should love to — I feel that I musn't escape. Your glimpse of the garden — all flying green and gold made me wonder again *who* is going to write about that flower garden. It might be so wonderful — do you see *how* I mean? There would be people walking in the garden — several *pairs* of people — their conversation their slow pacing — their glances as they pass one another — the pauses as the flowers 'come in' as it were — as a bright dazzle, an exquisite haunting scent, a shape so formal and fine, so much a 'flower of the mind' that he who looks at it really is tempted for one bewildering moment to stoop & touch and make *sure*. The 'pairs' of people must be very different and there must be a slight touch of enchantment — some of them seeming so extraordinarily 'odd' and separate from the flowers, but others quite related and at ease. A kind of, musically speaking — conversation *set* to flowers. Do you like the idea? I see the Pig of the Party — Mrs. Galloway — rooting in her little dark mind. And I see Bertie, who hasn't the remotest idea of getting them into harmony. Perhaps thats not fair. But its full of possibilities. I must have a fling at it as soon as I have time.[1] I am sitting writing to you in the kitchen. I cannot *bear* at present, my studio with its great Thou-God-Seest-Me window. It is far more tolerable to sit up here with the saucepans & the nutmeg grater & the big swinging tree so close against the pane. Confound my poverty! How I long to buy an exquisite room, absolute privacy, a devoted black woman, and some ravishing perfume. And I've been groaning for half an hour at having to pay the window cleaner four and sixpence! And all the ugly makeshift furniture in the studio seems to be scrawled over with 1/11¾.

At that moment, appropriately enough the window cleaner caught at my feet which weren't by any means flying and asked if it would be convenient to have 'em done again now. And since then a whole day has gone by — and I have read a long letter from Lawrence — He has begun to write to me again and quite in the old way — all about the leaves of the melon plant 'speckled like a newt', and all about 'the social egg which must collapse into nothingness, into *non being*'. I am so fond of him for many things — I cannot shut my heart against him and I never shall. I had also a most urgent letter from Virginia reminding me that Id sworn to go to Asheham to-morrow. My God, it is true. I shall *have* to go some time and another

from Sydney Waterlow asking me to Marlborough & another from
Anne Rice and 'Eve' asking me to Cromer Sands.[2] How desperate it
is! I shall have to run fresh ribbons in the legs of my petits pantalons
& leap in and out of holiday trains — when all I *want* to do is to sit
in a dark, warm, dusky room and write — Virginias letter more or
less says that she & Lytton sit all day surrounded by *hawks* and
mushrooms. Also S.F.[3] is there too: I wish she were a little less
anthracite.

       To Hell with the Blooms Berries.

       Dont you think one really must run away as soon as possible and
as far as possible —
Goodnight, dearest dearest

Yours
Katherine.

Do write if you feel inclined — — Your adorable letters . . .

MS Texas. *LKM* I. 78-9.

[1] KM did not write the story, although her poem 'Night-Scented Stock' was written at
this time about the garden at Garsington. (See *Poems*, 1923, 59-60.)
[2] KM's cousin, Sydney Waterlow (1878-1944), educated at Eton and Trinity College,
Cambridge, was a scholar and diplomat; his mother was Charlotte Beauchamp, a daughter
of Henry Herron Beauchamp. 'Eve' was perhaps KM's name for Anne Estelle Rice's husband, O. Raymond Drey.
[3] Alix Sargant-Florence, a Cambridge graduate whom the Woolfs took on as an appren-
tice printer at the Hogarth Press; she later married Lytton Strachey's brother James.

To R.C. Trevelyan,[1] *19 August 1917*

Asheham House, Rodmell | Lewes (Sussex)[2]
Sunday Aug. 19 1917

We the undersigned, wish to say that we have read the Pterodamozels
with great pleasure, & wish to thank the author.

Virginia Woolf[3]
Katherine Mansfield
Lytton Strachey
Edward Garnett

MS (postcard) Sussex. *LVW* II. 175.

[1] Robert Calverley Trevelyan (1872-1951), poet, essayist, and translator, published
Pterodamozels, An Operatic Fable, a play in two acts, in 1917.
[2] KM was the Woolfs' guest at Asheham from 18 to 22 Aug 1917.
[3] The message on this postcard is in Virginia Woolf's hand, with KM's and the other
signatures appended.

To Virginia Woolf, [c. 23 August 1917]

[141A Church Street, Chelsea]

Dear Virginia

I had a last glimpse of you just before it all disappeared & I waved: I hope you saw.

Thank you for letting me see wonderful Asheham. It *is* very wonderful & I feel that it will flash upon one corner of my inward eye for ever.

It was good to have time to talk to you. We have got the same job, Virginia & it is really very curious & thrilling that we should both, quite apart from each other, be after so very nearly the same thing. We are you know; there's no denying it.

But dont let THEM ever persuade you that I spend any of my precious time swapping hats or committing adultery — I'm far too arrogant & proud.[1] However, let them think what they like. Theres a most wonderful greengage light on the tree outside and little white clouds bobbing over the sky like rabbits. And I wish you could see some superb gladioli standing up in my studio very proud & defiant, like indian braves.

Yes, your Flower Bed is *very* good.[2] Theres a still, quivering, changing light over it all and a sense of those couples dissolving in the bright air which fascinates me —

Old Mother Gooseberry, my char from Ludgate Hill has hung up her beetle bonnet "please m'm if you would let me have the place to myself." So I am chased off, to sit among those marble pillars of brawn at the Library & read *not* Henry James.

Murry hasn't appeared yet, but I have asked my painter friend about the woodcuts & he wants to do them.[3] But he says he would like to read the story before going to Scotland next week. Can you let me have those pages? I haven't another 'fair copy' & then Ill send you the compleat artikel. Have you got your coffee mill down there? Would you like me to send you some of the coffee we once talked about. You remember? I have to go into Soho & get some for myself & Id like to make you a small present at the same time. Let me know.

Yours ever
Katherine.

MS Berg. *LKM* I. 80.

[1] This could refer either to the occasion a few weeks earlier, when Maynard Keynes and Clive Bell had gossiped with Virginia Woolf about KM (*DVW* I. 67, n. 42), or the unflattering remarks Virginia was said to have passed on from Bell and Desmond MacCarthy (*LVW* II. 179, n.2).

[2] Virginia Woolf had shown KM her story 'Kew Gardens', published by the Hogarth Press in May 1919. The story, as Alpers points out (1980, 249-52), has obvious similarities to a passage in KM's letter to Lady Ottoline of 15 Aug 1917, (see p. 325) and presumably

also to a letter of KM's to Virginia which has not survived, but to which Virginia refers in herself writing to Lady Ottoline on 15 August: 'Katherine Mansfield describes your garden, the rose leaves drying in the sun, the pool, the long conversations between people wandering up and down in the moonlight. It calls out her romantic side; which I think rather a relief after the actresses, A.B.C's, [teashops] and paint pots.' (*LVW* II. 174.)

³ When *Prelude* came from the Hogarth Press in July 1918, a few of the copies carried woodcuts by J.D. Fergusson on the blue paper wrapper. The Woolfs did not like the designs, which were dropped from most of the edition.

To Lytton Strachey, [? late August 1917]

[141A Church Street, Chelsea]

Dear Lytton

I wish you would come and see me when you are in London again.

my address is

141A Church Street
Chelsea

Please do.
I am bitten to death.

Herzlichen Gruss
Katherine.

MS Strachey.

To Ottoline Morrell, [23 September 1917]

[141A Church Street, Chelsea]
Sunday Night.

I feel as though I have returned from the seaside with one hot cheek and a feeling of sand between my toes, as I sit down to write to you, my dearest Ottoline. Your wonderful letter which seemed with its spray of verbena to come flying through the gold and green September air dropped in my lap and I read it and sniffed and sniffed the sweet spray and put it at the bottom of a blue jar.

Murry has had a holiday this last week and we've been so immensely occupied that I have had no time "to myself" at all. I havent been able to shut a gate or a window or a door — and now at the end of these exquisite days I feel that it is High Time to lie down & be covered with these fresh fallen yellow leaves. But — to discover that it still is possible to laugh so much, to linger, to gaze in at shop windows and burn so ardently for that lovely mirror, to walk under these bright trembling trees and high, tumbling clouds, to watch children, and to lean over bridges.

Ottoline: "But dear Katherine. This is like Walt Whitman *too dreadfully* in the home!"

Yes, I feel it is. But what am I to do, dearest? I am hung about with memories like these and cannot move for them — Next week I must be abominably sober but *this* week is still here, and no, I cannot be calm —

(A dreadful, cold thought: can this be all hypophosphites?)[1] Ah well! I must think that over carefully, "profoundly question it" (as B[ertrand] R[ussell] might say) and if I feel it is true do not be surprised upon opening the Daily Mirror to find a picture of me with my hair parted down the middle & a black velvet band round my neck: Portrait of Katherine Mansfield, 141a Church Street . . . You may make what use you like of this letter . . .

But I had rather think that it was something quite, quite different —

I am so glad to think that Mrs. Galloway is to be uprooted and flung over the wall — I hated to think of her; she was a poisonous little weed — Clive, that plump marrow, hiding under the leaves, and every leaf an ear, cant be taken seriously — Do you think? In fact none of *those people* ought to be "considered"; it is only consideration which makes them swell so huge and loom so large. They cannot spoil September — Ah, Ottoline, will there really be winter again after all this rich beauty? Cold and rain again, dark little days, dingy little days gripping one with frigid fingers like those hateful little dressmakers of my childhood. Must one really stand passive to them and be draped and pleated and folded into a kind of awful mackintosh parcel again? . .

London has a lap so full of pears and plums that every mean child hath a bellyful —

But B. and H.[2] says in the Evening News: Now is the time to think of those cosy bloomers . . .

What Can One Do?

Dearest, forgive a fool of a girl tonight. I long to talk to you — I should not be half so silly if you were here —

Are you coming to London — soon?

I am always your
Katherine —

MS Stanford. *LKM* I. 80-2.

[1] Components sometimes used in medicinal syrups.
[2] Probably Bourne & Hollingsworth, the store in Oxford Street.

To Dorothy Brett, [11 October 1917]

[141A Church Street, Chelsea]
Thursday

My dear Brett,

It is a cold sharp day — I can see the sun flying in the sky like a faint far-away flag — My Japanese doll has gone into boots for the winter and the studio smells of quinces. I have to write all day with my feet in the fringe of the fire — and Oh Alas! it is sad to think that I shall be warm in front and cold behind from now until next June. It seems to me so extraordinarily right that you should be painting Still Lives just now. What can one do, faced with this wonderful tumble of round bright fruits, but gather them and play with them — and *become them*, as it were. When I pass the apple stalls I cannot help stopping and staring until I feel that I, myself, am changing into an apple, too — and that at any moment I may produce an apple, miraculously, out of my own being like the conjuror produces the egg. When you paint apples do you feel that your breasts and your knees become apples, too? Or do you think this the greatest nonsense. I don't. I am *sure* it is not. When I write about ducks I swear that I am a white duck with a round eye, floating in a pond fringed with yellow blobs and taking an occasional dart at the other duck with the round eye, which floats upside down beneath me.[1] In fact this whole process of becoming the duck (what Lawrence would, perhaps, call this "consummation with the duck or the apple") is so thrilling that I can hardly breathe, only to think about it. For although that is as far as most people can get, it is really only the 'prelude'. There follows the moment when you are *more* duck, *more* apple or *more* Natasha than any of these objects could ever possibly be, and so you *create* them anew. Brett (switching off the instrument)[2]: "Katherine I *beg* of you to stop. You must tell us all about it at the Brotherhood Church[3] one Sunday evening." K: Forgive me. But that is why I believe in technique, too (you asked me if I did.) I do, just because I don't see how art is going to make that divine *spring* into the bounding outlines of things if it hasn't passed through the process of trying to *become* these things before recreating them.

I have left your letter unanswered for more days than I could have wished. But don't think it was just because I am so careless & faithless. No, really not. I enjoyed keeping silent with the letter just as one enjoys walking about in silence with another until a moment comes when one turns and puts out a hand and speaks.

I threw my darling to the wolves and they ate it and served me up so much praise in such a golden bowl that I couldn't help feeling gratified.[4] I did not think they would like it at all and I am still astounded that they do. What form is it? you ask. Ah, Brett, its so difficult to say. As far as I know its more or less my own invention. And how have I shaped it? This is about as much as I can say about it. You know, if the truth were known I have a perfect passion for the island where I was born. Oh, I out-Chili Chili [Guevara] any day! Well, in the early morning there I always remember feeling that this little island has dipped back into the dark blue sea during the night only to rise again at beam of day, all hung with bright spangles and glittering drops — (When you ran over the dewy grass you positively felt that your feet tasted salt.) I tried to catch that moment — with something of its sparkle and its flavour. And just as on those mornings white milky mists rise and uncover some beauty, then smother it again and then again disclose it. I tried to lift that mist from my people and let them be seen and then to hide them again. . . Its so difficult to describe all this and it sounds perhaps overambitious and vain. But I don't feel anything but intensely a longing to serve my subject as well as I can — But the unspeakable thrill of this art business. What is there to compare! And what more can one desire. Its not a case of keeping the home fire burning for me. Its a case of keeping the home fire down to a respectable blaze and little enough. If you don't come and see me soon there'll be nothing but a little heap of ash and two crossed pens upon it.

Are you coming to London soon — Let me know. Let us meet. Shall I see you float across my window upon a chariot of bright umbrellas?[5]

Venus Laughing From the Skies. Isn't it a beautiful title, when all is said and done — Goodbye goodbye goodbye. It is all *too* wonderful.

Katherine.

MS Newberry. *LKM* I. 82–4.

[1] Cf. section IX of *Prelude*, where KM writes of ducks in a very similar vein.

[2] Brett was deaf, and frequently used an ear trumpet.

[3] Two months earlier, on 28 July 1917, Bertrand Russell had been confronted by an angry crowd at the Brotherhood Church in Southgate, south London, when he spoke in favour of the Russian Revolution.

[4] The Woolfs, with whom KM had dined the evening before, had just taken proofs of the opening pages of *Prelude*.

[5] Brett must have been working on "Conversation Piece at Garsington", a painting of several of her friends under parasols. It is reproduced in *Carrington, Paintings, Drawings, and Decorations*, ed. Noel Carrington, 1980, 33.

To Ottoline Morrell, *[22 or 29 October 1917]*

[141A Church Street, Chelsea]
Monday

I waited until the policeman said: 'Five minutes to three', and then

I fainted by the way. I could not have borne Shirely Kellog's grin or George Robey's leer a moment longer.[1] How can I have missed you? For I was there at twenty five minutes past two, with my outward eye upon the ticket office and my inward one upon the wonderful clouds sailing over the Charing X road upon 'a solemn breath'. *They* bore me away at last. Yes, I must confess what you already know. I am no longer a fit companion for any sort of a fling . . . Even the Bangos were only *really* lovely once and last time I felt that I was playing Cook to your Duchess in Alice in Wonderland.[2] How plainly I realised as we sat in that tumble of music the dull dog you thought me! But the Bangos were more dividing than seas and I could not even *hail* across them. . .

No, I saw myself whirling away from you like a twig upon the Swannee River,[3] and I saw you standing on the bank with the cotton fields behind you saying: 'It is a pity that K. did not learn to dance when she was a child!' May I try to explain?

The truth is that every time I return from one of my voyages I feel less 'sociable' and less able to take an interest in Guten Morgan[4] and Company. No, no, I don't altogether want solitude, but I do long, when I am in 'port', as it were, to seek out my few friends and to take my ease with them and they with me — a kind of mutual refreshment and a renewing of a precious compact and an exchange of what treasure we have discovered.

Does that sound to you a pompous arrogant programme? I don't mean it so.

God knows I have sharpened as keen a tooth upon the old Gossip Bone as any, in my time; but I cannot make even the feeblest snap at it again. Nor am I in the least tempted to taste of the pleasures of the Town. No, I still love to watch people, to observe and remark and try to understand, but not 'in the spirit of a jaunt'. . .

You picture me writing this, of course, in a hair net and dress improver, with my elbow leaning upon a Life of George Eliot. But in very truth, life seems to me so thrilling, so intensely wonderful that I feel quite hopelessly ardent before it.

But you see I cannot be content with anything less. I'd rather be entertained by a fallen leaf than by George Robey and I cannot feel amused by Teddie Gerard when my mind is so full of Natasha's singing[5] . . .

I am confessed —

Goodnight.

K.

MS Texas.

[1] Shirley Kellogg and George Robey were playing in *Zig-Zag*, a revue with music by Dave Stamper, at the Hippodrome in Charing Cross Road.

² Both KM and Lady Ottoline were admirers of minstrel bands, and had apparently been to hear one on an earlier occasion. Cf. KM's letter to Lady Ottoline of 17 May 1916 (p. 267) in which she used the same comparison from Lewis Carroll. A distorted account of the present letter got back to Virginia Woolf, who noted on 12 Nov 1917, '. . . listened to some Garsington gossip. K.M. has broken with Ott. in a letter which says "You shan't play the Countess to my cook any more" or words to that effect.' (*DVW I. 75.*)

³ Cf. Stephen Foster's song 'Old Folks at Home' (1851).

⁴ Evan Morgan (1893–1949), later 2nd Viscount Tredegar, a minor poet, wealthy, was a frequent visitor to Garsington. He was at this time private secretary to the Parliamentary Secretary of the Ministry of Labour.

⁵ The comedian Teddie Gerard was then playing in *Bubbly!*, a musical by J. Hastings Turner and Philip Brahan, at the Comedy Theatre. Natasha Rostov sings on several occasions in Tolstoy's *War and Peace*. It tells something of Garsington relationships that Lady Ottoline must have shown this letter to Mark Gertler, for he wrote to her on 10 Nov 1917, after she had paid a visit to Siegfried Sassoon at Craiglockhart War Hospital, Slateford, Midlothian: 'How did you get on in Scotland with S.S. I wonder. "Not a word" "Not a word" Ah! Hah! Hem! Hem! as George Robey would say. But I forget, we must not talk of George Robey "whilst Natasha still sings!"' (Texas.)

ꝏ

The next month, November 1917, saw both KM and Murry struck by ill-health. When Murry was given leave from the War Office, he went to rest at Garsington, and soon recovered. KM visited him for a weekend, and her journey in a dog cart from the station brought on the chill that flared into a serious lung condition, and the medical order that she spend the rest of the winter in the South of France. From now on, there was to be no period of even a few months when KM's health could be called good. She began the protracted convalescence that was in fact a gradual decline for the next five years.

ꝏ

To Daniel Rider,¹ [16 November 1917]

141a Church St | Chelsea S.W.3.

Dear Dan,

Don't think I have forgotten or grown cold. But the fact is that the lad Murry is down with

Flu +

Fever +

That giddy feeling

and I am nursing him and running about with a covered basket trying to buy half a chicken for him *and* to get on to the bus with it after. Etc. Etc.

I cant leave him just for the present, but as soon as he is on his own legs again I want to 'get busy'. I did so enjoy our talk the other evening. Please remember me to Mrs Rider. Kindest regards from Murry & me

Yours ever
Katherine Mansfield.

MS Stanford.

[1] Daniel James Rider (b. 1869), whose bookshop at 36 St. Martin's Court, off St. Martin's Lane, had been a centre for writers when KM and Murry first lived together. He published several books on the legal relations between landlords and tenants, as well as *The Wit and Wisdom of Lloyd George* (1917).

To Dorothy Brett, [19 November 1917]

[141A Church Street, Chelsea]

Dearest Brett

I left an envelope on my doorstep today for fear lest you should call & find me gone. I should *love* to see you while you are in town and so let us try to manage it somehow. But the facts are these. Murry is in the throes of that long expected breakdown. He is no longer at the office, he has to go away for some time to some place where the SUN shines,[1] and at present I am as you may imagine, rather tied. He has been appallingly, terrifyingly weak and ill — and is much wasted away — I don't think he will be back in London at work all this winter, but he talks of being alright again in 6 weeks. My dear girl — I shall be at his place for T tomorrow — at 47 Redcliffe Road. Will you come there? Or will you dine with me tomorrow in town? Anywhere. The Sceptre,[2] par exemple. But he would just *love* to see you if you can manage tomorrow. Bus *no 14* passes the end of his road. (Tomorrow of course means Tuesday.)

I am sorry the Wolves are at Garsington. There will be a rare bone dragged into the light before they are gone —

I agree with all you say about Ottoline — yes with every word. She *is* all that — she *is* like music. But if *my* letter[3] hurt her she must know how *she* hurt *me* — I do hope that we shall see you tomorrow at T time. We speak of you so often.

Brett darling. | I am yours as ever
Katherine.

MS Newberry.

[1] Murry was given two months' sick leave from the War Office when his doctor said he was threatened with tuberculosis.

[2] The location of this restaurant, presumably a Bloomsbury haunt, is untraced.

[3] The 'Cook to your Duchess' gibe in KM's letter of ? 22 or 29 Oct 1917 to Lady Ottoline (see p. 332) would have been particularly wounding to her friend.

To Ottoline Morrell, [20 November 1917]

[141A Church Street, Chelsea]

Ottoline, my dear one —

Murry is VERY ill. The doctor says he must go away for at least five weeks and perhaps for longer. One of his lungs is slightly affected, but the principal thing is fever, COMPLETE exhaustion — a collapse at last after this appalling depression and overwork. The doctor says his mental condition (his depression) has been caused absolutely by his weakness which is very great. He has been really WASTING AWAY. I simply turn to you —

Would you have him at the cottage for a little while? And let him get better there? I feel that if he is there and you are near all will be well but if he has to go away to a strange place I dare not think what might happen.

He longs to come. It is his idea that if he could just have the room he could arrange with Mrs. Trench (or Miss Crozier) to look after him and give him his food.[1] Brett is also writing to explain, and what he wants is quiet without solitude — you understand? —

Do you feel that you could have him? That he has not been too draped in gloom? Now that I realise that he has had fever, pain and infernal weakness for so long I understand why the poor creature has been so utterly gloomy. He is as pale as a moth and his great gaunt eyes have reproached me — & terrified me all these days.

I shall send you a telegram tomorrow — & ask you — See how I *believe* believe — and yet I have no right to — perhaps —[2]

Katherine.

MS Stanford.

[1] KM was proposing that Murry stay in the bailiff's cottage at Garsington, which Lady Ottoline had offered her the previous July (see p. 320, n.1), and that women from the village might cook for him there so that he would not be an imposition at the manor house (where in fact he did stay).

[2] Lady Ottoline wired back the next day, 21 Nov 1917, 'OF COURSE DELIGHTED HAVE YOU BOTH DEAREST KATHERINE COME SOON WHY NOT TODAY OTTOLINE' (ATL). Later she recalled that Murry, after his mischief-making of a few months before, 'became like a ghost of a friend. He came several times on fairly long visits, generally when he was ill or run down. Katherine would write and ask us to take him and feed him up — but on these visits he hardly dared speak to me!' (Morrell, 192).

To Dorothy Brett, [21 November 1917]

141A [Church Street, Chelsea]

Dearest Brett,

I spent AT LEAST ½ an hour in the Chelsea Post Office this evening trying to get through to you on the 'phone. First they said you were engaged & then that "there was no reply from the number". I told them that you *were* there, did my utmost, but it was simply hopeless. They finally refused to answer my ringing at all — and I came out of the box positively gasping with rage.

Here is, dearest girl, the full report from Head Quarters.

I wrote Ottoline last night & wired her at dawn. This is her perfect answer. It really is a masterpiece of an answer — don't you think? I wired then again.

Murry wrote fully, too, explaining his little self. But here is the Great Brick. He cannot travel till Saturday. I have urged and implored him to go tomorrow, but he says simply that he cant, and please to "tell Brett what a brute I feel and to ask her to forgive me." He says he must arrange his affairs here — that I cant do it — and Saturday is the first moment he can get away. So don't wait for him. I am so infinitely sorry that it has kept you in town another day, but what can I do?

On Saturday I whisk him to Paddington & put him into that morning train. Brett, he really is ill. Do look after him. I felt quite terrified about him today — he is so pale and frail-looking. And explain just what we have decided to O. won't you? But I know you will. What a winged messenger you were yesterday — & how you *comforted* me. Bless you for it.

Always as ever your
Katherine.

MS Newberry.

To Anne Estelle Drey, 23 [November] 1917

141A Church Street | Chelsea | S W 3.
23 X[1] 17

Chère et charmante femme,

C'est que je regrette infiniment de vous dire que mon projet — de rester a Londres pendant l'absence de mon ami est, d'une haute necessité — tres modifié. Il m'a demandé, et vraiment je n'ai pas le coeur de lui refuser, d'aller passer un ou deux "week-ends", avec lui. Puis, pensant à son état de santé je me suis persuadée que, moi-même, je ne serais pas tranquille de le laisser pour si longtemps seul, et privé de cet coup d'oeil mère.

Alors, en ce cas, et bien tristement, je ne vois plus la possibilité charmante de garder chez moi votre delicieuse Madame Blinks[1] — Pendant mes voyages de samedi a lundi je ne peux pas la laisser toute seule même avec ma gosse japonaise, et bien sur c'est insupportable pour une chatte serieuse de passer les heures trop longues et trop frequentes dans un panier sous les faux coussins d'une compartiment de chemin de fer!

Hélas la petite pensionnaire n'est pas pour moi — et j'ai tant esperée!

Avez vous songé à Madame Paker[2] pour mère de lait? Je sais qu'elle adore les chats; elle m'a souvent parlée de la votre.

Mille remerciements, encore, ma chère amie pour mon cadeau de guerre! Je trouve cet beurre bien bon et le blancheur, apres ce jaune sinistre du margarine est tres appetisant! Et les oignons! Ah, ils demandent tout un livre! Apres un repas virginal d'oignons au lait bouillant, j'ai passé toute une nuit dans les rêves les visions splendides des voyages dans le metro —

> Boulevard St.Michel
> La Cité
> Chatelet —

Ces mots touchants, mêlés aux oignons me fait presque pleurer.

Ne voulez vous pas venir prendre une tasse de thé chez moi avant la repetition demain? Je serais enchantée de vous voir — et de feliciter Drey sur son convalescence —

Ah ma chère amie, la tête me tourne, tellement je suis fatiguée. Je vous écris dans le salon de Murry, et j'ai un seul desir — c'est de me coucher chez moi avec ma boule de l'eau chaude pour — au moins — la reste de l'hiver.

> A bientôt | Tres tendrement
> Katherine.[3]

MS ATL. *Adam* 300, 88-9.

[1] Anne Drey's cat.

[2] Mrs Bates, who was KM's charlady at Clovelly Mansions in 1911, and again in Church Street, worked also for Anne Drey; she was the original of KM's story 'Life of Ma Parker', written in 1921.

[3] (Translation)
Dear charming lady,
   I infinitely regret to tell you that my plan — to stay in London during my friend's absence has, through absolute necessity — been greatly changed. He has asked me, and truly I haven't the heart to refuse him, to go and spend one or two weekends with him. Then, thinking about his state of health I'm persuaded that I too would not be happy to leave him on his own for so long, without a motherly eye.
   So, as a result, and very sadly, I can no longer entertain the delightful possibility of having your charming Madame Blinks to stay. I cannot leave her all alone during my trips away from Saturday to Monday even with my Japanese urchin, and it is quite intolerable

for a dignified cat to spend too many hours too often in a basket under the cushions of a railway carriage!

Alas, the little boarder is not for me, and I had hoped for [her] so much.

Have you thought of Mrs Parker as a foster mother? I know she loves cats; she has often spoken to me about yours.

Many many thanks, once again, my dear friend for my spoils of war. I find this butter very good and its pale colour, after the sinister yellow of margarine, is very appetizing. And the onions! They deserve a whole book! After a virginal meal of onions boiled in milk, I spent a whole night dreaming splendid visions of trips on the metro —

     Boulevard St.Michel

     La Cité

     Chatelet —

These moving words, mixed with onions, almost make me cry.

Would you like to come and have a cup of tea with me before the rehearsal tomorrow? I would be delighted to see you — and to congratulate Drey on his recovery —

Ah dear friend, I am so tired my head is spinning round. I am writing to you in Murry's sitting room, and I have only one desire — to go to bed in my own home with a hot water bottle for — at least — what is left of the winter.

       See you soon | Yours affectionately

           Katherine.

To J.M. Murry, [25 November 1917]

[141A Church Street, Chelsea]

Dearest

It was not until you had gone yesterday that I realised what a great wind was blowing. I hope you kept tight hold of the strap of the railway carriage and were not wafted in and out of window on your way — — What strange first moments those are when the train has gone & the one who remains walks backward — as it were, into *the same city?* . . . They must be remembered. I must 'register' them.

Your telegram — for which I waited about 365 hours, heart beats and sighs, didn't, after one blissful second, perfectly satisfy me after all. Was it quite understood between us that you were not on any account to write first chop just to 'comfort' me? No, now I have begun waiting for your letter. So do not forget to post it, my precious, beloved boy. I am thankful that you are away from those cursed rooms. If you knew how I hate them, how I feel the very soles of my feet burning up the coconut matting on the stairs. As to that bedroom with that great gaunt bed so infernally high out of water — the dog howling outside the window & the linen hanging below in the yard — it always terrified me.

(By the way — isn't *Furnished Rooms* a good title for a story which plays in the Redcliffe Road — I cant resist it. Come & look over my shoulder — — The meeting on the dark stairs — you know, someone is coming down & someone is coming up — IS someone there? The 'fright' — the pause — the unknown in each other glaring through the dark & then passing (which is almost too terrifying to be borne). Then the whole Street — And for back cloth the whole line of the street — and the dressmakers calling to the cat, the chinamen, the dark gentlemen, the babies playing, the coal cart, the line of the sky above the houses, the little stone figure in one of the gardens who carries a stone tray on his head, which, in summer is filled with flowers & in winter is heaped with snow, the lamenting piano, and all those faces hiding behind the windows — & the *one* who is always on the watch. I see the heroine, very small, like a child with high heeled boots & a tiny muff of *false* astrakhan — & then the restless despairing hero for whom "all is over". She cannot understand what is the matter with him. Does she ever know? And what happens? . . .

It is the extreme coldness of my room, love, and the brown paper wagging over the sooty fire place which gives me such a 'veine'. Nothing will go up the chimney while this tempest lasts & I begin to feel the blighted Mongol stir and clamour in me.

It *was* a good thing that you did not step next door with me last night. Heavens above — a party! M. Bourlet, Mrs. Bustle, Mrs. Maufe,[1] Major Jardine, Miss Francis — etc — etc — etc. And "thank you so much", and "should we play German music during the war" & "do you ever get anonymous letters" and "will it, *can* it last another year?" M. Bourlets voice was true 'bourlet'. Instead of stopping a hole to keep the wind away it let the wind in. I was very unhappy, and felt a strange, unreasonable desire to pretend to be a german and cry 'wunderbar' after the french songs. There was a boiled fowl for dinner & such great tumblers of cold water that I more than once suspected a gold fish of flicking through mine. But 'Heron'[2] pulled me through.

12 oclock — I must go & make myself something hot. L.M. is still in bed — dreaming of Webb[3], I expect, & saying that she never never could be kissed on the mouth but did not mind the cheek —

Do not forget to take care of yourself — to go slow — to drift — to eat — to sleep — and to keep warm. Do not forget how I love you — and write me — more than one line.

I am going to turn into a female Balzac — this week — house hunt by day[4] and write by night.

Goodbye for now, my soul

Tig.

MS ATL. *LKM* I. 84-5, *LJMM*, 94-6.

[1] Gladys Prudence (later Lady) Maufe, KM's neighbour and friend at 139 Church Street. Her husband Edward Maufe (1882–1974) was later the architect of Guildford Cathedral.

[2] Usually the 'dream house', but sometimes the 'dream life', that KM and Murry hoped for after the war. The name of course came from her brother Leslie's second name, which was also given to the small private press Murry and his brother Richard began the next year. On 6 Mar 1918 Murry wrote to KM: 'What a moment it was in your studio last September when we sat together and discovered the Heron'. The same letter said, 'my life is absolutely built on it, because it is to me the solid symbol of our love, the fortress, the hiding place.' (ATL.)

[3] A fellow employee of Ida Baker's at the munitions factory. Ida frequently slept on the gallery in KM's studio.

[4] KM and Murry had decided on living together again, which meant finding a new flat.

To Ottoline Morrell, [7 December 1917]

[141A Church Street, Chelsea]

Dearest Ottoline,

My beastly cough and general feeling as though I had been shot in the wing will I am afraid, tie me to my fireside this weekend. I don't dare to make the journey again while I feel like this[1] and am trying to stay in one temperature until my water wings will bear me swimming again. I am so sorry. But I do hope that when you are in town you will come here — It is just round the corner from Ethel Sands[2] and I should love to see you and have a talk over *my* fire.

I am in a furious working mood. This always happens to me when the flesh is weak — but it is such superb fun to sit here and write and write and think stupid things like: I burn to call her Lillah, but I cant because of that MacCarthy woman.[3] What shall I do? Kill the MacCarthy woman. . .

I am sending you a few of the Morris notices in case you care to go. Perhaps you would put one in Clive's way or Fredigondes. And I wish Brett would stick a pin in little Tommy Earp and make *him* go. I wonder what you think of the drawing.[4]

Do write to me dearest Ottoline and let me know if I may expect to see you —

I hope little Murry is being good, & is not prolonging the war.

It has been such a divine day. . .

Katherine.

MS Stanford.

[1] KM had caught a bad chill while visiting Garsington the previous weekend — a visit of which Lady Ottoline recorded: 'Katherine came for a week-end while Murry was here. I felt very doubtful about her and she left me with rather a feeling of distrust. Her curious smooth unruffled face, like a Japanese mask. I am afraid she really dislikes me underneath and envies the comfort and comparative luxury of our home, and laughs at us all and thinks we are negligible. . . .She is too dreadfully lacking in human kindness ever to be very sympathetic to me. . . . She enjoys mocking and I recoil from it.' (Morrell, 236–7.)

² The wealthy American painter Ethel Sands (1873-1962), who became a British citizen and was one of the founders of the London Group, lived at 15 The Vale, Chelsea.

³ The actress Lillah McCarthy (1875-1960), married to the director and critic Harley Granville-Barker from 1906 to 1917, and in 1920 to Frederick (later Sir Frederick) Keeble, Professor of Botany at Oxford.

⁴ The notices were for Margaret Morris's Club in Chelsea — perhaps with a drawing by J.D. Fergusson. Fredegonde Shove (1889-1949), daughter of Virginia Woolf's cousin Florence Fisher and the historian F.W. Maitland, was the wife of the economist Gerald Shove, Fellow of King's College, Cambridge. A conscientious objector, Shove worked on Philip Morrell's farm during the war, until his socialist principles provoked a minor insurrection. Thomas Earp, son of a Newark manufacturer, was an Oxford undergraduate introduced to Garsington by Aldous Huxley.

To Dorothy Brett, [7 December 1917]

[141A Church Street, Chelsea]
1.45 A.M. Very quiet and attentive prior to Bombs dropping.[1]
Dearest Brett,

I have been writing all the evening & now, with a ten minutes interval, I should like, so to speak, to walk up and down the corridor with you, before the curtain rings up again.

I really can't travel this weekend. It is 2 cold and I am 2 cold and my cold is 2 bad. So I am hugging the cave and sitting wrapped up in a rug, very self contained and luxurious. How are you? Are you in a working mood? We had no talk at all really. I did feel (as you jolly well know) uncommonly awkward *down there* & then lying in Mademoiselle's little cubby hole[2] seemed to remove me miles and miles away from you. It is another house up there. And then one did so tend to talk politics. Rather comic to use the little Welshman as a fan and hide behind him. . .[3]

Miss D. Brett — has painted a companion picture to the Gamps. It is called *Politics*. Scene: the fireplace in the red room. Mademoiselle in left hand corner, profile holding a tray of coffee. Someone with his back turned helping himself. Philip in the middle of the fireplace, very bland and double breasted, smoking a cigarette in a long holder. Ottoline in armchair in right hand corner with a tangle of bright wools spilling out of her lap. Brett on the floor in brocade shoes, holding the bellows and in the foreground Murry seated, black *beyond measure* & Henry Bentinck with his legs crossed, his hand shading his eyes. You might, if you were particularly devilish call this *The Great War* instead. But I *do wish*, Miss, as how you would paint it.

Why does one get so peckish in the stilly watches? I have just summoned the waiter and ordered the wing of a chicken, very hot, with a rum omelet to follow and half a bottle of wine. He has gone

away, but I am afraid he will be a long time executing the order. . .
In Heaven the waiter will always come back within five minutes —
don't you feel?

This is only a note by the way, a pin stuck in to make you write
me one of your pearls of letters. I shant write any more. Ill go
to bed.

> My bed is waiting Cool and Fresh
> With linen White and Fair
> And I must off to Sleep-sum-bye
> BUT — not forget my prayer!

And my neapolitan ice pyjamas wrapped round the water bottil.

The Lord be with you. Hug the lad for me, & tell me if you think
he is putting on our mysterious enemy Flesh.

Brett: Katherine, you are very silly tonight.

I am. But if you knew how hard I have been working you'd forgive
me and not disdain the honest worker's palm of

Katherine qui vous aime.

MS Newberry.

[1] After several weeks' respite, German air attacks had resumed over England in the
early hours of 6 Dec 1917. Six Gotha aircraft reached the suburbs of London, killing seven
civilians and injuring twenty.

[2] On her visit to Garsington 1-2 Dec 1917 KM had slept in an attic room usually occupied by Juliet Baillot, the Swiss governess of Lady Ottoline's daughter Julian (see p. 361,
n.1) and later the wife of Julian Huxley.

[3] The Welsh Liberal MP David Lloyd George (1863-1945), after serving as Chancellor
of the Exchequer, as Minister of Munitions, and as Secretary of State for War, had replaced
Herbert Asquith as Prime Minister in December 1916.

To Virginia Woolf, [mid-December 1917]

141A, CHURCH STREET, | CHELSEA, S.W.

My dear Virginia,

I have not been able to get to a telephone even. For I am alone
here — & nobody has visited me — Murry is at Garsington and my
bloody rheumatism has ramped and raged — When it really descends
on me — I become a crawling thing without the power of doing anything except cursing my fate. The attack ought to be over in a day or
two when I will come & make my apologies in person if I may —
but Lord! what a curse the flesh can be — or the bones rather. I am
so down in the depths that I cant imagine anything ever fishing me
up again. That is why you havent heard from

Yours ever
Katherine.

MS Sussex. *LKM* I. 84; *Adam* 370-375, 21-2.

To Dorothy Brett, [12 December 1917]

[141A Church Street, Chelsea]

Dearest Brett.

Snow use. My medicine man[1] will not let me stray into wild pastures I shant be able to meet you in the Lyons [tea-room] den on Friday. I am so sorry. I would have loved a bone and a chat but my left water wing has played up — curse its eyes! How long will you be in Town? Shall you feel inclined to alight on this doorstep — isn't it a devil of a way out — but youll be heartily welcome — a bright fire and a nice hot cup of tea —

Ill write you at length another time — Theres tons I want to say but I am catching a post — making a kind of dash for it. The tooth is *out* & Ottoline & I have had a rare giggle at it. Bless you. Kiss your hot water bottle for me.

Ever yours.

K.

MS Newberry.

[1] William Bradshaw Ainger, the doctor KM was now consulting.

To J.M. Murry, [13 December 1917]

[141A Church Street, Chelsea]

Cher and charmant jeune homme:

You must not be so agitato, though indeed I well understand the state of mind. But you can't afford to feel in the least shattered. Take a long breath & think of the sea at full tide & a little boat riding in ever so slowly — to a little bay with white sand and wild cherries growing nearly down to the water. No, thats a silly recipe. It dont calm me. Au contraire down I run to the waters edge with my heart beating like a drum. Your song is very lovely indeed — exceedingly lovely. So wild and shy and ardent — & the measure of it beautifully fitting. One line brings me up sharp.

White is her hair.

I don't like that a bit. I know that it is not your meaning & I know I am an upstart but *unbind* or bind up — or unbraid — or cover, all seem to me 'easier'. And as light hands are tending her I think one of those wouldn't be out of place. I (1) simply don't feel her hair was ever white — it does away with the ageless beauty idea (2) I feel a little crack where this line joins the others; its not part of them. I may be quite insolently wrong. I'd *bracket* the line if that was a help. What do you feel?[1]

H[er] L[adyship] hasn't been near again, has not mentioned Xmas. If she dont I shall stay here & you there. For 1 want to begin moving as soon as I can. I wrote to Fraulein Palmer last night about Mrs J's flat, which Ive seen & like enough to take.[2] It suits me, & then you can dine with me every night & go up & work after — and I am on the spot if you want me. We mustnt start houses or big flats. Beaufort Mansions has nothing under £80 & then only ground floor. We should be bound to live differently & spend more. This is best, for then we *are* so free to fly.

Johnny [J.D. Fergusson] came yesterday. He was so very particularly nice, measuring his drawings with a little compass & saying "yes, it looks pretty good to me". Have you ever heard him refer to a person's state of health as "one foot in the grave and the other on a banana skin".[3] Oh! that does make me laugh so. Please *do* give his address to Lord H. [Henry Bentinck] I made sure I said so & I have a feeling that he was immensely cheered by the idea. H.L. says she'd like a portrait. I told him yesterday. Of course he said *No.* (Burn this letter. Burn it to bits, please). The fact that you had put on 2 lbs was "as it should be". "That is what's wanted". I loved the little drawing. Don't you think that you & I draw very well? Or is it just my fancy — I think we both have a real talent, but then I always think I can do everything — don't I?

The doctor is coming today. I never felt such a fraud — dancing about and eating every leaf and blade within sight. He'll put me into the army I should think. However I will keep a page clean to tell you how he turns up his eyes and admires me.

I am still feeling *prestissimo.* In fact I cant sleep for a nut. I lie in a kind of *furious bliss*! & the room in the firelight looks like some encampment, with the stairs for a sort of chemin de mouton.

Ma Parker yesterday went to my heart. She said suddenly "Oh Miss, you do make the work go easy." What could be a sweeter compliment. Its one I could pay to you & to J.D.F. but nobody else alive.

L.M. is simply loathing me — Here I am, supposed to be ill and bristling at every point with independence & *hard* where I should be *soft* & snorting when she says "I woke up this morning feeling a little blue and heart sick. . ." "Ah Putney!"[4] I cried & knew I was horrid — but she exasperates me *trop.*

Goodbye for just now. I shall come back later.

That man has just been — the doctor, & thumped away. He says I must lie very low for a week. I have taken it beautifully in time and *all is well* — He is so fearfully nice & kind & has read Tolstoi. What a pearl to find in these oceans of sillies. I feel an atom bit dashed I confess —

Knock. Now I really *am* dashed. Two loathsome females have come to look over the studio FROM MISS WRIGHT.[5] Is that legal? I thought only 6 weeks beforehand. I'm jiggered! They made my floor filthy — said it was a quaint little place!! but not big enough for *real* furniture.

Oh, Hell. Oh, how I loathe these english.

Courage. Keep calm Wig. It ain't so bad, but I feel a snip furious I must allow.

Its alright. I am angry but not in the you and me country. There, all is radiant. If I shut my eyes will the train carry me away. No. So keep them open & try to be sensible. But it was a push in the face — I must say. Let me end on a clear note — a real note — *con amore.* My darling boy — I am

Wig.

MS ATL. *BTW*, 449; *LJMM*, 96-8.

[1] Murry took KM's advice in altering the last line of stanza 2 in his 'Song of the Cinnamon's Guards' in *Cinnamon and Angelica* (1920), the verse play he was working on.

[2] KM had decided to rent rooms next to Murry's in Redcliffe Road. Miss Palmer was Murry's landlady.

[3] Murry's note (*LJMM*, 97) says that the quip was originally that of James Pryde, a journalist friend.

[4] Ida Baker's factory was near Putney.

[5] The owner of KM's studio flat.

To J.M. Murry, [14 December 1917]

[141A Church Street, Chelsea]
Friday.

My darling Boy,

My temper is serene again. I am so sorry that I let fly yesterday but it did and *does* seem to me a bit steep de la parte de Miss Wright — I have a lot of 'things' to say . . . Miss Palmer came here last evening. I have taken that flat for a year for 11/- a week. She is having it colour washed cleaned swept, painted where necessary. Not badsome. . She was very nice and decent. Je suis très contente. I don't know just when I shall move my bits of things for I want to have the floors & curtings done & the kitchen dresser painted etc before I do. However it is amicably arranged. I like the place. I feel so free there. I have *adored* this cubby hole & that is a fact. Im not unfaithful to it even now but its plain to see that it is over.

About the South of France — please don't mention it, Betsy. I just *couldn't.* I am really not in the least seriously ill. It would be a pure joke to pretend that I was, and I am a little lion as you know most times. The South of France must joliment attendre. But this is exceedingly important. Dont you DARE come back here until you have to. Youd undo all the good youve done, and worry me to death. I should have to spend all my time collecting food for the Xmas season & so on — and where you are all is so simple. Oh, my love, PLEASE BE REASONABLE FOR JUST THIS ONE XMAS. Praps Ill come down *or* I shall stay here but the idea that you should post up simply horrifies me. I implore you, most seriously to be wise about this. When I think of your coal, housekeeper during the holidays, shops shut, etc. etc. I feel quite hysterical. I should be tortured. I, of course, here have got coal. L.M. & Chaddie & Belle[1] have stuffed this place with food for me. I eat like a warrior, and drink pints of milk a day. But if I have to feel that you are neglecting yourself in your rooms I shant bite another crust and Ill throw the milk down the drain, my temper will be vile. Bogey stop torturing me *at once*, or I'll tell.

I feel much better today except for this worrying idea. In fact I feel, simply dandy. I ate nearly ½ lb. steak last night & Ive got 9 newlaid eggs 1 lb butter, dates, filletted haddock, cream — etc etc in the larder. I shall be as fat as butter and as brown as a maori if only you will behave. But of course you will — darling.

X X X X
X X X X

I have an idea that your hair will never grow until you take it to New Zealand — Then it will sprout up and wave in the breedge like a little fern tree — all one lovely crinkle. I feel that if Mother were only to pat it with her tiny white hands and frown at it there would be no holding it. I hope that is true.

What a nice letter from Milne. He is a rare nice boy. He must come and make a long stay with us when Sullivan is there too.[2] There is something *shy* and *loving* in this letter which endears him to me — and he is "serious" — Thank you for letting me see it. I send you a kind of cabbage from Anne [Drey] — bless her — "Pantalons solides" might be the title of all her pictures.

I did not do any work yesterday — That was another reason why I felt jumpy. But today I am going it & shall have to make an effort to be nice to Brettushka. H[er] L[adyship] hasn't been here again. I wonder what has happened to her? She seems to have quite disappeared — Its a nice day here. Very quiet — and warm. Even the milkman crying milk sounds to me like a bird trying its note — a funny sort of big bird you know — a bird penguinian.

The clock ticks on tiptoe and the yellow curtains wave gently — I love such a day — It is such a rest — not having been outside for these days. I love to be out of the streets and buses — out of the nudging crowds — Oh, I must work. The very shadows are my friends. Dont forget to weigh yourself again when the week is up — &

if you are not heavier you must melt a horseshoe in your next glass
of milk so as not to disappoint me. Dearest of all. I am

Your loving, cautious playfellow

Wig.

MS ATL. *LKM* I. 85-6; *LJMM*, 98-100.

[1] KM's sister Charlotte Perkins, now living in London and working in the War Graves
Registration office, had called to see her with their Aunt Belle Trinder.

[2] Murry's friend H.J.M. Milne later worked in the Department of Manuscripts in the
British Museum. Another friend, and a colleague in the War Office, was the scientist and
journalist J.W.N. Sullivan (1886-1937) who married Vere (Evelyn) Bartrick-Baker, KM's
friend at Queen's College. As well as many works on popular science, Sullivan was the
author of *Beethoven: His Spiritual Development* (1927), and an autobiographical novel,
But for the Grace of God (1932).

To J.M. Murry, [15 December 1917]

[141A Church Street, Chelsea]

Dearest Boy

I am spending an idle day in bed — Ribni[1] sits by me and I have
made myself a sort of Pirate cap which I think, hope, nay am sure
will startle the doctors young eye. Its all sunny outside and I am
bored. After he is gone Ive a mind [to] throw away my wings & go
off for a frisk. But I wont. I am almost terrifically well again. H[er]
L[adyship] has asked me for Xmas, so Ill come — and if you don't
get your usual paralysis down there & I my usual feeling that I ought
to [be] in the little room we may have some fun. Mrs. Maufe came in
last night & wanted to whisk me off to her house for a few days. Oh
what a dread prospeck! The amount of whisking that people want to
do with me and awrapping of me up in bundils is quite terrifying. I
said I was being superbly looked after by my old Mrs HARRIS who
was a very good cook — a woman I had known for years & couldn't
be more comfortable with. Oh! what fun. Do you know who I
meant? Sairey Gamp's friend.[2] I laughed so much inside that I
thought she would hear the laughs running up & down in me. Even
to write it makes me laugh again & Ribni stuffed the ends of his
necktie in his mouth stood on his head & waved his feet when
I told him.

I wish I had made more time to work though. You see L.M. is
here nearly always at the weekends & Chaddie is coming this afternoon, and Johnnie this evening, and then there is such a fearful lot
to eat in this house that it does take time to get through with it.
L.M. is so hopeless though well intentioned. One has to issue
directions all the time — A plague on it. I wish you & I were away.
Oh I long to be away, just we two. Weren't we happy in our [Villa]

Pauline. Do you remember? And do you remember the drawing you made on a big stone. Your feet were bare & very pink from standing on that flat rock. Oh, Jag, we must GO OFF you and I again. I am so frightened that the idea rather fills you with horror, and that you cling to this little island. Tell me the truth and don't spare me. There is a fragrance on the wings of your play which fills me with childish longings. It sounds to me a heavenly play. Now I must call you to account. If you dont like the other aloe bud I sent you[3] or if you cant read the (I confess) awful writing — well tell me. I wont be offended. That I promise you. But majestic silence or 'wait a bit' I cant stand. I dont mind what you say, but *do say something.* Look at me. I criticise you like a shot and never keep you waiting. You know I am *most impatient.* And I almost expected a peal of bells at least. Ill finish this letter after that man has been —

Later. Really. I am very nearly in love with this old doctor. He *is* such a find. No, thats not my feeling. What I do feel [is] that hes the sort of man we might all be talking to in a café in the good Paris days — I don't have to alter my vocabulary or pretend a bit, and Ah you know how rare *that* is. He is coming again on Monday — so you can see how careful he is. He says I am much better and look much better and I've no temperature at all — but I must still go a bit slow and not go out. I think he thought I was a pirate — yoho! yoho! so don't you worry a bit. I am almost 2 lively and gay.

Oh, here is L.M. who wants to post this letter my precious darling. Excuse the funny writing but the bed is all hills and valleys.

I am always your own
Tig.

MS ATL. *LKM* I. 89-90; *LJMM*, 100-1.

[1] A favourite doll, named after Colonel Ribnikov, in a story of that title by Aleksandr Kuprin (1870-1938). While she was living in Acacia Road KM collaborated with Koteliansky on his translation of this, the first story in Kuprin's *The River of Life, and Other Stories* (1916), otherwise translated by Koteliansky and Murry.

[2] Sairy Gamp, the cockney midwife in Dickens's *Martin Chuzzlewit* (1844), attributed a good deal to her imaginary friend, Mrs Harris.

[3] Murry's note (*LJMM*, 101) identifies the 'bud' as 'Another part of *The Aloe*, of which *Prelude* was part.'

To J.M. Murry, 17 December 1917

[141A Church Street, Chelsea]

My dear precious one

I am writing fully tomorrow. This is just a note to say what my wire said that all is well. Yes I sent you the Aloe Bud on Tuesday for a surprise. where it is the devil only knows. I dont — But for some extraordinary reason I cant take in the fact that it is lost — or even going to be lost.[1] So dont you worry either.

Your poem [*Cinnamon and Angelica*] — Ah your poem is simply wonderful — Yes it is really great — Do not hesitate to believe that. It is simply thrillingly good —

My own. I cant come for Xmas. That is what I want to write about fully tomorrow — The doctor says I would be so very mad to travel, even in a car from this door to that and wont hear of it. So let my other letter stand & *believe me* that to know that you are there & fed & warm is the greatest possible relief to me & just makes me well. If you came here I should worry my life out. The doctor is awfully nice & sensible. He says Im better. I *am* indeed but I must be very careful of this wing. Belle saw him today & she asked if she could take me to her place *de luxe* — fur coats motorcars from here to there, but he still said *no*. So you see! Rib & I must hang up our own stockings. Half the world is keeping me supplied with eggs & fish & everything — & crowds are looking after me — It is absurd — You just stay where you are — Bogey & believe that your Wig is doing every single thing. These silly people have kept me from writing to you today — that is why this is such a breathless rush. Don't worry my precious own — Take care of yourself. We must turn into giants. This is preposterous. I will write fully fully tomorrow. A huge big letter.

But none could contain more love than this one to you from

Wig.

I will write Ottoline & everybody, too, tomorrow. Oh my treasure you just be all jokey & when we meet again we shall crinkle up our eyes and laugh at all this silly affair. I am writing this in a sort of *telegraphic* way that you & that I understand — a sort of signal to say yes the flag is flying — So full report tomorrow Sir — But I want to write miles about *Angelica*.

MS ATL. *LJMM*, 101-2.

[1] Murry had 'a hazy memory that it was eventually recovered and formed the opening pages of *At the Bay*' (*LJMM*, 101).

To Ottoline Morrell, [18 December 1917]

[141A Church Street, Chelsea]

Dearest Ottoline

I am so sorry. But I shall not be able to come to Garsington for Christmas. My medicine man simply refuses to let me travel, under *any* circumstances, anywhere. So I shall have to stay here under the shadow of the Rhodesian Mountain.

He is an awfully sane and unalarming person but he says definitely that I may be very seriously ill if I catch a chill, and that even if I could catch a train from this door to that I must not 'risk the air'. It is *too* maddening. For I had so looked forward to being with you. Do, if you feel inclined write me one of your heavenly letters dearest, for just at this moment with the shock fresh I feel horribly *low*. The trouble is my left *wing* which is still so inclined to be a C.O. He has it up before the tribunal every other day but no — no — no — it is firm in its wickedness for the moment. However all this is quite temporary, and I cannot be too grateful to you for appealing to me through my vanity and making me go to him.

I feel the greatest fraud imaginable, little carthorse that I am writing to *you* like this. What you told me about your dreadful headaches has been at the back of [my] mind ever since. I do *hope* that you will give Maurice Craig[1] a serious trial. It is impossible to go on like that especially with these black English months ahead. *Do* tell me how you are.

I am so *dull* but I have not really un cafard. Only I am tired of counting the stairs and the stair-eyes.

With fondest love, | *Ever*,
Katherine.

MS Stanford.

[1] Maurice Craig, a Harley Street physician and psychiatrist, author of *Psychological Medicine* (1905). Lady Ottoline continued to suffer from headaches, which may have been related to the severe emotional depression she experienced in 1917, or to the facial neuralgia which, ten years later, was diagnosed as necrosis of the jaw.

To J. M. Murry, [? 20 December 1917]

[141A Church Street, Chelsea]

Dearest

Now that you have been here everything seems quite simple and straightforward again. You were in every possible and impossible way, *too* lovely and never was I happier than then. I do only hope that you are not overtired — Weigh yourself again and don't forget to let me know the result.

I really ought to be seeing about my passport straight away — oughtn't I?[1] Because it takes ages. I will ask the doctor for the certificate on Sunday — and then you tell me what to do. You can find out from Brett — can't you? I feel hopelessly vague about what must be done but I *do* think it ought to be put in hand without delay — Chaddie came yesterday. I did up your present in white paper & tied it with violet heart stamped ribbon. She was enchanted. She brought me an IMMENSE apple green padded silk dressing gown from Belle — big enough for at least three Wigs great with child. The ugliness and inappropriateness of it was a severe blow. I shall have to change it somehow — And Johnnie spent the evening. He was very depressed and subdued. We talked about places. He says you *can* get little houses down there at about £10 or £15 a year. I feel so stupid and bald in the head & lie here wrapped up falling asleep over Dombey & Son. That man strapped me up so tight yesterday that the wind out of my sail, I am too becalmed for words. My love, if only you will get better still, stronger and fatter — Go on faithfully with the treatment wont you. I would kiss H.L.s hands for all that she has done for you. What rare luck it was that you went there! This letter is so feeble and dull that I must put the cosey on it. Forgive me, dear love — I am longing to hear from you. And Ah! my dear Bogey

I am forever your
Wig.

MS ATL. *LJMM*, 104.

[1] Murry had come to London for a brief visit, when it seems they agreed that KM should leave England in the New Year.

To J.M. Murry, [21 December 1917]

[141A Church Street, Chelsea]
Friday.

How shall I begin this letter? All the love names in the world are not enough. But you are to feel as you read these lines as though I held your head in my hands, and were looking at you — a long long look, before we kiss each other. It is absurd to say that I love you *more*. How could that be? And yet I do love you more. My precious one, love like ours hath no equal on this earth. I could not love you more; I always love you more — — —

A letter from you by this afternoons post. I am only praying that you have got one from me by now. Curse these posts; they are hopelessly disorganised and we must expect them to be more so at Xmas.

'Something' in your letter worries me. You say you *dread* this Christmas at G[arsington] so much. Did I ever urge you to stay? And yet if you come up how shall we go down together again? Can you stick it without hating it too much? Can you swim over its head? Please tell me this. I cannot bear to think that I have begged you to endure something intolerable. I think it is always understood that you keep aloof.

And now darling, about your having paid this rent in advance for me. I shall have to pay you back by degrees. You know I will. When I am well I shall save *by pennies* simply but save I mean to, and you shall have it. You know my feelings about money. It is appalling that I should cost so much just now, but believe me I will repay you in the not too long run, my own. I shudder at the thought of your journey. God! what a terror it must have been. Was there no fire in the waiting room? Or couldn't you have sat in the tearoom? I suppose you were on the *qui vive* for the train and didn't dare to. I should have liked the country lad better if he had carried his suitcase quite alone; your rucksack was quite enough, but the walk must have been in its way, wonderful.

Mrs. Maufe brought me her maufling for tea yesterday. She left him with me. I think it is the first time I have spent an hour alone with a thoroughly modern enlightened child. I found out that the method practised on him had been to treat him exactly like a grown-up *on a small scale*. You can imagine the result. I sat and gaped at him. He had brought with him a dairy farm from Heals[1]   exactly like a real dairy farm *on a small scale*. And of course he did not play with it because he cant play. He ran it as a little going concern and I bet he made it pay. God forbid that any child of mine should fall into modern ways — I was thankful when his mother took him away.

I have spent nearly the whole day lying on the sofa fast asleep. I cant think why — but I just got up, wrapped in a rug, lay down again and would be sleeping still if the boy from Andre Sleigh & Angus hadn't woke me up. They charged me 10/10 for those two little blocks.[2] I was staggered. I had thought they would have been 1/6 each.

It is cold and quiet here, but I feel so much better for that long sleep.

Pleurisy has just the same effect as fever. It tires you out almost without your knowing it.

Are you walking again in your enchanted country.[3] That is what I long to hear.

I am like you in your dislike of people. But the mania is more advanced. I think we shall live, a long time, one day, absolutely alone. Thats my idea of Heaven.

I am yours for ever
Wig.

MS ATL. *LKM* I. 89; *LJMM*, 102-4.

¹ Heal & Son Ltd., furnishers and upholsterers, 195-198 Tottenham Court Road.
² The blocks of J.D. Fergusson's designs for *Prelude*, made by André, Sleigh & Anglo
Ltd., photo-process engravers in Milford Lane, Strand.
³ That is, progressing with his verse play *Cinnamon and Angelica*.

To Anne Estelle Drey, [22 December 1917]

141a Church Street, | Chelsea | S W 3
Saturday.

My dearest Anne,
The reason why I have not replied before to your letter & Book
& to Drey's Souvenir of Love has been that I have been strictly in
bed for days, nearly weeks, with my left water-wing (alias my lung)
entirely out of action for the time and strapped up in plaster which
gives off waves of smell like new varnish on an inside cabin wall.
Dry pleurisy, ma chère, an old complaint of mine! It has been most
hellishly annoying as you know my views on the subject of ill health
— Picture me, lying very close to the wall, with my darling Japanese
doll for an innocent — all too innocent — bed companion, dressed in
a pair of pyjamas which look as though they ought to take off and
on with a spoon, they are so like a glace neapolitaine, with one
immense faux nichon — i.e. the one that the strapping goes over and
that is therefore (fleur delicat) mounted in cotton wool, and upon
which the eyes of my visitors are immediately rivetted. However the
worst is over and I am up today, feeling as light and airy as what
Ma Bates used to call a *gash* balloon, and still quite unable to grasp
the fact that life really has given me such a cuff & a kiss as this old
attack. *For* the doctor says I must never stay in England for another
winter but must leave in September & not come back until April,
and at present as soon as I am well enough he has given me a medical
certificate for the South of France, and I hope to be able to leave in
January. This must sound like an absolute plant to you. It did to
me. When I heard the medicine man say: "You ought to go to some
place like Teneriffe or Madeira, but as you cant go there Spain or the
South of France *will do* —" I would not have swopped my lung with
any man alive. If I stay in England he says I may become con-
sumptive. Alors, je m'en vais! But I cant really believe that this will
happen and I wont until I see a pink house with two cedars in front
of it. It is too good luck. But talk about the knock out blow — Ive
had it! Why cant you come too? I mean to find a little house somewhere down there with a good garden and really make it a pied à
terre so that my *rare* darling friends can camp in it too and always

feel that it is there if they want to come. I shall beat along the coast slowly this spring, *if if if* I ever do get there . . .

London has been just lately like a big brimming bowl of the very best pea soup. One looks up at the studio window at a kind of green thick mixture with the tree outside swimming in it like a bunch of dry herbs. There has not been a breath of wind, but if you put your hand out of bed a cold whistling draught from nowhere blows it back again. Through it the rag and bone man has cried up and down the road with quite peculiar relish and just when the fog was at its highest and best some carol singers started: "Christians! Awake! Salute the Happy Morn . . ." Quel pays! When you are living "as you might say three hundred and sixty four days under an umberellar like any dratted mushroom." Since the raid the gas supply is almost cut off and the gas man informed me yesterday that if these raids go on there will be no knowing whether London will have any gas at all.[1] So nice plus the coal shortage.

Looe sounds a real find. I am thankful you are there and out of this. If you should meet a tall man with a pointed grey beard, Irish eyes, and a voice like the sky at evening, salute him from me. His name is Charles Palliser,[2] and he was a love of my salad days.

Murry is still in the country, putting on 3 lbs a week. I am going down to him for a week before I pack and *begin to get ready*.

A thousand thanks for Nanette. My God after a visit from *well meaning* relatives and friends who assailed me with: "don't you think Lloyd George is *too splendid*?" "I do think the King has behaved *splendidly* during the war. Don't you?" "It must be *too splendid* to be a man at a time like this, don't you think?" I have simply lain in bed gasping and fanned myself with ce livre charmant. It breathes of France.[3] I shall be here until about the second week in January. I'd simply love a poulet and its very sweet of you to think of sending me one. I wanted to send you some candies, but they are not to be had, so I shall send dates instead. Quelque chose de bien sucré —

Forgive a dull dog of a letter. My mind feels so bald — and my faithful Lesley Moore who has all the intentions of an angel has almost made me an imbecile with this sort of thing.

She: Which would you rather have. Hot milk or Oxo.
Me: Oxo please.
She: Oh, don't you think you'd rather have hot milk?
Me: No thanks. Oxo please.
She: But don't you think hot milk is more nourishing.
Me: Oxo, please.
She: I wish you would have hot milk, just to please me.
Me: Oxo, please.

She: Very well dear. But what about having Oxo in the hot milk. Isn't that a good idea?

Me: Plain Oxo, please.

She: (from the kitchen) Oh, Katya dear, I find there isn't any Oxo left. Will you have milk?

Me: !!!!!!

Salute Drey for me. I do hope I shall see you again soon. Ah ma chère et ma charmante, je vous aime bien tendrement, et je vous embrasse bien serré.

Katherine.

MS ATL. *LKM* I. 86-8.

[1] London was bombed by half a dozen German planes early in the evening of 18 Dec 1917, leaving six dead and seventy injured.

[2] Harold Beauchamp's friend Charles Palliser (see p. 7, n.6) had settled in Cornwall.

[3] Possibly *Nanette, ou la jolie écosseuse. Ecrit par elle-même* (1798).

To J.M. Murry, [22 December 1917]

[141A Church Street, Chelsea]

Dearest and Wonderful Boy,

Your letter with the Poem came today. I simply pray that you have got some of mine by now. The poem is extraordinarily good. It has such ease. Something has changed so in your work — You do seem now so, to "begin and somewhat loudly *sweep* the string".[1] Yes, that is just, just what I mean.

Every new thing that you send me seems to be surer to be more absolutely *poetry*. Ah God! why cant you simply give yourself up to your power *now*. Why must your bird be still chained to your wrist when it is so ready for flight. But, my soul, it won't be for long, and nothing can stop you. I feel, with quite a new, 'special' feeling you are a *poet*. You have, finally and for ever, taken me up to the top of a hill and shown me your Kingdom, not wreathed in mist, not with the promise of towers and fountains, but all touched with that strange infallible light of dawn . . .

What these few weeks have meant to you and how they have taught me far more about you! My heart could fly out of my body with pride of you. The world is only the water that flows under the bridge. It may rush and roar, but we are two shining children leaning over that arc of light and looking down undaunted.

I love you.

It is not so cold today, and I feel a great deal better. I will tell you what the medicine man says tomorrow. I am sure he will be surprised.

I feel quite different — rather quiet still — rather like a doll that has been mended but put on a high shelf to dry before it can be played with again.

God above! How I do love you!!

I cant send any presents this year Bogey. Does it matter? I cant get out to buy them and I dont trust L.M. I will try and write a sketch for Brett & perhaps for H.L. and praps for you. Anne, with rare sense has sent me a Big FAT FOWL.

Johnnie is going away for Xmas to Fisher White.[2] That is a relief off my mind for then I know he will be fed. Sullivan comes to-morrow. I think JDF, too, and I pray *not* Meg [Margaret Morris]. For though I do like her so much — Oh — why dont she talk more quietly and why does she roar?

Here is L.M. — waiting for this letter & interrupting me as I write.

A fool today beyond words. But she has brought me a flower or two. That is comfort.

Here she is. I am quarrelling with her, too. & she keeps saying it is because she is always sleepy. One in the eye for me.

Lovely one — Dearest.

I am your own
Wig.

NO LM ON ANY FARM.[3]

MS ATL. *LJMM*, 105-6.

[1] Cf. Milton, *Lycidas,* II. 15-17: 'Begin then, Sisters of the sacred well / That from beneath the seat of Jove doth spring, / Begin, and somewhat loudly sweep the string.'
[2] Fisher White is unidentified.
[3] The proposed 'Heron' cottage was to have a small farm of its own.

To J. M. Murry, [23–24 December 1917]

[141A Church Street, Chelsea]
Sunday

My dearest —

Here is the certificate which the doctor has just given me. Is it alright? He says that left lung of mine that had the *loud deafening* creak in it is "no end better" but there is a SPOT in my right lung which "confirms him in his opinion that it is absolutely imperative that I go out of this country & Keep out of it all through the future winters". It is evidement rather a bad 'un of its kind — at any rate it would become so if I did not fly. About Oxfordshire. He says it is far wiser that I stay here until I am well enough to travel & dont attempt the country; that was even when I explained about the hot pipes and glasses of hot milk on trays. The programme seems to be (if I don't want to do this mysterious crocking up) to sit tight, pack and make for the sun. See? What do you think? Although I am still snapping up fishes like a sea lion, steaks like a land lion, milk like a snake (or is that only a 'tale'?) and eggs honey, creamb, butter and nourishing trimmings galore, they seem to go to a sort of Dead Letter Office. However he has given me a tonic today which will put that right. Of course I feel now that Ive only to get into the sun and Ill simply burst into leaf and flower again. It is this old place that does it to me and I keep sweeping out *our* house with a branch of acacia tree, picking a rose to tuck into my bodice and then hurrying off just in time to catch the train which tumbles you, my treasure, in my arms. And I keep going into that room and putting my arm round you and saying: "Look theres that diamond of light in the shutter" —

I know quite well, I appreciate absolutely that you must be faithful to England. Hell it would be to know you were away & felt its call, but all the same you will have to have two homes & we shall have to have all our babies in pairs, so that we possess a complete 'set' in either place.

Je t'aime! Je t'aime!!

This man is coming again on Thursday to unstrap me and overhaul me. In the meantime I think that the passport affair should be got under way & the Hotel Beau Rivage written to — to make sure — don't you? I thought — tell them Madame will be there for 2 months at least so she will require une belle chambre avec vue sur la mer & beaucoup de soleil — & to reply immediately. You, who write so much better than I had better send that letter & don't forget your *name problem*. But don't mention LUNGS or they will take fright. You know the french. They'd imagine I had come there to gallop away.

Should I forward you my old passport. Tell me. I shall send *this* and if you need it *that* registré of course. I was so glad of your wire this morning; it put a flower on my sunday.

These my present letters are really such *self engrossed dull* matron affairs that I groan to think about them after they are gone. But you see I feel that life has changed so and it has all happened so quickly — all my plans are altered — all my future is touched by this, all *our* future rather. Its like suddenly mounting a very fresh, very unfamiliar horse — a *queer queer* feeling.

As to 'working' I cant just now. However I have heaps to read and to think over against the time when I shall get down to it again — What is so difficult to realise is that this has happened to *me* and not to *you*. That seems just nonsense. And oh dear, what a serious talk I shall have to have with you before I do go, about taking care of *yourself.* Its almost funny in a way — isn't it? One thing — which must be your idee mère — is don't you worry about me. Keep happy! We can afford to be happier than anybody — you and I. And just think how I shall write. I wish we could have been married before I go[1] — but it don't really signify. (*Burn my letters*) You are so grown into my heart that we are like the two wings of one bird.

Goodbye for now, my own. Have you weighed yourself again? I am sorry to plague you but you know how one feels. And dont dare not to tell the ABSOLUTE TRUTH. I am ever your own

Wig.

P.S. If the certificate is not right I think you had better write to Ainger direct. Tell me if you do. I notice for one thing he has left the date out. Ribni says "Happy Xmas" & hes going to take off his kimono & hang up one of the sleeves tomorrow. And he says weve got two oranges & 2 tangerines & nuts and flowers in this place — see? *And* you are not to forget him or he may creep into your pocket next time you're here & give you an awful fright. *And* "tell that Old Mousey that I like him."

Monday.

Dearest

This letter could not be registered yesterday so I am adding a word. Also, as you see I am sending you the passport. I do hope all this will not take too long. As I am going I have a great longing to be ready — and I feel today absolutely strong enough to travel — The spiritual fact qu'on voyage vers le soleil is such a staff!

Sullivan came last night. He was particularly nice. And he told me a story about you which is so *frightfully good.* Do you know it — Allen's[2] remark about you? I'll not repeat it in case you do.

Johnny & Meg then came, but Meg was very bored and went her way. (Sullivan and I talked mainly about music — Beethoven chiefly and why these people fail in art.) Then Sullivan left & J.D.F. and I had a long talk. Dearest, Bentinck went to see him, bought his *best* picture & is going up to Leeds to see his others. Isn't that perfectly stunning of him. You can imagine Fergussons quite extraordinary pleasure that this had happened "and, between you and me, just at the right moment. Its meant a great deal!" Of course his pleasure was doubled because Lord Henry chose his best — That proved him the sort of buyer that he delighted in having. Fergusson wants to show you & me his work all that he has got there. I have a sort of idea he is going to give you summat. If we can manage to get to the studio before I go — we must. But I wish you could get into touch with Lord Henry — *really* into touch. No letter today yet. It will I fondly hope come later, and no parcel from H L. I am writing this in bed, the bath is running. I had a devilish night & feel as though during the night I had slept in a furniture van. Also L.M. said in the middle of *my* wakefulness & *her* sound sleep: "It really was a delicious tapioca pudding. But I really do prefer elderly men. Funny isn't it?" That gave me quite 'a turn' —

I have just seen Miss Wright about letting my place. I am going to have a board put up immediately —

L.M. is now doing the floor. My spirit faints. I must go. Darling I am

Wig

MS ATL. *LKM* I. 88-9; cited *BTW*, 450, 451; *LJMM*, 106-8, 110.

¹ At George Bowden's prompting, divorce proceedings had begun; the case was heard in London on 17 Oct 1917, but the decree nisi was not to become absolute until the end of April 1918.

² Percival 'Porky' Allen, a friend of Murry's since his school days at Christ's Hospital, had been killed in action in 1916.

To J.M. Murry, 24 December [1917]

[141A Church Street, Chelsea]
Christmas Eve 8.P.M.

My precious love.

A knock at the door and the postwoman hands me your Sunday letter & a card saying my Gs are no go. If all my letters lie in Carsington . . . For I have written to you every day. AMEN. And L.M. does not eat them (strange!) And I am sure she posts them in live letter boxes. It really is *simply* awful. But perhaps by now they do lie in your bosom. I cant bear the thought of strangers looking under their wings. *Arent* my Gs alright really? However Ill never make another. Boge (Hum! Ha!) Fergusson is away just now & when he comes back he has some special work to do on a big picture that will keep him busy pretty indefinitely. He is thinking of going up to *Leeds* after the New Year. He is porte close absolutely. Please tell H.L. *Who* sent me the most exquisite pink silk eiderdown — you know the sort of padded silk quilt qui fond sur le coeur — It is perfect for now and ever. I can also see myself wrapping up future generations in it & hurling them in a pink parcel out of the window to you in the meadow below (But 'not a word to the wife' about that!) It is, at any rate a staggering gift. I thought she'd send me some mittens.

You are an appalling bad boy to send me a jacket. Stop it! It has not come yet & I know it will be perfect but you MUST not buy me anything more or pay any more for me. Save, my lovely one, please. You have simply covered me with presents lately & Ive given you nothing. L.M. gave me a petticoat — rather like raspberries & currants. Very nice. I let her. It must have cost a lot I suppose, but perhaps it didn't. The *food* in this studio makes one reel. I ought to get heavy again if I only bite off a corner of it but at present if you charcoaled my bones I would be a very useful anatomical specimen.

At 10 o'clock this morning — just as L.M. went out, the lad *Sullivan* turned up — He was playing the wag I think for he said he had not got a holiday — but might he spend part of the day with me. All this *dead* serious as though there were already a posse of police in the front garden. He was awfully nice to me and made up the fire and all that and went out for a bottle of wine. At four o'clock (I sent him away for lunch) he went back to Watergate House. He really is immensely anxious to join us, and I rather think he will — that we will let him. But I was so tired after he had gone that I fell asleep.

I feel much better tonight — but a funny feature about this sort of illness is ones temper. I get so irritable so nervous that I want to *scream*, & if many people start talking I just lose my puff and feel my blood getting black. Perhaps thats just because one is a bit weak. I only tell it to you to put in your symptom book.

Julian [Morrell] has sent me a dear little Kalendar Buch. I shall write her and H.L. I wish you could have eaten half my steak & stout tonight. That *is* the thing. One is very peaceful here — and very independent. You know — I feel that I have got written on my chest: PLEASE DO NOT FUSS! If the doctor says I may begin to go out at the end of this week what shall we do? Do you feel inclined to come up for another day. Thats so expensive unless we think it necessary — And do tell me all that must be done about my passport and WHEN I MAY EXPECT TO GET IT THROUGH. It ought not to be difficult. I posted you a registered packet today.

I am a brute about L.M. who is really being amazingly good & kind.

Love these are only dull jottings — Read them as such — Ribni is all bound up with gold ribbons and he has got the postman's Christmas box ready & the dairy boy's.

I love you. I am your woman
Tig.

MS ATL. Cited *BTW*, 450-1; *LJMM,* 108-9.

To Julian Morrell,[1] *24 December [1917]*

141A Church Street | Chelsea | S W 3.
Christmas Eve.

Dearest Julian,

It really is quite monstrously kind of you to have sent me the little book and the card. The little book is Enchanting. I keep turning over the pages and wondering what is *gay* enough to catch ones life after all those lovely twirling lines on the cover. I think I shall have to keep it for a pocket drawing book to use in the South of France. Its a perfect little trap to catch a sunbeam!

Was the little boy on the card meant to be Murry? It was very like him about the *feet*. I shall have to send you my present for the New Year for I am still in my cage. Its a great bore. I hope you have a very happy Xmas and if there should be crackers pull one with Murry for me, will you?

Much love, dear Julian
from
Katherine

MS Texas. Cited *Exhibition*, 34.

[1] Julian Morrell (b.1906), later Mrs Igor Vinogradoff; Lady Ottoline's only child.

To Ottoline Morrell, 24 December [1917]

141a Church Street | Chelsea | S W 3
Christmas Eve

Dearest Ottoline,

I was quite staggered by your lovely present to me this morning. It is exquisite — as sweet as balm as soft as air — as gentle — — — You cannot imagine how I have enjoyed curling up under it today, instead of under my old travelling plaid — a vile object which always reminds me somehow of a beach and a bun and a band.

I have sent you nothing — for I am still tied by the wing to my studio, and I expect Murry has told you that as soon as I am 'fit to travel' I must go off to the South of France and stay there — Then I shall send you flowers or a flat yellow basket of oranges and leaves . . .

Life has given me such a strange cuff and a kiss since I saw you that I feel really bewildered — rather — Now that I *know* that I must never stay in England between September and April, and though perhaps after the war I wouldn't have done so — a command and a real live danger signal is a very different affair — — —

I am longing to hear from you? Did you have a letter from me a little while ago. I sent one — And how are you dearest — *Please* let me know.

I think of you so much.

> My fondest love | Yours ever
>
> Katherine.

MS ATL.

To Ottoline Morrell, [28 December 1917]

> 141A [Church Street, Chelsea]
>
> Friday.

Dearest,

I was so *more* than glad to hear from you yesterday . . . Yes, indeed I appreciate what Xmas cares are yours and I didn't really expect a letter (though I longed for one).

Murry & the Mountain have just gone off to the Foreign Office, armed with medical certificates enough to ensure one a State Burial — The Mountain has to come too and knock down the English and French policemen on the way.[1] She has a month's leave from her factory for the purpose — and by the end of that time I really shall be well enough to run about the farmyard & pick up grain for myself again. Its an absurd situation —

I *shall* miss you. I shall be awfully lonely at times — wanting a talk with you and wanting to have you there in the sunlight away from this hideous, evil England —

If it would not be too much trouble may I come down to Garsington on Tuesday for a few days? The doctor wants me to go away before I "make the journey" and my flat has to be dismantled and done with next week. I should *hate* to go anywhere except to you — if you will have me — and then I thought my passport will be ready in a few days time and I could come up to London just for one night with M. before I go away. I am not an invalid really — I am up and 'bobbish'. Would I worry you too much?

It's extraordinary how *changed* life feels to me now that I know that this life in England will not be mine, even as little as it has been. I simply don't feel that I shall ever come back again if only they will let me go. But perhaps that is partly because it is winter and because I have sat so long in this studio listening to the rag-and-bone man and the man crying coals . . .

M. *seems* a changed being. He has so immensely enjoyed himself, too. I think he is very much better and as well as he ever will be. *What* you have done for him — it is past telling. I am so happy that he and Mark [Gertler] have come together. He talked of Mark so much last night and wants to be a friend of his. I wish I could see him again. It is years since I have. Brett has evidently painted me *out out* of her picture.

Dearest this is not a letter — I am still gasping rather after trying to move the Mountain *in time*.

Always, yours,
Katherine

MS Newberry. *LKM* I. 90-1.

[1] The plan that Ida Baker accompany KM to France was thwarted when she was refused a travel permit by the Foreign Office. After a short stay the next week at Garsington, KM left alone for Bandol on 7 Jan 1918.

INDEX OF RECIPIENTS

GENERAL INDEX

Reference to the page and the footnote giving biographical details about individuals immediately follows their names and is printed in italics prefixed by *B*. References to place names and addresses are given in the Mansfield entry.

'A Dill Prickle' (Mansfield): 305
'A Ship in the Harbour' (Mansfield): 305, 306
Abercrombie, Lascelles: 125
Adam: 83n
Ainger, W.B.: 343n, 344, 348, 349, 358, 360; sends KM to France, 353, 356
All Blacks rugby tour, 1905: 39
Allen, Grant: 99
Allen, Maud: 61, 62n
Allen, Percival ('Porky'): 358, 359n
Amiel, Henri-Frederic: *B17n4*, 48
Amores (Lawrence): 281n
'An Indiscreet Journey' (Mansfield): 148, 181n
Andersen, Hans Christian: 48, 49n
'Apple Tree Story' (Mansfield): 198n
Arlen, Michael ('the Armenian'): *B248n1*, 247
Arnim, Felicitas Joyce von: 15n, 22, 23
Asquith, Emma Alice Margaret (Margot): 88, 89n
Asquith, Herbert Henry: 342n
At the Bay (Mansfield): 349n
Athenaeum: 52n9
Aubanel, Theodore: 306
Austin, Alfred: 104, 107n

Baillot, Juliet: 324n
'Bains Turcs' (Mansfield): 127n
Baker, Ida ('Lesley Moore', 'L.M.'): *B90n1*, xi, 90, 91n, 122, 123, 126, 135, 137, 138n, 176, 180, 183, 184, 225, 226, 346, 348, 356; at Queen's College, 11n, 13, 17, 25n; writing to KM in New Zealand, 40n, 41; at Ridge Cap, 51; with KM in London, 57, 74; 'Godmother', 64, 65n, 73; with KM at Rottingdean, Sussex, 97; gifts to KM, 102n, 131, 132, 237, 360; hair brushing business, 110, 111, 133; in Rhodesia, 139, 190n; burns KM's letters, xxiii, 139; KM's assessment of, xii, 189; 'Rhodesian Mountain', 291, 349; war work, Chiswick, 293n; KM's irritation with, 324, 344, 347, 354, 359; shares KM's studio, 339, 340n; war work, Putney, 344, 345n; as companion for KM in France, 362, 363

Balfour, Lady Eve: 179n
Balfour, A.J.: 179n
Balzac, Honoré de: 46, 47n
Banks, Georges: 122, 123
Barrie, J.M.: 119n
Bartrick-Baker, Evelyn ('Vere'): 46, 47n, 347n
Bashkirtseff, Marie: x
Bates, Mrs (original of 'Ma Parker'): 337, 344, 353
Beauchamp, Annie, born Annie Burnell Dyer (KM's mother); *B32n1*, vii, 3, 88, 43, 47, 53, 110, 131, 140n, 143n, 212, 213, 245, 247, 251, 346; influence on KM, x; in England with Harold Beauchamp, 18; plans for KM in England, 42; and clothes, 50; takes KM to Wörishofen, 89; 'Janey', 93n; illness, 141; and Leslie Beauchamp, 197, 233, 252
Beauchamp, 'Aunt Louey': *see* Lassetter, Elizabeth Weiss
Beauchamp, Charlotte Mary ('Chaddie'; KM's sister): *B30n1*, 3, 9, 33, 34, 35n, 38, 42, 46, 50, 53, 111n, 132, 141, 219, 225, 226, 252; at Queen's College, 5n, 19; 'Marie', 30n; at Days Bay, 41; marries John Campbell Perkins, 120, 121n; sends KM money, 228, 229; trip to Europe, 243, 245, 246; widowed, 247n, 254; living in London, 346, 347, 350
Beauchamp, Connie (Harold Beauchamp's cousin): 17n
Beauchamp, Esterel (daughter of Cousin Henry Beauchamp): 15
Beauchamp, Ethel (Harold Beauchamp's niece): 251, 252n
Beauchamp, Gwendoline Burnell (KM's sister): 208n
Beauchamp, Harold (KM's father): *B143n1*, vii, x, 3, 5, 7n, 20n, 23n, 24n, 27, 32n, 42, 45, 53, 111, 144, 245, 355n; relationship with KM, viii, 41; as benefactor to the Trowells, 16n; in England, 18; and KM's writing, 26n, 47n; and KM's return to England, 35, 36n, 52n, 57; as 'Pa man', 120; later marriage to Laura Kate Bright, 140n; cited as an example